National Saving and Economic Performance

A National Bureau
of Economic Research
Project Report

National Saving and Economic Performance

Edited by   B. Douglas Bernheim and
John B. Shoven

The University of Chicago Press

Chicago and London

B. Douglas Bernheim is the John L. Weinberg Professor of Economics and Business Policy at Princeton University and a research associate of the National Bureau of Economic Research. John B. Shoven is a professor of economics at Stanford University and a research associate of the National Bureau of Economic Research.

The University of Chicago Press, Chicago 60637
The University of Chicago Press, Ltd., London

Library of Congress Cataloging-in-Publication Data

National saving and economic performance / edited by B. Douglas
  Bernheim and John B. Shoven.
     p.   cm.—(A National Bureau of Economic Research project
  report)
     "Papers presented at a conference held at . . . Maui, Hawaii,
  January 6–7, 1989 . . . part of the Research on Taxation program of
  the National Bureau of Economic Research—P.
  Includes bibliographical references and indexes.
  ISBN 0-226-04404-1 (cloth)
  1. Saving and investment—Case studies—Congresses. 2. Economic
  policy—Case studies—Congresses. 3. Economic history—1971– —
  Congresses. I. Bernheim, B. Douglas. II. Shoven, John B. III. National Bureau of Economic Research. IV. Series.
  HC79.S3N38   1991
  339.4'3'0722—dc20   90-26131
                                                                    CIP

Relation of the Directors to the
Work and Publications of the
National Bureau of Economic Research

1. The object of the National Bureau of Economic Research is to ascertain and to present to the public important economic facts and their interpretation in a scientific and impartial manner. The Board of Directors is charged with the responsibility of ensuring that the work of the National Bureau is carried on in strict conformity with this object.

2. The President of the National Bureau shall submit to the Board of Directors, or to its Executive Committee, for their formal adoption all specific proposals for research to be instituted.

3. No research report shall be published by the National Bureau until the President has sent each member of the Board a notice that a manuscript is recommended for publication and that in the President's opinion it is suitable for publication in accordance with the principles of the National Bureau. Such notification will include an abstract or summary of the manuscript's content and a response form for use by those Directors who desire a copy of the manuscript for review. Each manuscript shall contain a summary drawing attention to the nature and treatment of the problem studied, the character of the data and their utilization in the report, and the main conclusions reached.

4. For each manuscript so submitted, a special committee of the Directors (including Directors Emeriti) shall be appointed by majority agreement of the President and Vice Presidents (or by the Executive Committee in case of inability to decide on the part of the President and Vice Presidents), consisting of the three Directors selected as nearly as may be one from each general division of the Board. The names of the special manuscript committee shall be stated to each Director when notice of the proposed publication is submitted to him. It shall be the duty of each member of the special manuscript committee to read the manuscript. If each member of the manuscript committee signifies his approval within thirty days of the transmittal of the manuscript, the report may be published. If at the end of that period any member of the manuscript committee withholds his approval, the President shall then notify each member of the Board, requesting approval or disapproval of publication, and thirty days additional shall be granted for this purpose. The manuscript shall then not be published unless at least a majority of the entire Board who shall have voted on the proposal within the time fixed for the receipt of votes shall have approved.

5. No manuscript may be published, though approved by each member of the special manuscript committee, until forty-five days have elapsed from the transmittal of the report in manuscript form. The interval is allowed for the receipt of any memorandum of dissent or reservation, together with a brief statement of his reasons, that any member may wish to express; and such memorandum of dissent or reservation shall be published with the manuscript if he so desires. Publication does not, however, imply that each member of the Board has read the manuscript, or that either members of the Board in general or the special committee have passed on its validity in every detail.

6. Publications of the National Bureau issued for informational purposes concerning the work of the Bureau and its staff, or issued to inform the public of activities of Bureau staff, and volumes issued as a result of various conferences involving the National Bureau shall contain a specific disclaimer noting that such publication has not passed through the normal review procedures required in this resolution. The Executive Committee of the Board is charged with review of all such publications from time to time to ensure that they do not take on the character of formal research reports of the National Bureau, requiring formal Board approval.

7. Unless otherwise determined by the Board or exempted by the terms of paragraph 6, a copy of this resolution shall be printed in each National Bureau publication.

(Resolution adopted October 25, 1926, as revised through September 30, 1974)

Contents

Acknowledgments

This volume consists of papers presented at a conference held at the Stouffer Wailea Hotel, Maui, Hawaii, January 6–7, 1989. The conference is part of the Research on Taxation program of the National Bureau of Economic Research. The conference was supported by the Pew Charitable Trusts. The editors are grateful to Ilana Hardesty and Beverly Gustafson for organizational and editorial assistance for the conference and volume.

Any opinions expressed in this volume are those of the respective authors and do not necessarily reflect the views of the National Bureau of Economic Research or any of the sponsoring organizations.

Introduction

B. Douglas Bernheim and John B. Shoven

According to official government figures, rates of saving in the United States declined precipitously during the 1980s and are currently much lower than in any other comparable period of our history. During the second half of the last decade, net national savings amounted to a paltry 2.7 percent of net national product, compared with 7.9 percent for the 1970s and 8.6 percent for the 1960s. The United States saved a much smaller fraction of its national income than other industrialized countries throughout the postwar period. While the last decade witnessed a decline in saving throughout the developed world, the United States had the dubious distinction of leading the way.

There is widespread agreement among economists that the consequences of low saving are severe. When an individual fails to save, he jeopardizes his own economic security. Following retirement, serious illness, or involuntary job loss, he may well find that his resources are insufficient to maintain his accustomed standard of living, and at times he may experience significant hardship. Even if his luck holds out during his own lifetime, he will contribute little to the enrichment of his family line.

Inadequate rates of saving have also been blamed for a variety of chronic macroeconomic problems. When a society fails to save, each and every individual may ultimately pay the price for collective profligacy. Traditionally, many economists have been concerned about the link between saving and capital accumulation. If chronically inadequate rates of saving depress investment, then the economy must follow a growth path on which output, income, productivity, and wages are all lower than they would be in a more frugal society. Relatively recent developments have also stimulated interest in the relationships between saving and international economic transactions. Some have argued that low rates of saving have compelled the United States to sell large chunks of its capital stock to foreign investors at "fire sale" prices. Others insist that excessive consumption is primarily responsible for the

1

staggering U.S. trade deficits of recent years and has indirectly brought about the deteriorating competitiveness of American industry. In short, it can be argued that inadequate saving threatens the foundations of economic prosperity.

The task of restoring acceptable rates of saving in the United States poses a major challenge to those who formulate national economic policy. During the 1980s, widespread concern over various economic woes spawned a series of sporadic attempts to stimulate saving and investment through policies that were designed to make these activities more rewarding. These policies included liberalized individual retirement accounts (IRAs) and Keogh Plans, the special treatment of some reinvested dividends, reductions in capital gains taxes, and increased investment incentives at the corporate level. The results were, to say the least, disappointing. Despite the existence of ample economic incentives, rates of saving continued to decline steadily.

Disillusioned with this approach, Congress eliminated many of these special incentives in the Tax Reform Act of 1986. Unfortunately, rates of saving failed to rebound significantly in the second half of the 1980s. This has generated considerable support for the reinstatement of several special provisions, such as the favorable treatment of capital gains, that were dropped only a few years ago. The Bush administration has even proposed the creation of "family savings accounts," which would considerably broaden the current scope of IRA-like investments.

The 1980s provided a humbling experience for economists and policymakers alike. Certainly, we learned many lessons about the economy, but foremost among them was the realization that we still understand very little about the factors that motivate people to save. There are few areas within the field of economics where the need for continuing research is quite so urgent.

This volume contains papers presented at an NBER conference on saving, held in Wailea, Hawaii, on January 6 and 7, 1989. The conference was part of the NBER's Project on Saving and Investment. The goal of the conference was to further our understanding of the determinants of saving, as well as the relationships between saving and various macroeconomic aggregates. The papers in this volume may be grouped into five areas: (1) the measurement of saving, (2) the effects of corporate saving, (3) the impact of taxation on saving, (4) the relationship between saving and international capital flows, and (5) the relationship between saving and growth. The remainder of this introductory section contains a brief summary of each paper.

The Measurement of Saving

A number of economists are skeptical about the validity of the official data on saving. Some contend that international comparability is a severe problem, despite efforts by the OECD and other organizations to standardize national accounts. Others argue that arbitrary accounting conventions result in the exclusion or mismeasurement of certain forms of saving. Some revisionists have even gone so far as to suggest that, once one adjusts the official figures appropriately, saving rates during the 1980s were not significantly below historical averages.

In "Market Value versus Financial Accounting Measures of National Saving," David F. Bradford argues that notions of saving based on the National Income and Product Accounts (NIPA) are seriously defective. These measures are similar in spirit to the financial accounting concepts that are used to derive the "net worth" of business enterprises. It is well known that accounting concepts provide imperfect measures of economically meaningful variables. In particular, investment (and therefore saving) in NIPA is limited to acquisitions of tangible property, and depreciation is calculated mechanically as a function of historical cost.

Bradford argues that it is more appropriate to measure saving as the change in the market value of net wealth. Certainly, expenditures on intangible assets such as advertising and R&D constitute investment, since they enhance a firm's command over future economic resources. Likewise, since individuals regard capital gains on existing assets as current income, unrealized or reinvested gains should be thought of as saving. Changes in the market valuation of an enterprise reflect both the value of intangible investments and capital revaluations. Bradford therefore concludes that, if one is interested in explaining saving behavior through conventional microeconomic theories, then a market-value notion of saving rather than the NIPA accounting measure, is appropriate.

Bradford considers several potential objections to the use of market-value accounting. Chief among them is the claim that no reliable market-value data exists. In response, he points out that the National Balance Sheets, compiled under the auspices of the Board of Governors of the Federal Reserve, are a largely underexploited resource. In particular, the National Balance Sheets carry land and corporate assets at market value and, in addition, contain information about the stock of consumer durable goods.

Measures of saving based on market-value accounting prove to be much more volatile than conventional accounting measures. Indeed, Bradford's time series for household and aggregate saving bear very little resemblance to the official numbers. He does find evidence of a long-term declining trend in the growth rate of real wealth per capita. However, his calculations also suggest that recent performance has been less disappointing than NIPA figures would lead one to believe. Indeed, the current level of wealth per capita is slightly above its long-term trend.

Bradford acknowledges that there are a variety of problems with the National Balance Sheets data and that his calculations provide imperfect measures of market-value concepts. However, he argues that these calculations represent a distinct improvement over NIPA data and an important step toward more informative measures of national saving.

The Effects of Corporate Saving

Two papers in this volume examine the question of whether the decision by corporations to retain or distribute earnings affects household-level consumption and saving. Do investors pierce the corporate veil and treat retained earnings as if they were their own income? Understanding this issue would certainly be important if one wanted to design policies to increase national saving. If the corporate veil is completely pierced, then any engineered increase in corporate saving would be completely offset at the household level. On the other hand, if it is not, aggregate saving would presumably be positively related to increases in its individual components.

In "Dividends, Capital Gains, and the Corporate Veil: Evidence from Britain, Canada, and the United States," James M. Poterba addresses the question of the corporate veil by estimating aggregate consumption functions for three countries: the United States, the United Kingdom, and Canada. If there were no corporate veil, household consumption should be invariant to firms' policies regarding the distribution of earnings (holding the earnings themselves fixed). Instead of using changes in dividend payments (which might signal improved prospects for the future and not simply a new payout policy) in his consumption regressions, Poterba uses a variable constructed to reflect the relative tax burden faced by dividends and capital gains brought about by retentions. He also examines whether involuntary capital gains resulting from corporate restructurings affect aggregate consumption and saving.

Poterba's results provide some evidence against the no-corporate-veil hypothesis. Under that hypothesis, one expects that increased dividends (holding all else equal) or increased cash received from involuntary capital gains realizations would simply be offset by the additional acquisition of financial assets by the recipients. The new payout behavior would leave consumption unchanged and would not change the composition of the assets of households. Poterba's econometric regressions suggest that increases in dividend payouts increase consumption, particularly when that variable includes the expenditures on household durables. For the United States and the United Kingdom the coefficient reflecting the impact on consumption of reducing the relative tax penalty on dividend payments is consistently positive over a fairly large number of specifications, although only occasionally statistically significantly different from zero. The point estimates are about twice as large when consumption includes the purchase of durables as they are when only nondurables and services are used as the dependent variable. This suggests that much of the additional cash received by the investors is used to purchase household durables, which contradicts the predictions of the pure life-cycle model. The point estimates indicate that nondurable consumption also increases when dividends are raised. The results for Canada show less of an impact of cash receipt on consumer behavior (in fact, the point estimate of the relative dividend tax variable is negative for some specifications), so in the Canadian case the analysis is more consistent with the no-veil hypothesis.

Poterba's analysis of the effects of the involuntary capital gains realizations due to mergers and acquisitions in the United States suggests that consumer spending increases due to these payments, although once again at least half of the increase in spending takes the form of the purchase of consumer durables. For both the United States and the United Kingdom, Poterba finds that between 50 and 60 percent of the proceeds of these cash mergers are spent and not reinvested in financial markets. The implication is that there is a fairly strong "mailbox effect." That is, checks in the mailbox affect spending far more than gains that simply show up on the stock listings in the newspaper.

Poterba's results are admittedly only suggestive. However, what they suggest is that corporate financial policies may have important implications for the aggregate saving rate in the economy. More research on this topic would seem desirable, particularly a more microeconomic evaluation of investor response to cash receipts. In the meantime, policymakers should be aware that the corporate veil may not be completely transparent.

In "Corporate Savings and Shareholder Consumption," Alan J. Auerbach and Kevin Hassett also test for the presence of a corporate veil, again using aggregate macro time-series information. The authors argue that previous papers claiming to have found evidence of a corporate veil have not completely neutralized the analysis from the informational content that may be conveyed by dividend increases. The life-cycle theory does not imply that consumption should not respond to changes in dividends, but only that consumption should be unaffected by wealth-neutral changes in payout policy. They are skeptical as to whether previous investigators have appreciated this distinction and state that Poterba's results in this volume are difficult to interpret because they are unsure whether the switch to a dividend tax preference variable (rather than dividends themselves) solves the problem. Poterba offers no evidence that changes in dividend taxes are independent of wealth changes.

Auerbach and Hassett derive their econometric specification from a representative agent intertemporal utility optimization model. Unlike Poterba, they only examine consumption exclusive of the acquisition of durables. Using quarterly and annual aggregate data from 1947 to 1986, the authors estimate that expected changes in dividends, holding wealth constant, do not cause a statistically significant change in consumption in their Euler equation framework. This is taken as evidence against the presence of a corporate veil and implies that wealth-neutral changes in dividend payout behavior would not affect aggregate national saving. The authors are quick to point out, however, that their tests are not powerful enough to dispose entirely of the possible existence of a corporate veil.

Auerbach and Hassett proceed to investigate the observed excess sensitivity of consumption to short-term changes in income, particularly labor income.

They find that their evidence is consistent with a considerable fraction of the population being subject to liquidity constraints. However, they doubt that the liquidity-constrained consumption case applies to the distribution of corporate earnings because equity ownership is so concentrated among the highest income households in the country.

Finally, Auerbach and Hassett test whether the marginal propensity to consume out of corporate equity wealth is as high as the marginal propensity to consume out of other forms of wealth. If the marginal propensities are different, then a new form of corporate veil is introduced, because a shift in wealth from corporate equity to other forms will change aggregate consumption and saving. In this part of their paper, Auerbach and Hassett come up with a startling result. They find that there is no apparent effect of corporate wealth on consumption. The marginal propensity to consume out of such wealth is not significantly different from zero. This implies that transferring wealth out of corporate equities might indeed increase consumption and decrease saving. The authors concern themselves with the distribution of the holders of equities in trying to explain this result, but it clearly deserves more research and may mean that the corporate veil does exist in a somewhat different form and should be a consideration in the design of prosaving policies.

Taxation and Saving

The next group of papers looks at the effect of taxation on saving. Tax policy is one of the governmental instruments that is most often considered to alter saving behavior. A long literature exists arguing that an income tax discourages saving by taxing it twice: first, earnings that are saved are subject to tax, and second, the return on the savings is also taxed. The elimination of this double taxation is one of the appeals of saving via pension vehicles and individual retirement accounts. If the country adopted a consumption tax rather than an income tax, the double tax would be eliminated.

In "The Saving Effect of Tax-deferred Retirement Accounts: Evidence from SIPP," Steven F. Venti and David A. Wise examine a new source of data regarding households' responsiveness to the availability of tax preferred individual retirement accounts (IRAs). Using the Survey of Income and Program Participants (SIPP) panel data set, the authors document the low levels of financial assets held by most households at all ages and levels of income. The overall median level of household financial assets (including saving and checking accounts, stocks, bonds, etc.) was $1,600 in 1985. They further show that most IRA accounts are held by households with incomes less than $50,000 and with only modest amounts of financial assets. They find that families who contributed to IRAs after they became available in 1982 had not, prior to that time, accumulated financial assets at a rate even close to the IRA contribution ceiling. They also find no evidence that IRA contributions have been funded by borrowing. The overall conclusion from a descriptive look at the SIPP data is that most IRA saving represented new saving and not a re-shuffling of existing accounts.

Venti and Wise propose that IRA saving and other forms of saving are not perfect substitutes, largely because of the liquidity restrictions placed on IRA accounts. They present a model that permits these two forms of saving to be treated as separate goods. The model is estimated with the SIPP data and the perfect-substitutes hypothesis is rejected. They simulate the impact of a $1,000 increase in the IRA contribution ceiling. This affects only those who are already contributing at the maximum level. For those households, the model of Venti and Wise predicts that the $1,000 increase in the limit would result in an average increase in IRA contributions of $856 and an average decrease in other saving of only $22. Immediate tax proceeds would fall by $269, but the total effect of the increase in the ceiling would be an increase in the national saving rate.

In "Consumption Taxation in a General Equilibrium Model: How Reliable Are Simulation Results?" B. Douglas Bernheim, John Karl Scholz, and John B. Shoven seek to determine the confidence one can have in the point estimate results of computational general equilibrium models used to evaluate the impact of the U.S. switching from a personal income tax to a consumption or expenditure tax. Most general equilibrium evaluations of this issue have come to the conclusion that such a switch would increase saving and the long-run capital-labor ratio and substantially enhance economic welfare. However, these general equilibrium models require a large number of parameter valuations (particularly behavioral elasticities) that are not known with certainty. The research question that the authors address is how the uncertainty regarding input parameters translates to uncertainty about the model's predictions.

Bernheim, Scholz, and Shoven use the Fullerton-Shoven-Whalley model to examine this question. They present a technique of linearizing the model to get an approximation of the variances in the model's predictions given the variance-covariance matrix associated with the underlying parameters. The consumption tax is modeled as an income tax with complete deductibility of saving (similar to unlimited IRA accounts with no withdrawal penalty). The United States currently does not have a pure income tax, but rather a hybrid tax somewhere between an income tax and a consumption tax. This is due to the fact that at least half of saving is sheltered from taxation either through such vehicles as pension accumulations or through saving that takes the form of investment in owner-occupied housing.

The results of Bernheim, Scholz, and Shoven are mixed. It does appear that the short- and medium-run results regarding the effects of the adoption of a complete consumption tax on saving are tied down fairly precisely. One can at least rule out the possibility that the effect is zero or of the opposite sign with a reasonable degree of certainty. The predicted impact of the tax policy change on the present value of utility or economic welfare is positive, but the point estimate is between one and a half and three times the standard deviation for this variable. The authors conclude that the results lend some support to the case for a consumption tax, but that they also emphasize the need for more precise econometric estimates of the various key elasticities in the economy (such as the saving and labor-supply elasticities) that are inputs to the general equilibrium models.

In "Taxes and Capital Formation: How Important Is Human Capital?" James Davies and John Whalley study the dynamic effects of taxes on saving and investment. Their analysis departs from most of the preceding literature on this subject by considering both human and nonhuman capital formation.

The accumulation of human capital is of enormous quantitative importance in the U.S. economy. Moreover, human and nonhuman capital may function as substitutes, at least to some extent. For example, when the returns to physical capital are taxed at higher rates, it is conceivable that individuals simply shift their resources toward education and training without actually lowering their overall levels of saving. Thus, the omission of human capital seriously limits the usefulness of many previous models that have been used to study the welfare effects of capital income taxation.

Davies and Whalley simulate the effects of various tax policies, using a fully dynamic, overlapping generations model of the U.S. economy. The structure of the model is conventional, except that the authors have incorporated a process governing the accumulation of human capital. The model is calibrated to a stylized data set that is intended to represent the position of the U.S. economy in the mid-1970s.

For their dynamic general equilibrium model, Davies and Whalley find that the inclusion of human capital increases the short-run impact of taxes on saving. However, they also show that the transition to a steady state is much more rapid than in the absence of human capital, and that there is very little distortion of human capital investment in the steady state. Consequently, they conclude that the incorporation of human capital does not significantly alter the full dynamic welfare effects of most tax reforms. This conclusion stands in sharp contrast to previous partial equilibrium results, which have suggested that the endogenization of human capital substantially increases the welfare effects of various tax policies.

National Saving and International Capital Flows

In a well-known study published in 1980, Martin Feldstein and Charles Horioka documented extremely high correlations between domestic saving rates and domestic investment for industrialized OECD countries. This finding was widely interpreted as evidence of international capital market imperfections. Although the Feldstein-Horioka analysis was subjected to a variety of criticisms, their basic finding appeared to hold up rather well.

During the 1980s, foreign nationals demonstrated a phenomenal appetite for assets in the United States. Although the United States was a net supplier of capital to the rest of the world in the 1950s, 1960s, and 1970s, net inflows of foreign capital climbed seven-tenths of a percentage point (relative to GNP) in the early 1980s, and then shot up another two-and-a-half points in the late 1980s. At year-end 1988, the Commerce Department estimated that foreigners had accumulated nearly $1.8 trillion worth of assets in the United States. This number exceeded the value of American-owned foreign assets by more than half a trillion dollars.

These developments imply that the correlation between domestic saving and investment noted by Feldstein and Horioka may have declined significantly during the 1980s. Anecdotal evidence suggests that this may have occurred because international capital markets became increasingly well integrated: governments reduced artificial barriers to capital flows, extensive new markets for hedging exchange-rate risks were developed, and financial institutions became increasingly sophisticated. One might therefore expect national policy regarding saving and capital income taxation to have very different effects in the 1990s than in the 1960s or 1970s. Two of the papers in this volume are concerned with evaluating the Feldstein-Horioka result and its interpretations in light of recent experience.

In "National Saving and International Investment," Martin Feldstein and Philippe Bacchetta examine correlations between domestic saving and investment for the period 1980–86, and compare these results with correlations for earlier periods. They find a substantial decline in the correlation between gross saving and gross investment and a somewhat smaller decline in the correlation between net saving and net investment. In addition, they document significant differences between EEC and non-EEC countries. Specifically, correlations between saving and investment for EEC countries have historically been lower than for non-EEC countries and declined more rapidly between the 1970s and 1980s. This evidence is consistent with the view that capital markets among the EEC countries have become highly integrated over the last decade. Even so, the impact of domestic saving on domestic investment remains substantial. The evidence indicates that, during the 1980s, a one dollar increase in domestic saving added more than 50 cents to domestic investment.

Feldstein and Bacchetta argue that high correlations between saving and investment are likely to persist even with full integration of international capital markets. With perfect integration, each investor would have to receive the same return, contracted in his domestic currency, on all equally risky investments, domestic or foreign. This need not imply equality of real ex ante interest rates, where returns on investments in each country are denominated in its own currency, unless expected changes in exchange rates equal the difference between expected inflation rates. Empirical violations of purchasing power parity imply that this condition is often not met. Moreover, even though purchasing power parity might hold in the long run, investors may be highly sensitive to exchange-rate fluctuations and political risks. Consequently, net international capital flows may respond very little to apparent interest-rate differentials.

Several economists have proposed alternative explanations for the high correlation between saving and investment. It is extremely important to test the validity of these competing explanations, since each has different implications for public policy. One hypothesis, originally advanced by Maurice Obstfeld, is that the Feldstein-Horioka results are spurious and reflect the common influence of economic growth on both saving and investment. Feldstein and Bacchetta's analysis corroborates Obstfeld's claim that this is a theoretical possibility, but their empirical analysis demonstrates that the relationship between investment and saving remains equally strong even when one includes measures of growth. An alternative hypothesis, popularized by Lawrence Summers, is that governments actively seek external balance by manipulating fiscal policy. Feldstein and Bacchetta point out that Summers's evidence on the endogeneity of government deficits is also consistent with the hypothesis that deficits are exogenous, and that they crowd out private investment.

Since the Feldstein-Horioka results concern long-run correlations between saving and investment, it is still possible that international capital flows absorb a substantial fraction of short-run fluctuations in domestic saving rates. Feldstein and Bacchetta investigate this possibility by estimating dynamic adjustment processes for both saving and investment. They find that a gap between domestic saving and investment raises investment in subsequent years but leaves saving unaffected. In particular, a saving-investment gap equal to 1 percent of GDP causes the ratio of investment to GNP to rise by roughly one-quarter of a percentage point in the following year.

In "Quantifying International Capital Mobility in the 1980s," Jeffrey A. Frankel discusses four distinct definitions of perfect capital mobility: the Feldstein-Horioka definition, real interest parity, uncovered interest parity, and closed interest parity. He argues that full integration of financial markets would produce closed interest parity, but would not necessarily yield any of the other three conditions.

Closed interest parity holds when interest rates are equalized across countries for financial contracts that are written in a common currency. This condition would be violated only if there were significant barriers to the flow of financial capital across countries, such as transactions costs, information costs, capital controls (actual or potential), tax laws that discriminate by country of residence, or default risk. Frankel tests this condition by using data on forward exchange rates for 25 countries to construct covered interest rate differentials. His calculations reveal that financial markets became increasingly integrated during the 1970s. Barriers to flows of financial capital remained for a few developed countries until the late 1970s and even mid-1980s. However, by 1988, integration of financial markets had virtually eliminated all covered interest rate differentials for the major industrialized countries.

Uncovered interest parity holds when an investor who has not hedged against exchange-rate risk expects to receive the same rate of return, denominated in his own currency, on the bonds of all countries. This requires both closed interest parity, as well as risk neutrality with respect to variations in exchange rates. Since investors are probably quite sensitive to exchange-rate risk, it would be rather surprising if this condition was satisfied in practice. More generally, uncovered interest rate differentials measure exchange-rate risk premiums. Frankel's decomposition of interest rate differentials provide a measure of these risk premiums. He finds that they have been both substantial and variable.

Real interest parity holds when real interest rates are equalized across countries. Frankel points out that this requires uncovered interest parity, plus the assumption that there can be no expected real depreciation of a country's currency. This assumption is satisfied only when goods markets are completely integrated. In practice, transportation costs for some goods are high, and many countries impose quotas and tariffs. Thus, the well-documented failure of real interest parity need not have anything to do with the efficiency of financial markets. Frankel provides new evidence on expected changes in real exchange rates and concludes that these expected changes explain a significant fraction of observed real interest rate differentials.

Finally, the Feldstein-Horioka notion of capital mobility requires real interest rate parity, plus the assumption that national saving is uncorrelated with other determinants of national investment. Frankel notes that the validity of this assumption has been disputed but argues that the Feldstein-Horioka results are nevertheless quite robust. He also updates previous estimates of the saving-investment correlation using data from the 1980s. In contrast to Feldstein and Bacchetta, he employs time-series data for the United States rather than a cross section of different countries. His results suggest that the Feldstein-Horioka result has broken down to a much greater extent than is indicated by the work of Feldstein and Bacchetta.

Taxes, Saving, and Growth

The final three papers in this volume deal with national saving and economic growth. In a closed economy, it is saving that funds and permits investment. While there is some debate about the exact magnitude of the contribution, it is universally agreed that one of the key contributors to economic growth is a rapidly growing capital stock. In such a closed economy, the question of the adequacy of saving is the same issue as the adequacy of investment. In an open economy situation, there is no reason why investment and saving in a particular country should be equated. Savers simply would look all over the world for the highest return on their investments, taking account of the various risk factors.

In "A Cross-Country Study of Growth, Saving, and Government," Robert J. Barro develops several theoretical models of the determinants of long-term growth rates and saving rates for economies. He first presents a model in which public goods and services, jointly with private capital, determine per capita output. The model features an infinitely lived representative agent who maximizes intertemporal utility. Public goods and services are financed by proportional income taxes and the government runs a balanced budget. With some assumptions regarding technology, Barro finds that the growth rate of per capita output initially increases with increases in the level of government investment, but that at higher levels of government investment and taxes, growth is eventually retarded. Government consumption, in contrast to government investment, does not enter into production functions and definitely depresses economic growth and saving rates in his model.

Barro extends his initial model to include endogenous population growth and adds a distinction between physical and human capital. Human capital consists of two components, raw unskilled labor and accumulated human capital. Population growth is in effect a form of saving and investment, as is skill acquisition or extra human capital. Higher rates of population growth require adults to spend more time raising children, which in the model lowers the return to human capital investments.

Barro's empirical work in the paper involves the cross-country estimation of four interdependent endogenous variables. The dependent variables that he is trying to explain are per capita GDP growth, the ratio of physical investment to GDP, human capital acquisition (measured through the rate of secondary school enrollment), and population growth. The independent explanatory variables include five classes of government expenditures (measured as a ratio to GDP), a proxy for the treatment of property rights, dummies for socialist and mixed economies, and one for violent war or revolution.

Barro's results are often consistent with his theoretical models. For example, public consumption spending is systematically inversely related to growth and investment. On the other hand, public investment tends to be positively correlated with growth and investment. The results regarding property rights tend to indicate that they stimulate growth and both physical and human capital investment. Finally, there appears to be a strong negative interaction between population growth and investment in human capital. Barro refers to this as the trade-off between the quantity and the quality of children. He characterizes his paper as a progress report on a large research project to gain a better understanding of the determinants of economic growth.

In "Consumption Growth Parallels Income Growth: Some New Evidence," Christopher D. Carroll and Lawrence H. Summers also deal with cross-country issues of growth and saving, although without Barro's concentration on government expenditures. Carroll and Summers challenge the empirical validity of representative agent life-cycle theories, or the modeling of the economy as infinite horizon optimizers as in the theoretical sections of Barro's paper. They find that the aggregate consumption and saving implications of these fashionable representations of aggregate behavior are grossly inconsistent with the features of cross-country and cross-section data on consumption and saving. The authors begin with the inference of the infinite horizon representative agent model that consumption growth should depend on the difference between the real interest rate and the rate of time preference. The growth rate of consumption should also be related to the elasticity of substitution of consumption, but the theory says that it should be independent of the rate of growth of income. When Carroll and Summers examine the cross-country data, they find that they do not conform to the predictions of the model. In particular, they observe a very high correlation between the rate of growth of consumption and the rate of growth of income. Further, the predicted positive correlation of consumption growth with real interest rates is not readily apparent.

Carroll and Summers examine several possible ways to reconcile long horizon optimization models with the international empirical evidence. One by one, the attempted reconciliations are rejected. The authors find that consumption tracks income more closely than these theories would predict, both at the aggregate level and at the individual level. The pattern of the consumption of the elderly relative to that of the young across countries also is inconsistent with what the long horizon optimization models would predict. Ultimately, the authors reject all models with lifetime or longer horizons.

Carroll and Summers conclude with two suggestions. First, they think that the evidence favors Milton Friedman's original view that permanent income should not be regarded as lifetime income (or income over even a longer horizon), but simply as the mean or expected income over a much shorter horizon, perhaps several years. They think that a model in which most households are liquidity constrained or only hold a "buffer stock" of saving may be descriptive of the real world. Second, the authors suggest that the bulk of saving in most economies is done by a very small minority of the population and that these households may behave differently than others. That is, they suggest that the consumption and saving behavior of "savers" is possibly quite different than the consumption and saving choices of the vast majority of the population. They offer this insight as a guide for additional research on this topic.

In "Saving Behavior in Ten Developing Countries," Susan Collins documents cross-country differences in rates of saving, as well as within-country trends over time for a sample of developing countries. She also attempts to explain the observed differences of saving behavior. In particular, she explores the roles of economic growth, standard of living, and the age distribution of the population.

Collins's calculations reveal that the experiences of developing countries have been quite diverse. For the period 1960–84, gross saving (expressed as a fraction of GNP) ranged from a low of 11.9 percent in Indonesia, to a high of 24.3 percent in Singapore. Countries with higher rates of saving also tended to grow more rapidly. Her analysis of the data suggests that there is very little relationship between saving and income inequality, and that standard of living only affects the rate of saving in relatively poor countries.

One striking feature of the data is that four of the 10 countries experienced massive increases in rates of saving during the 1960s, 1970s, and 1980s. Singapore, Taiwan, Korea, and Hong Kong all eventually achieved gross saving rates in excess of one-third of GDP, despite the fact that all saved very little in the early 1960s (e.g., Hong Kong saved only 2% of GNP in 1960). This evidence calls into question the importance of "cultural" determinants of saving, since it indicates that many Asian countries achieved high rates of saving through rather dramatic behavioral changes.

Collins develops a formal model of life-cycle saving and uses it to motivate an econometric analysis of the data. She emphasizes that, according to theory, one needs to control for interactions between the various determinants of saving (such as growth, income, and age distribution). Her estimated equations bear this prediction out. Moreover, they account for a substantial portion of the differences in saving behavior both across countries and over time. On the basis of these estimates, Collins concludes that there appear to be fundamental, structural differences between the determinants of saving in low- and middle-income countries.

Finally, Collins conducts a detailed analysis of rates of saving in Korea. She argues that the trend toward collective frugality has, to a large extent, been driven by the household sector. This conclusion is supported by household survey data that decomposes saving into rural and urban components. Collins interprets the Korean experience in light of her econometric estimates. This allows her to speculate about the special determinants of rising saving in Korea.

1   Market Value versus Financial Accounting Measures of National Saving

David F. Bradford

1.1   Introduction

This essay is a venture into well-trodden terrain: the definition of saving. Because so many others have thought about the same issues, probably nothing I say here has not been said before by someone else. J.R. Hicks (1946) mapped the territory in a particularly well-known theoretical treatment. More recently, Auerbach (1985), Boskin (1986, 1988), Eisner (1980, 1988), Goldsmith (1982), Peek (1986), Ruggles and Ruggles (1981), and Shoven (1984) have discussed many of the points raised here in connection with empirical explorations of saving and wealth. In his presidential address to the American Economic Association, Eisner (1989) included the main theses argued here in a broadside indictment of the divergence between measurement and theory to be found in economics. This paper differs, perhaps, in degree of emphasis of two propositions. The minor theme is that saving should be defined by reference to the underlying concept of wealth to which the saving is an increment. The major theme is that the most useful wealth concept is the market value of

David F. Bradford is professor of economics and public affairs at Princeton University and Director of the Research Program in Taxation at the National Bureau of Economic Research.

This is a revision of a paper prepared for an NBER conference on saving held January 6–7, 1989. The author would like to thank Alan Auerbach, William Beaver, Michael Boskin, John Campbell, Angus Deaton, Bronwyn Hall, Robert Hall, Alan Huber, Robert Lipsey, James Poterba, Robert Shiller, John Shoven, Scott Smart, Frederick Yohn, Jr., and conference participants for helpful discussions of various aspects of this research and Kathleen Much for editorial advice. This paper was completed while the author was a fellow at the Center for Advanced Study in the Behavioral Sciences, Stanford, California. The author is grateful for financial support provided by Princeton University; the John M. Olin Program for the Study of Economic Organization and Public Policy, Princeton University; National Science Foundation grant BNS87–00864; the Alfred P. Sloan Foundation; and the National Bureau of Economic Research.

assets, not the cost-based measure of capital implied by the use of national income and product account (NIPA) saving. Whereas NIPA investment measures tell us something about the margin of productive additions to the stock of wealth in a particular form, the (definitionally equal) saving measures are neither those that the microeconomic theory of consumption explains nor those appropriate to assess national economic performance.

Inspection of a sample of the extensive literature commenting on and analyzing national saving has surprised me by the diversity of positions, often implicit, on these issues. It appears that the macroeconomists are truer to microeconomic principles than are many of those who approach the subject from a public finance perspective. The fact that so much research is carried out making use of statistical measures of saving that seem to me to bear so little relationship to economic theory suggests there is a place for a review of fundamentals and display of some basic data related to them.

1.1.1   Income, Saving, and Wealth

Beginning students are taught that saving is a residual, what is left from personal income after deducting consumption and taxes or after deducting from aggregate income consumption by households and governments. But saving is also conceived of as an addition to wealth, and it is not always recognized that the three ideas—consumption, income, and wealth—are not independent. Defining any two determines the definition of the third. The Schanz-Haig-Simons (SHS) conception of income familiar to public finance takes the ideas of consumption and wealth as fundamental and *defines* income as the sum of consumption and the change in wealth during an accounting period. The basic notion of wealth, in turn, is the market value of a household's (or household aggregate's) stock of claims on goods and services in the future.[1] This is the approach to saving taken by the microeconomic theory of household behavior.

Most commentary on and analysis of national saving, by contrast, start with a NIPA definition of income. To make life confusing, the term "income" in the national income account context is attached to factor payments and makes distinctions between taxes regarded as falling on factor payments and those that do not (indirect business taxes). It is doubtful that there is an economically meaningful distinction between taxes that bear on factor payments and those that do not. We can cut through the problem if, for the concept of income in the SHS sense, we read "product" in the national accounting sense.

Which of the three notions—product, consumption, wealth—are fundamental in the case of national income accounting is not immediately obvious. As is well known, national income accounts involve two conceptions of product, gross and net. Gross national product, "the market value of the goods and services produced by labor and property supplied by residents of the United States (U. S. Department of Commerce, Bureau of Economic Analysis 1986), and consumption, personal and governmental, can reasonably be described as the fundamental ideas. Together (by subtraction) they define gross investment and saving. To reach *net* product, *net* investment, and *net* saving, it is necessary to subtract an allowance for the "using up" of the reproducible capital stock, a wealth notion. Here, then, it is the wealth and consumption ideas that are fundamental: we can think of net product (income) as definitionally equal to the sum of consumption (personal and governmental) and the change in the reproducible capital stock owned by U.S. residents.

1.1.2 NIPA Saving and Financial Accounting

In its treatment of business investment and its yield, the NIPA net income concept can be loosely characterized as a consolidation of the account books of business firms. This is not to suggest that the NIPA accountants actually aggregate the income statements and balance sheets of firms. It is rather to emphasize that investment (and therefore saving) in the national income and product accounts consists of acquisitions of tangible property and is, furthermore, cost-based, constructed from historical data on expenditures for machines, structures, and inventories. Increments in the value of intangible property and (what may be the same thing) revaluations of tangible property arising from its location within going businesses are excluded from the NIPA income and saving concepts. Net saving in the national income and product accounts constitutes the change in the stock of reproducible business capital.[2] The NIPA capital data can be thought of as the figures financial accountants would present if they used the NIPA depreciation conventions and adjusted their historical cost-based entries on tangible assets (including inventories) annually to what they would be had historical prices been instead at current levels.

The main difference between the two conceptions of wealth corresponds roughly to the difference between financial accounting for the net worth of business firms, on the one hand, and the market valuation of those firms on the other ("roughly" because financial accounts include intangible assets acquired by purchase from another firm). The difference is sometimes summed up as that between recognition or not of "capital gains," but this description hides as much as it reveals. The market value of the equity of a firm may differ from the "book" value of its tangible property for many reasons, including changes in the supply price of the capital items in question (for which national income accounting makes a correction), changes in discount rates, and changes in the beliefs about the future upon which market valuation of assets depends—all of these give rise to capital gains in the popular sense of the term. But the two values also may differ because of the genuinely stochastic character of the returns on investment and the conservative quality of business accounts, which result in little or no tracking of the accumulation of intangible capital and of such assets as proven oil reserves.

1.1.3   Empirical Relevance: A First Look

Available data suggest that the difference in definition corresponds to a significant difference in aggregate wealth measures. Table 1.1 shows estimates of the net worth of nonfinancial corporate business in the United States (including corporate farms) and of the market value of the equity claims on those firms. The figures are derived from the Balance Sheets for the U.S. Economy (hereafter, National Balance Sheets) prepared by the Board of Governors of the Federal Reserve System (1988).[3] Net worth consists of the difference between assets and liabilities on the account books after various adjustments. Assets in this case include reproducible assets at replacement cost (i.e., after adjusting valuation based on historical cost for changes in the acquisition prices of the same assets), land at market value, and direct investment abroad by U.S. firms. Liabilities include all the usual sorts of debt (at book value), profit taxes payable, and foreign direct investment in the United States. I would emphasize that in its treatment of fixed investment the net worth in table 1.1 is essentially the concept implicit in NIPA accounting for saving. The market value of equity is essentially that appropriate for the SHS saving concept, which, in turn, is in the concept "explained" by microeconomic theories of saving behavior.

It is evident from table 1.1 that the market value of equity and the net worth on firms' books are very different. The column titled "Market Value/Net Worth Ratio" shows the ratio of the market value of the equity claims to the consolidated nonfinancial corporate sector to the consolidated financial accounting measure of net worth, that is, the sum of tangible and financial assets (including direct investment abroad) less the sum of debt claims (at book value), profit taxes payable, and foreign direct investment in the United States. Since 1948 this ratio has varied over a remarkable range, with a high of 110.1 percent at the end of 1968 and a low of 36.7 percent at the end of 1978.

To put the divergence between accounting and market values of corporate equity in perspective, the column of table 1.1 headed "Net Worth Less Market to GNP" shows the ratio of the difference to the GNP. The difference ranges between an excess of over 7 percent and a shortfall of over 62 percent, with a substantial decrease on average. Figures 1.1 and 1.2 make the points graphically.

It seems clear that the basic objective of the National Balance Sheets, to measure wealth at market value, is the one appropriate for discussions of saving. Nevertheless, economists widely accept and use for this purpose the NIPA saving data. Distinguished examples (and I make no claim to a systematic review of the literature) include Blades and Sturm (1982), Boskin and Lau (1988), Campbell (1987), Lipsey and Kravis (1987), most of the contributors to Lipsey and Tice (1989), Poterba (1987), and Summers (1985).

In at least some of these instances, lack of market-value wealth data is taken

Table 1.1   **"Book" Net Worth and Market Values of U.S. Nonfinancial Corporate Business, Year End, 1948–87**

Year	Net Worth of U.S. Nonfinancial Corporate Business ($ millions)	Market Value of Corporate Equities ($ millions)	Market Value/ Net Worth Ratio (%)	Net Worth Less Market to GNP (%)
1948	209,615	83,862	40.0	48.1
1949	219,672	92,205	42.0	49.0
1950	244,190	116,647	47.8	44.2
1951	269,211	138,250	51.4	39.3
1952	285,071	149,941	52.6	38.4
1953	300,142	144,776	48.2	41.8
1954	315,117	216,033	68.6	26.6
1955	342,531	269,173	78.6	18.1
1956	378,078	289,169	76.5	20.8
1957	403,297	242,470	60.1	35.7
1958	419,289	342,082	81.6	16.9
1959	439,972	361,299	82.1	15.9
1960	448,422	354,114	79.0	18.3
1961	461,733	428,294	92.8	6.3
1962	475,580	389,171	81.8	15.0
1963	489,970	456,076	93.1	5.6
1964	513,321	509,516	99.3	.6
1965	543,746	553,720	101.8	−1.4
1966	583,906	504,223	86.4	10.3
1967	621,655	651,678	104.8	−3.7
1968	668,880	736,506	110.1	−7.6
1969	729,963	646,230	88.5	8.7
1970	784,634	648,492	82.6	13.4
1971	856,111	758,897	88.6	8.8
1972	934,346	855,233	91.5	6.5
1973	1,048,013	678,436	64.7	27.2
1974	1,337,118	499,098	37.3	56.9
1975	1,491,060	684,337	45.9	50.5
1976	1,647,452	787,807	47.8	48.2
1977	1,817,268	748,002	41.2	53.7
1978	2,107,859	773,143	36.7	59.3
1979	2,419,386	933,373	38.6	59.2
1980	2,780,531	1,293,116	46.5	54.4
1981	3,109,641	1,214,845	39.1	62.1
1982	3,230,025	1,382,773	42.8	58.3
1983	3,327,399	1,638,730	49.2	49.6
1984	3,447,798	1,617,733	46.9	48.5
1985	3,503,026	2,022,648	57.7	36.9
1986	3,560,138	2,332,629	65.5	28.9
1987	3,657,167	2,331,322	63.7	29.3

Source: See text. Based on Board of Governors of the Federal Reserve System (1984).

Fig. 1.1   Market value of corporate equity/corporate net worth, 1948–87

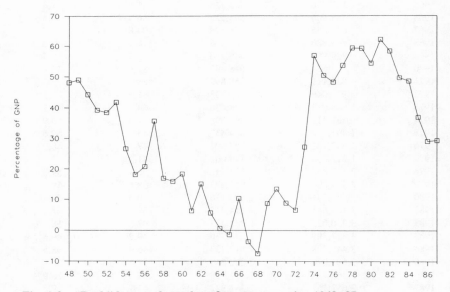

Fig. 1.2   "Book" less market value of corporate equity, 1948–87

to justify resort to NIPA concepts, and some analysts (e.g., Auerbach 1985; Boskin 1986, 1988; Poterba and Summers 1987) have noted the potential role for the market-value data provided in the National Balance Sheets. Summers and Carroll (1987) explicitly analyze aggregate saving in the National Balance Sheets sense (although they do not regard it as preferable to the NIPA measure). Noting that "national income account (NIA) data provide notoriously poor proxies for the economic concepts of saving and investment," Obstfeld (1986, 82) explores some of the biases that may result from the use of NIPA data in comparing saving and investment behavior of countries. Some macroeconomists—for example, Hall (1978, 1988) and Campbell and Deaton (1988)—go out of their way to avoid measuring saving. Hall, in particular, has argued that income aggregates are misplaced in macroeconomics; focus should instead be on aggregate consumption and labor earnings. Granting some such exceptions in the literature, I think it is fair to say that there is wide acceptance of NIPA saving measures.

In this paper I argue that wealth and consumption are both important variables in economic models and important measures of economic performance, that income should be viewed as a derivative concept in this connection, and that the appropriate concept of wealth is measured at asset market value. We should use NIPA *saving* measures only to the extent that they serve as reasonable proxies for the market-value measures. (This is not to suggest that the corresponding investment concepts are not useful in the analysis of production.) Although it is ultimately a statistical question whether the NIPA saving measures are reasonable proxies, the evidence from the National Balance Sheets leads me to doubt it.

In the next part of the paper I review the relationship between the two notions of wealth (and therefore of saving): market value of assets and financial accounting net worth. I then take up objections to the use of market-value wealth. The fourth section presents time-series data on the behavior of national saving in the U.S. economy, and the fifth raises, without solving, some significant problems with the National Balance Sheets data as measures of market value.

Much attention has been paid in recent years to the saving performance of U.S. residents, which has been generally judged disappointing. My contention, that the NIPA saving aggregates and ratios of NIPA saving to NIPA income measures are poor indicators upon which to base conclusions, is neither inherently in favor of this assessment nor opposed to it. One may still be dissatisfied with the U.S. saving record when it is looked at in the framework suggested by microeconomic theory. The sixth section presents some observations on this issue.

1.2   Concepts of Wealth

1.2.1   Market Value of Assets

The SHS notion of income underlying the base of an income tax (or at least generally accepted by academic commentators as the *proper* base of an income tax) is the sum of the change in the wealth and the consumption of the taxpaying unit, be it an individual or a family. Consumption and wealth are the primitive concepts, which need to be given operational substance to produce a tax system. Although the general ideas seem obvious enough, both pose difficult problems of definition at the margin. Within limits, the standard to which the operational definitions refer in a tax policy context is essentially normative—one starts with a notion of ability to pay and designs the income measure to implement it. (The limits relate to the substitutability of different forms of wealth in taxpayer portfolios.)

In *Untangling the Income Tax* (Bradford 1986) I suggested that the usual arguments justifying the SHS income concept as a tax base imply a definition of a person's wealth as "the maximum amount of present consumption he could finance currently by selling or otherwise committing all of his assets" (22). If this definition is accepted, the operational focus shifts to the identification of "assets" and quantifying the opportunities of "selling or otherwise committing" them. Examples of significant but hard-to-quantify assets are human capital (the present value of a person's future earning power) and the discounted value of inheritances. It is interesting that these two are also examples of assets that are difficult to sell or "otherwise commit." Proponents of SHS income taxation normally exclude both human capital and the value of great expectations from the wealth component of the definition of income.

Experience with tax administration gives us numerous examples of the fact that it is the market value of wealth, rather than its accounting value, that figures in individual behavior. If tax on accruing market value (capital gains) is deferred, taxpayers will concentrate their portfolios in assets that generate accruing value rather than cash income. If accounting measures of depreciation are different from actually accruing changes in value of assets, taxpayers respond in well-known ways.

A simple two-period model of a person's intertemporal budget constraint will help clarify the role and nature of wealth in the analysis of behavior, in this case the explanation of consumption levels. For the purpose, we can imagine a world in which there is just one consumption good and in which labor is supplied inelastically, with no welfare significance. We conceive of people as born into this world with inherited resources (to be specified), working one unit of time during the first period to earn the wage w_1 (measured in consumption units), consuming an amount C_1, and applying any excess of the wage over consumption to purchase assets. In the second period, the person also works one unit of time to earn the wage w_2 and consumes that amount plus the results of liquidating the assets. The problem is to choose an amount of first-period consumption and a portfolio of assets.

In the most basic model, there is no uncertainty (so there is no information problem). The second-period wage is known and there is a single asset available, which we may think of as a discount bond paying one unit of consumption in period 2. The going price for the asset is p_2. The person is born holding B_1 units of the bond and, in the course of period 1, chooses the number of units of the asset to buy (or sell) so as to carry B_2 units into period 2. Two equations—(1) and (2)—define the lifetime budget constraint.

(1) $C_1 + B_2 p_2 = w_1 + B_1 p_2.$

(2) $C_2 = B_2 + w_2.$

The intermediate asset position, B_2, can be eliminated between (1) and (2) to yield a single lifetime budget constraint, (3).

(3) $C_1 + C_2 p_2 = w_1 + w_2 p_2 + B_1 p_2.$

The right-hand side of equation (3), $w_1 + w_2 p_2 + B_1 p_2$, is the market value of "opening wealth" (*including* human capital). We see from (3) that in this simple world we can specify the person's opportunity set completely with two numbers, opening wealth and p_2, the price of claims on period-2 consumption (or the interest rate). To specify the opportunity set without capitalizing labor services, we need four numbers, $B_1 p_2$, w_1, w_2, and p_2: opening *nonhuman* wealth, wages in the two periods, and the interest rate.

This simple formulation reminds us that if we are looking forward from a point in time and want to explain consumption levels, wealth is a needed piece of information. It also demonstrates that it is not the only piece of information we need to explain consumption or, a related problem, to assess a person's welfare, even under the simple, perfect market conditions of the model. In general, information about prices is needed—here, wages and the interest rate and in a multiperiod setting, wages, relative prices of goods, and a term structure of interest rates. By inspection of condition (3) we see that in the simple model the welfare of the individual is increasing in opening wealth including human capital and decreasing in the price of future consumption (i.e., increasing in the interest rate). But even in this case, when human capital is excluded, although welfare is still increasing in opening wealth, the effect of an increase in the interest rate on the assessment is indeterminate and hinges on the taste for consumption in period 2. Simply put, a high interest rate is bad for someone who wants to borrow against tomorrow's earnings to consume more today.[4]

Initial nonhuman wealth is a given, a parameter, in the model described above; wealth along the way (initial wealth augmented by saving) is chosen, endogenous. A complete model would explain initial wealth, too, so it would drop out of the analysis. Wealth would return as an explanatory variable, though, with the introduction of uncertainty. Then the wealth along the way is the result of the individual person's choice and luck, so second-period consumption would depend upon the market performance of the portfolio. The same would be true for the aggregate of individuals.

The model reminds us that to predict the level of consumption we need to take into account the market value of nonhuman wealth, the interest rate, and current and future wages. In a stochastic setting the distribution of future wages could be correlated with the value of nonhuman wealth, marketed and unmarketed. In particular, one might expect workers observing prosperity (high market value of wealth) to raise their forecasts of future wages. If we take into account that lifetime labor supply is chosen along with consumption levels, it is far from clear what sort of consumption behavior one ought to expect to see associated with movements in the market value of wealth.[5]

With enough simplifying assumptions, though, one can derive from the general approach outlined above the conclusion that a person's current consumption will be a function of his forecasted labor earnings and current wealth, for example,

$$C_t = aE_t[w_{t+1}L_{t+1}] + bW_t,$$

where a and b are constants, E_t is the expectation conditional on information at time t, and W_t is the (stochastic) market value of nonhuman wealth.[6] Such a model will generate a time path of consumption and wealth, and hence of saving, defined as the change in wealth. The point to emphasize here is that such regularity as the models do lead us to look for is in the relationship among consumption, labor earnings, and wealth at *market value*.

1.2.2   Net Worth as an Accounting Idea

We can capture in a crude way the role for financial accounting in the simple model of behavior by adding an explicit, real asset, say a certain number of machines, M_1, as another element of endowment. In the typical financial accounting context, there is no readily observable market for fixed capital. Assume, therefore, that the machines are inalienable (i.e., they cannot be sold). The number of machines is tracked by the financial accounts. A machine generates output $\bar{O}$ in period 2 ($\bar{O}$ would be stochastic in a realistic model). Then the budget constraint is expressed by equations (4) and (5); the single-constraint version that eliminates the financial assets carried over is expressed by (6).

(4) $$C_1 + B_2 p_2 = w_1 + B_1 p_2.$$

(5) $$C_2 = w_2 + \bar{O}M_1 + B_2.$$

(6) $$C_1 + C_2 p_2 = w_1 + w_2 p_2 + B_1 p_2 + \bar{O}M_1 p_2.$$

It is evident from (6) that, in a world of certainty, with unlimited borrowing and lending of the financial asset, the only use of the financial accounting information is to provide a basis for estimating what the market value of the machines would be $(\bar{O}M_1p_2)$. If one knows the market value of the machines, the accounting information is superfluous.

Complicating the model by introducing an explicit treatment of uncertainty and asymmetries of information does not suggest a further role for financial accounting information. With complete Arrow-Debreu contingent claim markets, the market value of wealth continues to define the position of the budget constraint. Owing to the increased number of prices, ambiguities about the signs of derivatives multiply in welfare comparisons or positive predictions of the effect of changes in parameters on consumption or labor supply. Missing markets, asymmetries, liquidity constraints, and the like render budget sets nonlinear and reduce the information contained in any single parameter, such as initial wealth, of the individual's problem. Nevertheless, there does not appear to be a general role for accounting information except as the basis for estimating implicit market values.

The function of financial accounting for a business firm is not to duplicate market valuation. A clear statement of this point is presented in an official pronouncement of the Financial Accounting Standards Board: "Financial accounting is not designed to measure directly the value of a business enterprise, but the information it provides may be helpful to those who wish to estimate its value" (Financial Accounting Standards Board, 1978, as excerpted in Gibson and Frishkoff, 1986, 19). Financial accounting for asset value and market value converge where there is an actual transaction that renders the market value objectively measurable. Between transactions, accounting rules prescribe transformations (depreciation, amortization, etc.) of the original market-value data to describe the stock of assets involved.

It is tempting, and I think even usual among economists, to attribute to the accounting measure of net worth (appropriately corrected to some sort of replacement-cost basis) the status of a kind of "permanent income" measure, a stationary point in the noisy world of asset revaluations. I am not aware, however, of any empirical evidence in support of this characterization of accounting net worth in relation to the valuation of firms (nor of the related characterization of accounting depreciation).[7]

There are really two reasons we should expect accounting values to differ from market values of firms. First, accounting practices clearly lay no claim to tracking the market values of those assets that are carried on the books. Thus, for example, the depreciated accounting value of fixed investment neither is, nor claims to be, a stand-in for market value for the assets involved.[8] Intangible assets acquired by purchase are generally amortized according to formula.[9] Depreciation or amortization deductions for retirements from the stock of assets, based on the amounts paid for the assets, are needed to account for the fact that *some* systematic effect can be expected with the passage of time. These allowances are, to be sure, based on experience with the physical or otherwise determined useful lives of similar assets in the past, but to serve their purpose they must be formally prescribed in accounting rules.

They do not refer to assessments of current market value in the context of the firm, which may deviate up or down from the path implied by accounting rules of thumb.

Second, important intangible assets created by the activities of a firm (i.e., not bought from another firm) are typically not carried on the balance sheet at all. As is well known, research and development and advertising outlays are expensed currently. Successful efforts do not generate assets on the books unless there is an actual transaction, such as a sale of patent rights. The value of a firm that discovered the laser or the transistor and could appropriate the resulting value would surely jump in market value. Its accounting net worth, however, would not change. The same is true for an economy under NIPA capital accounting practices. Since the inventor of a new idea may have difficulty capturing the rents, there is a better basis for excluding the value increase from company books than for excluding it from a national aggregation. Technological and market surprises of many kinds (oil price shocks, technological breakthroughs, discovery of a new oil field) are excluded from company books and from NIPA income and capital accounts. Observation of the histories of firms such as computer, automobile, and pharmaceutical companies makes clear that large movements in value are associated with the success or failure of ideas (including marketing) and organizational innovations. Such value changes are clearly of great quantitative significance, quite stochastic, and weakly, if at all, related to investment in fixed capital.

In short, the accounting net worth of the firm is a measure of *some* of its past inputs. It represents the solution to an intractable statistical problem: how to aggregate information about financial commitments through time embodied in property of one sort or another. It is not a shortcoming of accounting net worth that it does not perfectly match the valuation of the firm by those making use of accounting information. Accounting data are designed to inform, rather than duplicate, market evaluation.[10]

1.2.3 NIPA Saving and Investment

Gross investment in the national income and product accounts is the sum of net exports of goods and services (as emphasized by Eisner and Pieper 1989, a measure of the accumulation of claims on foreigners, not a measure of the change in market value of net claims on foreigners), business expenditures on fixed investment (structures, including residential structures, and producers' durable equipment), and the change in business inventories. If we think of gross national product as a flow of physical goods and current services, we can think of gross investment as the portion of that flow devoted to adding to the stock of wealth. This may be an interesting measure; it is arguably the appropriate horizontal axis on a marginal efficiency of investment schedule. (This is not the place to develop the point, but it may be that a market value aggregate belongs in a production function for SHS income. When a firm purchases a piece of real estate for a "revalued" price, presumably it expects to obtain as much extra value of output as it does when it constructs a new building for the same amount.)

It is a further issue whether there is a useful aggregate, called the capital stock, that can be sensibly employed in a production function.[11] The idea that there is such an aggregate that generates a flow of productive services underlies the capital stock figures compiled by the Bureau of Economic Analysis. Although value data provide the starting point, like GNP itself, the capital stock is conceived of as a physical quantity. The depreciation estimates ("capital consumption allowances with capital consumption adjustment") in the NIPA are intended to capture the loss over time in the current productive service flow potential embodied in the accumulation of fixed investment. Other things equal, we might expect the profitable investment opportunities to increase with increases in depreciation allowances, which would signal the need for "replacement" investment. If this model captures the essence of the flow of investment opportunities, it is net investment, not gross, that belongs on the horizontal axis of a marginal efficiency of investment schedule.

NIPA depreciation allowances are not intended to represent the decline in market value of the assets in question and would not do so even if there were no measurement problems except under very special assumptions about the time path of discount rates and about the way productive capacity of the assets declines over time. (Basically, what is required is constancy of discount rates and exponential decay of productivity.[12]) The actual rules used in constructing the depreciation allowances are rooted in studies of retirement and other measures of physical life.[13]

"Economic depreciation" is defined to be the decline in market value of a piece of equipment or a structure between the beginning and end of the accounting period. As it happens, Hulten and Wykoff (1981) have concluded that the U.S. Department of Commerce capital consumption estimates are reasonably similar to the average historically experienced economic depreciation for a subset of assets for which there is an active second-hand market. It is difficult to know, however, how relevant such ex post data on a subset of assets are to the forward-looking market valuation of the bolted-down assets of business firms. A striking implication of the data in table 1.1 and figures 1.1 and 1.2, taken at face value, is that the NIPA capital consumption allowances for the nonfinancial corporate sector differed sharply and unsystematically from economic depreciation over the 1948–87 period.[14] (I take up below some of the reasons one might not take the figures at face value.)

1.3   Objections to the Use of Market-Value Measures of Saving

Various objections are sometimes raised to the use of asset market-value data, rather than NIPA measures, in analyzing saving.

1. Asset markets are too volatile. They register paper gains and losses, not the steady accumulation of real things.

To a degree that seems often unappreciated, the determinants of wealth are psychological. We need only be reminded of Ponzi schemes and tulip manias, not to mention stock market crashes, to bring home how dependent asset values are upon beliefs about the future. The modern literature on the rationality of expectations and the efficiency of pricing in asset markets has emphasized in a refined way the unpleasant difficulty of rooting asset values in "fundamentals."

Asset valuation is also inherently dependent upon the structure of information. I like to illustrate this dependence with the case of a building that is destined to be destroyed by a meteor on a certain date. As long as no one knows when and where the meteor will strike, the building has the same value as others like it. At the moment the astronomers make public a prediction, the building loses value (to a degree dependent on the distance into the future of the catastrophic event and on the confidence the public places in astronomers' forecasts). It is clear that the owner of the structure suffers a fall in wealth at the point the information is revealed, and presumably we would say that "society" suffers the same fall in wealth, even though, in a sense, nothing is changed by the knowledge that causes the loss in value. The meteor was going to crash into the building in any case.[15]

An interesting intermediate case arises if the information about the future is revealed only to the owner of the building. (The analogous situation is not unusual—it gives rise to the "lemons" problem.) If he keeps the matter a secret and sells the structure, he suffers no loss, nor is there any observable private or social loss until the meteor strikes.

As the examples suggest, the market value of assets has a kind of ephemeral quality that may, for example, lead to doubts about the efficacy of capital markets as institutions of resource allocation.[16] Unfortunately, the ephemeral quality of market assessments of value does not alter the role implied for them in.economic theory. Real risk and uncertainty about the future are apparent facts of life that cannot be avoided by focusing on inputs that can be measured with relative precision. The purpose of asset measures produced by financial accountants is to assist in the estimation of market values. The usual argument applies that the market price will incorporate whatever information the accounting data contain. There is, presumptively, no money to be made by betting on accounting net worth against the market.[17]

2. Asset market value changes incorporate price effects. What we need are real saving and wealth stock concepts that are independent of discount rates and other relative asset value changes.

Various examples suggest the importance of taking into account price effects, especially in using wealth measures to draw conclusions about welfare. One of the most important is the effect of changes in the discount rate. At any moment the stock of claims to future goods and services is heterogeneous with respect to the time and contingencies under which the claims pay off. When the prices of future consumption claims change, so does the value of an unchanged stock of assets. In his discussion of the concept of income, Hicks (1946) favored a wealth measure that would be unchanged if the steady-state level of consumption did not change.

The increasing site value of land that we might expect to accompany population growth provides another example. When the value of all houses (including mine) increases, I may be no better off, in spite of my higher wealth, because I have to live somewhere. A third example was suggested to me by John Shoven: discovery of a new technology that made computers of enormous power virtually costless and instantaneously producible would render the existing stock of computers valueless (while we are at it, assume that all software transfers costlessly to the new machines).

These are index number problems of the classic sort.[18] A financial accounting measure of saving appears attractive in the particular instances because they seem to call for no change in the real-wealth measure in the face of actual changes in market value. (I have not actually tried to sort out whether a real-wealth measure would not change in the examples.) But this is surely fortuitous. Dealing with the index number problem requires transforming market-value data, and it is only by chance that financial accounts may sometimes give the right answer.

The discount-rate change problem is a particularly important one. When we assess performance, it would make sense to look at both wealth and discount rate data. There is no basis, however, for presuming that financial accounting measures of wealth perform adequately as indices of real wealth.

3. There are no reliable data on market value of wealth, therefore, we have to use the NIPA saving measures.

There may be problems with existing data on market values, although very extensive and accurate data are available on assets such as corporate equities. The National Balance Sheets data seem to me an underexploited resource. Furthermore, as in other contexts, an objection such as this one should be grounds for devoting efforts to improving the data and to establishing the adequacy of the proxies we use if direct measurements are not at hand.

1.4 Time-Series Data on Wealth at Market Value

Figures derived from the National Balance Sheets cast doubt on the adequacy of NIPA saving measures as a proxy for changes in the market value of assets. Table 1.2 shows the time series of various wealth aggregates. The nominal dollar figures have been reduced to common units using the implicit GNP deflator (taking the average of fourth- and first-quarter values to approximate the year-end figure corresponding to the balance sheet observations). The aggregate net worth of households includes the market valuation of corporate shares and of land. The National Balance Sheets value fixed investment

Table 1.2   Household Net Worth and Aggregate Wealth, 1948–87

Year	Net Worth of U.S. Households (millions $1982)	Government Net Worth (millions $1982)	Aggregate Wealth at Market (millions $1982)	Aggregate Saving (millions $1982)	Aggregate Saving to GNP (%)
1948	3,487,654	− 857,494	2,630,160		
1949	3,671,501	− 889,339	2,782,162	152,002	13.7
1950	3,883,883	− 819,665	3,064,218	282,056	23.4
1951	4,189,833	− 790,067	3,399,766	335,548	25.3
1952	4,287,324	− 795,849	3,491,475	91,709	6.6
1953	4,377,281	− 825,250	3,552,031	60,556	4.2
1954	4,687,899	− 840,255	3,847,644	295,613	20.9
1955	4,938,926	− 814,882	4,124,044	276,400	18.5
1956	5,075,169	− 780,335	4,294,834	170,791	11.2
1957	4,984,653	− 770,061	4,214,592	− 80,242	− 5.2
1958	5,427,604	− 806,349	4,621,255	406,663	26.4
1959	5,571,610	− 809,815	4,761,795	140,541	8.6
1960	5,680,642	− 808,103	4,872,539	110,744	6.7
1961	6,086,197	− 824,849	5,261,347	388,808	22.8
1962	5,928,471	− 832,285	5,096,186	− 165,161	− 9.2
1963	6,274,049	− 833,201	5,440,848	344,662	18.4
1964	6,576,652	− 837,694	5,738,958	298,110	15.1
1965	6,871,566	− 823,076	6,048,490	309,532	14.8
1966	6,833,612	− 806,728	6,026,885	− 21,605	− 1.0
1967	7,370,297	− 831,246	6,539,050	512,166	22.5
1968	7,827,453	− 825,822	7,001,631	462,581	19.6
1969	7,493,648	− 790,676	6,702,972	− 298,659	− 12.3
1970	7,432,952	− 790,358	6,642,595	− 60,377	− 2.5
1971	7,752,823	− 817,570	6,935,254	292,659	11.8
1972	8,190,783	− 815,700	7,375,083	439,829	16.9
1973	7,889,046	− 758,254	7,130,791	− 244,291	− 8.9
1974	7,457,661	− 712,663	6,744,998	− 385,793	− 14.1
1975	7,830,318	− 794,411	7,035,907	290,909	10.8
1976	8,348,919	− 834,194	7,514,726	478,819	16.9
1977	8,642,746	− 837,706	7,805,040	290,315	9.8
1978	9,111,741	− 816,502	8,295,239	490,198	15.7
1979	9,631,709	− 784,075	8,847,635	552,396	17.3
1980	10,046,585	− 790,784	9,255,800	408,166	12.8
1981	10,064,616	− 812,292	9,252,323	− 3,477	− 0.1
1982	10,061,786	− 925,358	9,136,427	− 115,896	− 3.7
1983	10,544,681	− 1,067,194	9,477,487	341,060	10.4
1984	10,731,277	− 1,188,518	9,542,759	65,272	1.9
1985	11,372,752	− 1,328,645	10,044,108	501,349	13.9
1986	11,907,562	− 1,473,725	10,433,837	389,729	10.5
1987	12,257,233	− 1,596,916	10,660,317	226,480	5.9

Source: See text. Based on Board of Governors of the Federal Reserve System (1984); U.S. Department of Commerce (1986, 1987).

owned directly (in unincorporated businesses and in the form of owner-occupied housing and consumer durables) at replacement cost (using the NIPA data).[19]

The column titled "Government Net Worth" in table 1.2 is simply the aggregate debt of local, state, and federal governments held by the public (of course, it is a negative number). Government debt is, directly or indirectly, included on the asset side of household balance sheets: to avoid double counting, the column headed "Aggregate Wealth at Market" sums the household and government net worth to produce an aggregate wealth measure. Notice that no attempt at all has been made to evaluate the real asset position of governments.[20]

The difference in aggregate wealth from one year to the next gives us "Aggregate Saving" in table 1.2. Given what we know about the volatility of the stock and real property markets, we should expect significant volatility in the wealth and saving measures, and we find it. Figure 1.3 displays the wealth time series graphically, and figure 1.4 shows the saving series, normalized by dividing by GNP. For comparison, as described numerically in table 1.3, figure 1.4 also displays the ratio of net national saving to GNP, a figure derived from the national income and product accounts. As we might expect, the market-value measure is much more variable than the NIPA measure. The measure based on the National Balance Sheets oscillates over a range from a low of almost − 15 percent to a high of almost 25 percent of GNP. The NIPA

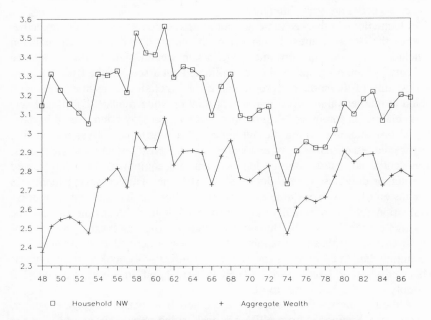

Fig. 1.3   Household and aggregate wealth, 1948–87, ratio to GNP

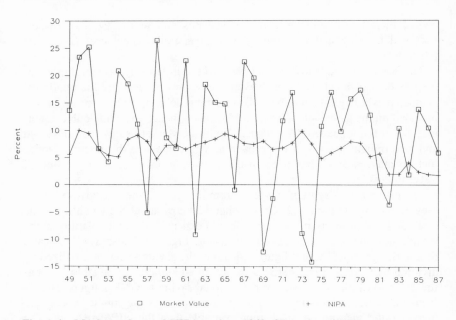

Fig. 1.4   Market value and NIPA saving, 1949–87, ratio to GNP

measure drifts from a high of 10 percent in 1949 to a low of 2 percent in 1987. The two series are very different.

Fluctuations in market value are not all that accounts for the difference between the two measures. In particular, the National Balance Sheets concept includes the stock of consumer durables in wealth. The National Balance Sheets include estimates of the "consolidated net assets" of the United States, consisting of the sum of reproducible assets (including consumer durables), land at market value, U.S. gold and special drawing rights (SDRs), and certain claims on foreigners.[21] Subtracting government debt and excluding land from this total and taking the difference from year to year gives us a saving figure purged of market revaluations. It consists mostly of reproducible assets: residential structures, nonresidential plant and equipment, inventories, and consumer durables. It thus differs from NIPA net national saving mainly in inclusion of consumer durables, and, in avoiding the inclusion of market revaluations, it is conceptually directly comparable to NIPA saving. Indeed, the figures are taken from the Bureau of Economic Analysis tangible-wealth tabulations. To emphasize that this hybrid series is derived from financial accounting data (although it is far from the historical-cost book values on firms' balance sheets), I refer to it as "'Book' less Land" in figure 1.5 (fig. 1.5 simply adds the new series to fig. 1.4).

Although the resulting series is smoother than that of aggregate wealth, significant differences from NIPA national saving remain. Exploration of the

Table 1.3   **Net National Saving in the United States, NIPA Basis, 1948–87, Ratio to GNP (in percentages)**

Year	Gross Saving	Capital Consumption Allowances	Net Saving
1948	19.4	7.8	11.6
1949	14.0	8.4	5.6
1950	18.2	8.2	10.0
1951	17.6	8.2	9.4
1952	14.9	8.3	6.6
1953	13.7	8.3	5.4
1954	13.9	8.7	5.1
1955	16.9	8.5	8.4
1956	18.1	8.9	9.2
1957	17.1	9.1	8.0
1958	14.1	9.4	4.8
1959	16.2	9.0	7.2
1960	16.3	9.0	7.3
1961	15.5	9.0	6.5
1962	15.9	8.6	7.3
1963	16.3	8.5	7.8
1964	16.7	8.3	8.4
1965	17.5	8.1	9.4
1966	16.9	8.0	8.8
1967	15.9	8.3	7.6
1968	15.6	8.3	7.4
1969	16.5	8.4	8.0
1970	15.2	8.7	6.5
1971	15.6	8.8	6.7
1972	16.5	8.9	7.7
1973	18.5	8.7	9.8
1974	16.8	9.3	7.5
1975	14.9	10.1	4.8
1976	15.9	10.1	5.8
1977	16.9	10.1	6.7
1978	18.2	10.2	7.9
1979	18.3	10.6	7.7
1980	16.3	11.1	5.2
1981	17.1	11.4	5.7
1982	14.1	12.1	2.0
1983	13.6	11.6	2.0
1984	15.1	11.0	4.1
1985	13.3	10.9	2.4
1986	12.7	10.8	1.9
1987	12.4	10.6	1.8

Sources: 1948–84: *Economic Report of the President,* February 1988; 1985–87; *Survey of Current Business,* July 1988.

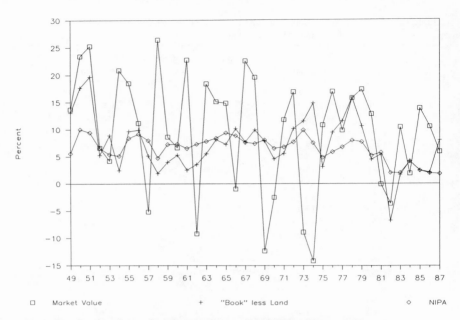

Fig. 1.5   **Comparison of saving measures, 1948–87, ratio to GNP**

reasons for the remaining differences would be a side excursion from my principal line of argument. The evidence from the National Balance Sheets data clearly supports the conclusion that financial accounting saving misses significant amounts of the value change that is revealed in asset markets.

1.5   Caveats on the National Balance Sheets Wealth Figures

Several problems with the National Balance Sheets data should be recognized.

1. The market value of equity incorporates the capitalized value of certain variations in tax liabilities that are not balanced by offsetting measured asset values. An instance is the "trapped-equity" problem.[22] Corporate payouts in the form of dividends are subject to tax at the shareholder level, and shareholders ought to discount this tax in bidding for shares. A considerable (and inconclusive) literature now exists developing the technical ins and outs of the tax and securities law and practice in relation to the trapped-equity argument. To the extent that dividend taxes are discounted in the price of equity, the value of a corporation's shares will be below the market value of the assets owned by the firm.

Another instance is the value of tax liabilities accrued by corporations via such tax rules as accelerated depreciation. An increase in such accruals ought to lower the value of corporate equities.[23]

A possible third instance is the tax consequence of changing corporate financial structure. The tax system has set up incentives, which have varied through time, bearing on the choice between debt and equity. One view of the current intense leveraged-buyout activity in the United States is that it is strongly motivated by such tax considerations, and the gradual realization of the private profit (at the expense of public revenue) to be made by financial restructuring accounts for some of the bidding up of equity prices.

There is, in all of these instances, a balancing asset "owned" by the public through the public's "ownership" of the government, which we might describe as accrued tax liability. Unfortunately, however, we cannot observe the value of this asset in the market, and so the empirical problem does not go away with aggregation across sectors.

2. Anticipated tax claims are also important in assessing pension reserve assets, which are viewed as belonging to households. Presumably, the great bulk of these claims is subject to income taxation upon distribution. When household and government financial claims are netted in reaching a national wealth figure, this problem goes away.

3. As Auerbach (1985) has emphasized, unfunded pension liabilities of corporations represent unmeasured assets of the households that are presumably offset by an effect on measured corporate equity value in the market. This component of wealth is missed in the National Balance Sheets.

4. Debt is carried on the National Balance Sheets at book value. Corporate debt liabilities are thus incorrectly valued. Correcting for inflation, of course, is relatively easy. But there is also a divergence between book and market value in current dollars that varies through time. Tax incentives plus simple changes in the nominal discount rates result in such divergences. Furthermore, the leveraged buyout wave may be responsible for a systematic divergence between book and market valuation of debt. The large premiums paid for equity claims in corporate takeovers are sometimes explained by the implied expropriation of the interests of bondholders. The value of the bonds of RJR Nabisco is said to have fallen by 20 percent as a consequence of the successful takeover of the firm in a leveraged buyout in December 1988.

It might be thought that the misstatement of the value of bonds as liabilities on the books of corporations would be balanced by their misstatement as assets in the hands of the public in an aggregation across sectors. This would be so if the aggregation were in terms of financial accounting concepts. But aggregation to national saving will sum the market values of equity with the book value of debt. To correct for this problem will require gathering data on the market value of bonds. (Brainard, Shoven, and Weiss, 1980 have developed such estimates for the debt of a large population of U.S. corporations.)

5. I have mentioned above the likelihood that some of the recent increase in equity value has come at the expense of bondholders and of the government (through lost tax revenues otherwise expected). Shleifer and Summers (1987) have suggested that other "stakeholders" in corporations have also lost wealth

in the wave of corporate acquisitions. We would probably describe the wealth effects on noncorporate, nonbondholder stakeholders as impacts on human capital; the effects are in any case presumably not reflected in asset market data.

6. The National Balance Sheets present no estimates of the market value of businesses owned directly by households. The data in table 1.1 show a large and variable divergence between book and market values of property owned by corporations. There is no obvious reason there should not be a similar degree of divergence in the valuation of noncorporate firms.

7. The Flow of Funds staff of the Federal Reserve Bank expresses reservations about the adequacy of the estimated market value of land, which is built up using ratios of assessed to market values from real estate tax administration reported in censuses of governments taken once every five years. I have no independent basis for evaluating these reservations. (Corporate holdings are presumably captured in equity values, but corporations own a small fraction of U.S. land.)

1.6 The Saving Performance of the United States

It is usual to assess aggregate saving behavior by reference to saving "rates," ratios of saving to aggregate income. Although dividing the aggregate saving by a national income measure is a natural method of normalizing for the size of the economy, one should be cautious in drawing conclusions about economic performance from trends in, or comparisons across countries of, such ratios. Saving rates thus defined do not obviously relate to the objective of assessing the level of aggregate consumption against a standard either of consistency with past behavior or of prudence with respect to future welfare. For these purposes, measures of wealth per capita are called for or, more generally, measures of the wealth of various subgroups in the population.[25]

Table 1.4 displays wealth per capita data for the United States, where wealth is interpreted in the National Balance Sheets sense of household net worth (at market value) minus government debt. Saving per capita is simply the first difference of wealth per capita, and thus incorporates population growth. Figure 1.6 displays the saving series expressed as the year-to-year growth of wealth per capita (labeled "Growth in Wealth per Capita" in table 1.4).Because wealth is a stochastic variable, a particular year's experience conveys limited information.

It is not clear what one should regard as either a normal or a "good" rate of increase in wealth per capita. If productivity were stationary we would probably expect wealth per capita to be constant, and welfare considerations would also presumably prescribe constancy. In general, both predicted and optimal accumulation would be related to technological progress and demographic structure. As shown in figure 1.6, there appears to be a long-term

Table 1.4   **Per Capita Wealth and Saving at Market Value, 1948–87**

Year	Wealth per Capita ($ 1982)	Saving per Capita ($ 1982)	Growth in Wealth per Capita (%)
1948	17,937		
1949	18,649	711	4.0
1950	20,123	1,475	7.9
1951	21,951	1,828	9.1
1952	22,161	209	1.0
1953	22,175	14	.1
1954	23,601	1,427	6.4
1955	24,854	1,253	5.3
1956	25,428	574	2.3
1957	24,506	−922	−3.6
1958	26,425	1,919	7.8
1959	26,777	352	1.3
1960	26,969	192	.7
1961	28,642	1,673	6.2
1962	27,320	−1,323	−4.6
1963	28,751	1,431	5.2
1964	29,908	1,157	4.0
1965	31,129	1,221	4.1
1966	30,662	−467	−1.5
1967	32,907	2,245	7.3
1968	34,885	1,978	6.0
1969	33,072	−1,813	−5.2
1970	32,395	−678	−2.0
1971	33,397	1,002	3.1
1972	35,137	1,740	5.2
1973	33,650	−1,487	−4.2
1974	31,540	−2,110	−6.3
1975	32,578	1,038	3.3
1976	34,466	1,888	5.8
1977	35,439	973	2.8
1978	37,268	1,829	5.2
1979	39,313	2,045	5.5
1980	40,639	1,326	3.4
1981	40,203	−436	−1.1
1982	39,293	−910	−2.3
1983	40,364	1,071	2.7
1984	40,265	−100	−.2
1985	41,977	1,712	4.3
1986	43,184	1,208	2.9
1987	43,705	521	1.2

Sources: See text. Based on Board of Governors of the Federal Reserve System (1984); U.S. Department of Commerce (1986, 1987).

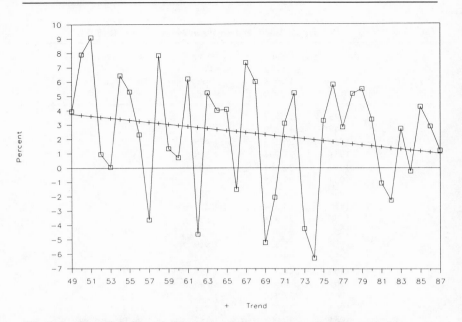

Fig. 1.6   Growth in household net worth less government debt per capita, 1949–87

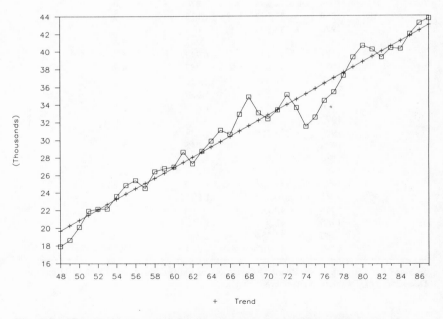

Fig. 1.7   Household net worth less government debt, 1982 dollars per capita

declining trend to the rate of growth of real wealth per capita. Interestingly, the performance of the most recent three years is on or slightly above trend.

For those looking for good news (bearing in mind the caveats mentioned above about the use of wealth as a measure of welfare), figure 1.7 displays the trend in real wealth per capita. The picture shows that, on average, since 1948 U.S. residents have been adding to the stock of wealth per capita about $700 (1987 price level) per year. According to figure 1.7, the current level of wealth per capita is just a bit above its long-term trend.

1.7 Conclusion

Although the NIPA saving measures, and especially NIPA saving rates, are widely used in both scholarly and journalistic treatments, their shortcomings as representations of the saving concepts derived from economic analysis should not be controversial among economists. Saving is the change in a stock of wealth. NIPA saving describes the change in a cost-based measure of some past resource commitments. Households, individually and in the aggregate, measure their situations instead by reference to a forward-looking assessment of the success or failure of those and other resource commitments. These assessments find expression in the capital market's valuation of enterprises, broadly conceived. The annual change in that value is the measure of saving.

Whatever their usefulness as measures of a certain class of inputs, the NIPA saving and wealth measures are not good proxies for the market-expressed assessments of results. The National Balance Sheets present the conceptually appropriate measures of national wealth and saving. It is clear, though, that much needs to be done to improve the quality of the statistics and to refine their interpretation.

Notes

1. For discussions of the SHS income concept, see Bradford (1986) or Institute for Fiscal Studies (1978).

2. For this purpose, owner-occupiers can be thought of as in the business of providing housing services. Other household-owned and household-employed capital (consumer durables) is excluded from the NIPA investment and capital concepts, but that is not my main concern here.

3. To derive the aggregate accounting net worth of the corporate sector, I have added the net worth of corporate farms (line 46 of the Sector Balance Sheet for the Nonfinancial Business Sector) to the nonfarm, nonfinancial total (line 43).

4. The importance of intertemporal prices (interest rates) is often overlooked in assessments of welfare. Summers (1983) develops a cost-of-living series corrected for interest rate changes, applicable to a person with a given amount of wealth (and no anticipated earnings).

5. For examples of more refined intertemporal models see Breeden (1979), Campbell and Deaton (1988), Ingersoll (1987, Chap. 11), Merton (1971, 1973).

6. For a classic example of such a model, see Ando and Modigliani (1963). For recent examples, see Blinder and Deaton (1985), Deaton (1987), Hall (1978, 1988), West (1988).

7. See Beaver and Ryan (1985).

8. See Gibson and Frishkoff (1986, 44).

9. See Gibson and Frishkoff (1986, 46).

10. See Foster (1986) for a survey of the accounting literature on the information content of financial statements.

11. For an overview see Brown (1980).

12. See the clear discussion in Hulten and Wykoff (1981).

13. See U.S. Department of Commerce, Bureau of Economic Analysis (1987); also Musgrave (1983, 1986a, 1986b).

14. Using National Balance Sheets data, Bulow and Summers (1984) have emphasized this point in their discussion of the failure of income tax rules to recognize wealth changes in the form of asset revaluations. They suggest that the ex ante depreciation allowances for tax purposes should be increased to compensate the investor for the risk of asset revaluations that are unrecognized by the tax rules.

15. James Poterba has reminded me that, quite apart from discounting, the aggregate market value of wealth may not fall by the full prior value of the doomed building when the meteor news arrives. The aggregate value will depend upon the general equilibrium response of all asset prices, even if the asset in question is a tiny part of the aggregate stock. Bradford (1978) illustrates the point.

16. See Stiglitz (1972, 1979).

17. Summers (1986) has emphasized how difficult it may be to establish the "rationality" of asset markets, i.e., to tell whether one can make money be selling short when prices are too high by some internal standard. But presumably those who would use NIPA saving figures rather than asset market values are not talking about small, hard-to-detect, effects.

18. Pollak (1975) has worked out the index number theory applicable to an intertemporal setting. See also Summers (1983).

19. The figures for household net worth (sector basis) included in this paper incorporate an adjustment to deal with an error discovered in the course of this work by Frederick O. Yohn, Jr., of the Flow of Funds section of the Federal Reserve Board. In the published series, household claims on noncorporate private financial institutions have been omitted from household net worth. I have added the "approximate share of noncorporate companies" in the net worth of the private financial institution sector (line 50 in the Sector Balance Sheet of Private Financial Institutions) to the published household sector net worth.

20. Boskin, Robinson, and Huber (1987) and Eisner (1986) have developed government real asset series.

21. Perhaps because it is not clear how one would allocate accounting values, the National Balance Sheet's "total consolidated net assets" of the United States excludes U.S. holdings of foreign equities and makes no deduction for foreign holdings of U.S. equities (other than via direct investment). The household sector net worth does include holdings of foreign equities. The two wealth concepts are thus not quite parallel.

22. See Auerbach (1979, 1983b) and Bradford (1981).

23. Auerbach (1983a, 1989) and Auerbach and Hines (1987) show that the capitalized value effects of tax law changes can be large.

24. Kotlikoff (1984, 1986, 1988) has emphasized a similar point with respect to assessment of the national debt.

References

Ando, Albert, and Franco Modigliani. 1963. The "Life-Cycle" Hypothesis of Saving: Aggregate Implications and Tests. *American Economic Review* 53 (May): 55–84.

Auerbach, Alan J. 1979. Wealth Maximization and the Cost of Capital. *Quarterly Journal of Economics* 93:433ff.

———. 1983a. Corporate Taxation in the U.S. *Brookings Papers on Economic Activity,* No. 2.

———. 1983b. Taxation, Corporate Financial Policy, and the Cost of Capital. *Journal of Economic Literature* 21:905–40.

———. 1985. Saving in the U.S.: Some Conceptual Issues. In *The Level and Composition of Household Saving,* ed. Patric Hendershott. Cambridge, Mass.: Ballinger.

———. 1989. Tax Reform and Adjustment Costs: The Impact on Investment and Market Value. *International Economic Review* 30 (November): 939–62.

Auerbach, Alan J., and James R. Hines, Jr. 1987. Anticipated Tax Changes and the Timing of Investment. In *The Effects of Taxation on Capital Accumulation,* ed. Martin Feldstein. Chicago: University of Chicago Press.

Beaver, William H., and Stephen Ryan. 1985. Do Statement Thirty-three Earnings Explain Stock Prices? *Financial Analysts Journal* 61, no. 5 (September–October): 66–71.

Blades, Derek W., and Peter Sturm. 1982. The Concept and Measurement of Savings: The United States and Other Industrialized Countries. In *Saving and Government Policy.* Boston: Federal Reserve Bank of Boston.

Blinder, Alan S., and Angus S. Deaton. 1985. The Time Series Consumption Function Revisited. *Brookings Papers on Economic Activity,* no. 2, 465–511.

Board of Governors of the Federal Reserve System. 1988. *Balance Sheets for the U.S. Economy, 1948–87.* Washington, D.C., October.

Boskin, Michael J. 1986. Theoretical Issues in the Measurement, Evaluation and Interpretation of Postwar U.S. Saving. In *Savings and Capital Formation,* ed. F. Gerald Adams and Susan M. Wachter, 11–43. Lexington, Mass.: Lexington Books.

———. 1988. Issues in the Measurement and Interpretation of Saving and Wealth. NBER Working Paper no. 2633. Cambridge, Mass., June.

Boskin, Michael J., and Lawrence J. Lau. 1988. An Analysis of Postwar U.S. Consumption and Saving. Center for Economic Policy Research, Stanford, Calif., August. Mimeograph.

Boskin, Michael J., Marc S. Robinson, and Alan M. Huber. 1987. Government Saving, Capital Formation and Wealth in the United States, 1947–85. In *The Measurement of Saving, Investment, and Wealth,* ed. Robert E. Lipsey and Helen Stone Tice, 287–353. NBER Studies in Income and Wealth, vol. 52. Chicago: University of Chicago Press.

Bradford, David F. 1978. Factor Prices May Be Constant but Factor Returns Are Not. *Economics Letters* 1:199–203.

———. 1981. The Incidence and Allocational Effects of a Tax on Corporate Distributions. *Journal of Public Economics* 15: 1–22.

———. 1986. *Untangling the Income Tax.* Cambridge, Mass.: Harvard University Press.

Brainard, William C., John B. Shoven, and Laurence Weiss. 1980. Financial Valuation of the Return to Capital. *Brookings Papers on Economic Activity* no. 2, 453–511.

Breeden, Douglas T. 1979. An Intertemporal Asset Pricing Model with Stochastic

Consumption and Investment Opportunities. *Journal of Financial Economics* 7 (September): 265–96.

Brown, Murray. 1980. The Measurement of Capital Aggregates: A Postreswitching Problem. In *The Measurement of Capital,* ed. Dan Usher, 377–420. NBER Studies in Income and Wealth, vol. 45. Chicago: University of Chicago Press.

Bulow, Jeremy I., and Lawrence H. Summers. 1984. The Taxation of Risky Assets. *Journal of Political Economy* 42: no. 1 (February): 20–38.

Campbell, John. 1987. Does Saving Anticipate Declining Labor Income? *Econometrica* 55, no. 6 (November): 1249–73.

Campbell, John, and Angus Deaton. 1988. Why Is Consumption So Smooth? Woodrow Wilson School, Princeton University, January. Mimeograph.

Deaton, Angus. 1987. Consumers' Expenditure. In *The New Palgrave: A Dictionary of Economics,* ed. John Eatwell, Murray Milgate, and Peter Newman, 1:592–604. New York: Stockton.

Eisner, Robert. 1980. Capital Gains and Income: Real Changes in the Value of Capital in the United States, 1946–77. In *The Measurement of Capital,* ed. Dan Usher, 175–344. NBER Studies in Income and Wealth, vol. 45. Chicago: University of Chicago Press.

———. 1986. *How Real Is the Federal Deficit?* New York: Free Press.

———. 1988. Extended Accounts for National Income and Product. *Journal of Economic Literature* 26 (December): 1611–84.

———. 1989. Divergences of Measurement and Theory and Some Implications for Economic Policy. *American Economic Review* 79, no. 1 (March): 1–13.

Eisner, Robert, and Paul J. Pieper. 1989. The World's Greatest Debtor Nation. Typescript. Department of Economics, Northwestern University, January 13.

Financial Accounting Standards Board. 1978. Objectives of Financial Reporting by Business Enterprises. FASB Statement of Financial Accounting Concepts no. 1. FASB, Stamford, Conn.

Foster, George. 1986. *Financial Statement Analysis,* 2d ed. Englewood Cliffs, NJ: Prentice-Hall.

Gibson, Charles H., and Patricia A. Frishkoff. 1986. *Financial Statement Analysis,* 3d ed. Boston, Mass.: Kent Publishing.

Goldsmith, Raymond W. 1982. *The National Balance Sheet of the United States, 1953–1980.* Chicago: University of Chicago Press.

Hall, Robert E. 1978. Stochastic Implications of the Life Cycle-Permanent Income Hypothesis: Theory and Evidence. *Journal of Political Economy* 86 (December): 971–87.

———. 1988. Intertemporal Substitution in Consumption. *Journal of Political Economy* 96, pt. 2: 339–57.

Hicks, John R. 1946. *Value and Capital,* 2d ed. Oxford: Clarendon.

Hulten, Charles R., and Frank C. Wykoff. 1981. The Measurement of Economic Depreciation. In *Depreciation, Inflation and the Taxation of Income from Capital,* ed. Charles R. Hulten, 81–125. Washington, D.C.: Urban Institute.

Ingersoll, Jonathan E. 1987. *Theory of Financial Decision Making.* Totowa, N.J.: Rowman & Littlefield.

Institute for Fiscal Studies. 1978. *The Structure and Reform of Direct Taxation: The Report of a Committee Chaired by Professor J. E. Meade.* London: George Allen & Unwin.

Kotlikoff, Laurence J. 1984. Taxation and Savings: A Neoclassical Perspective. *Journal of Economic Literature* 22 (December): 1576–1629.

———. 1986. Deficit Delusion. *The Public Interest* 84 (Summer): 53–65.

———. 1988. The Deficit Is Not a Well-Defined Measure of Fiscal Policy. *Science* 241 (August): 791–95.

Lipsey, Robert E., and Irving B. Kravis. 1987. Is the U.S. a Spendthrift Nation? NBER Working Paper no. 2274. Cambridge, Mass., June.

Lipsey, Robert E., and H.S. Tice, eds. 1989. *The Measurement of Saving, Investment, and Wealth*. NBER Studies in Income and Wealth, vol. 52. Chicago: University of Chicago Press.

Merton, Robert C. 1971. Optimum Consumption and Portfolio Rules in a Continuous-Time Model. *Journal of Economic Theory* 3, no. 4 (December): 373–413.

———. 1973. An Intertemporal Capital Asset Pricing Model. *Econometrica* 41, no. 5 (September): 867–87.

Musgrave, John C. 1983. Fixed Reproducible Wealth in the United States, 1972–82. *Survey of Current Business* 63, no. 8 (August): 62–65.

———. 1986a. Fixed Reproducible Tangible Wealth in the United States, 1972–82, Revised Estimates. *Survey of Current Business* 66, no. 1 (January): 51–75.

———. 1986b. Fixed Reproducible Tangible Wealth in the United States, 1982–85. *Survey of Current Business* 66, no. 8 (August): 36–39.

Obstfeld, Maurice. 1986. Capital Mobility in the World Economy: Theory and Measurement. *Carnegie-Rochester Conference Series on Public Policy* 24 (Spring): 55–103.

Peek, Joe. 1986. Household Wealth Composition: The Impact of Capital Gains. *New England Economic Review* (November/December): 26–39.

Pollak, Robert A. 1975. The Intertemporal Cost of Living Index. *Annals of Economic and Social Measurement* 4, no. 1 (Winter): 179–95.

Poterba, James M. 1987. Tax Policy and Corporate Savings. *Brookings Papers on Economic Activity*, no. 2 (December): 455–503.

Poterba, James M., and Lawrence H. Summers. 1987. Recent U.S. Evidence on Budget Deficits and National Savings. NBER Working Paper no. 2144. Cambridge, Mass., February.

Ruggles, Richard, and Nancy Ruggles. 1981. Integrated Economic Accounts for the United States, 1947–1980. Institute for Social and Policy Studies Working Paper no. 84. Yale University, New Haven, Conn., October.

Shleifer, Andrei, and Lawrence H. Summers. 1987. Breach of Trust in Hostile Takeovers. NBER Working Paper no. 2342. Cambridge, Mass., August.

Shoven, John B. 1984. Saving in the U.S. Economy. In *Removing Obstacles to Economic Growth*, ed. Michael L. Wachter and Susan M. Wachter, 187–223. Philadelphia: University of Pennsylvania Press.

Stiglitz, Joseph E. 1972. On the Optimality of the Stock Market Allocation of Investment. *Quarterly Journal of Economics* (February): 25–60.

———. 1979. The Inefficiency of the Stock Market Equilibrium. Princeton University, April. Mimeograph.

Summers, Lawrence H. 1983. Observations on the Indexation of Old Age Pensions. In *Financial Aspects of the U.S. Pension System*, ed. Zvi Bodie and John B. Shoven, 231–51, 257–58. Chicago: University of Chicago Press.

———. 1985. Issues in National Savings Policy. NBER Working Paper no. 1710. Cambridge, Mass., August.

———. 1986. Does the Stock Market Rationally Reflect Fundamental Values? *Journal of Finance* 41, no. 3 (July): 591–601.

Summers, Lawrence H., and Chris Carroll. 1987. Why Is U.S. National Saving So Low? *Brookings Papers on Economic Activity*, no. 2, 607–35.

U.S. Department of Commerce, Bureau of Economic Analysis. 1986. *The National Income and Product Accounts of the United States, 1929–82*. Washington, D.C.: Government Printing Office, September.

———. 1987. *Fixed Reproducible Tangible Wealth in the United States, 1925–85*. Washington, D.C.: Government Printing Office, June.

West, Kenneth. 1988. The Insensitivity of Consumption to News about Income. *Journal of Monetary Economics* 21: 17–33.

Comment   Joseph E. Stiglitz

This paper raises a fundamental issue for those engaged in both theoretical and empirical work in macroeconomics: What should be the appropriate concept of savings and income, and how should it be measured? Bradford challenges the conventional wisdom by putting forward two propositions:

1. "Saving should be defined by reference to the underlying concept of wealth, to which the saving is an increment."
2. "The most useful wealth concept is the market value of assets, not the cost-based measure of capital implied by the use of national income and product account (NIPA) saving."

Bradford's paper makes an important contribution in providing us a cautionary tale on the use of time-series macroeconomic data. Some of us have wondered how much information could be extracted from the standard six or seven time series, which by now have been analyzed exhaustively. If data mining was ever a problem, surely it must be here. This must be a pit that has been exhausted—at the very least the quality of the ore can hardly justify sinking many more resources down what surely must be a bottomless hole.

It has now been widely recognized that macroeconomics must be based on microeconomic foundations. And, if that is so, surely we must base much of our econometric research by focusing on microeconomic units, not the aggregate series that (so many) macroeconometricians have so long taken as their principal province.

Bradford focuses on the difficulties associated with determining saving, the contrasting figures one obtains from looking at national income and product accounts and estimates based on wealth accounts, with saving's being defined as the change in the value of wealth. He argues forcefully that the appropriate measure should be the change in the value of wealth, using current market values.

The magnitude of the discrepancy between the two—even after account of certain obvious differences between the two—makes one pause and ask, Which series should we be using and for what purposes?

Bradford bases his analysis on well-received principles of microeconomics, principles that have long been employed in other branches of economics. In public finance, the Haig-Simon definitions of income reflect the same under-

Joseph E. Stiglitz is a professor of economics at Stanford University, a senior fellow at the Hoover Institution, and a research associate at the National Bureau of Economic Research. He is also the editor of the *Journal of Economic Perspectives*.

lying concerns that give rise to the first proposition. And in finance, the efficient markets hypothesis, holding that the current market value is an unbiased estimated of the future returns, has reigned supreme for more than a decade.

It has also long been recognized that it makes a difference, both to economic theory and econometric practice, what concept of income, saving, and wealth one employs and how these variables are measured. More than two decades ago, Karl Shell, Miguel Sidrauski, and I (1969) analyzed the dynamics of an economy in which savings—measured in a way similar to that suggested by Bradford—was related to income (again, measured in the corresponding way). The dynamics were markedly different from that of the standard growth model.

Still, I am not convinced by Bradford's conclusions. One needs to begin by asking, for what purpose do we want the measure of savings or wealth. Here, I want to distinguish two broad uses. The first is in making predictions. For a variety of reasons, we may want to be able to predict, say, consumption next period. Consumption is related to income, but what concept or measure of income? The second, to which I will turn later in my comments, is for purposes of welfare analysis.

The decades since Keynes have taught us that the concept of income on which consumption is supposed to depend is indeed elusive. Emphasis centered around life-time and permanent income considerations. These neoclassical theories actually argued that one could dispense with income and focus attention on wealth—human plus nonhuman capital. (Of course, general theories, noting the different stochastic properties of human and nonhuman capital, suggested that one could not simply add the two together.)

Recent theoretical and empirical work has cast doubt on this basic conception. Hall has observed, for instance, that if consumption really depended on permanent income, then changes in consumption should be a random walk. Subsequent empirical work seems to have supported the conclusion that consumption is not as volatile as the permanent income theory would suggest.

At the same time, theoretical work has emphasized the importance of capital market imperfections (derived from information asymmetries), providing a rationale for why individuals can smooth their consumption only imperfectly and why shortfalls in current income may be reflected in current consumption (see, e.g., Stiglitz and Weiss 1981, and Greenwald, Stiglitz, and Weiss 1984). These theoretical arguments are bolstered by observations concerning the small reserves of liquid assets held by most households, even in a a wealthy country such as the United States.

These views suggest that a simple measure of wealth such as that envisaged by Bradford has little claim for being *the* measure of wealth to employ in econometric studies.

There are further objections to Bradford's second proposition, that the measure of wealth to be employed should be based on stock market value. From the first perspective, what measure provides a good prediction of, say, consumption, the question is simply an empirical one: the proof is in the pudding. If this measure provides a better "consumption function", then the Bradford consumption function will replace the Friedman and Modigliani-Ando consumption functions in basic macroeconometric models. Bradford has not provided us with the econometric evidence. Here, let me say why I am skeptical.

It would, undoubtedly, be unfair to begin the argument with that dramatic event, the October 1987 stock market crash, but I cannot resist: in that one day, a quarter of the value of America's corporate "wealth," as Bradford would have us measure it, was wiped out. This should have had an instantaneous and large effect on consumption. It was an event which did not go unnoticed. And yet, it did not seem to have such a large effect.

There are strong reasons to believe that individuals do not believe the efficient markets hypotheses. How else can we explain their gambling (investing) behavior? (See Stiglitz 1982.) There is also direct corroborating evidence that they may be well advised not to: the persistent discrepancies in the value of closed-end mutual funds and the value of their underlying securities, and the volatility in that discount, is perhaps the best documented of these pieces of evidence. If individuals do not believe the stock market fully reflects the value of the assets, then the stock market value will not provide the best predictor of their behavior.

There is, by now, a well established, if somewhat controversial, literature on the excess volatility of the stock market. Moreover, volatility varies with the level of prices on the stock market. This evidence too is consistent with individuals not acting simply on the basis of the market value of their assets. (If individuals are risk averse, of course, market value will not be a "sufficient" statistic summarizing all the information that is relevant for their making their consumption decisions.)

Bradford, in his paper, focuses more on saving than on consumption. I am inclined to agree with Bob Hall that it makes more sense to talk about consumption, about the purchases of goods and services, than about savings, which is usually defined negatively as that part of income which is not consumed. Obviously, if we have a good theory of consumption, we can figure out what any particular savings construct will be. And conversely. But focusing on consumption enables us to avoid some of the difficulties associated with defining savings.

Bradford presents one example where his constructs may be of considerable help in understanding what is going on. He argues that savings, as conventionally measured, may be low in the United States not because there has been any change in underlying time preferences. Rather, more of savings has taken the form of an accretion in the value of owner-occupied houses (and real estate more generally). I cannot help but think that there is some truth in that argument, but is seems far from the whole matter. Are (conventionally measured) savings rates in Iowa, Texas, and Oklahoma, which have experienced declines in house prices and real estate values, markedly higher than in the rest of the country? Have saving rates increased dramatically in the past year, as the rate of increase in real estate prices have declined? I have no doubt that wealth variables (including housing wealth) should enter the consumption function, but I am skeptical whether doing so will explain away all of the current U.S. savings puzzle.

Let me now turn to the second use to which such numbers can be put: welfare analysis, making judgments about the future economic prospects of the economy. Does "savings"—an increase in wealth, as measured in the way that Bradford would have us measure it—provide the best predictor of the increase in the economy's present discounted value of future output? Or does NIPA provide a better measure?

NIPA provides an estimate of the gross investment, but it has long been recognized that the estimates of net investment—that is, the depreciation on existing capital stock—are not reliable. If the economy is growing steadily, with little change in the pace of innovation, then there might be a regular relationship between net and gross investment, and hence the errors committed by focusing on NIPA accounts might not be too serious. But when the economy faces large changes in relative prices, and consequently large changes in the value of various assets, the NIPA accounts might be misleading. The changes in the price of oil might have lead to much capital being economically without value, and focusing on NIPA investment accounts would have, accordingly, led us to overestimate the future productivity of the economy.

The questions is not whether NIPA is a perfect measure. That has never been an issue. The only question is, Would using a market based measure be more reliable? Again, I am skeptical. Besides all the reasons listed above for why one might not believe in the efficient markets hypothesis, there is one more: changes in the market value will also reflect changes in the real rates of interest and in risk discount factors. These present difficult index number problems for any national income accountant. But I am not sure that simply ignoring them—as the Bradford measure would have us do—is appropriate.

The theory of the valuation of national income developed over the past century (see, e.g., Samuelson 1950) is based on a competitive theory with perfect risk markets and, if not perfect information, at least no informational asymmetries. These theories can no longer be taken seriously. There is, accordingly, a fundamental lacuna in the foundations of the theory of the valuation of national income. In the absence of such foundations, we should take a catholic view on how to proceed with both theoretical and empirical work in this area: we should think deeply about what the appropriate variables are and how they can be measured. Bradford has performed a valuable service in focusing our attention on these fundamental questions.

References

Greenwald, B., J. E. Stiglitz, and A. Weiss. Informational Imperfections in the Capital Markets and Macro-economic Fluctuations. *American Economic Review* 74, no. 1 (May): 194–99.
Samuelson, P. A. 1950. Evaluation of Real National Income. *Oxford Economic Papers*. January.
Shell, K., M. Sidrauski, and J. E. Stiglitz. 1969. Capital Gains, Income and Savings. *Review of Economic Studies* 36 (January): 15–26.
Stiglitz, J. E. 1982. Information and Capital Markets. In *Financial Economics: Essays in Honor of Paul Cootner,* ed. William F. Sharpe and Cathryn Cootner, 118–58. Englewood Cliffs, N.J.: Prentice Hall.
Stiglitz, J. E. and A. Weiss. 1981. Credit Rationing in Markets with Imperfect Information. *American Economic Review* 71, no. 3 (June): 393–410.

2   Dividends, Capital Gains, and the Corporate Veil: Evidence from Britain, Canada, and the United States

James M. Poterba

Whether households pierce the corporate veil is a fundamental issue for evaluating the radical changes in both tax policy and corporate financial behavior that have occurred in the United States during the 1980s. The share of pretax corporate earnings that are distributed to the owners of corporate capital—either as dividends, share repurchases, or interest—has increased significantly during this period. Reductions in dividend taxes coupled with increased tax burdens on capital gains have lowered the incentive to accumulate profits within the corporation and encouraged dividend payout. Tax changes have also affected optimal capital structure. Net equity issues by U.S. firms have been *negative* in each year since 1984, as firms have replaced equity with debt finance. This paper investigates the effects of increased cash payout, and of "forced realizations" of capital gains in corporate control transactions, on the level of aggregate consumption.

The standard neoclassical paradigm suggests that these changes should not affect consumption, except through their effects on the cost of capital facing firms. Since households base consumption on their net worth, the question of whether capital gains are realized and whether cash is paid out of the firm or retained and reflected in higher asset values should not affect spending decisions. Numerous empirical studies have failed to reject the null hypothesis that the division of corporate earnings between cash distributions and reten-

James Poterba is professor of economics at the Massachusetts Institute of Technology and a research associate of the National Bureau of Economic Research.

The author is grateful to Mervyn King, Jack Mintz, and Patrick O'Hagen for providing data; to Alan Auerbach, Olivier Blanchard, Martin Feldstein, Robert Hall, Lawrence Summers, and seminar participants at Boston University, Columbia, Queens University, Toronto, and the NBER Conference on the Economics of Saving for helpful discussions, and to the National Science Foundation and NBER for financial support. A data appendix for this project has been deposited at the ICPSR in Ann Arbor, Michigan.

tions does not affect consumption and, therefore, have concluded that there is no corporate veil.

An alternative view, supported as much by anecdotal evidence as by formal theoretical models, argues that households respond differently to different accretions to wealth. Malinvaud (1986) argues that "households must consider one franc of retained earnings as being less permanently gained than that same franc if it had been distributed as a dividend. In other words, even perfectly informed and rational households will not fully compensate by their consumption private corporate saving, not to speak of less well-informed or more careless shareholders" (119).

The corporate veil might also be due to investor reliance on rules of thumb or other behavioral principles. Shefrin and Statman (1985), for example, suggest that households often draw arbitrary distinctions between consuming out of principal and consuming out of income. Investors may be myopic, may fail to devote the necessary resources to monitor developments within firms, or may otherwise fail to completely pierce the corporate veil.[1] If such behavior is widespread, the division of corporate income between cash payout and retained earnings could affect spending decisions. It is nevertheless difficult to determine the importance of such investor behavior on a priori grounds. The transparency of the corporate veil is therefore an empirical issue.

Identifying the link between corporate cash flows and consumption is complicated by the fact that many factors that raise corporate profits and therefore corporate saving, such as technological shocks that increase the productivity of capital, also affect the opportunity set facing households. Finding that dividends raise consumption may simply indicate that positive news about future cash flows increases consumer spending. The central problem is, therefore, finding a source of variation in corporate cash flow that does not directly affect consumption. I argued (Poterba 1987a) that shifts in the relative tax burdens on corporate payouts and retentions alter corporate financial policy but are unlikely to have large direct effects on household behavior. My empirical results for the United States suggested that raising corporate payout by one dollar was associated with an increase of thirty cents or more in consumption spending.

This study extends my previous investigation in two directions. First, it exploits the tax policy variation in Britain and Canada, as well as the United States, to develop further tests of whether investors pierce the corporate veil. Second, it tests another link between cash flow and consumption by exploring whether forced capital gain realizations in takeover transactions affect consumer spending.

This study is divided into five sections. The first outlines previous work on the question of whether households pierce the corporate veil. Section 2.2 describes my consumption function specification and discusses econometric issues. Section 2.3 presents the aggregate data on the United States, Britain, and Canada that are used in estimation. Section 2.4 reports consumption functions for each of the three countries and analyzes whether changes in dividend tax rates affect consumption. The results are not conclusive, but for each country they point toward the presence of a corporate veil. The fifth section examines how forced capital gain realizations affect consumption, in this case focusing exclusively on the United States. The findings suggest that such realizations may raise consumption by as much as 40 cents on the dollar, primarily by increasing outlays on durables. The final section suggests directions for future work.

2.1 Previous Evidence on Consumption and Corporate Cash Flow

The hypothesis that households pierce the corporate veil received initial empirical support from studies on the stylized pattern of U.S. saving rates through time. Denison's (1958) pioneering study observed that gross private saving was a remarkably stable fraction of GNP for the United States during the decade after World War II. David and Scadding (1974) confirmed this finding using a longer time series and generalized it by noting that the sum of the gross private saving rate and the government saving rate had varied very little over the previous century.

Most subsequent studies have tested for the presence of a corporate veil by estimating either consumption or saving functions on aggregate time-series data. Modigliani's (1970) study examined the cross-national correlation between corporate saving rates and total private saving rates. His point estimates generally suggested that higher retained earnings led to higher private saving rates, but the standard errors were too large to reject the null hypothesis of no effect. Feldstein (1973) studied U.S. consumption data for the period 1929–66, and found convincing evidence that households raise consumption in response to retained earnings. He rejected the strict Keynesian hypothesis that disposable income matters to the exclusion of retained profits, but his point estimates suggested that the propensity to consume dividends (approximately 76 cents per dollar) was larger than the comparable propensity to consume retained earnings (about 50 cents per dollar). In a parallel study for the United Kingdom, Feldstein and Fane (1973) found that a pound of dividend income raised consumption by 75 pence, while a pound of retained earnings had a 25-pence effect.

The same pattern—higher marginal propensities to spend from dividends than from retain earnings—emerges in other, more recent, studies. In some cases the differential was too small, or the standard errors were too large, to reject the null hypothesis of equal consumption effects. Howrey and Hymans (1978) conclude that a one dollar decrease in corporate saving caused by higher dividend payout would raise consumption by 25 cents.[2] However, von Furstenberg's (1981) estimates suggest a change of between 40 and 60 cents. Both studies conclude that households pierce the corporate veil, a finding which is true to a degree.

None of the studies that reject the corporate veil provide strong evidence that households *completely* pierce the corporate veil. In contrast, two studies by Bhatia (1979) and Hendershott and Peek (1989) claim to find evidence *for* a corporate veil. Bhatia (1979) followed Feldstein's (1973) methodology, adding several additional years of data and modifying some of the data series in minor ways. He found no evidence that retained earnings-induced capital gains on corporate stock affect consumption any more than other capital gains, which implies that an increase in dividends financed by reduced retentions would have a large positive effect on consumption. Hendershott and Peek (1989) adjust both personal and corporate saving for inflationary mismeasurement and conclude that previous evidence of a negative correlation between the two was primarily the result of opposite-signed inflationary biases.

None of the foregoing studies address the potential endogeneity of corporate saving in regression equations explaining aggregate consumption. If profit rates vary through time, changes in corporate saving may in part reflect shocks to the economic environment that could affect consumption even if households do not pierce the corporate veil. One could even develop models with transactions costs for selling shares and imperfect credit markets where shocks to consumption affect corporate saving through the demand for cash dividends.

The only studies that recognize the potential endogeneity of corporate saving are Poterba (1987a) and Auerbach and Hassett (in this volume). These studies employ U.S. data for 1929–86, and for the postwar period, respectively. The former study used changes in dividend taxation to identify exogenous shifts in the level of corporate saving and found weak support for the view that corporate saving affects total private saving. Auerbach and Hassett work in the Euler-equation framework (surveyed in Hall 1989) and test whether *forecastable* movements in dividends affect spending. If households were liquidity constrained, then even forecastable dividend changes would affect spending. Auerbach and Hassett's evidence that forecastable changes in dividends do not affect consumption is therefore strong evidence against the liquidity-constraints account for the corporate veil. It is weaker evidence against some of the alternative explanations based on myopia or other considerations.[3]

2.2   Consumption and Corporate Cash Flow

An extension of the Ando-Modigliani (1963) aggregate consumption function provides a useful shorthand to formalize the hypothesis that cash receipts affect consumption more than accruing capital gains. The standard life-cycle–permanent income formulation relates consumption to human wealth, the present discounted value of after-tax labor earnings, as well as financial and nonfinancial net assets. Demographic variables, such as the fraction of the population in their retirement years, may also alter the level of per capital consumption. Generalizing this framework to allow for the possibility that dividends affect household expenditures, the consumption function may be written:

(1) $C_t = \alpha_0 + \alpha_1 A_t + \alpha_2 HW_t + \alpha_3 SHR65_t + \alpha_4 DIV_t + \varepsilon_t.$

In (1), C_t denotes real per capita consumption, A_t the household sector's beginning of period stock of nonhuman wealth, HW_t human wealth at the beginning of the period, SHR65 the fraction of the population aged 65 or greater, and DIV_t cash dividend receipts. If households pierce the corporate veil and dividends convey no information about future corporate profits that is not also reflected in share values, then α_4 should be zero.

It is critical to focus on variation in DIV_t that is uncorrelated with other news that may affect consumption. Variation in tax policy induces such movements in dividends and may be used to identify α_4. The tax treatment of dividends versus retained earnings can be summarized in a "tax discrimination variable," θ_t, defined as

(2) $\theta_t = \Sigma w_{it}^*[(1-m_{it})/(1-z_{it})],$

where m_{it} denotes the marginal dividend tax rate on investor i in period t, z_{it} the effective capital gains tax rate for this investor, and w_{it} the share of corporate equity held by this investor.[4] Provided dividend policy is determined by equating the marginal benefit of paying dividends, whether from reduced agency costs or improved signaling, to the tax cost of payout, θ_t should affect dividend distributions. This yields an equation for firm behavior:

(3) $DIV_t = \beta_0 + \beta_1 \theta_t + Z_t \gamma + \mu_t,$

where $Z_t \gamma$ includes corporate profits and other variables that may be correlated with the residuals in the consumption function. My identifying assumption is that θ_t has no direct effect on consumption but operates only through its influence on payout.[5] This implies that equation (1) can be estimated by instrumental variables, using θ_t as an instrument for DIV_t.

Equation (1) is exactly identified. One could therefore test for the presence of a corporate veil by estimating (1) by instrumental variables, using θ_t as an instrument for DIV_t. A more direct (but equivalent) test for the presence of the corporate veil is to include θ_t in the consumption equation and test for the significance of this variable:[6]

(4) $C_t = \alpha_0 + \alpha_1 A_t + \alpha_2 HW_t + \alpha_3 SHR65_t + \alpha_5 \theta_t + \varepsilon_t.$

This approach avoids the need to specify a detail model of corporate payout, an important virtue since no such model is generally accepted.[7]

Two empirical difficulties arise in estimating (4). First, human wealth is unobservable. Hayashi (1981) addresses this problem by quasi differencing (4) and focusing on consumption responses to the unanticipated change in labor income (and its associated forecast power for human wealth). Since α_2

is only an incidental parameter in this study, I adopt the simpler approach of assuming that human wealth is a constant multiple of current after-tax labor income:

(5) $$HW_t = YL_t/\rho.$$

The HW_t in equation (4) can thus be replaced with YL_t, with the resulting coefficient reinterpreted accordingly.[8]

The second econometric difficulty is that real per capita consumption and some of the nontax explanatory variables in (4) are nearly nonstationary time series.[9] Differencing (4) to achieve stationarity may eliminate much of the useful low-frequency variation in the tax discrimination variable, raising its noise-to-signal ratio and biasing the estimated coefficient toward zero. I therefore estimate (4) both in levels and differences. I present levels estimates with and without a time trend, and differenced estimates with and without an intercept, since these are parallel specifications. The estimated standard errors in the level equation are corrected for serial correlation using the Newey-West (1987) algorithm allowing for correlation at one lag.

A similar approach can be used to study whether other forms of cash income from capital investments affect consumption. One particularly interesting cash flow, in light of the recent growth in corporate share repurchases and takeover transactions, is the stream of realized capital gains that result from "involuntary" stock sales when firms are taken over or go private. Bagwell and Shoven (1989) report that, in 1986, when cash dividend payments were $77.1 billion, share repurchases by U.S. corporations totaled $41.5 billion, and merger and acquisition expenditures were $74.5 billion.

There are many reasons for expecting a positive effect of involuntary realizations on consumption. In models with costly trading or other frictions in portfolio adjustment, for example, a forced realization may catalyze consumption spending. Evidence that realized gains are correlated with consumption outlays is not informative on the general issue of whether forced realizations spur consumption, since most gain realizations are voluntary. The same factors that impinge on consumption decisions may therefore affect realizations. Asset sales in many corporate control transactions, however, are involuntary. Households who own shares in firms that are purchased for cash (as opposed to with securities swaps) receive cash for their shares, even if they had planned to hold their shares for a long period.

Equation (4) can be augmented to test whether the value of cash payouts in control transactions, $CASHMERG_t$, affects consumption:

(6) $$C_t = \alpha_0 + \alpha_1 A_t + \alpha_2 HW_t + \alpha_3 SHR65_t + \alpha_5 \theta_t + \alpha_6 CASHMERG_t + \varepsilon_t.$$

The contemporaneous level of corporate takeovers may be correlated with the error in (6) because it may lead to asset revaluations as investors decide that other stocks are "in play." I therefore modify (6) in some cases, replacing A_t

with A_{t+1}. The total value of assets dated *after* the news about control transactions should avoid the revaluation problem, although it raises other difficulties.[10]

2.3   Data Issues

Two criteria restrict the set of countries for which the aggregate consumption equations could be estimated. First, the countries need significant variation in the relative tax burdens on dividends and capital gains. Second, the tests require regularly available information on household net worth. The latter is a binding constraint for most countries. Three countries that satisfy these conditions and for which data are readily available are Canada, the United States, and the United Kingdom.[11] Since the principal novelty in my estimation is the tax variable θ_t, I begin by discussing it and then briefly mention the other data series.

2.3.1   Tax Discrimination Variables

For each country, the aggregate dividend tax preference variable is calculated as the weighted average of $(1-m_i)/(1-z_i)$ with weights based on equity ownership. In Britain the tax discrimination variable also allows for changes through time in the relative corporate tax burdens on retained versus distributed profits; these variables are described in more detail in Poterba and Summers (1985) and King (1977).

Table 2.1 presents time series for θ_t for each country. In the United States θ_t has increased over time. The increasing fraction of corporate shares held by nontaxable investors, the decline in personal marginal tax rates on dividends, and the recent increase in capital gains taxes have raised θ_t from approximately .60 in the early 1950s to roughly .85 in the late 1980s.

The United Kingdom both raised and lowered dividend taxes during the sample period. Adoption of a two-tiered rate of corporate taxation in 1958, with a higher rate on retained than on distributed profits, encouraged payout. This policy was changed in 1965 to a classical corporate income tax system of the type used in the United States, with the net effect of lowering θ_t and discouraging dividend payments. Another policy reversal in 1972, with the adoption of an integrated corporate income tax, made dividend payout more attractive.[12] The substantial increase in θ_t during the late 1970s reflects declining marginal tax burdens on individual investors, due to systematic reductions in tax rates at high income levels.

Data on the marginal tax burdens for Canadian shareholders were only available for 1963–86. The increase in the tax incentive for dividend payout beginning in 1972 results from introduction of a capital gains tax with a statutory rate of 27%. The discrete increase in payout incentives in 1978 is due to a change in the dividend tax credit scheme, which made dividend credits so generous that the tax system was "over-integrated." Beginning in 1982, and,

Table 2.1:   Dividend Tax Preference Variables

Year	United States	United Kingdom	Canada
1950	.650	.585	. . .
1951	.620	.519	. . .
1952	.607	.532	. . .
1953	.627	.539	. . .
1954	.635	.543	. . .
1955	.629	.532	. . .
1956	.632	.500	. . .
1957	.641	.535	. . .
1958	.644	.677	. . .
1959	.646	.725	. . .
1960	.656	.715	. . .
1961	.649	.709	. . .
1962	.658	.702	. . .
1963	.657	.678	.850
1964	.688	.602	.830
1965	.701	.544	.830
1966	.698	.430	.820
1967	.690	.427	.810
1968	.677	.432	.800
1969	.699	.444	.780
1970	.703	.434	.780
1971	.714	.456	.790
1972	.714	.486	.955
1973	.721	.705	.943
1974	.718	.615	.943
1975	.721	.640	.908
1976	.714	.655	.908
1977	.709	.605	.932
1978	.713	.748	1.068
1979	.691	.858	1.056
1980	.695	.855	1.033
1981	.699	.828	1.022
1982	.752	.796	.978
1983	.768	.832	1.024
1984	.780	.910	1.012
1985	.784	.900	.915
1986	.783	.885	.915
1987	.830	. .	. . .

Note: Each entry shows the ratio of after-tax income from one dollar of earnings paid out as dividends to one dollar of retained earnings. The data series for the United States is drawn from Poterba (1987a), that for Britain was furnished by Mervyn King, and the Canadian series was supplied by Jack Mintz.

more important, at the end of the sample, the dividend credit provisions were modified to eliminate the extraordinary incentives for dividend distribution, Jenkins (1986) discusses the various policy changes in some detail.

The most difficult part of estimating the tax discrimination variable is measuring the capital gains tax burden. Since gains are taxed only on realization, the effective tax burden depends on investor behavior. If gains are realized soon after they accrue, the tax burden will be higher than if gains are held for long periods. Estimates of z typically assume relatively simple rules for investor behavior; for example, that investors sell a fixed fraction of their assets each period. Since the capital gains tax rate is therefore measured with much greater error than the dividend tax rates, some of my empirical work explores the consequences of using *only* the dividend tax rate to measure relative tax burdens.[13]

2.3.2   Other Data Series

The remaining data series used in my analysis require less comment. Annual consumption in constant prices is drawn from the OECD National Income Accounts, and I estimate equations using both total consumption outlays and expenditures exclusive of durables. I focus on the postwar period for comparability across sample countries. Pretax labor income was defined as wages and salaries plus other labor income (employer contributions for pension plans and other benefits). An average tax burden on labor income was calculated as income tax payments divided by the sum of pretax labor income, property and entrepreneurial income, and the operating surplus of unincorporated enterprises. The results are relatively insensitive to the choice of tax rates and did not change when pretax rather than posttax labor income was used to measure YL_t in equation (4). When conversion from current to constant prices was needed, I used the price deflator for nondurable consumption.

Data on net worth of the household sector are drawn from national balance sheets. These data begin in 1948 for the United States, 1957 for Britain, and 1962 for Canada. For the United States and the United Kingdom, tangible assets such as residences and some financial assets, particularly equities, are measured at market value. Other financial assets, notably corporate and government bonds, are reported at book value. The Canadian data do not include any market value estimates; they are simply book-value estimates of asset holdings, and as such they are much less useful than the data for the other two nations. The net worth series are reported in appendix table 2A.1. Data were deflated to per capita terms using population data drawn from the U.K. *Annual Abstract of Statistics,* the *Historical Statistics of Canada,* and the *Statistical Abstract* for the United States. The fraction of the population aged 65 or older was also drawn from these sources and interpolated to create an annual series where necessary.

The final variable of interest is $CASHMERG_t$, the value of cash payouts in corporate control transactions. This variable was constructed for the United States using the W. T. Grimm & Company data series for cash merger and acquisition activity.[14] This data series is presented in appendix table 2A.2, and shows cash transactions doubling between 1977 and 1981 and doubling again by 1985. For the United Kingdom, a data series on total cash merger activity is published by the Department of Trade and Industry for the period since 1969. Data on total merger activity for earlier years was combined with information from Franks, Harris, and Mayer (1988) on the allocation of merger finance between cash and other securities to estimate the value of cash distributions. This data series, which displays a rapid increase in the mid-1980s, is also shown in the appendix table.

2.4   Estimation Results: Dividend Taxation and Consumption

This section presents the results of estimating equation (4) for the United States, Britain, and Canada. In table 2.2, parts A and B present the findings for the United States, using total consumption and total consumption excluding durables as the dependent variables, respectively. The coefficients on income and net worth are broadly consistent with the findings in earlier studies, although some equations evidence small net worth coefficients (around .01). In both the level and difference specifications the dividend preference variable, θ_t, has a positive effect on consumption. This is the direction predicted by the corporate veil hypothesis, since higher values of θ_t correspond to lower dividend tax burdens and higher levels of corporate payout. Only two of the specifications I present (one for levels, one for differences) yield coefficients on θ_t that are statistically significant at the conventional 95% confidence level. In all of the equations the estimated coefficients are positive, however, with t-statistics above 1.3.

The point estimates of the dividend tax effects vary substantially across specifications. They suggest that a ten percentage point increase in the dividend tax rate would reduce per capita consumption (in 1982 dollars) by between $100 and $400. More than half of this effect is on durable expenditures, as comparison between the estimates for total consumption (table 2.2, part A) and consumption excluding durables (table 2.2, part B) demonstrates. If one takes the view that expenditure on durables is essentially a form of saving, then the evidence is more favorable to the hypothesis that households pierce the corporate veil. In any case, it is clear that changes in the dividend tax rate affect the *allocation* of saving, shifting resources from business investment to household durables.[15]

Two other features of the results warrant comment. First, the estimated coefficients on θ_t usually decline when the equation includes a time trend (or an intercept when the equation is estimated in differences). Second, while the variable measuring the fraction of the population over age 65 does not significantly affect the other coefficients, its own coefficient is implausibly large. The coefficient in the last column suggests that a 10 percent increase in the share of the population over 65 would increase per capita consumption by $4,860 (in 1982 dollars). These unusual findings may be due to the short sample period and the trend in this variable, which may allow it to proxy for many time-varying effects. This is confirmed by the estimates in columns 2–3 of table 2.2, part A, where introducing the demographic variable induces a large change in the estimated coefficient on the trend variable.

Table 2.2   **Aggregate Consumption and Dividend Tax Preference, United States, 1950–87**

Explanatory Variable	A. Total Consumption Spending					
Constant	−2.558	−.559	−10.381	.054	. . .	. . .
	(.988)	(1.537)	(1.117)	(.018)		
Per capita after-tax labor income	1.010	.718	1.252	.828	1.021	.854
	(.131)	(.201)	(.067)	(.128)	(.125)	(.114)
Per capita net worth	.059	.019	−.006	.014	.019	.012
	(.025)	(.029)	(.013)	(.014)	(.015)	(.013)
Dividend tax preference (θ_t)	3.467	2.942	3.980	1.050	1.662	1.103
	(2.248)	(2.187)	(1.092)	(.801)	(.865)	(.749)
Time trend	. . .	.056	−.096	. . .	. . .	. . .
		(.028)	(.015)			
Percentage of population 65 or older	. . .	. . .	105.380	. . .	. . .	48.594
			(9.334)			(12.720)
Specification	Levels	Levels	Levels	Diffs	Diffs	Diffs
SEE	.216	.202	.092	.079	.088	.074
D-W	.260	.187	1.351	1.570	1.678	1.735
	B. Nondurable and Service Consumption					
Constant	−1.002	1.138	−4.627	.062	. . .	. . .
	(.697)	(.929)	(.858)	(.010)		
Per capita after-tax labor income	.846	.529	.823	.499	.721	.555
	(.091)	(.122)	(.067)	(.076)	(.094)	(.071)
Per capita net worth	.053	.009	−.005	.008	.014	.008
	(.020)	(.016)	(.009)	(.008)	(.011)	(.008)
Dividend tax preference (θ_t)	1.559	.988	1.562	.573	1.276	.720
	(1.644)	(1.414)	(.837)	(.476)	(.650)	(.464)
Time trend	. . .	.061	−.023	. . .	. . .	. . .
		(.016)	(.013)			
Percentage of population 65 or older	. . .	. . .	58.166	. . .	. . .	48.244
			(6.974)			(7.890)
Specification	Levels	Levels	Levels	Diffs	Diffs	Diffs
SEE	.148	.119	.065	.047	.066	.046
D-W	.471	.165	1.007	1.712	1.642	1.876

Note. Estimates are based on annual data, 1950–87. Standard errors are shown in parentheses; for the level specification they are corrected for the presence of first-order serial correlation using the Newey-West (1987) procedure.

To explore the sensitivity of these results to tax variation during the 1980s, I reestimated each equation for the sample period ending in 1980. The estimated coefficients on θ_t in the level specifications declined substantially, but the estimates from differenced models were virtually unchanged. The standard errors for all for the estimated coefficients increase and the null hypothesis that households completely pierce the corporate veil is no longer rejected, even at quite low confidence levels. Including a dummy variable for the period after 1980 has the same effect on an equation estimated for the full sample period, causing a substantial decline in the coefficient on the tax discrimination variable.

Table 2.3 reports estimates of equation (4) for the United Kingdom. In the level specification for both total and nondurable consumption, the no-veil hypothesis is rejected at standard confidence levels. These results are stronger than the comparable findings for the United States. When the equation is estimated in differenced form, however, the estimated coefficient on the dividend tax burden is again statistically insignificant, though it remains positive and suggests that lower dividend tax rates raise consumer spending. The importance of durable expenditures is also confirmed by these results: the estimated coefficients on total consumption are roughly twice as large as those on nondurable spending.

The final set of estimates, for Canada, are reported in table 2.4. Once again the estimated coefficients on net worth and after-tax labor income seem broadly plausible, while the large coefficients on the demographic variable seem implausible. The results on dividend taxation for Canada are different from those in the United States and the United Kingdom: in the level equations, the estimate of α_5 is *negative*. The differenced equations yield small and statistically insignificant positive coefficients. I explored the findings from the level equations somewhat further by separating the Canadian θ_t series into one component related to the marginal tax burden on dividends, and another arising from the tax burden on capital gains. When I assume that the capital gains tax rate is zero, estimates of α_5 in levels are positive and lead to rejection of the "no veil" null hypothesis at confidence levels similar to those at which the null hypothesis was rejected for the United States.[16]

A brief summary of the empirical import of these results is provided in table 2.5. Using 1986 as a benchmark, it reports the change in per capita consumption that representative estimates for each of the three sample countries would predict following a five percentage point increase in θ. This corresponds to a five percentage point reduction in the marginal dividend tax rate only when the capital gains tax rate is zero. The requisite change in the dividend tax rate is slightly smaller with positive capital gains rates. The estimated changes in total consumer spending from such a change vary from less than one-fifth of 1 percent in the United Kingdom, to one-half of 1 percent in Canada, to three-quarters of 1 percent in the United States. These changes are relatively large when compared with personal saving, which is typically between 5 and 10 percent of consumption. In the United States, for example, an .81 percentage point increase in consumption would correspond to a reduction of one-sixth in personal saving ($124 billion). A five percentage point increase in θ is of the order of magnitude of the changes due to each of the 1981 and 1986 tax reforms.[17]

Table 2.3   Aggregate Consumption and Dividend Tax Preference, United Kingdom, 1958–86

Explanatory Variable	Consumption							
	Total				Nondurable and Service			
	Levels	Levels	Differences	Differences	Levels	Levels	Differences	Differences
Constant	−1.182 (.106)	1.602 (1.424)	.067 (.039)	⋯	−.702 (.083)	1.665 (.893)	.051 (.025)	⋯
Per capita after-tax labor income	.329 (.060)	.334 (.051)	.530 (.157)	.588 (.160)	.345 (.044)	.342 (.035)	.441 (.099)	.485 (.103)
Per capita net worth	.048 (.008)	.037 (.004)	.024 (.010)	.028 (.010)	.033 (.006)	.024 (.003)	.017 (.006)	.021 (.006)
Dividend tax preference (θ_t)	.188 (.053)	.217 (.054)	.149 (.136)	.096 (.139)	.094 (.036)	.118 (.035)	.082 (.086)	.043 (.090)
Percentage of population 65 or older	20.651 (1.605)	−8.043 (14.77)	−22.734 (26.440)	22.170 (6.378)	16.940 (1.274)	−7.47 (9.31)	−15.553 (16.820)	18.214 (4.125)
Time trend	⋯	.046 (.022)	⋯	⋯	⋯	.039 (.014)	⋯	⋯
Specification	Levels	Levels	Differences	Differences	Levels	Levels	Differences	Differences
SEE	.040	.036	.039	.041	.027	.024	.025	.026
D-W	1.266	1.363	1.735	1.640	1.111	1.281	1.598	1.511

Note. Estimates are based on annual data, 1958–86. Standard errors are shown in parentheses; for the level specification they are corrected for the presence of first-order serial correlation using the Newey-West (1987) procedure.

Table 2.4   Aggregate Consumption and Dividend Tax Preference, Canada, 1963–86

Explanatory Variable	Consumption					
	Total			Nondurable and Service		
Constant	−.643	−1.030	.022	−2.268	−2.571	.062
	(.538)	(.502)	(.046)	(.314)	(.298)	(.030)
Per capita after-tax	.770	.734	.661	.643	.621	.343
labor income	(.065)	(.074)	(.145)	(.062)	(.051)	(.097)
Per capita net worth	.055	.061	.045	−.003	.001	.006
	(.023)	(.021)	(.017)	(.019)	(.015)	(.011)
Dividend tax	−.387	. . .	.148	−.263	. . .	.094
preference (θ_t)	(.374)		(.302)	(.229)		(.200)
Dividend tax	. . .	.731	. . .	. . .	.626	. . .
preference (no		(.496)			(.347)	
capital gains tax)						
Percentage of	25.570	24.737	28.046	46.426	45.886	20.652
population 65 or	(9.438)	(8.640)	(26.310)	(6.004)	(5.129)	(17.501)
older						
Specification	Levels	Levels	Differences	Levels	Levels	Differences
SEE	.093	.093	.074	.062	.059	.049
DW	.740	.804	1.162	1.038	1.200	1.833

Note. Estimates are based on annual data, 1963–86. Standard errors are shown in parentheses; for the level specification they are corrected for the presence of first-order serial correlation using the Newey-West (1987) procedure. Equations in levels do not include time-trend variables; these were estimated but always proved unimportant and did not affect the other coefficients.

Table 2.5   Estimated Consumption Effects from Changes in Dividend Tax

	Canada	United Kingdom	United States
Per capita consumption in 1986	11,475	4,171	11,611
Estimated consumption shift from	+53	+7	+95
five percentage point decline in	(34)	(7)	(49)
dividend tax burden (θ)			
Percentage change in consumption	+.46%	+.18%	+.81%

Source: Author's calculations based on estimated coefficients in tables 2.2–2.4. Point estimate assumptions are from table 2.2, part A, col. 5 for the United States, from table 2.3, col. 3 for the United Kingdom, and table 2.4, col. 2 for Canada. Prediction standard errors are shown in parentheses.

The results in this section provide substantial support for the view that changes in corporate financial policy between retained and distributed profits affect the private saving rate. Higher dividend payouts induced by lower dividend tax rates are likely to translate into higher consumption levels. These results suggest a substantively important, yet relatively neglected, channel through which changes in capital income taxes affect saving decisions.

2.4   Consumption and Realized Capital Gains[18]

This section undertakes the limited task of evaluating the statistical link between forced realizations and consumption.[19] The results of estimating (6) for the United States are shown in table 2.6. All of the equations are estimated in differenced form, with the measure of net worth in the first and third columns corresponding to beginning-of-period asset values while that in the second and fourth columns is the end-of-period value. The hypothesis that $\alpha_6 = 0$ is rejected at standard levels in the equation for total consumption outlays where wealth is measured at the beginning of the year. The point estimates suggest that one dollar of realized gains raises spending by roughly 60 cents. More than half of this is spending on durables, since the coefficient falls to .21 (a 21 cent per dollar increase) when the dependent variable is nondurable and service consumption. When the wealth variable is measured at the end of the period the coefficient also declines, falling to .34 for total consumption and virtually zero for nondurables and services. The hypothesis that cash payouts have no effect on consumption cannot be rejected at standard levels in these equations, but the point estimates continue to suggest a substantively important link between cash payout and consumption.[20] The dividend tax variable does not change very much with this modification of the equation, however, which suggests that my findings are not due to a correlation between tax rates and wealth.[21]

The remaining coefficients in the consumption function change somewhat when realized gains are included in the specification. The coefficient on θ in

Table 2.6   **Aggregate Consumption and Involuntary Capital Gains Realizations**

	Consumption			
Explanatory Variable	Total		Nondurable and Service	
Per capita cash	.586	.337	.213	.007
takeover transactions	(.265)	(.266)	(.172)	(.161)
Per capita after-tax	.792	.881	.532	.590
labor income	(.112)	(.089)	(.073)	(.054)
Per capita net worth	.013	.027	.008	.023
	(.012)	(.011)	(.008)	(.007)
Dividend tax	1.563	1.873	.887	1.130
preference (θ_t)	(.739)	(.695)	(.480)	(.421)
Percentage of	47.923	34.169	48.000	36.011
population 65 or	(12.050)	(12.820)	(7.832)	(7.775)
older				
SEE	.071	.066	.046	.040
DW	1.838	1.868	1.872	1.811

Note: Estimates are based on annual data, 1951–86. Standard errors are shown in parentheses. The net worth measure in cols. 1 and 3 is the beginning-of-period value of household net worth, while in cols. 2 and 4 it is the end-of-period value, which is dated after all news about takeovers has been revealed. Equations are estimated in differences.

the total consumption equation increase, although it is still within the bounds of the earlier estimates.

Since the data on cash takeovers show a sharp rise during the 1980s, there is a danger that the results are simply capturing the increase in consumption relative to income and wealth during the 1980s. To assess this possibility I reestimated the equations in table 2.6 for the sample period finishing in 1980. The coefficient on $CASHMERG_t$ declined and the estimated standard error rose sharply. It thus appears that pre-1980 data do not provide strong evidence on the link between realizations and consumption.

A second method of validating the findings is to estimate a similar equation for other countries. An analogue to the CASHMERG series was available for the United Kingdom since 1964, and the estimation results are remarkably similar to the findings for the United States:

$$C_t = .145 + .016*A_t + .627*YL_t - 74.893*SHR65_t$$
$$(.054)\ (.010)\quad (.166)\qquad (36.560)$$
$$+ .117*\theta_t + .569*CASHMERG_t$$
$$(.151)\qquad (.452)$$
$$R^2 = .719,\quad DW = 2.38,\quad SEE = .038,\quad 1964\text{--}86$$

Although the hypothesis that cash takeover expenditures do not affect consumption can not be rejected at conventional confidence levels, the point estimate implies that each pound of cash spending on takeovers raises consumption by approximately 50 pence.[22] The relatively short sample for this equation makes strong inferences difficult, but the similarity of the findings between the United States and the United Kingdom supports the view that forced realizations raise consumption.

The results in this section are suggestive, though hardly conclusive. They call attention to possible saving effects of the financial restructuring of U.S. industry during the 1980s. Even small effects operating through this channel could have potentially large effects on measured private saving. Assuming 80 cents of each dollar of cash outlays for takeovers is reinvested (the estimates above point toward values closer to 60 cents), the level of such spending in the mid-1980s could have depressed personal saving by approximately $15 billion per year. This effect is roughly half the size of the estimated effect of higher dividend payout in the last section.

2.5   Conclusion

The results presented here support, but are not definitive evidence for, the proposition that investors respond differently to cash receipts from firms and to accruing capital gains. Consistent but weak evidence for the United States, Great Britain, and Canada suggests that higher dividend tax rates lower consumption, an effect that I interpret as operating through reduced corporate dividend payout. Time series evidence from the United States and the United Kingdom suggests that forced realizations of capital gains in takeovers may also spur consumption.

These results point toward a host of interesting questions concerning the influence of fiscal policy on consumption. If investor behavior deviates from the neoclassical paradigm in ways that render corporate financial policy important for saving decisions, then tax distortions in financing acquire a new dimension and may play an important role in affecting personal saving.

The limited time-series data in each nation restricts the statistical power of single-country tests for a corporate veil. Future work should attempt to enlarge the sample of available data by confirming or refuting the patterns observed here with data from other countries. Searching for patterns across countries in the size of the dividend tax effect and the composition of the investor population, for example, could provide further insights on the link between corporate financing and consumption.

(Appendix follows on pages 66–67.)

Appendix

Table 2A.1   Household Net Worth, the United States, Canada, and the United Kingdom, 1950–87

Year	United States	Canada	United Kingdom
1948	820.6	. . .	. . .
1949	854.8	. . .	. . .
1950	955.9	. . .	. . .
1951	1,048.0	. . .	. . .
1952	1,102.2	. . .	. . .
1953	1,129.0	. . .	. . .
1954	1,239.1	. . .	. . .
1955	1,348.7	. . .	. . .
1956	1,441.0	. . .	. . .
1957	1,451.5	. . .	54.1
1958	1,615.4	. . .	61.0
1959	1,696.6	. . .	70.1
1960	1,742.9	. . .	71.2
1961	1,900.2	. . .	76.3
1962	1,889.9	112.8	84.7
1963	2,025.4	121.7	91.8
1964	2,164.6	131.3	93.9
1965	2,328.0	145.5	101.5
1966	2,401.9	162.8	104.9
1967	2,674.6	176.4	117.8
1968	2,995.3	188.7	138.9
1969	3,031.6	203.2	145.6
1970	3,161.8	216.3	157.9
1971	3,487.5	236.7	192.3
1972	3,853.3	263.1	277.8
1973	4,015.0	311.5	239.0
1974	4,195.4	370.8	249.8
1975	4,745.8	416.9	303.2
1976	5,364.9	469.2	335.7
1977	5,920.8	528.2	399.0
1978	6,755.5	606.3	480.1
1979	7,769.9	697.9	603.0
1980	8,931.1	811.8	689.8
1981	9,678.8	810.4	722.3
1982	10,139.8	974.3	812.6
1983	11,028.0	1,053.0	937.5
1984	11,587.3	1,135.8	1,046.4
1985	12,608.9	1,221.8	1,165.0
1986	13,592.2	1,336.9	. . .
1987	14,373.0	1,464.4	. . .

Note: Entries are measured in current prices, billions of units of local currency. Data for the United States are drawn from the *Balance Sheets of the U.S. Economy* (Board of Governors of Federal Reserve 1988), those for Britain from Bryant (1987) and Revell and Roe (1971), with interpolation by author between 1966–69 and 1970–72; those for Canada were provided by Patrick O'Hagen of Statistics Canada.

Table 2A.2   **Cash Merger and Acquisition Activity, the United States and the United Kingdom, 1950–86**

Year	United States	United Kingdom
1950	0.2	. . .
1951	0.2	. . .
1952	0.3	. . .
1953	0.6	. . .
1954	1.1	. . .
1955	1.7	. . .
1956	1.4	. . .
1957	0.9	. . .
1958	0.8	. . .
1959	1.0	. . .
1960	2.6	. . .
1961	3.3	. . .
1962	3.7	. . .
1963	4.1	. . .
1964	3.7	.71
1965	8.3	1.32
1966	8.3	1.23
1967	20.0	1.97
1968	37.2	4.45
1969	21.7	1.52
1970	14.1	1.22
1971	11.4	1.28
1972	14.7	2.08
1973	16.2	2.69
1974	12.8	1.15
1975	11.9	.46
1976	19.8	.74
1977	20.7	1.03
1978	27.5	1.21
1979	35.0	1.52
1980	29.4	1.06
1981	46.7	.97
1982	28.8	1.48
1983	34.1	1.13
1984	65.6	3.10
1985	103.1	2.85
1986	83.3	3.66

Note: Entries are measured in billions of 1982 dollars for the United States and billions of 1985 pounds for the United Kingdom. Data are drawn from W. T. Grimm *Mergerstat Review* with earlier data based on FTC tabulations for the United States and from the Department of Trade and Industry *Business Monitor* for the United Kingdom.

Notes

1. One traditional explanation of how cash flow may affect consumption, the presence of liquidity constraints, is unlikely to explain the corporate veil. Avery and Elliehausen (1986) report that 43 percent of publicly traded common stock is owned by households in the top one half of 1 percent, and 85 percent by those in the top 10 percent of the income distribution. Borrowing constraints are unlikely to be important for these investors, especially since they have a ready stock of equities to use as collateral.

2. Their subsample estimates in some cases suggest smaller consumption effects, in some cases even an implausible decrease in consumption.

3. The differences in results for the postwar period between the Auerbach-Hassett study (in this volume) and the present paper are largely due to differences in specification. My results suggest that much of the link between dividend payout and consumption operates through expenditures on durables, while their analysis focuses exclusively on nondurable and service consumption. In addition, my specification includes a number of demographic and other variables that they omit, and I omit variables (such as the rate of return) that they include. Although Auerbach and Hassett conclude there is no corporate veil, I show below that their point estimates of how changes in dividend payout would affect consumption are on the same order of magnitude as those in the current study.

4. The tax discrimination variable can also be affected by differential *corporate* taxation of retained and distributed profits as existed in the United Kingdom for part of our sample.

5. This assumption is open to question since much of the variation in the relative tax burden on dividends, especially in the United States, is due to systematic tax reforms that also affect the tax burdens on other types of capital income. Evidence from Hall (1988) and other studies, however, suggests that changes in after-tax asset returns are virtually uncorrelated with time-series movements in consumption growth. The identifying assumption is therefore unlikely to be seriously violated.

6. Auerbach and Hassett (in this volume) emphasize that it is essential to control for wealth in this equation since otherwise shocks to θ_t that affect wealth may provide spurious evidence of a corporate veil. Most of the equations in the present paper include household wealth at the *beginning* of the calendar year as an explanatory variable. This does not completely control for changes in share values that may be related to dividend tax changes. Several equations in sec. 2.4 include end-of-period wealth as an explanatory variable; this should avoid the problem of θ_t-induced changes in asset values.

7. I am grateful to Robert Hall, who discussed my earlier paper on this topic, for persuading me to adopt this approach. My decision was unrelated to his assignment as the discussant of the present paper.

8. I use the contemporaneous value of YL_t even though HW_t is the beginning of period value of human wealth; the results are not affected by use of the once-lagged value. The substitution based on (5) is valid only when the growth rate and discount rates applied to labor income are constant through time. I tried interacting after-tax labor income with various proxies for real interest rates, but the basic findings reported below were unaffected. The interest rate-YL interaction term usually had a negative but statistically insignificant coefficient.

9. Numerous studies including Campbell and Mankiw (1987) and Campbell and Deaton (1987) have investigated the stochastic properties of these data series.

10. End-of-period asset values are clearly affected by within-period shocks to consumption, so A_{t+1} and ε_t may be correlated.

11. Balance sheet data on household net worth are available for Japan since 1969, but that time series seemed too short to warrant study.

12. The U.K. tax rate on shareholders refers only to the tax burdens on individual investors, not a weighted average across all investor classes. Since most of the variation in θ_t arises from changes in either the corporate tax code or the tax rules affecting individuals, this data series is likely to track the "correct" θ_t series reasonably well.

13. More detailed discussion of the behavior of investors facing realization-based capital gains tax schemes can be found in McCarten (1988) for Canada and in Poterba (1987b) for the United States.

14. The Grimm series is extrapolated to the early years of the sample using information from the Federal Trade Commission and tabulations on form of payment in mergers from Franks, Harris, and Mayer (1988).

15. An issue that deserves further study is the extent to which corporate payouts affect the *timing,* rather than the level, of consumption. Dividend payouts and capital gain realizations may induce households to purchase durables they would otherwise have purchased at some future date.

16. The results for the United States and Britain were insensitive to setting the effective capital gains tax rate to zero. This is because there is more variation in *m* relative to *z,* and in the corporate-level tax discrimination variable, in these countries than in Canada.

17. Estimates in Poterba (1987a) suggest that a change in θ_t by .05, which is a 6.4 percent change, would lead to increased dividend payout of approximately 11 percent or $8.3 billion per year. Thus the consumption change is on the same order of magnitude as the change in dividend payout, and, if anything, the present point estimates suggesting that consumption changes by more than the change in dividends are implausibly large. In contrast, the Auerbach-Hassett (in this volume) findings imply this dividend change would raise nondurable and service consumption by .24 percent, or $6.7 billion. My results in table 2.2, part B (using the coefficient in col. 5) imply nondurable and service consumption rises by $17.6 billion. Thus although the papers reach quite different conclusions, the point estimates imply consumption changes of the same order of magnitude.

18. This section was stimulated by joint work with George Hatsopoulos and Paul Krugman.

19. Earlier studies have examined the influence of *accruing* capital gains on household saving. Hendershott and Peek (1989), for example, find a two cent decline in saving for each one dollar increase in corporate equity values.

20. This effect is somewhat stronger when the equations are estimated in levels rather than differences. Since the differenced specification is, however, less prone to spurious conclusions based on trending series, I focus on those results.

21. Auerbach and Hassett (in this volume) observe that one cannot rule out the possibility that wealth and θ_t are correlated, so my estimated tax effects may just be mislabeled wealth effects. This seems unlikely, not just because the results are insensitive to the dating of wealth, but also because they are too large. A 5 percent change in the dividend tax rate would cause a 6.8 percent increase in share values if the capitalized value of dividend taxes was exactly measured by my θ_t series and if dividend taxes were fully capitalized into prices. Using the 1986 stock market value of $2.2 trillion held by households, the wealth-induced rise in consumption would be $2.8 billion (.019*.068*2200, where .019 is the wealth coefficient in the consumption equation). This is far less than my estimated direct consumption effect from θ_t.

22. I examined the impact of using end-of-period wealth in these equations and, as in the United States, the estimated merger coefficient dropped substantially.

References

Avery, Robert B., and Gregory E. Elliehausen. 1986. Financial characteristics of high-income families. *Federal Reserve Bulletin* 72 (March): 175.
Board of Governors of the Federal Reserve. 1988. *Balance sheets of the U.S. economy.* Washington, D.C.: Federal Reserve Board.
Business Monitor. Various issues. London: United Kingdom Central Statistical Office.
Bagwell, Laurie, and John Shoven. 1989. Cash distributions to shareholders: Alternatives to dividends. *Journal of Economic Perspectives* 3 (Summer): 129–40.
Bhatia, Kul B. 1979. Corporate taxation, retained earnings, and capital formation. *Journal of Public Economics* 11:123–34.
Bryant, C. G. E. 1987. National and sector balance sheets. 1957–1985. *Economic Trends* 403:92–119.
Campbell, John Y., and Angus Deaton. 1987. Why is consumption so smooth? Working paper. Princeton University, Princeton, N.J.
Campbell, John Y., and N. Gregory Mankiw. 1987. Permanent income, current income, and consumption. NBER Working Paper no. 2436. Cambridge, Mass.
David, Paul A., and John L. Scadding. 1974. Private savings: Ultrationality, aggregation, and Denison's law. *Journal of Political Economy* 82 (March–April):225–49.
Dennison, Edward F. 1958. A note on private saving. *Review of Economics and Statistics* 40:261–67.
Feldstein, Martin S. 1973. Tax incentives, corporate saving, and capital accumulation in the United States. *Journal of Public Economics* 2:159–71.
Feldstein, Martin S., and George Fane. 1973. Taxes, corporate dividend policy, and personal savings: The British postwar experience. *Review of Economics and Statistics* 40:399–411.
Franks, Julian R., Robert S. Harris, and Colin Mayer. 1988. Means of payment in takeovers: Results for the United Kingdom and the United States. In *Corporate takeovers: Causes and consequences,* ed. Alan Auerbach, 221–64. Chicago: University of Chicago Press.
Hall, Robert E. 1988. Intertemporal substitution in consumption. *Journal of Political Economy* 96:339–57.
———. 1989. Consumption. In *Handbook of modern macroeconomics,* ed. Robert J. Barro. Cambridge, Mass.: Harvard University Press.
Hayashi, Fumio. 1982. The permanent income hypothesis: Estimating and testing by instrumental variables. *Journal of Political Economy* 90:895–916.
Hendershott, Patric, and Joe Peek. 1989. Household saving in the United States: Measurement and behavior. *Journal of Business and Economic Statistics* 7:11–19.
Howrey, E. Philip, and Saul H. Hymans. 1978. The measurement and determination of loanable-funds saving. *Brookings Papers on Economic Activity,* no. 3, 655–706.
Jenkins, Glenn P. 1986. The role and economic implications of the Canadian dividend tax credit. Working paper. Economic Council of Canada, Ottawa.
King, Mervyn A. 1977. *Public policy and the corporation.* London: Chapman & Hall.
McCarten, William James. 1988. Capital gains realizations and personal income taxation in Canada. Doctoral diss., Duke University.
Malinvaud, Edmond. 1986. Pure profits as forced saving. *Scandinavian Journal of Economics* 88:109–30.
Modigliani, Franco. 1970. The lifecycle hypothesis of saving and intercountry differences in the saving ratio. In *Induction, growth, and trade: Essays in honour of Sir Roy Harrod,* ed. W. A. Eltis et al. Oxford: Clarendon Press.
Newey, Whitney, and Kenneth West. 1987. A simple, positive-semi-definite, heteroskedasticity and autocorrelation consistent covariances matrix. *Econometrica* 55:703–6.

Poterba, James M. 1987a. Tax policy and corporate saving. *Brookings Papers on Economic Activity,* no. 2, 455–503.

———. 1987b. How burdensome are capital gains taxes? Evidence from the United States. *Journal of Public Economics* 33:157–72.

Poterba, James M., and Lawrence H. Summers. 1985. The economic effects of dividend taxation. In *Recent advances in corporate finance,* ed. Edward I. Altman and Marti G. Subrahmanyam. Homewood, Ill.: Irwin.

Revell, Jack, and Alan Roe. 1971. National balance sheets and national accounting—a progress report. *Economic Trends* (May):viii–xix.

Shefrin, Hersh M., and Meir Statman. 1984. Explaining investor preference for cash dividends. *Journal of Financial Economics* 13:253–82.

von Furstenberg, George M. 1981. Saving. In *How taxes affect economic behavior,* ed. Henry J. Aaron and Joseph A. Pechman. Washington, D.C.: Brookings.

Comment   Robert E. Hall

Two facts drive Poterba's interesting paper: First, in all three countries he studies, there has been a general decline in the bias of the tax system against dividends. The upward trend of the dividend tax preference index as shown in table 2.1 has diminished the disincentive to corporate dividend payout over the past four decades. Second, in the United States and Britain, consumption has risen in relation to the Ando-Modigliani life-cycle consumption function. Consumers spend more for given levels of wealth and earnings than they did earlier.

Poterba's conclusion is that the upward trend in consumption is the result of higher dividend payout, stimulated by the diminished tax disincentive. In the model he has in mind, consumers pay attention to cash receipts rather than just the present discounted value of corporate earnings as revealed in the stock market. When the tax bias changes and corporations switch to greater payout, consumption rises in that model. By contrast, in the standard Ando-Modigliani model, stock market valuation is all that consumers care about. Poterba's evidence adds to the growing literature that tries to make the case that consumers are more sensitive to current cash flows than they would be in the pure life-cycle model.

Though I do not think that Poterba's evidence can be dismissed, I find it a little fragile. First, much of the effect is in durables, a form of saving. The life-cycle model does not predict that consumers will respond to higher dividend payout by accumulating durables; rather, the extra cash flow should go into financial assets. But this failure of the life-cycle model should not be equated with simple excess consumption. Second, the standard errors of the effects are large. Even taken completely at face value, the results could have

Robert E. Hall is professor of economics at Stanford University and is also senior fellow at Stanford's Hoover Institution. He is a research associate of the National Bureau of Economic Research and serves as director of the bureau's Program on Economic Fluctuations.

arisen from purely random variation. Make only a modest allowance for topic selection (it was the coincident trends that led Poterba to run the regressions in the first place) and specification search, and the findings become statistically unconvincing. Third, the failure to find the relation in one of the three countries, Canada, weakens the case. There has been almost as much variation in the payout disincentive in Canada, but no variation in consumption around the Ando-Modigliani model resulting from those movements. Why are Canadian consumers not sensitive to cash flow in the same way that U.S. and British consumers are?

As Poterba notes, the fragility of the results is due in part to the slow-moving character of the changes in the dividend bias. Different combinations of other slow-moving right-hand variables, such as a time trend or the percentage of the population aged 65 and over, make large differences in the coefficient of the dividend bias variable. Further, putting a much lower weight on low frequencies, by using first differences, drastically reduces the coefficient of the dividend bias.

In view of the importance of slow-moving influences on consumption, further research on this topic needs to look at other well-known factors. These include, first, the dramatic increase in real asset returns in the 1980s. In principle, this increase should have had wealth and substitution effects on consumption. The omission means that the dividend bias coefficient is biased to the extent that changes in the tax system occurred at the same time that real returns rose, even if there is no casual link. Second, in the United States, the 1980s saw a dramatic increase in the likely volume of deferred taxation. Consumers were bombarded with news stories to the effect that current taxes were too low to pay for the government, so tax rates would have to rise in the future. This is another slow-moving omitted influence in Poterba's equation.

The paper assumes, without showing or citing evidence, that the dividend bias variable actually corresponds to changes in dividend payouts. It is possible (but, I believe, untrue), that consumption rises when the bias variable moves in the direction of higher payouts, but that payouts do not actually change. Such a finding would be paradoxical. It would be nice if Poterba would reassure us that payouts actually track changes in payout incentives. In this respect, his footnote 17 is an overreaction.

In the 1980s, corporations finally awakened to the folly of returning value to shareholders through dividends and began to return value predominantly through repurchase of shares. Poterba argues that repurchases that occur as part of changes in corporate control are exogenous to the consumer. Hence forced realizations from merger and related activity is another way to test the invariance of consumption to events that do not affect true wealth. Poterba moves rather quickly over the topic of how wealth is affected by cash buyouts. If the wealth variable in the consumption function measures the change in wealth associated with buyouts correctly, then the coefficient on the actual buyout proceeds should be zero, his null hypothesis. Even when the buyout occurs at a large premium to immediate past market value, consumption should respond only to the resulting increase in total wealth. However, in an economy where corporations are valued persistently far below their breakup values, there is room for a difference between shareholders' valuations and market value. Waves of buyouts, stimulated by changes in laws and regulations, could well enter the Ando-Modigliani consumption function because they raise shareholders' valuations in relation to current market value. Hence Poterba's null hypothesis is not obviously a correct characterization of rational consumer behavior.

In any case, the empirical findings on buyouts are at least as fragile as those for dividends. There is essentially no case that buyout cash stimulates nondurable and services consumption. There is a hint that the cash goes into consumer durables, contrary to Poterba's null hypothesis, which requires that the cash go entirely into replacement financial assets.

Given the imprecision of the findings for buyouts, it would be interesting to see if microdata on the behavior of actual recipients of buyout cash could give sharper results.

As a general matter, Poterba's results do not compel the rejection of the life-cycle consumption model. There are some hints that some of the failings of the model, especially at low frequencies, may be associated with changes in the dividend bias of the tax system and with rising buyout activity. But these hints are not strong enough to displace the life-cycle model from its dominant position in consumption economics.

3 Corporate Savings and Shareholder Consumption

Alan J. Auerbach and Kevin Hassett

3.1 Introduction

The 1986 Tax Reform Act markedly altered the relative tax burden of corporations and individuals while also changing the incentives for corporate dividend distributions. Over the period 1987–91, corporate tax revenues were projected to rise by $120.3 billion, with individual taxes being reduced by $121.9 billion (U.S. House of Representatives 1986, vol. 2, table A1). The act also repealed the 60% exclusion previously afforded capital gains and raised the top marginal tax rate from a high of 20% to a high of 33%. At the same time the top rate on dividends was cut from 50% to 33%.

The shift in after-tax income from corporations to individuals combined with the increased tax incentive to pay dividends has led some to predict profound reductions in corporate savings. Since corporate savings typically account for over half of private savings, this has prompted concern that aggregate capital accumulation will be adversely affected. Indeed, a recent Data Resources, Inc., publication predicts that: "Private Savings are likely to decline because of the massive shift of post tax income from businesses to individuals . . . over the 1986–91 interval, personal savings are thus expected to be only $5 billion higher while corporate savings are $24 billion lower" (Brinner and Abraham 1986, 17). This quote reflects the conception that the transfer of cash from corporations to shareholders will alter real activity, a view

Alan J. Auerbach is professor of economics and law at the University of Pennsylvania. Kevin Hassett is assistant professor at the Graduate School of Business, Columbia University.

The authors are grateful to the NBER and National Science Foundation for financial support and to Angus Deaton, Tarhan Feyzioglu, Fumio Hayashi, Greg Mankiw, John Shoven, Joel Slemrod, members of the NBER's Program in Financial Markets and Monetary Economics, and participants in workshops at the Columbia Business School and Wharton for comments on an earlier draft. The second author acknowledges the support of a Sloan Foundation dissertation fellowship.

consistent with the impression that shareholders do not "pierce the corporate veil" and recognize the full implications of the transfer. While the belief that transfers from corporations to individuals will have significant real effects may be commonly held, there is very weak supporting evidence for the proposition that *pure* transfer policies have any such effects.

This paper reexamines the implications of changing corporate savings. We begin with the straightforward proposition that the outcome depends crucially on the consumption behavior of shareholders. If, *holding wealth constant,* shareholders are perfectly rational and recognize reductions in corporate savings as a change in their own asset position, then they will counteract any changes in corporate retentions with increased personal savings, leaving private savings unchanged. It is this compensating response to *wealth-neutral* changes in corporate saving that we characterize as "piercing" the corporate veil. We use this simple observation about shareholder savings to develop a new test for the existence of the corporate veil.

The next section discusses the theory behind the corporate veil and argues that much of the previous literature lacked a proper focus. There are several reasons why changes in corporate saving might be associated with changes in national saving that are entirely consistent with a complete piercing of the corporate veil. Section 3.3 outlines and presents an Euler equation test for the existence of the corporate veil. The test supports the hypothesis that no such veil exists. Although the test's power is not strong enough to reject certain plausible alternative hypotheses, this finding still casts doubt on previous results purporting to demonstrate the existence of a corporate veil.

Because the Euler equation test is not powerful enough, by itself, to dispose entirely of the possible existence of a corporate veil, we then consider other approaches to the question. Using a switching-regressions model of consumption based on the Euler equation, we show in section 3.4 that the observed significant excess sensitivity of consumption to predictable changes in disposable income is associated with liquidity constraints rather than myopia or irrational behavior. This is further evidence against the existence of a corporate veil, because such liquidity constraints are almost certain not to apply to consumption supported by corporate wealth. Section 3.5 uses recent advances in the theory of cointegrated processes to shed new light on the time-series properties of consumption behavior and evaluate subtler tests for the presence of the corporate veil. A significant finding in this section is that the aggregate marginal propensity to consume out of corporate wealth is considerably lower than that from other tangible wealth. This could be associated with a corporate veil or with marginal consumption propensities differing across households according to wealth. Section 3.6 concludes the paper.

Because the previous literature has often been obscure on this point, it is useful to provide at the outset a precise statement of what a corporate veil would do. Our view is that a corporate veil would exist if a shift in the distribution of an individual's wealth among corporate and noncorporate forms, holding his overall wealth constant, affected that individual's consumption. We therefore rule out changes in relative asset values that also affect aggregate wealth or the distribution of aggregate wealth among individuals as useful in the search for a corporate veil.

As we shall discuss, tax-induced changes in corporate behavior can affect individual consumption behavior without a corporate veil: these policies could alter the overall value of private assets or the distribution of wealth among individuals.

3.2   The Corporate Veil

Reductions in corporate savings need not, of course, imply lower aggregate private savings. Corporate savings can be thought of as that investment that is financed out of retained earnings rather than with new debt or equity. Under certain well-specified conditions, this should, as first noted by Modigliani and Miller (1958) and Miller and Modigliani (1961), be of no consequence to the value of the firm. Any increase in dividends can simply be offset by a commensurate increase in the firm's debt or issues of new equity. The Modigliani-Miller analysis will hold in general equilibrium, provided that dividend recipients recognize that their apparent windfall is merely a time reallocation of their asset's dividend stream. Under perfect markets, consumption will not be altered, because the consumer's optimization problem is unchanged. Real behavior will not be affected by a financial version of musical chairs.

This "dividend irrelevance" view relies upon the shareholder's ability to "pierce the corporate veil", that is, to recognize wealth-neutral changes in financial policy for what they are. It further requires that shareholders can act to offset corporate savings decisions. If shareholders were liquidity constrained, then an increase in corporate distributions would relax this constraint and increase consumption, even with no change in perceived shareholder wealth. The case is analogous to consumption increasing without a change in human wealth if current labor income increases. However, there are two significant differences between the two cases. First, shareholders can sell stock or borrow against it to relax liquidity constraints, while such transactions are severely limited with respect to human capital. Second, as we discuss further below, the distribution of share ownership is so concentrated among wealthy individuals that the aggregate importance of liquidity constraints within this group is implausible.

If the value of the firm increases because of some underlying change in fundamentals, then a significant share of the concomitant increase in dividends may be consumed because the wealth or permanent income of the shareholder has increased. If, on the other hand, a firm reduces retained earnings and increases dividends by one dollar without any underlying change in the firm's real prospects, then, according to the permanent income hypothesis, consumption will not change in the absence of taxes because total wealth remains the same.[1] When markets are perfect, financial structure, or, equivalently, the timing of dividends, should have no effect on real economic behavior. This distinction is crucial to the proper understanding of the "corporate veil," and has been overlooked by much of the previous literature, which seems to interpret consumption responses to fluctuating dividends as evidence of a shareholder's inability to see through the corporate veil. To the extent that changes in dividends reflect real changes in the value of the firm, as indeed signaling models would suggest, consumption will, of course, change.

This point lends an interesting perspective to the passage already quoted from Brinner and Abraham (1986, 17). There, the shift in posttax income from corporations to individuals, in the aggregate very close to a wealth-neutral transfer, is predicted to reduce aggregate savings by $19 billion. This view suggests that simply carrying wealth across the corporate threshold induces massive changes in the consumption behavior of shareholders. Since it is implausible that liquidity constraints could explain so large a shift in shareholders' consumption, some other force must be perceived as operating here.

Proponents of this view may simply believe that some fundamental shareholder irrationality exists. Alternatively there may be a different experiment being implicitly considered, one that does not preserve the initial distribution of wealth among individuals. Changes in the distribution of wealth could well alter aggregate consumption, but one needs no corporate veil to explain such effects.[2] A problem one has in interpreting statements relating corporate and personal saving is that the experiment being envisioned is not explicitly specified. This vagueness has permeated the statistical evidence attempting to relate corporate and personal saving, in effect veiling the corporate veil.

The modern empirical study of corporate saving can be traced back to Denison (1958), who found that private saving was much smoother than its components, suggesting that personal and corporate saving may offset each other. Feldstein (1973) extended the inquiry by emphasizing that rational consumers should recognize retained earnings as wealth accruals and consume from them. Using a traditional consumption function, Feldstein found that retained earnings were significantly positively correlated with consumption. He interpreted this as evidence that consumers pierce the corporate veil. Subsequent research has come down on both sides of the issue.[3] An example of recent work finding evidence of a corporate veil is Poterba (1987). Poterba regressed private saving on several macroeconomic indicators and a dividend tax preference variable. A negative and significant coefficient on dividend taxes was interpreted as evidence that consumers do not completely offset changes in corporate saving induced by tax-related changes in dividend policy. A second test using dividend taxes as an instrument for changes in corporate saving, in an attempt to isolate wealth-neutral changes, found corroborative evidence. Since we have no a priori reason to believe that dividend taxes are orthogonal to wealth, Poterba's results are difficult to interpret.

Reexamination of the empirical methods used in existing studies of corporate saving reveals many shortcomings. Perhaps most important, previous studies have failed adequately to describe consumer behavior consistent with shareholder rationality. Because of this there has been an improper focus on simple changes in dividends or retained earnings, which are certainly correlated with changes in wealth. The response of consumption to these cannot be interpreted as a violation of the permanent income hypothesis and, as such, is irrelevant to the investigation of the existence of a corporate veil. In addition, by neglecting the duality of consumption and savings, some studies have needlessly introduced problems of measurement error as researchers have struggled over proper definitions for personal and private savings.[4] This focus on saving has also divorced the inquiry from breakthroughs in the study of consumer behavior and rational expectations which, as we shall illustrate, are particularly useful here.

Another problem with some previous research is from an econometric viewpoint. Results typically based on regressions using levels of aggregate time series are difficult to interpret because of underlying nonstationarity and the well-known accompanying spurious regression difficulties.[5] Significant correlation between corporate retained earnings or dividends and consumption may simply reflect common trends in the data.

In the following sections we illustrate that all of these shortcomings can be addressed through a straightforward application of the modern theory of the rational consumer. We test two related propositions implied by the absence of a corporate veil; first, that changes in dividend policy that are anticipated, and hence provide no new information to shareholders in estimating their wealth, do not affect aggregate consumption; second, that the response of changes in consumption to changes in different forms of wealth (corporate vs. noncorporate) are equal. Each test is based on the idea that, in the absence of a corporate veil, a shift in wealth should not affect consumption.

3.3   Euler Equations and the Corporate Veil

3.3.1   Rational Expectations and the Theory of the Consumer

Assuming a constant real interest rate and quadratic utility, Hall (1978) showed that one implication of the permanent income hypothesis is that consumption follows a random walk. If rational agents maximize a time-separable function of consumption, then all currently available information will already be included in current consumption. Hence, current consumption should provide the best available forecast of future consumption. Subsequent generalizations have allowed for interest rates to change over time.

Following the previous literature (e.g., Grossman and Shiller 1981; Hansen and Singleton 1983), consider a representative agent seeking to maximize the expected utility of consumption. If this consumer has a CES utility function with an intertemporal elasticity of substitution σ and a pure rate of time preference δ, then his optimal consumption path will obey the Euler equation:

$$(1) \qquad E\left[\left(\frac{C_t}{C_{t-1}}\right)^{1/\sigma}\left(\frac{1+\delta}{1+r_t}\right)\right] = 1,$$

where r_t is the after-tax rate of return to savings. Equation (1) may also be written:

$$(2) \qquad \left(\frac{C_t}{C_{t-1}}\right)^{1/\sigma}\left(\frac{1+\delta}{1+r_t}\right)\right] = 1 + \varepsilon_t,$$

where ε_t is a stochastic term with conditional mean zero at time $t - 1$. Taking logs of both sides of (2), and imposing the approximation that $\ln(1 + x) \approx x$, for x small, one obtains

$$(3) \qquad \Delta c_t = -\sigma\delta + \sigma r_t + \sigma\varepsilon_t,$$

where $\Delta c_t = \ln C_t - \ln C_{t-1}$. Since r_t and ε_t are potentially correlated, it is useful to decompose r_t into an expected component r_t^e uncorrelated with ε_t and a "surprise" term $r_t - r_t^e$, to obtain an estimable equation:[6]

$$(4) \qquad \begin{aligned} \Delta c_t &= -\sigma\delta + \sigma r_t^e + \sigma(\varepsilon_t + r_t - r_t^e) \\ &= \mu + \sigma r_t^e + e_t. \end{aligned}$$

Much recent debate has focused on the observation of Flavin (1981) that consumption seems excessively sensitive to anticipated changes in income, which have a positive and significant effect when included in equation (1). Interpretations of this positive coefficient have emphasized the idea that some fraction of consumers face liquidity constraints and consume their income in each period. To aid in this interpretation, Campbell and Mankiw (1987) consider a general model where λ individuals are liquidity constrained, "Keynesian" consumers, and $(1 - \lambda)$ individuals obey the permanent income hypothesis. In this case, if Δy_t^e is defined to be the expected current change in the logarithm of income of the liquidity-constrained group, equation (4) can be rewritten:

$$(5) \qquad \begin{aligned} \Delta c_t &= \lambda\Delta y_t^e + (1 - \lambda)[\mu + \sigma r_t^e + e_t] \\ &= \mu' + \sigma' r_t^e + \lambda\Delta y_t^e + e_t'. \end{aligned}$$

The implications of the permanent income hypothesis are straightforward in this context. Invoking rational expectations, that is, instrumenting with variables in the information set at the beginning of period t, should yield an estimate of λ insignificantly different from zero. Noting that, as first pointed out by Working (1960), time aggregation could induce an MA(1) error in equation (2), making period $t - 1$ variables inadmissible as instruments, Campbell and Mankiw use twice-lagged variables as instruments to obtain estimates of λ ranging from .413 to .668. They conclude that roughly 50% of income is held by consumers who face liquidity constraints.

Similar reasoning can be applied to consumers as stockholders. Predictable changes in dividends, already in the current information set, should be incorporated into consumption plans. Thus, expected dividends should affect only the consumption of the liquidity constrained. If we divide the income of liquidity-constrained households, Y_t, into dividend income D_t and all other income Y_t^*, then, in logarithms, $\Delta y_t \approx (1-\gamma)\Delta y_t^* + \gamma\Delta d_t$, where γ is the proportion of total income that dividends represent for these households. Thus, equation (5) may be rewritten:

(6) $$\Delta c_t = \mu' + \sigma' r_t^e + \lambda_1 y_t^* e + \lambda_2 \Delta d_t^e + e_t',$$

where $\lambda_1 = \lambda(1-\gamma)$ and $\lambda_2 = \lambda\gamma$.

The notion that liquidity constraints can be significant in explaining consumption out of expected dividends is, as we suggested earlier, difficult to support. Put simply, γ must be very small. Row 1 of table 3.1, taken from the 1983 Survey of Consumer Finances, gives estimates of the proportion of corporate equities held by individuals in different strata of the income distribution.[7] Our measure of income includes all money income received by the members of the sample in 1982. Notably, nearly all stock ownership is by those individuals at the top of the income distribution, with almost 78% of all corporate wealth held by the top 5% of the income distribution. In addition, as mentioned before, if stockholders did face constraints they could easily relax them by selling their stock.

Absent liquidity constraints, the coefficient on expected dividends, λ_2, should be zero unless the corporate veil exists. Since expected changes in dividends are already included in agents' current inferences about their asset positions, they should not affect consumption.[8] This is true regardless of the tax treatment of those dividends and whatever the process is that drives dividend changes. The coefficient on dividends, λ_2, measures the response of consumption to perceived wealth-neutral changes in dividends. If there is a corporate veil, this will be positive and significant.

As a final extension of the Euler equation approach we will further decompose disposable income into components attributable to capital and labor, keeping dividends separate. This will aid in the interpretation of excess sen-

Table 3.1   **Percentage of Total Wealth Held by Different Income Classes (taken from the 1983 Survey of Consumer Finances)**

	Income Class (percentile)						
	0–10	10–25	25–50	50–75	75–90	90–95	95–100
% Corporate wealth	.263	.385	2.511	4.396	7.919	6.866	77.661
% Other wealth	2.108	4.309	10.185	16.192	16.056	10.428	40.722

sitivity as liquidity constraints in the form of an individual's inability to borrow against future labor income. The equation we estimate is:

(7) $\Delta c_t = \mu' + \sigma' r_t^e + \lambda_1 \Delta y l_t^e + \lambda_2 \Delta y k_t^e + \lambda_3 \Delta d_t^e + e_t'.$

To guard against a possible aggregation-induced first-order moving average error term, we can estimate this equation using doubly lagged instrumental variables.[9]

3.3.2   The Data

For our estimation we use quarterly and annual data from 1948–85 taken from the Citibase dataset. For consumption, we use aggregate consumption of nondurables and services. Our interest rate variable is the average six-month Treasury-bill rate for the quarter less the inflation rate based on the implicit price deflator for nondurable consumption.[10] Income is defined as aggregate disposable income and excludes after-tax dividends when these are included in the Euler equation. After-tax aggregate labor income, capital income, and dividends are constructed in a manner similar to that used by Blinder and Deaton (1985). Variables are converted to real values with the aggregate deflator for nondurable consumption. Every variable but the interest rate is in logs and per capita. Further discussion of the construction of our variables is available in the data appendix below.

3.3.3   Results

We review first the results from our quarterly regressions. As a starting point, our estimation of equation (5) is reported in table 3.2, which reports the instrumental variable results based upon an instrument set that includes second, third, and fourth lags of consumption and income; the second lag of the six-month Treasury-bill rate; and second, third, and fourth lags of pretax corporate profits and the after-tax return to shareholders of a dollar distributed versus a dollar retained, taken from Poterba (1987).[11] Our finding of a σ insignificantly different from zero agrees with results reported in Hall (1988) and Campbell and Mankiw (1987). Our estimate of λ of .431 is very close to Campbell and Mankiw's reported estimates, which range from .413 to .668. The accompanying t-statistic is 3.56, implying that there is clear excess sensitivity of consumption to expected changes in disposable income.

The estimates of equation (6) are reported in the second row of table 3.2. We use the same set of instruments but include three lags of dividend changes, starting with the second lag. Again, our estimate of σ is insignificantly different from zero. Our estimate of λ_1 decreases slightly to .378 but is again statistically significant. The estimate of λ_2, our measure of the corporate veil, is slightly positive but insignificantly different from zero, indicating that consumption is not excessively sensitive to dividends.

Equation (7), a further generalization of the Euler equation, is reported in the third row of table 3.2. Again, second, third, and fourth lags of the differ-

Table 3.2   **Euler Equation Estimates (t-statistics in parentheses); Dependent Variable = Log-differenced Consumption (quarterly, 1947:1–1986:1)**

Equation	Constant	$\Delta y d_t^e$	r_t^e	Δdiv_t^e	$\Delta y k_t^e$	$\Delta y l_t^e$
(5)	.002	4.31	−.002	. . .	. . .	. . .
	(3.01)	(3.56)	(.137)			
D-W = 2.34, R^2 = .111, $\bar{R}^2$ = .093						
(6)	.003	.378	−.010	.065	. . .	. . .
	(3.20)	(2.89)	(−.503)	(1.16)		
D-W = 2.39, R^2 = .121, $\bar{R}^2$ = .095						
(7)	.004	. . .	−.058	.056	−.085	.458
	(4.15)		(−2.45)	(1.17)	(−1.09)	(3.67)
D-W = 2.27, R^2 = .177, $\bar{R}^2$ = .145						

Note: All variables, except the real interest rate, are expressed as differences of the logs of population-deflated variables.

enced variables and the second lag of the interest rate are used as instruments. Here, disposable income is broken down into its labor and capital components. The estimate of λ_1, interpretable as the proportion of labor income held by those who are liquidity constrained, is a statistically significant .458. Both coefficients on capital income are insignificantly different from zero, with the coefficient on nondividend capital income equal to −.085.

The annual results in table 3.3 use the same specification, but are based on instrument sets including once-lagged variables. We include such instruments because some variables are quite hard to predict using instruments lagged at least two years; our test of a corporate veil has little power unless a reasonable prediction of future dividend changes is possible.[12]

In comparing equations (5)–(7) in table 3.3 to those in table 3.2, we see few qualitative differences. The coefficients on disposable income are somewhat higher and those on dividends somewhat lower, but the conclusions are basically the same.

We have estimated these equations using different measures of the interest rate, different sets of instruments, different deflators, and different measures of consumption. In every case, we obtained results of a similar nature: we have found no evidence that consumption is excessively sensitive to changes in dividends, that is, no evidence of the existence of the corporate veil. In each case, the error is serially uncorrelated, making the standard error estimates used to calculate the reported t-statistics admissible.[13] All of the variables used in the estimation are difference stationary, so no problems of spurious regression are present.

How conclusive are these results concerning the existence of the corporate veil? The insignificance of the predicted changes in dividends is an important finding in light of previous claims to have "proved" the corporate veil's exis-

Table 3.3   Euler Equation Estimates (*t*-statistics in parentheses); Dependent Variable = Log-differenced Consumption (annual, 1947–85)

Equation	Constant	Δyd_t^e	r_t^e	Δdiv_t^e	Δyk_t^e	Δyl_t^e
(5)	.005	.472	−.017	. . .	. . .	. . .
	(2.39)	(5.42)	(−.284)			
D-W = 2.21, R^2 = .576, $\bar{R}^2$ = .537						
(6)	.008	.554	−.030	.022	. . .	. . .
	(2.414)	(4.888)	(−.453)	(.463)		
D-W = 2.28, R^2 = .586, $\bar{R}^2$ = .527						
(7)	.011	. . .	−.152	.025	.012	.492
	(2.229)		(−2.951)	(.555)	(.169)	(4.832)
D-W = 2.36, R^2 = .693, $\bar{R}^2$ = .631						

tence. The fact that predicted disposable labor income is consistently highly significant in these regressions while being no easier to predict shows that the insignificance of dividends is not due simply to the use of poor instruments.[14]

Yet, one must recognize that the results in tables 3.2 and 3.3 are not powerful enough to reject all alternative hypotheses corresponding to the corporate veil. For example, under the alternative hypothesis that the same fractions of dividend income and labor income accrued to households facing liquidity constraints and having a marginal propensity to consume current income of unity, we would expect the coefficient on expected dividends, λ_2, to equal the fraction of consumption accounted for by such households, λ, multiplied by the ratio of dividends to disposable income. Since this ratio is of the same order of magnitude as the coefficients of predicted dividends, we would be unable to reject the alternative hypothesis. We have already suggested, however, that there are fundamental inconsistencies with an alternative hypothesis based on liquidity constraints. The only plausible alternative must invoke myopia or irrationality to explain excess sensitivity. Thus, it is important to determine the source of the documented excess sensitivity of consumption to predictable changes in labor income. Unless a source compatible with the corporate veil is found, the results will support our conclusion against the veil's existence.

3.4 Credit Crises as Switching Regressions

As we have noted, there is more than one interpretation of the above result that consumption is excessively sensitive to changes in income. In this section we provide further evidence, based on a Markov switching model, that this excess sensitivity does indeed reflect the impact of liquidity constraints. We find that excess sensitivity has been episodic and confined to a relatively small number of postwar years, typically during recessions and/or credit crises.

In their concluding remarks, Campbell and Mankiw remark that the violation of the Euler equation is only a recent phenomenon. "The evidence against the permanent income model comes primarily from the second half of our sample period, 1969–85" (1987, 32). Since a portion of this period is one of increased national debt and higher real interest rates, it is not inconceivable that borrowing behavior somehow changed after 1969, but testing this is not straightforward, because, as Neftci (1984) noted, arbitrarily splitting data and testing for parameter differences may bias results in favor of finding multiple parameter regimes. This observation suggests an alternative specification of the model of the consumer: we consider a model where all consumers consume according to the permanent income hypothesis, except for occasional surprise episodes of nonoptimal consumption caused by economywide "credit crises." Specifically, we estimate the following switching model:

$$\Delta c_{it}^* = \sigma_i r_{it}^e + \lambda_i \Delta y_{it}^e + e_{it}$$
(8) $$\Delta c_{it} = \Delta c_{1t}^* \quad \text{if } i = 1$$
$$= \Delta c_{2t}^* \quad \text{if } i = 2,$$

where c_{it} is the logarithm of observed consumption, r_{it}^e is the expected interest rate, Δy_{it}^e is the expected change in the logarithm income, and e_{it} are independent, normally distributed errors. If liquidity constraints only appear occasionally, there will be two distinct states.[15] The liquidity-constrained state will have a large, positive, and significant coefficient on income. The unconstrained state will look like the random walk predicted by the permanent income hypothesis. Following Goldfeld and Quandt (1973) we model the transition from state 1 to state 2 as a first-order Markov process.

Even with the simplifying Markov assumption, the likelihood function for this model is quite cumbersome, since the likelihood of each possible "trajectory" through the data must be investigated. At first glance, this seems to require the summation of 2^t terms in the calculation of the likelihood, something infeasible even in small samples. But, as Coslett and Lee (1985) have shown, the likelihood function can be rewritten using a recursive relation that takes advantage of the assumed Markov structure and greatly reduces the computational burden.[16] Even with this simplification, the model is a difficult nonlinear estimation problem, with the usual accompanying problem of possible local maxima and minima. To estimate the model we use the same data used in the above Euler equations,[17] but in this case we use only annual data since our earlier results suggests that time aggregation will not alter the results significantly and the use of annual data further reduces the required computation time. Since our analysis is only meant to be suggestive of the benefits of this approach, we further simplify by approximating the expected interest rate with the actual lagged interest rate, and expected income with lagged income, rather than using instrumental variables. The Davidson-Fletcher-Powell nonlinear search algorithm was used to find the optimum. Since the likelihood function is very nonlinear, and may have numerous local maxima, different starting values were tried in order to assure that the maximum attained is global. Finally, the Coslett-Lee algorithm was started up by assigning the initial probability of being in each state its unconditional value.[18] The estimated matrix of second derivatives is used to construct the standard errors.

The results of the parameter estimation are reported in table 3.4. We find clear evidence of multiple regimes. In regime 1, the unconstrained regime, our estimate of σ is a statistically insignificant .047. The estimate of the coefficient on lagged changes in income is $-.023$, which is also insignificant. Sensitivity to the interest rate is slightly higher in the second regime, with a σ estimate of .082, but this coefficient is, given its standard error, still insignificantly different from zero. The liquidity constraint estimate for the second regime is .526. The accompanying t-statistic of 6.07 is significant at the .999 level of confidence. These estimates mesh quite well with previous estimates of the model's parameters, suggesting that our alternative nonlinear (because of the interaction of the switching model and the linear consumption model) specification and our simplifying assumptions are reasonable. The estimated transition matrix and the accompanying t-statistics are also given in table 3.4. Both regimes are significantly persistent. The probability of the economy being in the unconstrained state, given that it was unconstrained yesterday is .90. The probability of moving from a constrained state to a constrained state is .74. These values imply an unconditional probability of being in the constrained state of only .28.

To gain further insight into the nature of the two regimes, we calculate the conditional inference of the probability that the current year is in the constrained regime. The calculation of these probabilities follows the observation of Hamilton (1989), that time t information can be combined with our inference about the Markov probabilities to construct the best estimate of the state of the world at time t, conditional on our best guess about the state of the world at $t - 1$. For example, if the probability of being in each state at time $t - 1$ is .5, and the transition probabilities are also .5, then the conditional probability of being in state 1 at time t is simply the proportion of the total likelihood attributable to that state. If the Markov probabilities are different from .5, then the likelihoods are reweighed to account for the Markovian in-

Table 3.4   Maximum-Likelihood Estimation of Switching Regimes Model: Dependent Variable Is Log Change of Consumption (t-statistics are in parentheses)

	r_t	Δy_{t-1}	σ_i	P_{ii}
State 1	.047	$-.023$	1.079	.896
	(.60)	$(-.27)$	(7.52)	(2.28)
State 2	.082	.526	.510	.743
	(1.18)	(6.07)	(3.87)	(2.04)
Log-likelihood = 53.79				

formation about the likelihood of each path through the data. If, for example, we have a strong inference that yesterday was in regime 1, and the Markov probability of remaining in state 1 is very high, than we might classify today as regime 1, even if the state-2 model appeared to fit the current observation better. Starting at time zero, a chain of successive inferences can be used to estimate the most likely trajectory taken through the two underlying models.

Table 3.5 contains the conditional state probability for each year. The prob-

Table 3.5   **Conditional Probability of Being in the Constrained State**

Year	Probability	Credit Crisis	Average − Prime Rate
1949	.000		.70
1950	.000		.64
1951	.000		.75
1952	.039		.50
1953	.235		.53
1954	.000		.54
1955	.000		.47
1956	.023		.26
1957	.011		.10
1958	.270		.72
1959	.000		.54
1960	.041		.38
1961	.245		.50
1962	.097		.50
1963	.193		.50
1964	.000		.50
1965	.489		.52
1966	.739	*	.40
1967	.637	*	.36
1968	.574	*	.40
1969	.646	*	.25
1970	.668	*	.57
1971	.257		.60
1972	.480		.57
1973	.618	*	.27
1974	.000		.47
1975	.000		.40
1976	.008		.75
1977	.160		.85
1978	.314		.50
1979	.328		− .33
1980	.896	*	2.49
1981	.980	*	1.12
1982	.951	*	2.25
1983	.749	*	− .48
1984	.107		.41
1985	.000		− .03

Note: Asterisks confirm presence of a credit crisis.

ability estimates are in accordance with the view, expressed by Campbell and Mankiw, that liquidity constraints first emerged in that late 1960s. However, if we label a year a "credit crisis year" if the probability of being in the constrained regime is greater than .5, then the first constrained year is 1966, not 1969, with the probability of being in the constrained regime being quite low before that and for sustained periods after 1970 as well. After 1966, the economy switches periodically from a constrained to unconstrained regime. Overall, only 10 years in our sample are in the constrained regime. Table 3.5, column 4, lists an alternative measure of credit tightness, the differential between the average and prime lending rates. On average, this is much larger during the "credit crunch" periods providing further indication that the credit crisis interpretation of liquidity constraints is valid.[19]

3.5   A Time-Series Investigation of Consumption from Assets

3.5.1   The Consumption Function and Cointegration

In section 3.2 we showed that one implication of the piercing of the corporate veil is that wealth-neutral dividend changes should have no effect on consumption. Our findings in section 3.3 confirmed the absence of any such effect. In section 3.4, we supported the plausibility of this result by demonstrating that the observed sensitivity of consumption to other forms of current income than dividends is attributable to liquidity constraints, which are very unlikely to apply to corporate shareholders.

This section considers another implication of shareholders' piercing the corporate veil. We focus our attention on a question that was not easily addressed with our previous methodology: Is the marginal propensity to consume out of corporate wealth as high as the marginal propensity to consume out of other forms of wealth? A lower propensity to consume out of corporate wealth would imply a permanent increase in consumption as a result of a shift in resources from corporations to individuals. This heterogeneity of response could be seen as evidence of a subtler form of corporate veil than we considered above. Our previous test found that a change in the portion of existing wealth held in corporate form does not affect consumption. Our new tests address whether the composition of *changes* in wealth affect consumption. While such differences would be consistent with the presence of a corporate veil, there is at least one other potential explanation. Given the wealth distribution statistics reported in table 3.1, a lower aggregate marginal propensity to consume out of corporate wealth would be consistent with a marginal propensity to consume declining with the overall level of wealth. In such a case, a wealth-neutral transfer from corporations to individuals would increase consumption via distributional effects, not because of an effective corporate veil. This possibility is discussed further below.

The outcome of these new tests cannot be inferred directly from the findings to this point. For example, shareholders could understand and compensate for changes in dividend policy while at the same time being more reluctant to raise their consumption to respond to increases in share prices. This reluctance could be attributable to a lack of faith in efficient markets, for example, a belief that a market that had risen might be above its "true" value.

This distinction helps to clarify the alternative possible sources of a corporate veil. We have already dismissed the idea that shareholders are afflicted by the "bird-in-the-hand" fallacy, that a dollar distributed by corporations is intrinsically more valuable once in their hands (holding taxes and other real differences constant). However, dividend policy is but one very simply mechanism by which corporate share values could change. Shareholders might be reluctant to respond to other changes in corporate wealth, as just suggested. Alternatively, they might respond as we predict to changes in shareholder wealth, but the change in the market valuation of corporate shares may not accurately reflect "true" changes in corporate values. In either case, a corporate veil could exist, although by focusing on responses to changes in the market value of corporate wealth we do not consider the latter case.

To effect these alternative tests of the impact of corporate wealth on consumption, we take advantage of recent results concerning cointegrated time series.

One implication of the permanent income hypothesis is that, holding interest rates constant, consumption is a constant fraction of wealth. The concept of wealth, of course, is total wealth, and includes the present discounted value of returns to human capital, human wealth. According to the theory, there should be an equilibrium relationship between consumption and assets, or, in the terminology of Engle and Granger (1987), consumption and assets should be cointegrated.[20] The error term from the equation

$$(9) \qquad C_t = \mu(A_t + H_t) + e_t,$$

where H_t is human wealth, should be stationary. Any deviation from the long-run equilibrium relationship is stationary and short-lived. If current income affects consumption, and is itself not stationary, then the error term in equation (9) will not be stationary. Rather, the equilibrium relationship will be of the form:

$$(10) \qquad C_t = \mu(A_t + H_t) + \lambda Y_t + e_t,$$

that is, consumption will be cointegrated with assets and income. If interest rates matter, μ will change over time, and there need be no cointegrating relationship between consumption and assets.

We examine the relevance of the additional explanation of the corporate veil mentioned at the beginning of this section by estimating consumption functions similar to equations (9) and (10). If wealth is decomposed into its corporate, human, and noncorporate components, then we can relax the assumption that the propensities to consume from these are equal.[21]

If we difference equation (10) we obtain:

(11) $\Delta C_t = \mu(\Delta A_t + \Delta H_t) + \lambda \Delta Y_t + e_t - e_{t-1}.$

The presence of e_{t-1} could lead to inconsistent estimates because it is correlated with the explanatory variables. An alternative approach, if consumption, assets, and income are cointegrated, is to substitute the lagged estimate of the error from equation (10) as a proxy for e_{t-1}. In this "error-correction" model, we can also obtain consistent estimates of the coefficients on assets because the remaining error is orthogonal to the beginning-of-period explanatory variables.[22] For continuity, we exclude after-tax dividends from disposable income and include these separately in the regression. Notice that in these regressions, the coefficients on dividends no longer reflects simply the existence of a corporate veil. Actual current dividends are likely to include new information about future income and hence current wealth as well. The same is true of actual disposable income. However, our focus in this section is not on these coefficients, and the wealth coefficients should not be affected, since consumption responses to new information are assumed to be orthogonal to beginning-of-period wealth.

3.5.2   The Data

We construct our financial asset measure from the quarterly Flow of Funds tables supplied by the Board of Governors of the Federal Reserve Bank.[23] Noncorporate wealth includes total financial assets net of corporate equities and owner-occupied housing. From this we subtract total liabilities net of installment consumer credit. This is consistent with our exclusion of durables from our consumption measure, which is the same as that used in previous sections. Beginning-of-period values are used for all wealth variables. Corporate wealth is item 26 in the flow of funds table, "corporate equities." Our measure of human wealth is the present discounted value of future expected after-tax labor earnings, calculated as a rolling forecast. These earnings are discounted at the arbitrary rate of .015.[24] Specification tests indicated that this assumption was not crucial to the results. The time period considered is 1952–85.[25] Preliminary testing indicated that all of the variables used are difference stationary.

3.5.3   Results

Table 3.6, row 1, gives the result of the estimation of equation (6) using quarterly data, splitting off corporate equities, and not imposing equality of wealth coefficients. The coefficients on human wealth and noncorporate wealth are very similar, but the coefficient on corporate wealth is small and negative. The test for cointegration is essentially a test for the nonstationarity of the error term, that is, in the simplest case, a test of the null hypothesis the errors are first-order autocorrelated with a unit root. Following Sargan and Bhargava (1983), we test the null that the Durbin-Watson statistic is zero. The

Table 3.6   **Estimates of Consumption from Wealth in Levels and Differences (*t*-statistics in parentheses): Dependent variable = Quarterly Consumption**

	Constant	Human Wealth	Noncorporate Wealth	Corporate Wealth	YD	DIV
1. Quarterly levels:						
	.014	.100	.109	− .016		
	(.351)	(29.2)	(18.3)	(−4.31)	. . .	. . .
D-W = .316, R^2 = .99, Dickey-Fuller = − 2.75, Adjusted Dickey-Fuller = − 3.06						
2. Quarterly levels:						
	.286	.044	.067	− .001	.358	.307
	(8.55)	(9.46)	(12.55)	(− .319)	(13.65)	(.905)
D-W = .646, R^2 = .99, Dickey-Fuller = − 4.56, Adjusted Dickey-Fuller = − 4.51						
3. Quarterly differences:						
	.019	.007	.027	.006	.243	1.56
	(3.56)	(.302)	(1.91)	(1.24)	(6.57)	(2.90)
D-W = 1.82, R^2 = .49, error correction parameter = − .161 (− 2.07)						

Durbin-Watson statistic is a very low .316, which is close to the 5% critical value of the test of .28.[26] Since the relevant critical value depends upon the data used, this can only be interpreted as weak evidence of cointegration. Two further tests of cointegration shed more light on the issue. The Dickey-Fuller and augmented Dickey-Fuller tests reported in table 3.6, row 1, both accept noncointegration of assets and consumption. Row 2 of table 3.6 presents an estimate of this model with disposable income and dividends included. The coefficients on noncorporate assets and human wealth are somewhat smaller and more plausible. The coefficient on corporate equities is again small and negative. The inclusion of these variables has increased the Durbin-Watson statistic to .65,[27] leading to a clear conclusion that these variables are cointegrated. The Dickey Fuller and augmented Dickey Fuller tests both accept cointegration at the 10% significant level. (The 10% critical values from Engle and Yoo, 1987, are 4.26 and 4.06, respectively). Row 3 contains the estimates of the differenced error correction model. One lag of the error correction term is reported since no further lags were found to be significant in this specification. With the exception of the coefficients on corporate equities and dividends, the coefficients are all smaller. The large drop in the human wealth coefficient may well reflect the noisiness of our imputation method (see note 21).

Table 3.7 presents results for the same model using annual data. These results are quite similar to those based on quarterly data.[28] The pure life-cycle model rejects cointegration, and the inclusion of income leads to the acceptance of cointegration.[29]

Table 3.7   **Estimates of Consumption from Wealth in Levels and Differences**
(*t*-statistics in parentheses): Dependent Variable = Annual
Consumption

Constant	Human Wealth	Noncorporate Wealth	Corporate Wealth	YD	DIV
1. Annual levels:					
−.042	.105	.104	−.017	. . .	. . .
(.092)	(14.29)	(7.99)	(−2.03)	. . .	. . .

D-W = .95, R^2 = .99, Dickey-Fuller = −2.44, Adjusted Dickey Fuller = −2.73

2. Annual levels:					
.286	.039	.054	−.005	.412	.817
(3.73)	(3.64)	(4.70)	(−.698)	(6.87)	(1.09)

D-W = 1.32, R^2 = .99, Dickey-Fuller = 3.43, Adjusted Dickey-Fuller = −4.08

3. Annual differences					
.034	−.007	.039	.009	.412	.938
(1.46)	(−.260)	(1.89)	(1.25)	(5.94)	(.438)

D-W = 1.929, R^2 = .86, error correction parameter = −.813(−3.19)

The most startling conclusion in both sets of regressions is that the aggregate marginal consumption out of corporate equities is so close to zero.[30] As already suggested, this could simply be a reflection of a declining marginal propensity to consume as wealth increases, combined with the high position in the income distribution of shareholders. The distribution of corporate wealth is indeed more skewed than that of noncorporate wealth. Row 2 of table 3.1, again, taken from the 1983 Survey of Consumer Finances, shows the percentage of noncorporate wealth held by different strata of the income distribution. Contrasting this with the distribution of corporate equities depicted in row 1, it is clear that the distribution of noncorporate wealth is more equal, especially in the top brackets. Strong evidence of a declining marginal propensity to consume out-of-asset wealth is supplied in Hoyt (1988), who shows that differences in the ratio of wealth to permanent income across income classes grow dramatically over the life-cycle. Hoyt concludes that this indicates a much higher saving propensity among the wealthy. Other evidence of different propensities to consume across the income distribution is supplied in Drobny and Hall (1987), who use a relative tax variable to identify distributional effects in an aggregate consumption function. They find that the marginal propensity to consume is much higher among low-rate, that is, low-income, taxpayers.[31]

Given the existing evidence of differing propensities to consume among income classes, combined with the right-skewed distribution of corporate wealth, one may explain the very low observed coefficient on corporate wealth without requiring the presence of a corporate veil, as we have defined it. This explanation is entirely consistent with our rejection of the corporate veil in section 3.2, because the previous experiment of altering dividend policy holds constant the distribution of wealth across the population, while the current approach need not. Nevertheless, even without a corporate veil, such a low coefficient could still imply important consumption effects of shifts in the distribution of income away from corporate shareholders. However such distributional effects have little to do with the separate existence of corporate entities and depend very much on the particular policy experiment being envisaged.

3.6 Conclusion

This paper has used the modern theory of the consumer to devise a new test for the existence of the corporate veil. We find evidence that consumption is not excessively sensitive to fluctuations in dividends, reconfirming the view that shareholders successfully pierce the corporate veil. This finding is corroborated by other results suggesting that the significant excess sensitivity of current consumption to other forms of income is due to liquidity constraints that, unlike irrationality and myopia, cannot plausibly be associated with consumption from corporate equity wealth.

We find very little consumption from corporate assets in our consumption functions. This could be interpreted as evidence for a corporate veil. However, one may also explain this as representing the presumably very low propensity to consume of shareholders, 77% of whom are in the top 5% of the income distribution. For many purposes, this distinction could be important. Future research, perhaps using panel data to isolate differences in propensity to consume from various assets, should examine these distributional issues more closely.

Data Appendix

The variables used in our analysis are constructed as follows (all variables not taken from the Flow of Funds [FOF] tables are taken from the NIPA section of the Citibase dataset):

1. Consumption is personal consumption expenditures on nondurables and services.

2. Disposable income is broken down into its capital and labor components by assigning proprietors' income and personal income taxes to each according to its factor share. Dividends are also converted to after-tax values in this way. Capital income includes interest payments. Labor income also includes wages and salaries, other labor income, and transfer payments.

3. Human wealth is the present discounted value of all future labor income

(as defined above) and is calculated as a simple univariate forecast of labor income. This forecast is constructed by first regressing full-sample labor income on a constant and a trend, subtracting these, then performing an eight-lag VAR on the detrended series. These VAR coefficients are then used to forecast labor income given period t information, then the constant and trend are added back in.

4. Corporate wealth is item 26 of the FOF sector balance sheets for households. As there is a separate entry for pension fund reserves (item 30), our variable excludes equities held by pension funds. Such pension assets are included in our measure of noncorporate wealth.

5. Noncorporate wealth is also taken from the FOF sector balance sheets for households. It equals owner-occupied housing (item 4) plus total financial assets (item 11), less corporate equities (item 26), and total liabilities net of installment consumer credit (item 35 minus item 40). We exclude installment consumer credit and consumer durables for consistency with our consumption definition, which excludes durables.

6. The interest rates used are quarterly averages of the six-month and three-month Treasury-bill rates.

Notes

1. Even with dividend taxes present, consumption should change only to the extent that the dividend payment reduces the shareholder's wealth. This effect should be small, and under the "new view" of corporate equity valuation (Auerbach 1979) should be nonexistent. In any event, since the tests derived below examine the effects on consumption of changes in dividend policy, holding wealth constant, any effects on wealth of pure financial policy associated with taxes will be purged from the estimated consumption response.

2. Another possible channel for increased consumption effects would be wealth-induced changes associated with the shift in the tax burden. While there is a plausible theoretical argument that the provisions of the 1986 act should have increased the value of corporate shares (Auerbach 1989), this does not seem to be the mechanism the authors have in mind. However, this ambiguity highlights the problem in identifying the source of the perceived impact on consumption.

3. For further evidence of the existence of the corporate veil see Bhatia (1979) or Hendershott and Peek (1987). For recent evidence against the corporate veil see von Furstenburg (1981).

4. Indeed, corporate savings is extremely difficult to define. For example, an increase in share repurchases and reduction in dividends appears as an increase in corporate savings and a concomitant decline in personal savings.

5. See Phillips (1986) for a recent discussion of spurious regressions.

6. Several issues arise in considering whether it is acceptable to apply such "representative agent" equations to aggregate time-series data. Several authors have addressed these questions in the past with no clearly preferable alternative resulting. We do not claim exception from the usual criticisms, but neither do we view the current tests as especially sensitive to the types of aggregation bias involved, since the absence

of a corporate veil implies a particular zero restriction for each individual's consumption behavior.

7. We are grateful to Scott Hoyt for making this table available to us. In principle, one would prefer a distribution of corporate wealth by capital income classes, since individuals with low tangible wealth but high labor income would not be in a position to sell assets in order to consume. However, this change would probably not alter the table's basic message significantly.

8. An alternative test suggested to us would consider whether responses of consumption to *unanticipated* dividends were zero once unanticipated changes in wealth were accounted for. In principle, this test should yield the same results as ours, but it has the considerable disadvantage of requiring us to observe unanticipated wealth changes. (In our specification, this is not needed because observable lagged consumption is assumed to incorporate all information about wealth.) Otherwise, conditional dividend surprises are likely to convey positive information about wealth, and contaminate the test.

9. The use of doubly lagged instruments is also appropriate to correct for the presence of transitory consumption. If transitory consumption is white noise, then it will also cause differencing to introduce an MA(1) error component.

10. Alternative specifications using an after-tax interest rate yielded virtually identical results and are not reported.

11. This variable is only calculated (and only makes sense) annually, so in quarterly regressions the annual value for the corresponding year is used.

12. In the regressions presented, the first-stage $\bar{R}^2$ values for the changes in dividends are in some cases higher than those for other forms of disposable income. For example, in eq. (7) of table 3.2, the $\bar{R}^2$ is .06 for labor income, .05 for nondividend capital income, and .13 for dividends. For eq. (7) of table 3.3, the corresponding values are .33, .17, and .28. The annual estimates using doubly lagged instruments were similar to those reported in table 3.3, except for the coefficient on dividends, which was slightly negative. The fit of the first-stage regressions using doubly lagged instruments were quite poor, however, making the power of our test questionable. While aggregation problems most definitely still exist when using annual data, we report our estimates using singly lagged variables since these results are moderately more favorable to the existence of the corporate veil.

13. In this light, it should be unsurprising that application of the Hayashi-Sims (1983) correction for serial correlation also had little impact on our findings. For this reason, we do not report them.

14. We investigated a second alternative explanation for the insignificance, that dividend changes in general might have little influence on consumption, by including dividend surprises in the second-stage regression. We found the coefficient on unexpected dividends to be positive and significant.

15. Actually, consumer behavior in such a model would be different in the transition years between states, perhaps making a four-state model the proper specification. Unfortunately, the addition of two more states greatly increases the computational burden and will be pursued at a later date.

16. The basic idea is that the model is simply a mixture of two normal distributions, with the relative weight of each depending on all information upon to time T and the Markov probabilities. The algorithm passes through the data, using new information to recalculate the weights given each distribution at each time period.

17. The interest rate used is the annual average of quarterly three-month Treasury-bill rates.

18. For example, the unconditional probability of being in state 1 is: $p21/(p12 + p21)$. See Chiang (1980) for more details.

19. The differential reported is the average rate on short-term commercial loans

minus the prime rate, taken from the Federal Reserve Bulletin. We were unable to obtain a full series of another alternative measure of credit tightness attributable to Jaffee (1971). We interpret the relatively low differential during the 1960s credit crisis as reflective of the well-known quantity rationing in lending markets that occurred at that time, most notable the credit crunch of 1966. In an alternative specification, which interacted the differential with income in an Euler equation, we found that the interaction term had the correct sign but was not significantly different from zero. This is perhaps a reflection of the noisiness of the measure during the 1960s.

20. This assumes, of course, that they are both the same order of integration. All of the variables we use are integrated of the first order, or $I(1)$.

21. Since eqq. (6) and (7) also hold in differences, one might also make inferences about the relative speeds of adjustment to changes in different forms of wealth by comparing the estimates from the levels regressions to those using differences. Since differencing is equivalent to passing the data through a filter that gives little weight to the low frequencies in the data, one would interpret the differenced estimates as "short-run" coefficients and the levels estimates as the long-run coefficients. However, given the errors with which noncorporate assets and, especially, human wealth are computed, one would also expect differences to depress the coefficients of the variables. Separating these two effects (errors in variables and lagged adjustments) is not a simple task.

22. The error correction coefficient can also be interpreted as representing an estimate of $(\rho - 1)$, where ρ is the first-order serial correlation coefficient from the levels regression.

23. The quarterly FOF data were taken from the "Household Net Worth" tables published by the Board of Governors of the Federal Reserve Board, March, 1988.

24. This value of the discount rate might be slightly lower than the actual rate. Increasing the discount rate translates into a slightly higher coefficient on human wealth in our regression. Following Hayashi (1982), it is possible to construct a model to estimate the discount rate of human wealth. Our estimates of Hayashi's model were very unreliable, however, and quite sensitive to the detrending technique and convergence criterion used. Because of this, we omit reporting of these estimates in this paper.

25. We start at the later date of 1952 because that year marks the beginning of the availability of the quarterly wealth numbers from the FOF tables.

26. The choice of the proper test is quite a complicated issue. We use the Durbin-Watson test because of its ease of computation and intuitive appeal. The Dickey-Fuller and augmented Dickey-Fuller tests are also reported.

27. The 10% critical value reported in Engle and Yoo (1987) for a higher order model is .46 for sample size 100.

28. For the annual regressions, we also tried including estimates of social security wealth, kindly supplied by Selig Lesnoy of the Social Security Administration. However, this variable was computed only through 1974. The resulting reduction in degrees of freedom may in part explain the erratic results that followed.

29. The 10% critical values in this case are .83 (Durbin-Watson), 4.42 (Dickey-Fuller) and 3.85 (augmented Dickey-Fuller).

30. This result *is* consistent with earlier findings. Bean (1986) reports similarly small estimates of the impact of corporate wealth on consumption. Blinder and Deaton (1985) report only an estimate based on total net worth as a measure of wealth. Their estimate is approximately equal to our estimated coefficient for noncorporate wealth. In an alternative specification (not reported) that excluded human wealth, we obtained a slightly higher coefficient (.015) for corporate wealth, but interpret this simply as evidence that the stock market is useful in predicting future labor income. One potential explanation of this result in both sets of regressions is that the induced relationship between owner-occupied housing and the imputed rent on such housing raises the coef-

ficient on noncorporate assets above its true value. Leaving these two variables out of assets and consumption, respectively, actually leads to an increase in the gap between the two coefficients on assets. In eq. (3), the coefficient on corporate wealth goes from .009 to .010 and that on noncorporate wealth rises from .039 to .058.

31. Additional evidence on the effects of income redistribution on aggregate consumption is supplied in Borooah and Sharpe (1986).

References

Auerbach, A. J. 1979. Wealth Maximization and the Cost of Capital. *Quarterly Journal of Economics* 93 (August): 433–40.

———. 1989. Tax Reform and Adjustment Costs: The Impact on Investment and Market Value. *International Economic Review* 30:939–62.

Bean, C. R. 1986. The Estimation of "Surprise" Models and the "Surprise" Consumption Function. *Review of Economic Studies* 53:497–516.

Blinder, A. S., and A. S. Deaton. 1985. The Time Series Consumption Function Revisited. *Brookings Papers on Economic Activity,* no. 2, 465–511.

Borooah, V. K., and D. R. Sharpe, 1986. Aggregate Consumption and the Distribution of Income in the United Kingdom: An Econometric Analysis. *Economic Journal.* 96:449–66.

Brinner, Roger, and Jesse Abraham. 1986. Tax Reform Requires Gramm-Rudman-Hollings. *Data Resources U.S. Review* (September): 12–19.

Campbell, J. Y., and N. G. Mankiw. 1987. Permanent Income, Current Income and Consumption. NBER Working Paper no. 2436. Cambridge, Mass.

Chiang, C. L. 1980. *An Introduction to Stochastic Processes and Their Applications.* New York: Krieger.

Coslett, S. R., and L. F. Lee. 1985. Serial Correlation in Discrete Variable Models. *Journal of Econometrics* 27:79–97.

Denison, E. F. 1958. A Note on Private Saving. *Review of Economics and Statistics* 40:761–67.

Drobny, A., and S. G. Hall. 1987. An Investigation of the Long Run Properties of Aggregate Non-durable Consumers' Expenditure in the UK. Bank of England. Mimeograph.

Engle, R. F., and C. W. J. Granger. 1987. Co-integration and Error-Correction: Representation, Estimation and Testing. *Econometrica* 55 (March):251–76.

Engle, R. F., and B. S. Yoo. 1987. Forecasting and Testing in Co-integrated Systems. *Journal of Econometrics* 35:143–60.

Feldstein, M. S. 1973. Tax Incentives, Corporate Saving and Capital Accumulation in the United States. *Journal of Public Economics* 2, no. 2 (April):159–71.

Flavin, M. A. 1981. The Adjustment of Consumption to Changing Expectations about Future Income. *Journal of Political Economy* 89, no. 5 (October):974–1009.

Goldfeld, S. M., and R. E. Quandt. 1973. A Markov Model for Switching Regressions. *Journal of Econometrics* 1:2–16.

Grossman, S. J., and R. J. Shiller. 1981. The Determinants of the Variability of Stock Market Prices. *American Economic Review* 71 (May): 222–27.

Hall, R. E. 1978. Stochastic Implications of the Life Cycle–Permanent Income Hypothesis: Theory and Evidence. *Journal of Political Economy* 86 (December):971–87.

———. 1988. Intertemporal Substitution in Consumption. *Journal of Political Economy* 96:339–57.

Hamilton, J. D., 1989. A New Approach to the Economic Analysis of Nonstationary Time Series and the Business Cycle. *Econometrica* 57(March): 357–84.

Hansen, L., and K. Singleton. 1983. Stochastic Consumption, Risk Aversion, and the Temporal Behavior of Asset Returns. *Journal of Political Economy* 91 (April):249–65.

Hayashi, F. 1982. The Permanent Income Hypothesis: Estimating and Testing by Instrumental Variables. *Journal of Political Economy* 90 (October):895–916.

Hayashi, F., and C. Sims. 1983. Nearly Efficient Estimation of Time Series Models with Predetermined, but Not Exogenous, Instruments. *Econometrica* 51:783–98.

Hendershott, P., and J. Peck, 1987. Private Saving in the U.S., 1950–1985. NBER Working Paper no. 2294. Cambridge, Mass.

Hoyt, S. 1988. Wealth Accumulation in the 1983 Survey of Consumer Finances. Doctoral diss., University of Pennsylvania.

Jaffee, D. M. 1971. *Credit Rationing and the Commercial Loan Market.* New York: Wiley.

Miller, M., and F. Modigliani. 1961. Dividend Policy, Growth, and the Valuation of Shares. *Journal of Business* 34:411–33.

Modigliani, F., and M. Miller. 1958. The Cost of Capital, Corporation Finance and the Theory of Investment. *American Economic Review* 48:261–97.

Neftci, S. N. 1984. Are Economic Time Series Asymmetric over the Business Cycle? *Journal of Political Economy* 92: 307–28.

Phillips, P. C. B. 1986. Understanding Spurious Regressions in Econometrics. *Journal of Econometrics* 33:311–40.

Poterba, J. M. 1987. Tax Policy and Corporate Savings. *Brookings Papers on Economic Activity,* no. 2, 455–503.

Sargan, J. D., and A. Bhargava. 1983. Testing Residuals from Least Squares Regression for Being Generated by a Gaussian Random Walk. *Econometrics* 51:153–74.

U.S. House of Representatives. 1986. *Tax Reform of 1986.* Conference Report no. 99–841, vol. 2, table A1. Washington, D.C., September 18.

von Furstenburg, G., M. 1981. Saving. In *How Taxes Affect Economic Behavior,* ed. H. Aaron and J. Pechman, 327–90. Washington, D.C.: Brookings.

Working, Holbrook. 1960. Note on the Correlation of First Differences of Averages in a Random Chain. Econometrica 28:916–18.

Comment   Angus S. Deaton

It is a pleasure to be asked to discuss a paper such as this in which there is a real possibility of using econometric analysis to discover something that is of great significance for economic policy. Auerbach and Hassett quote the Data Resources, Inc. (DRI) prediction that the recent tax changes will reduce private savings by $19 billion, and, although none of us is very likely to accept that estimate, even a much smaller effect would indicate that this is an area where tax policy can have a dramatic effect on saving. Indeed, it is hard to imagine any other way in which apparently minor tax changes could be used

Angus S. Deaton is the William Church Osborn Professor of Public Affairs and a professor of economics and international affairs at the Woodrow Wilson School, Princeton University, and a research associate of the National Bureau of Economic Research.

to have such a large influence on saving and, presumably, capital formation. Unlike many other questions of equal policy import, this also seems to be one where we should have at least a fair chance of discovering something. The theoretical framework is clear and there are plenty of data. And there are also "the modern theory of the consumer" and "recent advances in time-series econometrics" waiting to be applied to give us clearer answers than ever before. I think that this paper does indeed take us further than we have been before, although it also leaves a number of problems and puzzles.

In the first part of the paper, that is "the modern theory of consumption" part, the authors use an Euler equation approach to derive a relationship between changes in consumption and the real interest rate, to which they propose to add anticipated changes in dividends. I think the Euler equation can be safely ignored. First, the relationship (1) is not an Euler equation and cannot be derived from one without ignoring important terms. Second, the authors use a pretax real interest rate, whereas the correct posttax rate behaves very differently. But of course we know that none of this is going to work whether it is done correctly or not; there simply is no relationship in the time-series data between changes in consumption and the real interest rate. The approach here is much more closely related to the literature following Flavin, who found that lagged income was correlated with the change in income, a result that has been widely ascribed to the presence of borrowing constraints for at least a fraction of the population. Auerbach and Hassett set out to show that this effect is not due to dividends. If it were, so that additional dividends significantly relaxed liquidity constraints, then changes in tax policy that discouraged retentions in favor of dividends could certainly decrease private saving.

The paper does not find any such effects. I believe the result, although the evidence in the paper is not overwhelmingly convincing. The problem is largely econometric. In order to avoid time-aggregation effects, only instruments lagged two periods or more are used in the regressions, but, for many of the variables, such instruments have only very poor explanatory power. In consequence the standard errors are large, so that in the conclusion that anticipated dividends do not significantly affect changes in consumption, it is the word "significantly" that ought to be emphasized, not the words "do not." While it is true that the significance of the income term survives the instrumentation, it is a good deal larger to start with, larger than we would expect the dividend term to be, even if we accepted some part of the DRI view, that dividends get spent.

Even so, it is implausible that many dividend recipients are liquidity constrained. Note that liquidity constraints are likely to be binding for those who have low nonhuman wealth and current labor income relative to their future anticipated labor income or inheritances, and such people are not exclusively poor. In consequence, table 3.1, on the fractions of wealth held by income groups, is not quite what we want, but I do not believe that the true picture would be very different. Of course, we do not really know that the sensitivity of consumption to anticipated income comes from liquidity constraints rather than something else. In the next part of the paper, Auerbach and Hassett buttress the liquidity story, and thus the implausibility of dividends affecting consumption. I have few quarrels with the modeling here, although it seems to me to make more sense to think of their probability that the economy is in a credit crisis as reflecting the proportion of consumers in the economy who are unable to borrow as much as they would like. Such a reinterpretation may require some reformulation, but I doubt that it would be very difficult to do so. The evidence in table 3.5, associating high probabilities of credit crisis with high real interest rates, is less strong than one would like. Indeed, if there really is such an effect, it should have been included in the model that was estimated.

In the last part of the paper, we come to the "recent advances in time-series econometrics." In particular, a good deal of attention is paid to the consequences of regression analysis when some or all of the right-hand-side variables are integrated processes. Although the regressions here look very similar to those that have often been run to test the corporate veil, the interpretations are different, and a good deal of necessary (and welcome) attention is paid to whether and when it is correct to use the OLS standard errors for inference. As Auerbach and Hassett note, the very low Durbin-Watson statistic when consumption is regressed on human wealth, noncorporate and corporate wealth, can be taken as evidence that the variables are not cointegrated, and though the introduction of income and dividends improves the cointegration tests, the distribution of the test statistics is still nonstandard, so that it is hard to infer much from these results. Instead, they focus attention on a first-difference specification with the induced moving average errors dealt with by inclusion of the lagged errors from the levels regression. Although the rapid convergence of the parameter estimates in the cointegrated regression implies that this two-stage procedure is asymptotically valid, recent Monte Carlo evidence suggests that there may still be problems in samples of the size used here.

But econometrics apart, the most surprising feature of these final results is that there is no apparent effect of corporate wealth on consumption. In the paper that Alan Blinder and I wrote for Brookings,[1] almost the only robust result was the effect of unanticipated changes in stock market wealth, and we did not think we were discovering anything that has not been found by many others over many years. Indeed, Hall's original rejection of the "random walk" consumption function concerned the influence of (lagged) stock market wealth on consumption, and others have replicated this result. Why then are

---

1. See A. S. Blinder and A. S. Deaton, "The Time Series Consumption Function Revisited" (*Brookings Papers on Economic Activity*, no. 2, 465–511).

the results of this paper so different? This seems like an important and urgent task for research.

If I put all three parts of the paper together, I find that there are results that I believe, and results of which I remain skeptical, at least for the time being. But there also remain some real problems in reconciling the results with any coherent story of the way in which changes in corporate wealth get through to households. I am prepared to believe that anticipated changes in dividends do not affect consumption, and I am prepared to believe that the anticipated changes in income that do affect consumption have nothing to do with dividends. But the last negative, that the stock market has no effect on consumption, is hard to swallow, partly because of previous evidence that it does, but also because it removes any link between corporate wealth and its owners. It is possible that stockholders do not accept the stock market's valuation as an accurate measure of corporate wealth, but if not, they must use some other measure, which, if we could identify, would affect consumption levels. We know it cannot be dividends, so what is it? In not providing an answer, the paper leaves us with as many puzzles as it resolves.

4 The Saving Effect of Tax-deferred Retirement Accounts: Evidence from SIPP

Steven F. Venti and David A. Wise

Individual retirement accounts (IRAs) rapidly became a very popular form of saving after they became available to all employees in 1982. Annual contributions grew from about $5 billion in 1981 to about $38 billion in 1986. Preliminary data indicate that contributions declined precipitously after the Tax Reform Act of 1986, even though the legislation limited the tax deductibility of contributions only for families who have annual incomes over $40,000 and who are covered by a firm pension plan. Whereas over 15 percent of tax filers made contributions in 1986, only 7 percent contributed in 1987. Two claims received considerable attention in the legislative debate over the tax treatment of IRAs. One was that the accounts were held primarily by the wealthy, a claim that is not supported by the data. Although wealthier households are much more likely than poor households to have IRAs, approximately two-thirds of accounts are held by households with incomes less than $50,000. The second claim was that IRAs produced no net saving; funds were simply transferred from other saving balances, or, if there was new saving, it would have taken place anyway. In earlier papers (Venti and Wise 1986, 1987a, 1987b, 1988b; Wise 1987) we analyzed the relationship between IRA saving and other financial asset saving. Those studies were based on household data from the 1983 Survey of Consumer Finances (SCF) and the 1980–85 Consumer Expenditure Surveys (CESs). At most, the evidence from these studies showed only a very modest substitution of IRA for other forms of

Steven F. Venti is an associate professor of economics at Dartmouth College and a research associate of the National Bureau of Economic Research. David A. Wise is John F. Stambaugh Professor of Political Economy at the John F. Kennedy School of Government, Harvard University, and a research associate of the National Bureau of Economic Research.

Financial support from the National Institute on Aging and the Hoover Institution is gratefully acknowledged. The authors are also grateful for discussion with Michael Rothschild, some of whose initial comments as a discussant have been incorporated in this version of the paper. The authors also thank Douglas Bernheim for his comments.

saving, indicating that the net saving effect was substantial. Recent analysis by Feenberg and Skinner (1989), using a panel of individual tax returns for 1980–84 also finds little evidence of substitution.

The results on IRAs are consistent with analysis of contributions to Registered Retirement Saving Plans (RRSPs) in Canada by Wise (1984 and 1985), and with the comparison of Canadian versus U.S. savings rates over time by Carroll and Summers (1987). A program comparable to the IRA has existed in Canada since 1956. In the early 1970s the contribution limits were increased substantially and the program was widely publicized. The maximum individual limit was $3,500. New limits will be as high as $15,000. Although the program has been in existence in Canada much longer than in the United States, and although the limits are based on income and for some are much higher than in the United States, Wise (1985) shows that the relationship between desired contributions and income is virtually the same in the two countries after accounting for the differences in the limits. Carroll and Summers (1987) show that after moving in tandem for almost 25 years the private savings rates in the two countries diverged dramatically after 1975, following expansion of the RRSP program. Corporate saving in the two countries, they find, has shown no long-term trend since 1954. The increase in the Canadian private saving rate and the decrease in the U.S. rate resulted from changes in the behavior of individuals, not corporations. Whether the increase in Canada was due to the RRSP program can only be judged by the coincidence of the two events and by the apparent lack of other explanations.

Nonetheless, simple forms of theoretical reasoning raise doubts about the net saving effect. Thus the question is reconsidered in this paper, based on data that are, in principle, better than the other data that we have used. The analysis here is based on the Survey of Income and Program Participation (SIPP). A total of almost 20,000 households were covered in the first nine waves—now available—of this panel survey. Each household in the survey is interviewed quarterly for 32 months. In principle, the data provide information on IRA contributions in two consecutive years, allowing statistical correction for individual-specific saving effects. Such effects may have influenced to some extent our prior results. Unfortunately, these data have not been entered on the data tapes released to us to date. Thus the analysis in this paper is based on contributions in a single year only, calculated as the difference between balances reported in the fourth (September–December 1984) and the seventh (September–December 1985) waves of the survey.[1]

We begin with descriptive data on IRAs and other forms of saving. Because the paper is directed to IRA contributions, self-employed persons and those over 65 and under 21 have been excluded.[2] Most of the descriptive data can be compared with information from the 1983 Survey of Consumer Finances and from the Consumer Expenditure Surveys, with no major inconsistencies. The following conclusions may be drawn from these data:

- The typical American family has very little financial asset saving, consistent with evidence from other surveys. The median of financial assets, including stocks, was only $600 in 1985. The majority of the saving of most families is in the form of housing.
- Families who have contributed to IRAs since 1982 had not, prior to that time, accumulated financial assets at a rate even close to the annual IRA limit.
- Comparison of IRA balances with other asset balances, or of the annual change in IRA balances with the change in other asset balances, provides no evidence of substitution of IRAs for other saving, even after controlling for several family attributes like age and income.
- These data apparently reveal individual-specific savings effects; individuals who save in one form are also likely to save in other forms as well.
- The data provide no evidence that IRAs have been funded by borrowing.

The incentive effects of IRA accounts are considered next. Attention is directed to the possibility that retirement saving and saving for other purposes may be treated by individuals as distinct "goods." That is, it may be incorrect to think of the IRA tax deduction as simply a subsidy to the one and only form of saving. To the extent that this is true it invalidates the simple theoretical reasoning that suggests little net saving effect of IRAs.

The formal statistical model that we estimate is summarized next and the estimation results are discussed. The conclusions are summarized by simulating the effect of an increase in the IRA limit.

- If the IRA limit of each family in the sample were increased by $1,000, the annual IRA contributions of families at the current limit would increase by an average of $856.
- About two-thirds of the increase would be financed by reduced consumption and about one-third by reduced taxes. Very little would be financed by reducing other saving or by increasing debt.

The last section contains a discussion and summary of the paper.

4.1 Descriptive Data

The SIPP data are organized by household and by subfamilies within households. Other surveys, like the SCF and the CES collect data only by household. Thus for comparative purposes most of the data presented here are also by household; the family data are also presented in most instances. In principal, the IRA information should be analyzed by family unit; they are most likely to correspond to tax units. In practice, however, the difference may be small. Data on accumulated wealth are presented first, then data on annual saving (change in asset balances). In each case the relationship between IRA and other saving is emphasized.

4.1.1   Accumulated Wealth

Household Assets

The data in table 4.1a confirm that the vast majority of the personal wealth of most households is housing equity.[3] The table shows the median of assets by type of asset and by income and age. The median of total wealth is

Table 4.1a   **Median Household Wealth by Type of Asset and by Income and Age in 1985**

Type of Asset and Age	Income (in thousands)							
	<10	10–20	20–30	30–40	40–50	50–75	>75	All
Total wealth:								
<25	0	838	4,425	7,797	16,794	58,469	285,476	2,031
25–35	0	2,053	7,394	12,488	22,535	35,450	53,775	6,325
35–45	500	8,569	26,850	34,108	41,400	60,375	111,488	30,112
45–55	1,500	14,275	36,200	42,242	61,850	88,675	129,236	45,724
55–65	10,175	38,750	58,500	71,284	81,700	99,730	171,715	56,241
All	500	5,822	21,340	30,850	43,329	68,197	120,483	25,067
Housing equity:								
<25	0	0	0	0	3,250	25,350	66,000	0
25–35	0	0	126	6,250	14,250	20,000	20,000	0
35–45	0	930	19,000	27,000	30,400	44,000	60,500	22,400
45–55	0	10,000	27,500	31,000	44,000	56,000	65,000	32,000
55–65	6,000	30,000	44,000	50,000	50,000	62,100	76,000	40,000
All	0	0	14,000	23,000	30,000	45,800	62,500	16,974
Financial assets, including stocks:								
<25	0	188	843	1,500	1,827	6,110	22,975	430
25–35	0	200	820	1,724	3,607	6,500	12,572	840
35–45	0	200	1,100	2,100	3,640	7,650	22,200	1,550
45–55	0	200	1,200	2,734	5,000	9,200	21,198	2,400
55–65	50	2,625	9,498	8,873	9,500	20,419	48,470	6,350
All	0	300	1,300	2,220	4,250	9,236	23,867	1,600
Financial assets, excluding stocks:								
<25	0	188	793	1,298	1,750	2,250	12,508	400
25–35	0	200	600	1,318	3,000	4,058	10,000	720
35–45	0	171	900	1,600	2,500	5,500	14,374	1,200
45–55	0	200	801	2,040	3,503	5,740	14,150	1,830
55–65	42	2,100	6,600	6,002	7,000	13,500	36,470	4,675
All	0	290	1,000	1,800	3,124	6,000	15,550	1,275
Debt:								
<25	0	492	1,170	1,700	2,105	2,290	3,556	800
25–35	0	606	1,000	1,600	1,765	3,000	4,050	1,000
35–45	0	500	1,000	1,400	1,600	1,600	3,050	1,000
45–55	0	213	545	1,025	1,560	2,300	3,025	849
55–65	0	47	195	442	600	1,240	2,000	200
All	0	350	700	1,200	1,540	2,000	3,075	750

Note: Sample is weighted to represent the national population of households with head age 21 to 65 and not self-employed.

$25,100.[4] The median of housing equity is $17,000. Including stocks, the median level of financial assets is only $1,600; excluding stocks it is only $1,275. Thus saving in the form of financial assets is typically very limited.[5] It is even smaller taking the family as the unit of analysis, as shown in table 4.1b.[6] Including stocks, the median of family financial assets is only $600. The median of total family wealth is only $8,100. Consistent with analysis

Table 4.1b   **Median Family Wealth by Type of Asset and by Income and Age in 1985**

Age	<10	10–20	20–30	30–40	40–50	50–75	>75	All
				Income (in thousands)				
Total wealth:								
<25	20	11,181	3,800	5,752	9,157	41,305	356,945	500
25–35	0	2,005	7,805	14,515	29,375	44,473	67,450	3,249
35–45	500	6,425	24,600	35,831	52,489	80,248	130,448	23,978
45–55	670	20,950	41,463	57,863	76,700	117,025	163,375	40,025
55–65	6,521	46,909	76,899	89,369	111,200	145,021	274,690	57,436
All	200	3,700	19,400	33,180	55,397	86,770	162,604	8,069
Housing equity:								
<25	0	0	0	0	0	23,000	0	0
25–35	0	0	0	5,300	15,500	18,025	33,000	0
35–45	0	0	13,250	25,000	32,250	46,000	63,500	13,500
45–55	0	10,000	30,000	36,500	48,398	57,000	70,000	25,000
55–65	0	30,000	45,000	54,323	57,000	70,000	86,500	35,000
All	0	0	8,000	20,000	32,000	46,000	69,500	0
Financial assets, including stocks:								
<25	12	300	843	1,200	1,827	7,750	351,570	150
25–35	0	200	950	1,800	3,698	6,349	10,000	400
35–45	0	200	1,196	2,120	4,025	8,200	20,099	1,000
45–55	0	399	1,500	3,309	6,000	11,500	20,698	1,284
55–65	0	2,358	8,048	12,785	17,279	35,400	79,700	3,700
All	0	314	1,325	2,500	5,000	10,453	30,100	600
Financial assets, excluding stocks:								
<25	10	251	750	978	1,300	1,189	1,570	125
25–35	0	200	737	1,400	3,000	4,457	7,499	350
35–45	0	200	955	1,548	2,800	5,600	14,374	800
45–55	0	350	1,200	2,499	4,400	6,800	13,450	1,000
55–65	5	2,000	5,235	9,000	10,500	25,300	47,900	3,000
All	0	300	1,030	1,898	3,510	6,500	15,000	500
Debt:								
<25	0	150	800	1,266	1,000	282	1,500	0
25–35	0	350	785	1,500	1,500	2,000	3,540	400
35–45	0	468	900	1,250	1,475	1,400	2,900	1,650
45–55	0	200	500	1,130	1,200	1,200	1,850	350
55–65	0	50	150	300	80	620	506	24
All	0	240	600	1,100	1,100	1,200	1,575	275

Note: Sample is weighted to represent the national population of households with head age 21 to 65 and not self-employed.

based on the SCF and the CES, these data make clear that the typical family was not, prior to the introduction of IRAs, accustomed to saving even close to the IRA annual limit, $2,000 per year per worker.

The Distribution of IRA Accounts by Age and Income

The percentage of households with IRA accounts and the mean balance in these accounts is shown in table 4.2, panel A, by age and income; comparable data for families is shown in table 4.2, panel B.[7] Overall, 25 percent of households have IRA accounts. The percentage increases with both age and in-

Table 4.2   **IRA Accounts by Age and Income**

Age	<10	10–20	20–30	30–40	40–50	50–75	>75	All
				Income (in thousands)				

				A. By Household				
Percentage of households with IRA accounts:								
<25	.0	4.1	6.8	7.5	8.7	29.0	29.6	6.2
25–35	1.1	6.2	11.5	17.0	27.5	33.9	54.8	14.1
35–45	1.2	8.1	22.5	21.8	34.8	48.3	70.4	24.4
45–55	8.3	13.8	25.3	29.7	40.3	56.6	68.6	32.6
55–65	9.8	257.1	40.6	43.5	54.4	67.2	76.9	38.6
All	4.7	12.1	22.0	24.5	36.6	51.2	68.3	25.0
Mean IRA balance:								
<25	0	162	80	258	419	3,372	2,346	342
25–35	16	195	391	526	1,378	1,886	3,810	607
35–45	18	367	1,022	1,222	2,240	3,787	6,540	1,588
45–55	551	660	1,574	1,976	2,858	4,924	8,010	2,588
55–65	562	2,028	3,415	3,817	5,314	6,908	8,674	3,495
All	260	691	1,314	1,508	2,593	4,343	7,071	1,818

				B. By Family				
Percentage of families with IRA accounts:								
<25	1.2	3.0	4.9	7.6	3.4	21.6	.0	2.4
25–35	1.5	6.6	12.7	17.9	28.9	33.3	62.5	10.9
35–45	2.4	9.4	23.4	22.4	37.0	53.8	74.4	22.2
45–55	6.2	16.2	27.6	35.2	49.8	66.7	74.2	29.4
55–65	8.6	26.8	42.9	56.5	67.5	74.6	74.1	34.9
All	3.3	10.8	22.4	27.5	40.8	56.1	72.6	18.8
Mean IRA balance:								
<25	22	86	65	166	136	228	0	52
25–35	34	195	445	572	1,441	1,791	4,889	427
35–45	49	374	1,048	1,273	2,313	4,288	7,314	1,359
45–55	360	848	1,680	2,170	3,903	7,124	8,929	2,305
55–65	464	1,854	3,660	5,320	6,961	7,848	8,951	3,081
All	141	551	1,322	1,747	2,979	5,067	7,974	1,290

Note: Sample is Weighted to represent the national population of households with head age 21 to 65 and not self-employed.

come. About 19 percent of families have accounts. Although wealthier households and families are much more likely than poorer households and families to have accounts, most account holders are not wealthy, as shown in table 4.3, panels A and B, for households and families, respectively. About two-thirds of households with at least one account have household income less than $50,000; these households own about 52 percent of IRA assets. Of families with accounts, about 76 percent have income less than $50,000 and these families own about 66 percent of IRA assets.

IRAs and Other Financial Asset Saving

IRA account holders also save more in other forms as well, consistent with evidence from other surveys.[8] In addition, IRA holders also have less debt. The data are shown in table 4.4, panels A and B, for households and families, respectively. These data provide no evidence that IRA saving substitutes for other financial asset saving. Nor do the data indicate that IRA accounts are funded by borrowing, as has been suggested by some commentators. Rather, these data apparently reflect individual-specific saving behavior; savers save more than nonsavers in all forms, including IRAs. And, almost by definition, savers borrow less. Even typical IRA holders, however, had not accumulated financial assets at close to the IRA annual limit, as is evident from the median balances.

Table 4.3   **Distribution of IRA Accounts and Balances by Income, 1985**

Income (in thousands)	Percentage with Accounts	Mean Balance		Cumulative Percentage	
		All	IRA > 0	All Accounts	Total Balances
A. By Household					
<10	4.7	260	5,754	2.6	2.0
10–20	12.1	691	5,628	12.8	10.0
20–30	22.0	1,314	6,058	31.8	25.6
30–40	24.5	1,508	5,887	48.2	39.4
40–50	36.6	2,593	7,091	63.8	54.6
50–75	51.2	4,343	8,408	87.4	82.1
75+	68.3	7,071	10,460	100.0	100.0
All	25.0	1,818	7,303	. . .	. . .
B. By Family					
<10	3.3	141	4,325	4.8	3.0
10–20	10.8	551	5,084	20.1	14.3
20–30	22.4	1,322	5,901	43.6	34.6
30–40	27.5	1,747	6,352	61.2	50.8
40–50	40.8	2,979	7,295	75.9	66.4
50–75	56.1	5,067	9,040	93.2	89.2
75+	72.6	7,974	10,982	100.0	100.0
All	18.8	1,290	6,873	. . .	. . .

Table 4.4   **Financial Assets and Debt of IRA Account Holders and Nonholders, by Income, 1985**

Income (in thousands)	Median Financial Assets Including Stocks		Median Financial Assets Excluding Stocks		Median Debt	
	IRA > 0	IRA = 0	IRA > 0	IRA = 0	IRA > 0	IRA = 0
			A. By Household			
<10	7,625	0	6,500	0	0	0
10–20	6,538	200	4,800	200	250	400
20–30	6,365	900	5,000	700	400	800
30–40	6,015	1,692	4,080	1,349	600	1,475
40–50	10,000	2,694	6,800	2,005	800	2,000
50–75	14,516	5,100	9,709	3,367	1,500	2,581
75+	36,085	9,735	21,475	6,687	2,613	4,425
All	10,800	728	7,641	600	900	700
			B. By Family			
<10	2,600	0	2,065	0	0	0
10–20	4,000	250	3,000	200	300	238
20–30	6,000	950	4,998	737	300	700
30–40	6,756	1,800	4,320	1,400	554	1,400
40–50	10,450	3,000	7,000	2,420	650	1,600
50–75	17,900	5,000	10,100	3,862	1,000	2,020
75+	37,700	11,000	19,000	6,877	1,400	3,000
All	8,600	300	5,922	270	500	200

Regression Summary of IRA and Other Saving

The relationship between IRA balances and other assets may be summarized by regressions of other wealth on IRA balances. The results are shown in table 4.5, panels A and B, for households and families, respectively. In addition to IRA balances, the regressions control for current income, age, age × income, education, marital status, and private pension coverage. It is clear that larger IRA balances are associated with greater wealth in all other forms, not less. Again, the data apparently reflect individual-specific saving effects.

4.1.2   Annual IRA Contributions and Other Saving

We next consider the relationship between IRA contributions (change in IRA balances) and the change in other saving balances between 1984 and 1985, first by considering summary tabulations and then by simple descriptive regressions.

Summary Tabulations

The relationship between IRA saving and other financial asset saving and debt is shown for households and families in table 4.6, panels A and B, respectively. The figures in the first two columns are the percentage of house-

Table 4.5   **Regression Parameter Estimates, Other Assets on IRA Balances, 1985**

Other Asset Category	IRA Balance Coefficient	Standard Error
A. By Household[a]		
Total wealth	2.80	(.26)
Housing equity	1.02	(.09)
Nonhousing wealth	1.78	(.24)
Financial assets, including Stocks	1.25	(.11)
Financial assets, excluding Stocks	1.00	(.05)
Debt	− .07	(.03)
B. By Family[a]		
Total wealth	2.48	(.17)
Housing equity	1.05	(.07)
Nonhousing wealth	1.44	(.14)
Financial assets, including Stocks	.76	(.09)
Financial assets, excluding Stocks	.82	(.04)
Debt	− .06	(.02)

[a]The regressions also control for current income, age, age × income, education, marital status, and private pension coverage.

Table 4.6   **IRA and Other Financial Asset Saving and Debt, 1984–85**

Income (in thousands)	% Non-IRA Saving >0[a] IRA > 0	IRA = 0	% Δ Debt > 0 IRA > 0	IRA = 0	Median Δ Debt IRA > 0	IRA = 0
A. By Household[a]						
<10	49	21	17	22	− 10.5	0
10–20	48	39	44	37	0	0
20–30	50	49	44	41	0	0
30–40	60	54	43	49	0	0
40–50	56	55	49	55	0	191
50–75	58	60	46	51	0	65
75 +	62	71	55	47	50	0
All	55	43	46	39	0	0
B. By Family[a]						
<10	42	22	21	19	0	0
10–20	53	40	30	36	0	0
20–30	55	51	42	42	0	0
30–40	60	55	44	50	0	50
40–50	53	56	42	48	0	0
50–75	58	61	49	47	0	0
75 +	71	74	53	39	325	0
All	56	40	42	34	0	0

[a]Excluding stocks.

Table 4.7   Regression Parameters, Change in Other Assets on IRA Saving, 1985–84

Change in Other Asset Balances	IRA Saving Coefficient	Standard Error
A. By Household[a]		
Total wealth	.65	(.24)
Housing equity	.23	(.13)
Nonhousing wealth	.42	(.19)
Financial assets, including stocks	.49	(.12)
Financial assets, excluding stocks	.31	(.08)
Debt	.07	(.07)
B. By Family[a]		
Total wealth	.85	(.18)
Housing equity	.26	(.12)
Nonhousing wealth	.60	(.14)
Financial assets, including stocks	.33	(.09)
Financial assets, excluding stocks	.21	(.07)
Debt	.05	(.04)

[a]The regressions also control for current income, change in incomes between 1984 and 1985, age, age × income, education, marital status, and private pension coverage. Total wealth and nonhousing wealth exclude IRAs.

holds with positive non-IRA saving, distinguished by whether the family was an IRA contributor (IRA > 0) or a noncontributor (IRA = 0).[9] Controlling for income, it is clear that IRA savers are at least as likely as non-IRA savers to save in other financial asset forms. The next four columns show the change in debt for IRA contributors and noncontributors. There is little relationship between IRA saving and debt; the data provide no evidence that IRA saving is accompanied by increased debt. Apparently, IRAs are not typically funded by borrowing. And there is no indication of substitution away from other financial asset saving. As emphasized above, the positive relationship between the two forms of saving is likely to reflect individual-specific savings effects. There is, however, no guarantee that inducement to fund an IRA account does not at the same time lead to increased consideration of future needs and thus to increased saving in other forms as well. In general, the virtual absence of saving among a large proportion of the population seems inconsistent with careful life-cycle planning.

Descriptive Regressions

The relationship between annual IRA saving and saving in other forms can be summarized by simple regressions of the change in other asset balances on IRA saving, controlling for other individual attributes. The results are shown in table 4.7, panels A and B, for households and families, respectively. Again these relationship show little substitution of IRA for other forms of saving. For example, the coefficient on total wealth (excluding IRAs) is 0.65, the coefficient on nonhousing wealth is 0.42, and the coefficient on debt is 0.07. The results for households and families are very similar. Because the regressions control for several individual attributes, the effect of individual-specific saving effects is less likely to have an important effect on these results than on the tabulations above.

4.2   The Incentive Effects of IRAs[10]

4.2.1   Promotion of IRAs

The widespread promotion of IRAs may have been the most important reason for their use, as emphasized in our previous work. Advertising of IRAs has typically emphasized the avoidance of current taxes, as well as the importance of prudent planning for retirement. They are available through almost any bank and through many other financial institutions. Recent evidence lends support to the speculation that promotion has been an important determinant of IRA purchasing behavior. First, according to preliminary IRS data, only 7.2 percent of those filing tax returns contributed to IRAs in 1987; in the previous year over 15 percent contributed. The reduction evidently reflects contributor misperceptions about the eligibility changes in the Tax Reform Act of 1986. Although the law affected IRA tax deductibility only for families who have both qualified pensions and incomes over $40,000, reporting of the 1986 Tax Reform Act and the less intense promotion by financial institutions has apparently left the widespread impression that the IRA has been eliminated. Indeed, a recent survey shows that about half of all persons who are in fact still eligible to contribute to an IRA think they are not.[11]

Another indication that promotion plays an important role is provided by Feenberg and Skinner (1989). Their data on tax returns suggest that families are often unaware of the actual contribution limits. A large fraction of families with legal limits of either $2,250 or $4,000 contribute exactly $2,000. In their view "the most compelling explanation for the false $2,000 limits is that the advertisements and brochures for IRAs common during the early 1980s made both a positive impression on consumers (encouraging them to buy IRAs) and a negative impression (that $2,000 was the legal limit)."[12]

Evidence on the role of promotion is also provided by the timing of IRA contributions. Contributors transferring assets from one account to another and seeking only to maximize the tax advantage of an IRA should contribute in January. Yet typically 40 to 50 percent of all contributions are made in March or April of the following year (Summers 1986). Such a response is undoubtably influenced by the intense advertising that coincided with the tax filing deadline.

4.2.2   Simple Economic Incentives

Two aspects of IRAs provide more traditional economic incentives to save through their use: one is that the contribution itself is tax deductible, the other is that the interest on the contribution accumulates tax free, with taxes paid only when funds are withdrawn from the account. On the other hand, once money is placed in an IRA account there is a 10 percent penalty for withdrawal before the age of 59.5. (The penalty is now 15 percent.) In this sense, the IRA is less liquid than a conventional account.

Some persons of course may consider the illiquidity of IRAs an advantage; it may help to ensure behavior that would not otherwise be followed. It may be a means of self-control. The fact that the opportunity is lost if a contribution is not made in the current year may serve the same purpose. One cannot, as with conventional saving, put it off—possibly a self-delusion—until the next year.[13]

On the other hand, because of the higher return on IRAs, to achieve any given level of retirement income requires less saving if funds are placed in an IRA account than if they are placed in a conventional account. This "income" effect raises the possibility that there could in fact be less saving with than without IRAs. The effect of IRAs on saving is the net result of all of these factors, including their promotion, and will depend on the distinction that investors make between IRA saving for retirement and other saving, as explained below.

4.2.3   One Form of Saving or Two

It may be tempting to think of IRAs and conventional saving accounts as equivalent assets, or goods, simply with different prices, in which case one might think of IRAs as only a price subsidy of conventional saving with a limit on the quantity that can be had at the subsidized price. But to the extent that consumers treat them as different assets or goods—possibly because one is intended for retirement and the other for short-term saving or because one is less liquid than the other—and to the extent that the promotion has influenced their use, this view will not yield an adequate representation or forecast of the saving effect of IRAs. Indeed, our previous work indicates quite strongly that the two are not treated as equivalent by consumers.[14]

The idea may be made clear by the use of two graphs. Figure 4.1 is intended to represent a simple view of the effect of IRAs on saving. It shows the trade-off between the allocation of current income to current consumption versus saving for future consumption, for three current income levels. The dashed lines represent budget constraints without the IRA program and the solid lines the budget constraints with the program. In the latter case, saving is subsidized up to the IRA contribution limit, say $2,000. The more steeply sloped segment represents the availability of tax-advantaged saving up to the limit:

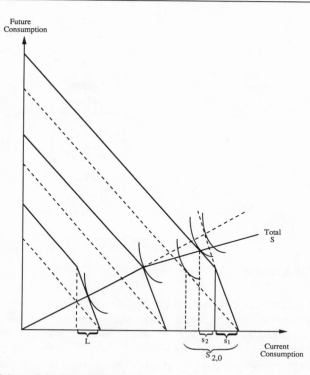

Fig. 4.1 IRAs and saving: A simple view

each dollar of consumption forgone yields more than \$1 of IRA saving. The line labeled "Total S" shows the relationship between income and saving. A family at the highest income level would, in the absence of the IRA program, save more than the IRA limit ($S_{2,0}$ measured from the intersection of the budget constraint with the horizontal axis). As the graph is drawn, the IRA program reduces saving out of current income, although retirement consumption is also increased. This is the income effect of the program. Without the program, non-IRA saving would have been $S_{2,0}$. With the program, IRA saving is S_1 and non-IRA saving $(S_1 + S_2) - S_1$. The addition of the IRA saving is more than offset by the reduction in non-IRA saving.

There are two potential flaws in this stylized reasoning. The first is the assumption that saving for retirement is equivalent to any other form of saving; that they are equivalent goods and treated as such by consumers. As emphasized above, they may not be. Indeed, the fact that IRAs are much less liquid than other forms of saving suggests in itself that they will not be treated as equivalent. Second, this simple view ignores the potential effect of the enormous promotion of IRAs discussed above.

In addition, other evidence suggests that personal saving behavior cannot

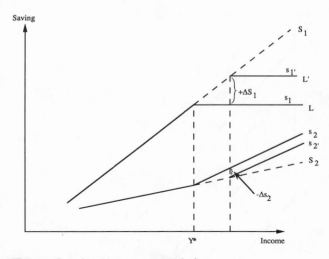

Fig. 4.2   IRAs and saving: A more general view

be explained by price effects, through the interest rate or tax laws. In general, the empirical evidence that saving behavior is noticeably affected by changes in the interest rate, at least over the range observed in the United States, is weak. In principal, whatever the effect of changes in the interest rate, the effect should also be reflected in the relationship between saving and the marginal tax rate, where interest payments are tax deductible. This reasoning would apply in particular to IRAs. The U.S. data, however, reveal mixed evidence on the effect of *existing differences* in marginal tax rates, after controlling for income.[15] Although direct evidence for IRAs is weak, the Canadian experience provides much stronger evidence. Analysis by Wise (1984) shows a very strong effect of income but the most appealing functional form specification shows no marginal tax rate effect, although functional forms that do not fit the data give the impression of a substantial effect.[16] Thus exclusive emphasis on price effects, through the marginal tax rate, may in general be misplaced.

Our analysis relaxes the assumptions reflected in figure 4.1. The two forms of saving are allowed to be treated as two goods. The IRA program may present a bargain on a distinct good, saving for retirement, not just a subsidized price on the one and only form of saving. But the general specification used in the analysis allows the data to reveal that they are treated as a single good, if that possibility is more consistent with observed behavior. This approach is summarized in figure 4.2. Here, IRA and non-IRA saving are treated as separate goods, S_1 and S_2, respectively. The heavy solid lines represent the saving that in figure 4.1 is represented by the single line "S." If the IRA limit were increased from L to L', persons with incomes below Y^* would be unaffected, since they are not constrained by the lower limit. If the increase were small, those with incomes above Y^* would increase IRA saving by ΔS_1 and would reduce non-IRA saving by ΔS_2. Our analysis is structured to determine to what extent the latter reduction offsets the increase in the former. The analysis takes account of the IRA limit and makes important use of the non-IRA saving of persons who are, as compared to those who are not, constrained by the IRA limits (either 0 or L). Our prior estimates strongly reject the figure 4.1 view.

4.3   Formal Estimates Based on the SIPP Data

Using the SIPP data we have obtained estimates based on the same model specification that we used in our prior analysis of SCF and CES data. The specification is summarized here, with further details in the appendix.

4.3.1   The Model

We concentrate on the potential substitution between IRAs and other liquid financial asset saving, assuming that, in the short run at least, IRAs are unlikely to be substituted for nonliquid wealth like housing. There are three key features of the model. First, the analysis uses individual attributes like age, income, and past saving behavior—as measured by accumulated assets—to control for individual-specific saving effects. Second, controlling for these attributes, the function S_1 and S_2 are estimated. Third, having determined S_1 and S_2, the results are summarized by the estimated change in the two forms of saving—ΔS_1 and ΔS_2—when the limit is increased. More formally, the budget constraint is given by

$$(1) \qquad C = Y - T - P_1 S_1 - P_2 S_2 = Y - T - (1-t)S_1 - S_2,\text{[17]}$$

where T represents taxes before saving, $P_1 = 1 - t$ is the price of IRA saving in terms of current consumption, and $P_2 = 1$ is the price of other saving in terms of current consumption, where t is the marginal tax rate. At times $Y - T$ is denoted by Y_T. Desired but not observed S_1 and desired as well as observed S_2 are allowed to be negative. In addition, the potential substitution between S_1 and S_2 is allowed to be quite flexible and distinct from the substitution between either form of saving and current consumption. Given current income, a decision function with these characteristics is

$$(2) \qquad V = [C]^{1-\beta}\{[\alpha(S_1-a_1)^k + (1-\alpha)(S_2-a_2)^k]^{1/k}\}^{\beta}.$$

This function has a tree structure with one branch current expenditure and the other saving. These two components are evaluated in a Cobb-Douglas manner with the preference parameter β. The two forms of saving are evaluated according to a constant elasticity of substitution subfunction.[18] The parameter α indicates the relative preference for S_1 versus S_2; if $\alpha = .5$, total saving is split equally between the two forms. The important feature of this functional form is that it allows greater substitution between the two forms of saving than between either of these and current consumption. The elasticity of substitution between S_1 and S_2 is $1/(1 - k)$.

It also allows the IRA advantage to be reflected first in a lower cost of saving in terms of current income, through the current budget constraint, and, in addition, through different preferences for the two assets, possibly reflecting the different rates of return. Although the distinction between current cost and return may be an artificial one in strict economic terms—that the ultimate difference is one of yield only—consumers may understand better, and be influenced to a greater extent, by the current tax saving than by the tax-free compounding of interest. Certainly the promotion of IRAs has tended to highlight the former. In practice, it is not possible to distinguish the quantitative effect of one from that of the other. Indeed, in practice it is not possible to distinguish with any precision the effect of the tax rate from the effect of other variables, income in particular. Nonetheless, both features of IRAs, as well as any effects of advertising or the contract-like nature of IRA saving provisions, are allowed to determine individual choices.

Maximization of (2) subject to the budget constraint yields unconstrained desired levels of S_1 and S_2

$$
\begin{aligned}
S_1 &= a_1 + d_1(Y_T - P_1a_1 - P_2a_2) \\
S_2 &= a_2 + d_2(Y_T - P_1a_1 - P_2a_2) \\
d_1 &= \frac{(P_1/\alpha)^{1/(k-1)}}{P_1(P_1/\alpha)^{1/(k-1)} + P_2[P_2/(1-\alpha)]^{1/(k-1)}}\beta \\
d_2 &= (\beta - d_1P_1)/P_2
\end{aligned}
$$

(3)

Two limiting versions of the specification are of special interest.

If k = 0

The limiting case of (2) as k goes to 0—yielding a Cobb-Douglas, or more precisely, a Stone-Geary specification—is a simpler model than the general one and is much easier to estimate. In fact, the estimated value of k is less than zero—indicating less substitution than a Cobb-Douglas specification would imply—and for simplicity many of the results are described assuming that it is zero. This specification is easily compared with the illustration in the previous section, graphed in figure 4.2. This case yields desired levels of S_1 and S_2, given by:

$$
\begin{aligned}
S_1 &= a_1 + \frac{\alpha\beta}{P_1} \cdot [Y_T - P_1a_1 - P_2a_2] \\
S_2 &= a_2 + \frac{(1-\alpha)\beta}{P_2} \cdot [Y_T - P_1a_1 - P_2a_2],
\end{aligned}
$$

(4)

and observed levels by:[19]

(5)
$$
s_1 = \begin{cases} 0 & \text{if } S_1 < 0, \\ a_1 + \dfrac{\alpha\beta}{P_1} \cdot [Y_T - P_1 a_1 - P_2 a_2] & \text{if } 0 < S_1 < L, \\ L & \text{if } L < S_1; \end{cases}
$$

$$
s_2 = \begin{cases} a_2 + \dfrac{(1-\alpha)\beta}{(1-\alpha\beta)P_2} \cdot [Y_T - P_2 a_2] & \text{if } S_1 < 0, \\ a_2 + \dfrac{(1-\alpha)\beta}{P_2} \cdot [Y_T - P_1 a_1 - P_2 a_2] & \text{if } 0 < S_1 < L, \\ a_2 + \dfrac{(1-\alpha)\beta}{(1-\alpha\beta)P_2} \cdot [Y_T - P_1 L - P_2 a_2] & \text{if } L < S_1. \end{cases}
$$

Here, abstracting from the prices, β is the total marginal saving rate and a is the proportion allocated to IRA saving. The lower-case s's represent actual saving and the upper-case S's, desired saving. The parameter β is the proportion of marginal income that is saved; α is the proportion of saving allocated to IRAs. The term $[(1 - \alpha)\beta]/[(1 - \alpha\beta)P_2]$ represents the marginal saving rate in the non-IRA form once the IRA limit L has been reached.

If the limit L is increased by one unit, the IRA saving of persons at the limit will be increased by $\Delta S_1 = 1$. Other saving will be reduced by $\Delta S_2 = -[P_1/P_2][(1 - \alpha)\beta]/(1 - \alpha\beta)$. If $\alpha = 1$, $\Delta S_2 = 0$. If $\alpha = 0$, $\Delta S_2 = -[P_1/P_2]\beta$.

If $k = 1$ *and* $\alpha = .5$

Under this assumption, the elasticity of substitution between S_1 and S_2 is infinite, and they are given equal weight in the preference function; they are perfect substitutes and are treated as a single asset. Because the price of IRA saving is lower, saving is only through S_1 if $S_1 < L$ and thereafter is through S_2. In this case, the IRA tax advantage simply creates a kink in the intertemporal budget constraint describing the relationship between forgone current consumption and future consumption, and inframarginal arguments could be used to represent the incentive effects of IRAs on persons who would in their absence save more than the IRA limit. This possibility is clearly rejected by the data, however. It is clear from the summary data that this extreme case is inconsistent with actual behavior; a large fraction of persons who have no IRA saving do have some non-IRA (S_2) saving. Saving behavior under this assumption is described in detail in Venti and Wise (1987b) and the relevant sections from that paper are reproduced as an appendix to this paper.

Other values of k

Unlike the $k = 0$ or $k = 1$ cases, there is no closed-form solution to the constrained S_2 function for other values of k. In this case, the constrained functions, $S_2^*(0)$ when $S_1 < 0$ and $S_2^*(L)$ when $S_2 > L$, are defined only implicitly, as described in the appendix

4.3.2 Parameterization of α and β and the Stochastic Specification

To capture the wide variation in saving behavior among individuals, α and β are allowed to depend on individual attributes X. In particular, we attempt to control for individual-specific saving behavior by using past saving behavior, as well as other attributes, to predict β. Both parameters are also restricted to be between 0 and 1 by using the form

(6)
$$\beta = F[X\underline{\beta}]$$
$$\alpha = F[X\underline{\alpha}],$$

where $F(\cdot)$ is the standard normal distribution function and $X\underline{\alpha}$ and $X\underline{\beta}$ are vectors of parameters.

Finally, we allow the S_1 and S_2 functions to be shifted by additive disturbances, ε_1 and ε_2, respectively.[20] The disturbances are assumed to be distributed bivariate normal with standard deviations σ_1 and σ_2, respectively, and correlation r.

There are three possibilities for the observed values of S_1: 0, between 0 and L, and L. A continuously measured value of S_2 is available for each person, yielding three possible joint outcomes for each observation. Estimation, based on these probabilities, is by maximum likelihood.

4.3.3 Results

Parameter Estimates

Estimation with k free to vary yields an estimated k of -1.67 with a standard error of 0.40, as shown in table 4.8b. Thus, although the data do not allow precise estimation of k, large values are clearly rejected.[21] In particular, the data are inconsistent with the limiting case of $k = 1$, which would indicate that the two forms of saving are perfect substitutes.[22] Thus to facilitate calculation, we concentrate on the simpler model, with k set to zero.

Parameter estimates with k set to zero are shown in table 4.8a. Several features of the results stand out: first, there is no relationship between the two forms of saving once family attributes, including past saving behavior, are controlled for. The correlation r between the disturbance terms in the two equations is essentially zero (.02). In particular, the data do not show that families who save more than the typical family in one form save less in the other.

Second, there is a wide range in saving behavior among families. This is summarized by the estimated values of β that range from .022 to .677. Recall that β is the total *desired* marginal saving rate. (Because the constant term a_1 is negative, however, estimated desired saving is negative for a large fraction of families.) Recall that to control for individual-specific saving behavior we have *predicted* β on the basis of individual attributes, including past saving behavior as measured by liquid and nonliquid assets. It is clear that these data

Table 4.8a   **Parameter Estimates with $k = 0$**

Variable	Estimate (Asymptotic Standard Error)	
Covariance terms:		
σ_1	4.68	(.13)
σ_2	7.11	(.03)
r	.02	(.01)
Origin Parameters:		
a_1	−13.00	(.79)
a_2	.02	(.07)

Determinants of β and α:	β		α	
Income	−.0125	(.0006)	−.0136	(.0019)
Age	.0098	(.0007)	−.0456	(.0043)
Liquid Assets	.0041	(.0002)	−.0048	(.0004)
Nonliquid Assets	.0013	(.0001)	−.0033	(.0003)
Pension	.0344	(.0152)	.2156	(.0670)
Education	.0087	(.0011)	−.0202	(.0056)
Children	−.0442	(.0075)	−.0219	(.0440)
Unmarried	−.0161	(.0171)	−.0322	(.0720)
Constant	−1.1441	(.0088)	4.7302	(.3128)

Predicted oversample: Parameter:	Mean	Median	SD	Minimum	Maximum
β	.210	.198	.060	.022	.677
α	.965	.991	.068	.067	1.000
d_1	.256	.246	.055	.038	.600
d_2	.010	.002	.026	.000	.612

For families predicted to be at the IRA limit:

Parameter:	Mean	Median
d_1	.296	.293
d_2	.028	.013
$d_2{}^*$	.037	.017

Log likelihood = −40,685.8
Number of observations = 9,524

do that to a substantial extent. Thus while the simple regressions above show a strong relationship between saving in one form and saving in the other, once the individual attributes that explain this relationship are controlled for there is no relationship between the amount of *new* IRA saving and *new* financial saving in other assets.

Third, like the total saving rate, the estimated desired IRA marginal saving rates, $d_1 = \alpha\beta$, also vary widely. The median is .246, the minimum is .038, and the maximum .600.

Table 4.8b   Parameters with k Estimated

Variable	Estimate (Asymptotic Standard Error)	
Covariance terms:		
σ_1	4.69	(.10)
σ_2	7.14	(.03)
r	.04	(.01)
Elasticity Parameter, k	-1.67	(.40)
Origin Parameters:		
a_1	−13.20	(.12)
a_2	−.01	(.08)

Determinants of β and α:	β		α	
Income	−.0125	(.0002)	−.0239	(.0036)
Age	.0095	(.0006)	−.0748	(.0102)
Liquid Assets	.0045	(.0002)	−.0101	(.0014)
Nonliquid Assets	.0014	(.0001)	−.0069	(.0009)
Pension	.0310	(.0147)	.4522	(.1195)
Education	.0093	(.0010)	−.0415	(.0099)
Children	−.0468	(.0072)	.0182	(.0734)
Unmarried	−.0128	(.0158)	−.0647	(.1002)
Constant	−1.1364	(.0344)	8.9030	(1.0039)

Predicted oversample:	Mean	Median	SD	Minimum	Maximum
Parameter:					
β	.214	.202	.061	.023	.705
α	.996	.999	.045	.005	1.000
d_1	.259	.249	.057	.038	.583
d_2	.011	.003	.027	.001	.635

For families predicted to be at the IRA limit:

Parameter:	Mean	Median
d_1	.301	.299
d_2	.033	.012
d_2^*	.022	.007

Log likelihood = −40,672.1
Number of observations = 9,524

Fourth, the desired marginal saving rate in other financial assets is typically very small, consistent with the low saving rates revealed by the summary data. Thus, according to these results, if it were not for IRAs, financial asset saving would be much smaller than it is.[23] Even among families predicted to be at the IRA limit, predicted marginal saving in other financial assets is very small on average, .028, and it does not change much when the possibility for IRA saving is exhausted. The estimated rate after the IRA limit is reached, d_2^*, is

.037. The small difference between these latter two estimates is important because it reveals the extent to which increased IRA saving—due to an increase in the IRA contribution limit, for example—would be offset by a reduction in other saving. (Fig. 4.2 makes this clear.)

Independent Estimates of Non-IRA Saving

Because the relationship between d_2 and d_2^* is fundamental to the results, it is informative to demonstrate that the result is not simply due to the functional form used in the analysis. An unconstrained version of the S_2 function, motivated by the piecewise linear illustration in figure 4.2, can be estimated by ordinary least squares. Let Y_2^* be the income at which a family with attributes X_i reaches the IRA saving limit. It is determined from the S_1 function estimates presented in table 4.8a and includes a randomly selected disturbance term for each family.[24] Define $Y_1 = Y$ if $Y < Y^*$ and Y^* otherwise, and $Y_2 = 0$ if $Y < Y^*$ and $Y - Y^*$ if $Y > Y^*$. Then $S_2 = c + \delta_2 Y_1 + \delta_2^* Y_2 + v$, where v is a disturbance term and the δ's are both linear functions of the same variables listed in table 4.8a. Thus δ_2 and δ_2^* correspond roughly to d_2 and d_2^*, respectively. The mean of the predicted values of δ_2 for families with $Y < Y^*$ is .060. For families with $Y > Y^*$, the mean of δ_2 is .066 and the mean of δ_2^* is .090. (The estimated value of c is $-.34$.) It is clear from this unconstrained approximation to the model specification that there is only a limited increase in S_2 saving after the S_1 limit has been reached, as the model estimates show.[25] Again, as a rough approximation, using the mean d_1 for families at the IRA limit (.296 from table 4.8a) and the δ_2 and δ_2^* estimates for families at the limit, an increase of .296 in IRA saving is associated with a .024 reduction (.090 − .066) in S_2 saving, about 8 percent of the IRA increase. If the elasticity parameter k were larger, the difference between d_2 and d_2^* (or between δ_2 and δ_2^*) would be larger and the substitution of IRA for non-IRA saving would be greater.

Simulations

To summarize the implications of the model estimates, we have simulated the effect of raising each families's IRA limit by $1,000. Only families predicted to be at the IRA limit are affected by the increase. For those at the limit, the simulated mean changes in consumption, taxes, and other saving associated with the IRA increase are as follows:

Change in IRA saving	+ $856	100.0%
Change in other saving	− $22	− 2.6%
Change in consumption	− $565	− 66.0%
Change in taxes	− $269	− 31.4%

Most of the new IRA saving resulting from an increase in the limit would represent a net increase in total saving; there would be little substitution away from other saving.[26] The average IRA saving of families at the limit before the increase is \$3,174; saving in other financial assets is only \$1,497. After the increase, IRA saving is \$4,030 and non-IRA saving \$1,475.

4.4 Conclusions

The SIPP data confirm that, with the exception of housing, the typical American family saves very little. In particular, financial asset saving of a very large proportion of families is close to zero. These data also indicate that most IRA saving is net new saving; it is not funded by substitution away from other saving or by increased debt. Thus if it were not for IRAs, personal saving would be even lower than it is. If the IRA limit were increased, most of the increase in contributions would be new saving. The model prediction of little substitution is consistent with the descriptive data that show very little non-IRA financial asset saving; there is little to substitute away from. These results are very similar to our findings based on the SCF and the CES. They are also consistent with the recent conclusions of Feenberg and Skinner (1989), based on panel tax data.

If the relevant data are released, the panel nature of the SIPP will allow control for individual-specific saving effects that is potentially better than the correction based on past saving behavior, the procedure followed in this paper. Judging from the work of Feenberg and Skinner (1989), however, it seems unlikely that the conclusions of this paper will be altered substantially. We can think of no reason why extensive substitution would not be revealed by the data.

Appendix
Special Cases of the Estimated Model

In addition to the limiting version of the model detailed in the text, two others are of interest. They are described under the second and third headings below.

1. If $k = 0$

This is the limiting case detailed in the text.

2. If $k = 1$ and $\alpha = .5$

Under this assumption, the elasticity of substitution between S_1 and S_2 is infinite, and they are given equal weight in the preference function; they are perfect substitutes and are treated as a single asset. The decision function (2) becomes

(A1) $$V = [C]^{1-\beta}[S_1 + S_2 - (a_1 + a_2)]^\beta.$$

Because the price of IRA saving is lower, saving is only through S_1 if $S_1 < L$ and thereafter is through S_2, with

$$
\text{(A2)} \quad
s_1 = \begin{cases}
0 & \text{if } S_1 < 0, \\
(a_1 + a_2) + \dfrac{\beta}{P}[Y_T - P_1(a_1 + a_2)] & \text{if } 0 < S_1 < L, \\
L & \text{if } L < S_1;
\end{cases}
$$

$$
s_2 = \begin{cases}
0 & \text{if } S_1 < L, \\
(a_1 + a_2 - L) + \dfrac{\beta}{P_2}[Y_T - P_1 L - P_2(a_1 + a_2 - L)] & \text{if } L < S_1.
\end{cases}
$$

In this case, the IRA tax advantage simply creates a kink in the intertemporal budget constraint describing the relationship between forgone current consumption and future consumption, and inframarginal arguments could be used to represent the incentive effects of IRAs on persons who would in their absence save more than the IRA limit.

3.   Other values of k

Unlike the $k = 0$ or $k = 1$ cases, there is no closed form solution to the constrained S_2 function for other values of k. In this case, the constrained functions, $S_2^*(0)$ when $S_1 < 0$ and $S_2^*(L)$ when $S_2 > L$, are defined only implicitly by the relationship

$$
\text{(A3)} \quad \frac{P_2(1 - \beta)[\alpha(m - a_1)^k + (1 - \alpha)(S_2^* - a_2)^k]}{(1 - \alpha)(S_2^* - a_2)^{k-1}} = Y_T - P_1 m - P_2 S_2^*,
$$

where m *is* either 0 or L. It is derived by maximizing (2) subject to the budget constraint and with the additional constraint that $S_1 = m$. The observed levels of saving are

$$
\text{(A4)} \quad
s_1 = \begin{cases}
0 & \text{if } S_1 < 0, \\
a_1 + d_1 (Y_T - P_1 a_1 - P_2 a_2) & \text{if } 0 < S_1 < L, \\
L & \text{if } L < S_1;
\end{cases}
$$

$$
s_2 = \begin{cases}
S_2^*(0) & \text{if } S_1 < 0, \\
a_2 + d_2(Y_T - P_1 a_1 - P_2 a_2) & \text{if } 0 < S_1 < 0, \\
S_2^*(L) & \text{if } L < S_1.
\end{cases}
$$

Notes

1. Analysis based on two consecutive years will be undertaken when the data are released.

2. More precisely, families with heads are who self-employed or over 65 or under 21 have been excluded. Household data are also considered. In that case the household head is used to determine whether the household is included.

3. The asset categories are defined as follows: *Housing equity:* Current market

value of home (including mobile homes) less the principal owed on remaining mortgage. *Financial assets excluding stocks and bonds:* Regular (passbook) saving accounts, money market deposit accounts, certificates of deposit or other saving certificates, NOW or other interest bearing saving accounts, money market funds, U.S. government securities, municipal or corporate bonds, other interest earning assets, noninterest bearing checking accounts. *Financial assets including stocks and bonds:* The above category plus the market value of stocks and mutual funds (less debt or margin account) and the face value of U.S. savings bonds. *Debt:* Store bills; credit card bills; bills from doctors, dentists, hospitals, or nursing homes that are not covered by insurance; money owed to individuals outside the family; loans owed to banks, credit unions, or other financial establishments (excluding loans to secure homes, vehicles, or stock and mutual fund shares); other money owed. *Nonhousing assets:* Financial assets including stocks and bonds (see above) plus motor vehicle equity, business equity, net equity in other property (vacation, commercial, or rental), money owed (including mortgages held), and equity in other financial investments, and less debt as described above. IRAs and Keoghs are not included unless otherwise noted. *Total wealth:* Housing equity plus Nonhousing assets as described above. IRAs and Keoghs are not included unless otherwise noted.

4. Based on the 1983 SCF, the median was $22,900.

5. The skewness of the distribution of wealth is reflected in the difference between the medians and the means. The total wealth mean is $48,241, housing equity is $29,398, financial assets including stocks and bonds $13,178, financial assets excluding stocks and bonds $8,395, and debt $3,035.

6. The family unit used is the IRS definition of the tax unit. Thus adult members of the household who are neither the household head nor spouse are classified as separate families. By this definition, there are approximately 40 percent more families than households in the SIPP.

7. Most of the medians are zero and are thus not shown.

8. See Venti and Wise (1986, 1987b).

9. The noncontributor category includes some cases where the difference in reported IRA balances between the two years is negative.

10. Much of the following discussion is drawn from our previous papers. See Venti and Wise (1987b) and Wise (1988).

11. *IRA Reporter,* vol. 6, no. 9 (September 30) 1988.

12. Feenberg and Skinner (1989, 12).

13. One might, for example, have a scheme in which the limit for the current year is added to next year's limit if a contribution is not made in the current year. Or, the contribution limit could cumulate more generally over time if contributions are not made during some period.

14. Especially Venti and Wise (1987b).

15. This may reflect in part an empirical identification problem. Income and marginal tax rates are closely related—although the correlation is by no means perfect—and most data do not provide accurate tax rates. Estimates are very sensitive to functional form. Venti and Wise (1988a) find little effect of the marginal tax rate. However, Feenberg and Skinner (1989) find a significant positive effect.

16. The analysis in Wise (1985) is based on tax records and thus very accurate marginal tax rates, which vary substantially given income. While there is some evidence that the marginal tax rate may affect whether a person contributes to an RRSP, there seems to be no effect on the amount of the contribution.

17. In principle, the marginal tax rate is determined in part by IRA contributions. But since the IRA limits narrowly restrict this influence, we treat t as exogenous.

18. This specification turns out to be a variant of the "S-branch" utility tree described by Brown and Heien (1972). See also Sato (1967) and Blackorby, Boyce, and Russell (1978).

19. Although it is illegal to borrow against an IRA, funds can be withdrawn subject to the 10 percent penalty. But since negative contributions are not observed in the data set, we adopt the assumption of a zero lower limit.

20. A random preference stochastic specification that makes each individual's choices formally consistent with the decision function (2) is obtained if a_1 and a_2 are assumed to be random, with additive disturbances. This specification is not tractable, however, when S_2^* must be solved for implicitly. Experience with both forms in Venti and Wise (1986, 1987a) shows that the results are not appreciably affected by this choice.

21. Because the likelihood function is rather "flat" with respect to k at its estimated value, it is informative to consider likelihood values at other selected values of k. For example, the value is $-40,707.1$ at $k \equiv .5$, $-40,685.8$ at $k \equiv 0$, $-40,677.5$ at $k \equiv -.5$, $-40,672.7$ at $k \equiv -1$, and $-40,672.1$ at $k \equiv -1.67$ (the maximum-likelihood estimate). Thus a likelihood ratio test rejects the hypothesis of $k = 0$ with a χ^2 statistic of 26. And of course larger values would also be rejected.

22. Two kinds of information in the data provide information on the degree of substitution between S_1 and S_2: one is the extent to which families who have no IRA saving, or who have IRA saving below the limit, save in other financial asset forms. Desired levels of saving S_1 and S_2 are observed as long as S_1 is less than the IRA limit. In addition, the degree of substitution between these two forms of saving is revealed in the data by comparing the share of the marginal dollar of income allocated to S_2 when the family is free to vary S_1 (that is, when S_1 is below the IRA limit) with the income share allocated to S_2 when desired IRA saving is constrained by the upper limit. That is, the extent of a "spillover" of desired IRA saving into non-IRA saving when the limit is reached also provides information on the degree of substitution between these two forms of saving.

23. In a previous paper based on CES data (Venti and Wise 1987b), we obtained very similar results on non-IRA saving. With those data we were able to test the model by using estimates based on the post-IRA period data (1982 and later) to predict saving before IRAs were introduced on a broad scale (1980–81). These estimates matched very closely the actual pre-IRA saving behavior.

24. It is the Y that solves the equation

$$s_1 = a_1 + [\alpha\beta/P_1] [Y^* - P_1 a_1 - P_2 a_2] + \varepsilon = L,$$

where ε is randomly drawn from the estimated distribution of ε_1, and α and β depend on family attributes X.

25. The results can not be expected to be the same as those from the model because the simple regression version does not account for the price of S_1 saving nor for the linear expenditure system parameters a_1 and a_2, as shown in eq. (5).

26. Even the very limited substitution suggested by these estimates is more than the data actually reveal. The data suggest a substitution parameter k that is in fact lower than the zero value used in making these calculations.

References

Blackorby, Charles, Richard Boyce, and R. Robert Russell. 1978. Estimation of Demand Systems Generated by the Gorman Polar Form: A Generalization of the S-Branch Utility Tree. *Econometrica* 46, no. 2 (March): 345–63.

Brown, Murray, and Dale Heien. 1972. The S-Branch Utility Tree: A Generalization of the Linear Expenditure System. *Econometrica* 40, no. 4 (July): 737–47.

Carroll, Chris, and Lawrence Summers. 1987. Why Have Private Savings Rates in the United States and Canada Diverged? *Journal of Monetary Economics* 20, no. 2 (September): 249–79.

Feenberg, Daniel, and Jonathan Skinner. 1989. Sources of IRA Saving. *Tax Policy and the Economy* 3:25–46.

Sato, Kazuo. 1967. A Two-Level-Constant-Elasticity-of-Substitution Production Function. *Review of Economic Studies* 34, no. 98 (April): 201–18.

Summers, Lawrence. 1986. Individual Retirement Accounts: Facts and Issues. *Tax Notes* 31, no. 10 (June 9): 1014–16.

Venti, Steven F., and David A. Wise. 1986. Tax-Deferred Accounts, Constrained Choice and Estimation of Individual Saving. *Review of Economic Studies* 53: 579–601.

———. 1987a. IRAs and Saving. In *The Effects of Taxation on Capital Accumulation,* ed. M. Feldstein, 7–48. Chicago: University of Chicago Press.

———. 1987b. Have IRAs Increased U.S. Saving? Evidence from Consumer Expenditure Surveys. *Quarterly Journal of Economics* 105 (August): 661–98.

———. 1988a. The Determinants of IRA Contributions and the Effect of Limit Changes. In *Pensions in the U.S. Economy,* ed. Z. Bodie, J. Shoven, and D. Wise, 9–47. Chicago: University of Chicago Press.

———. 1988b. The Evidence on IRAs. *Tax Notes* 38, no. 4 (January 25): 411–16.

Wise, David A. 1984. The Effects of Policy Change on RRSP Contributions. Prepared for the Tax Policy and Legislation Branch of the Canadian Department of Finance. Cambridge, Mass. Mimeograph.

———. 1985. Contributors and Contributions to Registered Retirement Saving Plans. Prepared for the Tax Policy and Legislation Branch of the Canadian Department of Finance. Cambridge, Mass. Mimeograph.

———. 1987. Individual Retirement Accounts and Saving. In *Taxes and Capital Formation,* ed. M. Feldstein, 3–15. Chicago: University of Chicago Press.

———. 1988. Saving for Retirement: The U.S. Case. *Journal of Japanese and International Economics* 2:385–416.

Comment   Michael Rothschild

This is one of a series of papers in which Venti and Wise have investigated effects of tax-deferred retirement accounts on aggregate savings. In the United States, almost all workers could make tax deductible contributions to individual retirement accounts (IRAs) from 1982 to 1986. Venti and Wise argue that the great bulk of contributions to IRA accounts during this period were net additions to aggregate saving. This seems odd, as the first theory that any economist would propose is that both IRAs and ordinary savings are ways of purchasing future consumption; the most important difference between the two is that IRAs permit this purchase on more favorable terms. Since the two goods are almost perfect substitutes, IRA saving should come in the first instance at the expense of other saving.

Michael Rothschild is professor of economics and dean of Social Sciences at the University of California at San Diego; he is also a research associate of the National Bureau of Economic Research.

The simple theory has, at least, three difficulties. First it is not strictly true. IRAs are different goods from savings accounts. IRA contributions are not as liquid as ordinary investment because the IRS discourages (with penalties and, more recently, with absolute prohibitions) their premature conversion into consumption. While IRAs are a good way to finance retirement, they are less attractive as a method of saving for one's children's education. Perhaps as important, but certainly less comfortable for the economist, banks and other financial institutions heavily promoted IRAs. Barrages of advertising may have made IRAs different goods in the minds of consumers from ordinary savings—advertising may indeed have made them appear to be a different good from what they actually were.

A second difficulty of the simple theory is that if it is true, then individual saving should be responsive to changes in interest rates. While some believe this to be true it is not one of the better-established truths of economic science.

A final difficulty with the simple theory is that if it is true it must be phrased in such a way as to take account of the great differences in personal saving behavior that survey and other data reveal. Venti and Wise convincingly demonstrate that different people save vastly different amounts. While controlling for demographic characteristics reduces some of the variability, it still remains true that some people save a lot, some save a little, and most save barely at all. Any theory of saving that is to survive a confrontation with cross-section data will have to allow for (and hopefully explain) individual differences.

The authors present and estimate an ingenious and illuminating theory. Unfortunately, their theory does not permit a clean test of the simple proposition that the two kinds of savings are perfect substitutes. A reformulation of their theory would allow such a test.

Venti and Wise's theory is a variant of the linear expenditure system.[1] In the standard linear expenditure system each good has associated with it a required level of consumption α_i and a share τ_i where $\Sigma\tau_i = 1$. For each good i the consumer must buy an amount α_i of good i. If income is Y, then disposable income is $Y - \Sigma\alpha_i$; the share of disposable income that the consumer spends on good i is τ_i. Venti and Wise use a variant of this system to estimate saving behavior. In their setup there are three goods: C, current consumption, S_1, IRA saving, and S_2, other saving. It is assumed that the intercept for C is zero, while those for the two kinds of saving are to be estimated. In their empirical work the intercept for IRA saving is negative. This implies that at low levels of income people take money out of their IRA accounts. However, Venti and Wise do not allow this; instead they require IRA saving to fall in the interval $[0, L]$ where L is the maximum contribution allowed by law. Heterogeneity is accounted for by allowing the share parameters, the τ's, to be determined by demographic characteristics, wealth, and income.

This functional form does not allow a test of the hypothesis that IRA saving

---

1. If the parameter k in eq. (2) is not equal to zero, then the form they estimate is more complicated; in their paper, most analysis focuses on the simpler case, when k equals zero.

and other saving are perfect substitutes. Ignore the nonlinearity introduced by letting the share coefficients, the τ's, depend on income. The Venti-Wise theory states that saving is a piecewise linear function of income. IRA saving is positive with a slope of τ_1 over an interval $I = [-\alpha_1, -\alpha_1 + (L/\tau_1)]$.[2] When income lies outside I there is no IRA saving. The slope of non-IRA saving depends on whether income is in I or outside of it. When income is in I, the share of the marginal dollar that goes to other savings is $\delta = \tau_2$, when income is outside I the share is $\pi = \tau_2/(1 - \tau_1)$. The theory that the two kinds of saving are perfect substitutes would have $\tau = 0$. However, it is clear that if $\pi = 0$, then $\delta = 0$. Thus, Venti and Wise do not really test the simple-minded perfect-substitutes theory.

I believe that this could be remedied by estimating the marginal share coefficients in the regression more freely and not constraining π to be a scaler multiple of δ. In a similar vein, the other assumptions of the theory could have been tested somewhat more. As we saw above, IRA saving is constrained to be zero when income is below $-\alpha_1$, the lower limit of the interval I, and when income is above $-\alpha_1 + (L/\tau_1)$, the upper limit of I. The Venti-Wise theory implies that the share of the marginal dollar spent on non-IRA saving is the same in both these regions. This is an easily tested hypothesis.

Finally, I wonder whether it would have been possible to allow for individual effects in the intercept terms (the α_1s) as well as in the slope terms.

Despite these quibbles, I want to stress that Venti and Wise have written a most interesting and ingenious paper. Simple aggregate models—which are the ones easiest to use to address such topics as savings—blind us to the great variety of economic situations in which people find themselves and the great variety of behavior that they exhibit. Venti and Wise have shown how this heterogeneity can be comprehended in a model that also has implications for aggregate policy.

2. Recall that α_1, required IRA savings, is negative, while IRA savings is restricted to be nonnegative. The price of IRA savings is unity.

5 Consumption Taxation in a General Equilibrium Model: How Reliable Are Simulation Results?

B. Douglas Bernheim, John Karl Scholz,
and John B. Shoven

5.1 Introduction

For years, various economists have argued that the taxation of capital income has a variety of detrimental effects, including the distortion of intertemporal decision making and the reduction of saving and capital accumulation. Many have called upon policymakers to abandon the current system of income taxation and to adopt a consumption (or wage) tax in its place. Recent concerns about the low level of saving in the United States has rekindled interest in the possibility of moving in this direction.

Unfortunately, the effects of consumption taxes are extremely complex and hard to evaluate. On theoretical grounds, the desirability of this alternative is not clear. It has long been recognized that, while consumption taxation reduces intertemporal distortions, it also contributes to the distortion of labor-leisure choices. A priori, there is no particular reason to believe that either effect is quantitatively more important than the other.

It is therefore necessary to evaluate consumption taxes on the basis of models that are somewhat "realistic." This observation has led to the emergence of a large number of papers (e.g., Summers 1981; Auerbach and Kotlikoff 1983; and Fullerton, Shoven, and Whalley 1983) that study various reform proposals in the context of reasonably complex models. These papers share an important feature: the impact of consumption taxation is determined computationally, rather than analytically.

B. Douglas Bernheim is the John L. Weinberg Professor of Economics and Business Policy at Princeton University, and a research associate of the National Bureau of Economic Research. John Karl Scholz is an assistant professor of economics at the Department of Economics and the Robert LaFollette Institute of Public Affairs at the University of Wisconsin—Madison. John B. Shoven is a professor of economics at Stanford University and a research associate of the National Bureau of Economic Research.

The authors would like to thank Charles Ballard, Glenn Harrison, and the discussant, Joel Slemrod, for helpful comments and suggestions.

In general, this literature suggests that our current policy of taxing income is rather costly. Summers (1981) found that a complete shift to consumption taxation might raise steady-state output by as much as 18% and consumption by 16%. Auerbach and Kotlikoff (1983) suggest that the steady-state capital-to-output ratio would more than double. Fullerton, Shoven, and Whalley (1983) studied the imposition of a progressive consumption tax and found that it would result in gains to the economy of roughly 1 percent of the present value of future national income.

Unfortunately, many economists have reservations about these general equilibrium calculations. There is often disagreement about the appropriate values of key parameters. In addition, these computations are usually based upon a large number of parameters, many of which are known with very little precision. It is certainly possible that the cumulative impact of uncertainty concerning these parameters may dwarf the quantitative effects predicted by these models.

This problem has been widely recognized in the general equilibrium literature. There are currently four different ways to deal with uncertainty about key parameters. One option, generally taken in the public finance and international trade literatures, is to conduct sensitivity analysis by varying the key parameters of the model, usually one at a time. At best, such calculations can illustrate policy effects under a few alternative sets of beliefs about the appropriate parameter values. It does not allow one to describe the quantitative importance about uncertainty concerning underlying parameters. A second option is to conduct Monte Carlo simulations. Unfortunately, this is extremely time consuming and expensive, and in practice, it has not been done. A third option is to take a discrete approximation to the underlying distribution of input parameters and *systematically* explore the sensitivity of the model to the choice of parameters. This approach has been developed and discussed in Harrison and Kimbell (1985), Harrison, Jones, Kimbell, and Wigle (1989), Harrison and Vinod (1989). Fourth and finally, for a linear model, if one knows the variance-covariance matrix associated with the underlying parameters, then it is possible to calculate *exact* variances for the model's output. For nonlinear models, one can approximate the variances of outputs through linearization. This approach was first suggested by Pagan and Shannon (1985).

In this paper, we elaborate on the advantages of the Pagan-Shannon approach. We then apply a variant of their methodology to the study of consumption taxation. Our basic objective is to answer the following question: Do we know enough about the underlying parameters in large-scale general equilibrium models to have any confidence about the effects of consumption taxes in these models?

We use the Shoven-Whalley computational general equilibrium model to study the impact of a switch to consumption taxation on four variables: labor supply, output, saving, and a measure of utility. We provide separate results for short-, medium-, and long-run effects, as well as for the overall impact on utility. Our calculations are based upon two different sets of beliefs concerning the precision with which the underlying parameters are known. We refer to these cases as "optimistic" (the uncertainty concerning parameters is small), and "pessimistic" (the uncertainty concerning parameters is large).

Our results are mixed. In the "optimistic" case, one can have a fairly high degree of confidence in many aspects of the basic simulation. Almost all short- and medium-run effects are known with reasonable precision (one can at least rule out the possibility that the effect is zero or of the opposite sign). In contrast, the standard errors of the long-run effects are almost as large as the associated central estimates. Nevertheless, the total (present discounted value) impact of consumption taxation on utility is estimated quite precisely—the calculated welfare gain (roughly \$600 billion) is approximately three times the size of its standard error.

Results based upon pessimistic beliefs are much less encouraging. Short-run effects on saving and utility, as well as medium-run effects on saving and output, are tied down fairly precisely. Unfortunately, one cannot have much confidence in the sign of any other effect. The calculated welfare gain turns out to be approximately 1.5 times its standard deviation. While this lends some support to the case for consumption taxation, it is hardly a ringing endorsement. Our results therefore emphasize the need for more precise econometric estimates of various key parameters used in the Shoven-Whalley model.

This paper is organized as follows. Sections 5.2 and 5.3 review the methodology and the Shoven-Whalley model, respectively. Section 5.4 considers uncertainty in assumed parameter values and proposes optimistic and pessimistic beliefs. Section 5.5 contains simulation and sensitivity results. The paper closes with a brief conclusion.

5.2 Methodological Framework

Computational general equilibrium models employ two types of inputs: a vector of economic parameters (such as price elasticities), henceforth labelled β, and a vector of policy parameters (such as tax rates), henceforth labelled θ. By solving for equilibria, one maps these parameters to outcomes. We will summarize outcomes as a vector of endogenous variables (such as labor supplies, production decisions, utilities, and so forth), henceforth labeled Y. The relationship between inputs and outputs can be summarized as some highly complicated implicit function, $G(\theta, \beta, \gamma)$.

Note the presence of the parameter vector γ in the function $G(\ )$. We will refer to γ as the "calibration" parameters. In practice, the value of γ is not taken from econometric studies, but rather is chosen to replicate base-case data. More formally, for any outcome vector Y and parameters β and θ, let $g(\theta, \beta, Y)$ be defined as the implicit solution to

$$Y = G(\theta, \beta, g(\theta, \beta, Y)).$$

Given some initial data Y_0, a vector of initial policy variables, θ_0, and an estimate $\hat{\beta}$ of the policy parameter vector β, one calibrates the model by setting $\gamma = g(\theta_0, \hat{\beta}, Y_0)$.

Typically, one is interested in the effect of some policy experiment on the equilibrium value of Y. Suppose this policy experiment entails changing the value of θ from its initial value of θ_0 to an alternative value, denoted θ_1. Taking the initial state and policy parameters as given, the change in Y can be written as a function of $\hat{\beta}$:

(1) $\psi(\beta) = G(\theta_1, \hat{\beta}, g(\theta_0, \hat{\beta}, Y_0)) - G(\theta_0, \hat{\beta}, g(\theta_0, \hat{\beta}, Y_0))$
        $= G(\theta_1, \hat{\beta}, g(\theta_0, \hat{\beta}, y_0)) - Y_0.$

For a specific model, set of base-case data, and policy experiment, the function Ψ summarizes the entire process of going from economic parameters to conclusions.

The usual research strategy is to obtain $\hat{\beta}$ from econometric studies and then evaluate Ψ at this specific set of point estimates. With a few notable exceptions, uncertainty that is reflected in the estimated standard errors of $\hat{\beta}$ is completely ignored. As a result, computable general equilibrium (CGE) exercises typically provide little information about the degree of confidence that one can have in the results.

In the past, CGE practitioners have eschewed costly Monte Carlo simulations and have attempted to document the robustness of their results in one of two ways. We refer to the first approach, taken in the public finance and international trade literatures, as traditional sensitivity analysis. By varying a few key parameters, it is possible to obtain a general feel for whether central qualitative results depend on the specific point estimate of β. Unfortunately, this approach suffers from a variety of problems. Lacking a formal methodological basis, it is inherently imprecise. Specific information contained in the variances of parameter estimates is simply ignored. The results of standard sensitivity exercises are very difficult to evaluate and summarize: one typically varies one parameter at a time, and there is no basis for aggregating sensitivity over separate parameters. One is forced by expositional and computational considerations to limit the sensitivity analysis to a relatively small set of parameters.

A second approach, taken by Harrison and Kimbell (1985), and Harrison et al. (1989), takes a discrete approximation of the underlying parameters of the model and systematically explores the possible combinations of input parameters. A distinction is drawn between unconditional and conditional systematic sensitivity analysis (USSA and CSSA). With USSA all potential combinations of the discrete approximation of parameters are explored. Under CSSA each parameter is altered assuming all other parameters retain their central values. With even a modest number of parameters and rough approximation of a parameter's distribution, the number of required solutions for USSA becomes prohibitive,[1] consequently, CSSA is generally performed.

Conditional SSA is a major improvement over standard sensitivity analysis. Its primary limitation is that, to conduct sensitivity analysis for alternative beliefs about the distribution of $\hat{\beta}$, one must start from scratch. In most cases, the assumed distribution of $\hat{\beta}$ is somewhat arbitrary. Different individuals may well have different beliefs about the precision of knowledge concerning any economic parameter. When one publishes the CSSA based upon a specific set of beliefs, readers with significantly different beliefs may not be persuaded by the results.

An alternative, seldom-used approach has been proposed by Pagan and Shannon (1985). If one knows the variance-covariance matrix for parameter inputs, then it is possible to calculate *exact* confidence intervals for linear CGE models. This observation suggests that one can calculate approximate standard errors for nonlinear models by linearizing around base-case equilibria.[2]

The practice of approximating standard errors through linearization can be justified formally, as follows. Suppose that we obtain $\hat{\beta}$ from econometric studies. In all but a few cases, only the asymptotic distribution of the estimate will be known. Suppose then that $\hat{\beta}$ is a consistent estimate of the true parameter value, β^*, and that its distribution is asymptotically normal. Let Σ denote the variance-covariance matrix for this asymptotic distribution. Suppose further that the function Ψ has continuous second derivatives (this is usually easy to guarantee—see the literature on regularity, e.g., Kehoe 1983). Then it follows that the distribution of $\Psi(\hat{\beta})$ is asymptotically normal, with variance-covariance matrix $\Psi_\beta \Sigma \Psi'_\beta$ (where the $[i, j]$th element of Ψ_β is the derivative of Ψ_i with respect to β_j, evaluated at β^*).

We can use this result directly to obtain an asymptotic variance-covariance matrix for our estimate of the policy's impact, $\Psi(\hat{\beta})$. Specifically, we calculate Ψ_β numerically at the initial parameter values. Note from equation (1) that we need only compute the derivatives of $G(\theta_1, \hat{\beta}, g(\theta_0, \beta, Y_0))$ with respect to β at $\hat{\beta}$ (because of the calibration, the second term in the formula for Ψ is always equal to Y_0, and its derivative is therefore zero). Accordingly, we may proceed as follows. First, calibrate the model using the base-case equilibrium. Second, find the equilibrium for the "revised" case (i.e., the equilibrium after the policy change). Third, vary a parameter slightly, recalibrate, and, starting from the revised case, recalculate equilibrium. Use the results of the "perturbed" case along with the revised case to compute the derivative of each output variable with respect to that parameter. Repeat for all parameters that are to be treated as uncertain. Finally, construct the variance-covariance matrix for the policy effect by performing the matrix multiplication described at the end of the preceding paragraph.

The procedure described above is justified whenever the parameter estimates β are known to be consistent and asymptotically normal. Unfortunately, as a practical matter this condition is rarely satisfied. On one extreme, CGE practitioners often discover that certain parameters have not been estimated econometrically. In contrast, the literature often contains many attempts to measure other parameters, and the existing estimates are rarely consistent across studies. In such cases, the analyst must exercise "casual Bayesianism," forming subjective beliefs based upon priors, indirect evidence, and judgments about the relative merits of different studies.

When Σ summarizes subjective beliefs rather than the second moments of an asymptotic distribution, this procedure for obtaining an approximate variance-covariance matrix for $\Psi(\hat{\beta})$ requires some reinterpretation. Suppose in particular that we approximate Ψ with a linear function F that is simply the first-order Taylor series expansion of Ψ around $\hat{\beta}$. Given Σ, it is then a simple matter to calculate the variance-covariance matrix for the distribution of $F(\hat{\beta})$. As long as the curvature of Ψ is not too great—or the variances of $\hat{\beta}$ are not too large—this will provide a good approximation to the variance-covariance matrix for the distribution of $\Psi(\hat{\beta})$.

Of course, if the curvature of Ψ is significant—or the variances of $\hat{\beta}$ are sufficiently large—the distributions of $F(\hat{\beta})$ and $\Psi(\hat{\beta})$ will be quite different, and the procedure will provide a rather poor approximation. It is possible to remedy this problem by modifying the Pagan-Shannon approach. Specifically, one would use higher-order Taylor series approximations to Ψ. In many cases, a second-order approximation may suffice. Thus, we write

$$H(\hat{\beta}) = \Psi(\hat{\beta}^*) + \Sigma_i(\hat{\beta}_i - \beta_i^*)\Psi_i(\beta^*)$$
$$+ \sum_i \sum_j (\hat{\beta}_i - \beta^*_i)(\hat{\beta}_j - \beta^*_j)\Psi_{ij}(\beta^*).$$

To evaluate the mean and variance of this expression, one must make some assumptions about the distribution of $\hat{\beta}$. First, we assume that this distribution is normal. This assumption is critical, since the variance of $H(\hat{\beta})$ will typically involve higher-order moments of the distribution of $\hat{\beta}$. Unfortunately, we know very little about these higher order moments, and intuition is a poor guide. However, with the normal distribution all higher-order moments can be expressed as functions of variance. The same kind of argument certainly applies to any two-parameter family of probability distributions. However, to the extent any parameter choices are influenced by econometric estimates, we would favor the normal distribution. While finite sample estimate of the parameters will not typically be normally distributed, asymptotic theory suggests that the normal often provides the best approximation.

Our second assumption is that the $\hat{\beta}_i$s are distributed independently. When $\hat{\beta}$ is taken from econometric estimates, this assumption is frequently justified.

Estimation error is a function of the idiosyncratic shocks in a particular set of data. To the extent shocks are independent across observations, they will also be independent across data sets. Parameter estimates based upon two distinct sets of data will therefore generally be uncorrelated. To illustrate, suppose that we have a single cross-section data set consisting of observations of the economic decisions of distinct households. Suppose these decisions are affected by idiosyncratic, unobservable preference shocks, and that these shocks are independent across households. If we estimate two parameters, say a labor-supply elasticity and an interest elasticity of saving, using the entire data set in both cases, the estimates will be correlated. However, if we randomly divide the data set into two subsamples, and then estimate the labor-supply elasticity with one subsample and the interest elasticity of saving with the other, these estimates will be statistically uncorrelated. Thus, as long as we rely on econometric studies that employ different data, it is arguable that the $\hat{\beta}_i$s are independent.

In practice, different parameters may be estimated with the same data, or with related data (e.g., time-series data for different variables covering the same time period). In addition, if certain techniques of estimation introduce systematic biases, then the use of similar techniques to estimate different parameters may create systematic relationships between the resulting estimates. Unfortunately, very little can be done about this. Short of reestimating all parameters of the model simultaneously, it is impossible to accurately measure correlations between the elements $\hat{\beta}$. At best, one can incorporate ad hoc correlations into subjective beliefs.

Under the assumption that the distribution of the $\hat{\beta}_i$s are independent normal, it is possible to show that

$$(2) \qquad E[H(\hat{\beta})] = \Psi(\beta^*) + \frac{1}{2} \sum_i \sigma_i^2 \Psi_{ii}(\beta^*),$$

and

$$(3) \qquad V[H(\hat{\beta})] = \sum_i \{\sigma_i^2[\Psi_i(\beta^*)]^2 + \frac{1}{2}\sigma_i^4[\Psi_{ii}(\beta^*)]^2\},$$

where σ_i^2 denotes the variance of $\hat{\beta}_i$ (i.e., the ith element on the diagonal of Σ). To implement these formulas, we require both first and second derivatives of Ψ, which we evaluate at $\hat{\beta}$. To calculate a numerical second derivative with respect to a parameter, one need only make two small changes in the parameter from the revised case rather than one change as before. Note that it is, in principle, possible to accommodate correlations between the parameters, but that this would necessitate calculating Ψ_{ij} for all i and j. When the set of economic parameters is large, this task would prove onerous.

This alternative approach to sensitivity analysis is necessarily approximate. The quality of the approximation depends upon the properties of CGE models and the degree of uncertainty concerning economic parameters. In another as yet unfinished project, we explicitly compare variance-covariance matrices based on first- and second-order expansions to the second moments of distributions generated by Monte Carlo simulations. It is much easier and certainly far less costly to implement these versions of the Pagan-Shannon approach than it is to conduct reliable Monte Carlo simulations. For first-order approximations, one need only calculate as many perturbed cases as parameters. In addition, one computes derivatives locally, so that the perturbed case equilibria are very close to the revised equilibria. By starting the equilibrium algorithm at the revised case, rapid convergence should in general be achieved. This same consideration may also imply that the computational cost of the Pagan-Shannon approach is lower than the corresponding cost for CSSA, even when one must solve for the same number of equilibria (generally, for CSSA, the discretized distribution places weight on widely divergent parameter values). For second-order approximations (assuming independence), one simply requires twice as many local permutations. These requirements are negligible in comparison to the task of performing Monte Carlo analysis. It is worth reiterating that second-order approximations become much more onerous if one wishes to allow for correlations between all parameters. With 100 parameters, one would require 10,000 perturbed cases to compute all of the second derivatives. It is, of course, relatively easy to incorporate a few select correlations without significantly adding to the computational burdens.

The Pagan-Shannon approach is also somewhat more flexible than USSA, CSSA, and Monte Carlo simulations. As mentioned earlier, the value of these alternative approaches is limited by the extent to which different economists agree about Σ. In contrast, variants of the Pagan-Shannon approach permit the researcher to report the vector of first and second derivatives. A reader can then supply his own beliefs about Σ, and, with relatively little effort, compute an approximate variance-covariance matrix for the outputs.

One final caveat is in order. Our discussion has focused on techniques for computing the variances of policy effects given a particular CGE model, data, and policy parameters. We have made no attempt to account for any uncertainty that one might have about the correspondence between the model and the real world. As a result, our estimates of variance reflect uncertainty concerning the impact of policy in the model and not in the actual economy.

5.3   Review of the Ballard-Fullerton-Shoven-Whalley Model

The model we use to investigate the consumption tax is a medium scale CGE model. It is completely documented in Ballard-Fullerton-Shoven-Whalley (BFSW) (1985) and is the same model used previously to evaluate a progressive consumption tax in Fullerton, Shoven, and Whalley (1983). Due to its previous documentation and use, we will only provide a brief description of the model here. If our purpose was simply to produce a new evaluation of the adoption of an expenditure tax, we would have developed a new data set and model structure. Our primary goal in this paper, however, is to assess the impact of uncertainty about parameter values on the certainty of model outcomes. For this purpose, the existing model and data suffice quite well.

While the BFSW model is not as dynamically sophisticated as more recent CGE models, it does have the essential structural features for evaluating a switch to a consumption tax. Within the model, consumers face both an intertemporal consumption decision and a labor-leisure decision. This means that both the intertemporal consumption and the labor-leisure margins are operative and subject to tax distortion. It also implies that there is no a priori presumption within the model that a consumption tax is superior.

The BFSW model has 19 producers and 12 consumer income classes. Consumer behavior is characterized by a nested CES-LES (constant elasticity of substitution/linear expenditure system) utility structure. The outermost nest uses a CES utility function to characterize the consumer's decision between present and future consumption. The parameter of substitution between present and future consumption is calibrated to be consistent with Boskin's (1978) 0.4 estimate of the interest elasticity of saving. The middle nest of the preference structure determines the allocation of the consumer's present consumption between goods and leisure, again, using a CES preference function. The substitution parameter of the preference function is calibrated to be consistent with a composite labor-supply elasticity of 0.128. The innermost nest of the preference structure allocates present consumption between 15 consumer goods according to LES preferences.

Producers use capital and labor to produce their output according to CES value-added production functions. They also use the output of other industries through a fixed-coefficient input-output matrix. The elasticity of substitution between capital and labor used to calibrate the production functions come from studies summarized by Caddy (1976). The 19 producer goods are transformed into the 15 consumer goods through a fixed coefficient transition matrix. The model is calibrated around a benchmark, general equilibrium data set from 1973. This data set defines an equilibrium in transactions terms. Value observations are separated into prices and quantities by assuming that a physical unit of a good or factor is the amount that sells for $1. All benchmark equilibrium prices are $1, and observed values are benchmark quantities.

Through their interaction, utility-maximizing consumers and profit-maximizing producers are assumed to reach a single-period competitive equilibrium where all profits are zero and supply equals demand for each good and factor. Single-period equilibria are sequenced through endogenous saving decisions that augment the capital stock of the economy. An exogenous labor force growth rate is assumed.

We calculate a benchmark balanced growth path that replicates the data, has constant prices, and implies that quantities grow at the labor force growth rate. A simulation is run by altering a tax parameter and calculating a revised sequence of equilibria. The model assumes markets are perfectly competitive with no externalities, quantity constraints, or barriers to factor mobility. Since a complete set of prices and quantities are calculated under different tax policies, we can calculate changes in national income, utility, income changes for consumers, and factor allocations among industries. The model is solved using the factor price revision rule of Kimbell and Harrison (1986).

The income tax system is modeled as a set of linear tax schedules for each of the 12 consumer groups. Each of the 12 income classes has a lump sum tax (or transfer in the bottom income class) that, along with a given marginal tax rate, yields average and marginal tax rates that are consistent with those the income class actually faces. This treatment captures the fact that average and marginal tax rates differ by group, that both are increasing, and that it is the marginal tax rate that causes the distortionary substitution effect of the income tax system.

A significant percentage of saving that occurs in households is channeled through tax deferred savings plans such as private, state, local, and federal pension plans, through individual retirement accounts (IRAs) and Keogh plans, or through the cash value of life insurance. These plans either allow for tax-free contributions and accumulation or taxable contributions with tax-free accumulation and withdrawal. Flow of Funds data indicate that in 1973, roughly 30 percent of all saving occurred through these vehicles and, thus, are taxed on a consumption-tax basis. This suggests that the income tax system is in fact a hybrid tax system that has some features of a consumption-based system. We model this system by allowing households to deduct 30 percent of their saving from the taxable income base. To move from this hybrid to a consumption-based system, we exclude the remaining portion of saving from the tax base. Thus, we act as if all saving occurred through IRAs or qualified savings account. By increasing the saving deduction the tax system moves from a progressive income tax to a progressive consumption tax while maintaining the 1973 structural features of the tax system.

There is a corresponding revenue loss associated with the move to the consumption tax. Since saving is excluded from the tax base, tax rates have to rise to maintain the current levels of revenue. The federal budget is balanced in the model so that in the absence of rate increases, government commodity purchases and transfer payments would be reduced. Since it would be impossible to separate tax effects from the expenditure effects of reducing commodity purchases and transfers, we maintain real government expenditure at a constant level. Therefore, we are doing differential incidence analysis. Given this, we examine three different methods of replacing the tax revenue lost in moving to a consumption tax. The first, lump-sum replacement, replaces the reduction by imposing lump-sum taxes or transfers by altering the zero-income intercept of the linear tax schedule. The second, additive-replacement, raises marginal rates by an equal, additive amount. The third, multiplicative replacement, increases marginal tax rates by a constant, multiplicative factor. The second and third methods allow us to recognize that frequently the replacement schemes necessary to maintain revenues are also distorting. We find that often the *method* of maintaining revenue balance is as important as the policy initiative that is being examined.

5.4   Sources of Uncertainty

In order to run the Ballard-Fullerton-Shoven-Whalley model described in section 5.3 one must supply a large number of parameters, as well as base-case data. Our current objective requires us to obtain variances, as well as point estimates for all parameters. In cases where point estimates have been taken from econometric studies, it should also be possible to obtain formal estimates of variances. Other parameter values are chosen somewhat arbitrarily; in these cases, variances must of necessity be somewhat arbitrary as well, and should be thought of as reflecting subjective beliefs.

We have divided the important model parameters into two sets, henceforth referred to as "group 1" and "group 2." This classification reflects two considerations. First, on the basis of economic reasoning and previous sensitivity analyses, we generally regard group-1 parameters as more important determinants of the effects of consumption taxation. Second, we obtain group-1 parameters from specific econometric studies and, consequently, for these parameters we also have estimated variances. In contrast, no econometric estimates of the variances for group-2 parameters are available. Given these distinctions, it seemed appropriate to present sensitivity calculations for group-1 parameters alone, as well as for all parameters jointly.

Group-1 parameters include the interest elasticity of saving, the labor-supply elasticity, the after-tax rate of return to physical capital, and the elasticities of substitution in production between labor and capital for each of the 19 industries described by the model. Parameter values, along with "optimistic" and "pessimistic" standard errors, are presented in table 5.1a. We discuss these in order.

The first group-1 parameter is the interest elasticity of saving. The key distinction between a consumption tax base and an income tax base is the inclusion of saving, and the main partial equilibrium claim regarding a consumption tax is its alleged neutrality with respect to intertemporal consumption. In a general equilibrium framework, with leisure an untaxed good and other taxes in the model, this appeal to intertemporal neutrality is not theoretically compelling. However, the sensitivity of behavior to the exclusion of saving from the tax base clearly depends on the interest elasticity of saving. This parameter will be the major determinant of the extent of capital deepening that occurs in the long run after the switch to a consumption tax.

Our estimate of the interest elasticity of saving is taken from Boskin (1978). Its standard error can be calculated through a simple transformation of the standard error for Boskin's consumption elasticity. We use this as our "opti-

Table 5.1a   Parameter Values and Associated Standard Error for Group-1
                    Parameters

Parameter	Value	Optimistic Standard Error	Pessimistic Standard Error
Interest elasticity of saving	.4	.109	.6
Labor-supply elasticity	.128	.095	.25
After-tax rate of return to capital	.0384	.0129	.015
Elasticities of substitution between capital and labor			
Agriculture	.6142	.057	.6139
Food	.7117	.0548	.5077
Clothing	.8152	.0416	.6727
Paper	.7682	.0466	.7881
Petroleum refining	.7411	.0792	.5463
Chemicals rubber & plastics	.8284	.0555	.9045
Lumber, clay & glass	.7902	.0375	.6552
Metals, instruments & miscellaneous manufacturing	.8782	.0298	.5480
Transportation equipment & ordinance	.6971	.1304	1.0079
Vehicles	.8207	.1175	1.0167
Others	1.00	.1304	1.0167

mistic" standard error. Under a more pessimistic view, each individual study contains some idiosyncratic bias, and uncertainty concerning this bias is not reflected in the estimated standard error. Thus, the 95% confidence interval around Boskin's point estimate includes both Denison's law (the elasticity equals 0—see Denison 1958), as well as much higher estimates, such as those obtained by Summers (1981). For our pessimistic scenario, we chose a standard error that is intended to subsume uncertainty concerning the idiosyncratic bias in Boskin's study. Given the wide range of prevailing beliefs about the interest elasticity, we take this standard error to be 0.6. Thus, the 95% confidence interval includes elasticities from roughly − 0.8 to 1.6.

The second group-1 parameter is the labor-supply elasticity. This is a key parameter in almost all general equilibrium tax policy simulations. Given that leisure is an extremely important untaxed good, the simple stories regarding a consumption tax being first best optimal are destroyed except in very restrictive circumstances that do not hold in the framework of the BFSW model. The labor-leisure decision is important, if only because labor accounts for roughly three-fourths of value added in the economy. There is a large preexisting tax distortion between goods and leisure, and an increase in that tax wedge can potentially cause large incremental welfare losses. The introduction of a consumption tax, via a saving deduction, at least at the time of its introduction, loses revenue. Given that we have assumed period-by-period revenue neutrality, this necessitates raising other taxes, almost certainly exacerbating the existing distortion in the goods-leisure choices.

In the model, the labor-supply elasticity reflects an average response for men and women. We use Mroz's (1985) estimated elasticity of .09 for women (with a weight of one-quarter), and MaCurdy's (1981) estimated elasticity of .14 for men (with a weight of three-quarters). The associated standard errors are .17 and .07, respectively. We obtain a standard error of .095 for the model parameter by applying the one quarter/three quarters weighting to the parameter standard errors. As with our estimate of the saving elasticity, we choose a pessimistic standard error that is intended to reflect, at least in part, the larger range of estimates available in the literature.

The third group-1 parameter is the after-tax rate of return to capital. This is not frequently thought of as a key variable in specifying a general equilibrium tax simulation model. Its importance here is due to the dynamic or intertemporal nature of the effects of an introduction of a consumption tax. While static models look only at the allocation of fixed factor supplies, the issue here is the productivity of the additional capital formation that a saving exclusion will encourage. Certainly, additional saving is more desirable the higher is the base-case rate of return to capital.

Our model, like almost all others, takes as a unit of capital that amount which earned one dollar net of tax in the base-case data or simulation. That is, capital is measured in capital service rental units. However, in the model, household saving results in the acquisition of physical investments or increments to the capital stock. By definition, the base-case after-tax rate of return to capital determines the number of rental units yielded (as a perpetuity) per unit of physical capital acquired. Also, by units definition, these rental units sell for one dollar in the base-case simulation. Their rental price, however, will differ from one dollar once policy alternatives are introduced. The base-case after-tax rate of return to capital thus determines the rate of conversion between capital in stock units and capital in service flow units.

Our estimate of the after-tax return to capital is taken from a paper by Feldstein and Jun (1987). Our optimistic assumption reflects their estimated standard error for this parameter. We have chosen the pessimistic standard error to yield a 95% confidence interval ranging from roughly 1% to 7%.

All other group-1 parameters are elasticities of substitution in production between capital and labor. These elasticities have always been key elements in the applied general equilibrium tax model, at least since Harberger's analysis. They are potentially important in the consumption tax case under examination here, due to the effect of the exclusion of saving from the tax base on relative factor prices. The change in relative factor prices will affect the various output prices differently depending on the factor intensities. All of these effects are made more important by the presence of other factor and partial taxes such as the corporation income tax and the social security payroll tax.

Estimates of these elasticities for 10 industries are taken from a survey paper by Caddy (1976). For each of these industries, Caddy compiles the results of a large number of studies, and provides both the mean estimate and variance of estimates. He reports the statistics separately for analyses that employed time-series data, and for those using cross-section data. He does not report the standard errors of estimates from individual studies. In order to avoid the need for reexamining all of these primary sources, we adopt a simplifying assumption: for each elasticity β, the ith estimate of this parameter is given by $\hat{\beta}_i = \beta + \varepsilon_i$, where the ε_i are distributed identically and independently. Under this assumption, it is appropriate to use the mean estimate as the value of the elasticity. Furthermore, we use the variance of this estimated mean (which is equal to the variance of the estimates divided by the number of studies minus one) for our optimistic beliefs.

These optimistic variances may significantly understate the true degree of uncertainty. In particular, Caddy's study indicates that there is a large systematic difference between results based on time-series and cross-section data. A more appropriate model might be that the ith estimate of the parameter β obtained using the technique k (henceforth denoted $\hat{\beta}_i^k$) is given by

$$\hat{\beta}_i^k = \beta + \mu_k + \varepsilon_i^k.$$

In this equation, μ_k represents the systematic bias inherent in the use of a particular approach to estimation. We assume that the μ_k are distributed identically and independently with mean zero, as are the ε_i^k.

One alternative is to estimate this relationship formally to obtain a point estimate and standard error. However, it is clear from inspection of Caddy's numbers that, given the size of the samples, the ε_i^k will essentially average out, while the μ_k will not. That is, if we estimate $\beta + \mu_k$ separately for each k (by taking the average estimated elasticity for time-series and cross-section studies, respectively), the standard errors of these estimates will be very small relative to the differences in the estimates for the two values of k. Accordingly, we obtain a very good approximation by acting as if $\beta_k = \beta + \mu_k$ is estimated without error for each k. We then have, essentially, two observations on β plus noise. It is then appropriate to use the average of these two numbers as our estimated parameter, and to use the variance of this average (which is $[\beta_1 - \beta_2]^2 / 2$) as our estimate of the variance. This calculation forms the basis for our pessimistic scenario.

Estimates of the elasticity of substitution are not available for nine of the 19 industries represented in the model. Following previous practice, we take this elasticity to be unity (i.e., the production function is Cobb-Douglas). It is natural to assume that our uncertainty about these elasticities must be at least as great as those that have been estimated. Accordingly, we take the standard errors of the elasticities for these nine industries to equal the largest standard error for the other 10 industries.

Group-2 parameters include export demand elasticities, the ratio of labor endowment to labor supply, the preference parameters on the LES inner nest of the utility specification, the minimum required purchases in the LES inner nest, the marginal tax rates for the linearized income tax schedules, and the percentage of capital income that is taxable by the individual income tax for each industry. As econometric estimates of standard errors are unavailable for these parameters, we must impose somewhat arbitrary subjective beliefs. Assumed parameter values, along with optimistic standard errors, are given in table 5.1b. While these assumptions are largely self-explanatory, some clarifying comments are in order.

The preference parameters on the LES inner nest of the utility specification must sum to unity. Accordingly, we cannot allow them to vary independently. One alternative is to allow one to be determined as a residual. However, the choice of a residual parameter would be extremely arbitrary, and it would imply a peculiar covariance structure. Instead, we define a new set of parameters ϕ_i, and let the LES parameters β_i be given by

$$\beta_i = \frac{\phi_i}{\sum\limits_i \phi_i}.$$

Initially, we normalize so that the sum of the ϕ_i equals unity. We suppose that we know something about the variances of the ϕ_i, and that these are distributed independently. This implies a more natural covariance structure for the β_i—as one β_i rises, all others decline proportionately. In table 5.1b we have given the standard errors for these LES parameters as a percentage of their assumed values.

We have also parameterized the LES specification by assuming that the minimum required purchase for each consumption category is $2,500. Rather than vary each of these independently, we assume that all minimum purchases equal a common parameter, and we define beliefs over this common parameter.

We follow a similar practice for marginal tax rates. In this case, we assume that each rate is equal to some constant times a common parameter, and we normalize so that the base value of this parameter is unity. A standard error of 0.1 for this parameter therefore signifies that the standard error of each marginal tax rate is 10% of its assumed value, and that all of these tax rates are

Table 5.1b   **Parameter Values and Associated Standard Error for Group-2 Parameters**

Parameter	Value	Optimistic Standard Error	Pessimistic Standard Error
Export demand elasticity	-1.4	.28	.56
Supplemental export parameter (v)	-10.0	2.0	4.0
Ratio of labor endowment to labor supply	1.75	.1	.25
LES preference parameters (%)	. . .	10	20
LES minimum purchase parameter	2,500	250	500
Marginal tax rate scaling parameter	1	.1	.2
Scaling parameter for proportion of capital income subject to ITT	1	.1	.2

perfectly correlated. While perfect correlation is probably too strong an assumption, it does seem likely that factors that lead us to under- or overestimate effective marginal tax rates for one class of consumers are likely to do likewise for all other classes. We follow exactly the same practice for the fraction of capital income subject to the individual income tax in each industry.

5.5 Simulation Results

5.5.1 Standard Point Estimates

When the consumption tax is simulated we find there are large returns to moving the 1973 tax system from a hybrid to a consumption based system. As reported in table 5.2, the efficiency gain with additive replacement is $557 billion or roughly 1.1 percent of the present value of future expanded national income. These efficiency gains are calculated as the present discounted value of the sum of equivalent variations for each representative household in the model. Using the expenditure function for each household, we calculate the income changes, at old prices, that would allow each group to obtain the same pattern of instantaneous utility over time in the new tax regime. This instantaneous utility excludes saving (to avoid double counting), and is based on current consumption and leisure.

With additive and multiplicative replacement, the price of capital relative to labor falls immediately after a consumption tax is implemented. Saving increases by 30 percent in the first equilibrium. This savings is used directly for investment. Investment, however, is more labor intensive than other com-

Table 5.2   **Dynamic Welfare Effects in Present Value Equivalent Variation over Time (in billions of 1973 dollars)**

	Types of Scaling to Preserve Tax Yield		
	Lump-sum	Additive	Multiplicative
Consumption Tax	643	557	540
	(1.243)	(1.076)	(1.044)
Time Path for the ratio of the rental price of capital to the wage rate:			
Year:			
0	1.0042	.9678	.9650
10	.9344	.9116	.9103
20	.8901	.8750	.8745
30	.8608	.8504	.8503
40	.8411	.8336	.8336
50	.8275	.8219	.8220

Note: The numbers in parentheses represent the gain as a percentage of the present discounted value of consumption plus leisure in the base sequence. This number is $51.766 trillion for all comparisons and accounts only for the initial population.

ponents of aggregate demand. Therefore, the increase in savings generates an indirect increase in the relative demand for labor and thus, an indirect decrease in the relative price of capital. The time path of prices, given in the bottom of table 5.2, gives an indication of how long the economy takes to resettle into a steady-state growth path. With additive and multiplicative replacement, roughly 45 percent of the total price change occurs in the first 10 years, and 70 percent of the change in 25 years. The corresponding figures for lump-sum replacement are 34 and 64 percent. The patterns of intersectoral change that emerge from the model suggests that industries that are relatively capital intensive, such as real estate and agriculture, prosper over time, as capital deepening occurs.

A somewhat different look at our central case is given in table 5.3. There, the impact of the consumption tax on saving, labor supply, output, and utility are presented from the short- (impact effect), medium- (15 years) and long- (steady state) run perspective. Under this model specification, the consumption tax has very little effect on labor supply. The tax has an ambiguous effect on net wage rates. To the extent labor income is consumed, tax rates rise; to the extent it is saved, tax rates fall. Each of these net effects have corresponding income and substitution effects, the outcome of which is to leave labor supply virtually unchanged.

The impact effect on savings and investment is very strong. However, after the initial increase the rate of saving is steady. Capital prices adjust slowly in the model; therefore, some time has to pass before the increase in investment can be reflected in increased output. In the initial period, consumer demand is reduced by approximately the value of saving. Consequently, aggregate demand and output are roughly constant. After 15 years, output starts reflecting the increased level of capital formation generated by the investment. In the new steady state, the level of production in the economy is roughly 7 percent higher than in the base-case equilibrium. It might seem surprising that, at the

Table 5.3	Change in Base-Case Quantities of Imposing a Consumption Tax with Additive Replacement and Saving Elasticity of 0.4 (in millions of dollars)		
	Short Run	Medium Run	Long Run
Saving	32,114	46,303	437,258
	(30.5)	(29.2)	(27.2)
Labor supply	6,642	4,428	− 23,423
	(.7)	(.4)	(− .2)
Output	17,121	99,592	2,040,690
	(.8)	(3.2)	(6.6)
Utility	− 30,425	2,725	681,467
	(− 2.8)	(.2)	(4.2)

Note: The percentage change from base-case quantities are given in parentheses. The short run is the impact effect, the medium run is 15 years, the long run is the new resulting steady state.

same time output is increasing and labor supply is holding steady, utility, which is based on consumption and leisure, fails to increase in the medium run. Output increases in the medium run primarily in response to the investment component of aggregate demand. Consumer demands, and hence consumption, have not yet increased sufficiently to increase utility. In the new steady state, however, sufficient capital deepening occurs so that consumers have more income, consume more, and take the same amount of leisure. This is reflected in higher levels of final period utility.

We also find that, in the long-run, the policy is a Pareto improvement, all income classes are better off. There is far more output in the economy, consumers save more, consume more, and have an equivalent amount of leisure. Though all classes gain from the consumption tax, poorer households are somewhat better off when taxes are replaced in a multiplicative fashion than under additive replacement. The rate increases necessary under a consumption tax are smaller for low-income households under multiplicative replacement and, therefore, consumers are better off.

5.5.2   Standard Sensitivity Analysis

As a point of reference we will describe the conventional sensitivity analysis that is typically done in the Ballard-Fullerton-Shoven-Whalley CGE model. Sensitivity analysis for the consumption tax is generally performed on the interest elasticity of saving, since benefits that occur from a consumption tax are generally thought to be the result of reducing the price of capital. In table 5.4 we vary the interest elasticity of saving from 0.4, the level consistent with Boskin (1978), to 0.0, the level consistent with Denison's law (Denison 1958), and 2.0, a magnitude roughly comparable to those derived in Summers (1981). The magnitude of the results are quite sensitive to the choice of savings elasticity. They range from $416 billion with multiplicative replacement and a 0.0 interest elasticity of saving, to $935 billion with a 2.0 saving elasticity and lump-sum replacement. The last figure is roughly 70% of 1973's national income.

In table 5.4, we also present price ratios of the rental price of capital to the wage rate under different elasticity assumptions. From these results it is clear that the degree of substitution in the economy makes a great deal of difference in how quickly the economy responds to tax changes. With a saving elasticity of 2.0, the transition from steady states occurs quite quickly, despite there being a larger adjustment to make. Sixty-seven percent of the price adjustment occurs in the first five years; after 10 years, 85% of the adjustment has occurred. The adjustment paths are much slower with lower saving elasticities. It takes roughly 15 years for the price of capital to adjust halfway to its steady-state level with a saving elasticity of 0.0, while it is 10 years for the 0.4 saving elasticity.

Table 5.4   **Dynamic Welfare Effects in Present Value Equivalent Variations over Time (in billions of 1973 dollars) with Differing Interest Elasticities**

A. Consumption Tax

Saving Elasticity	Types of Scaling to Preserve Tax Yield		
	Lump-sum	Additive	Multiplicative
.0	521	436	416
	(1.006)	(0.842)	(0.803)
.4	642	557	540
	(1.243)	(1.076)	(1.044)
2.0	935	835	819
	(1.808)	(1.613)	(1.582)

B. Time Path for the Ratio of the Rental Price of Capital to the Wage Rate under Different Saving Elasticities (additive replacement)

Year	Interest Elasticity Saving		
	.0	.4	2.0
0	.9677	.9678	.9681
10	.9284	.9116	.8467
20	.8994	.8750	.8056
30	.8776	.8504	.7884
40	.8611	.8336	.7807
50	.8485	.8219	.7770

Note: The numbers in parentheses represent the gain as a percentage of the present discounted value of consumption plus leisure in the base sequence. This number is $51.766 trillion for all comparisons and accounts only for the initial population.

5.5.3   Formal Sensitivity Results

Following the methodology outlined in section 5.2, we have calculated standard errors for policy effects using both first- and second-order approximations. We provide results for both optimistic and pessimistic beliefs for group-1 parameters alone, as well as for all parameters. Accordingly, we have generated eight sets of results. These are summarized in tables 5.5 through 5.12. Each table indicates the impact of a shift to consumption taxation on four variables (saving, labor supply, output, and utility) in three different time frames (the short, medium, and long runs). In the context of our model, the medium and long runs correspond to about 15 and 100 years, respectively. We also provide an index of the overall impact of consumption taxation on welfare. Each table includes approximate standard errors for all these effects.

We begin with results that reflect uncertainty concerning the values of group-1 parameters alone. Table 5.5 provides standard errors from a first-order approximation under optimistic assumptions. One immediately notes

Table 5.5   **Expectations and Standard Errors of the General Equilibrium Output in the Short, Medium, and Long Run Using Group-1 Elasticities (in millions of dollars)**

	First-Order Approximation, Optimistic Standard Errors		
	Short Run	Medium Run	Long Run
Saving	32,114	46,303	437,258
	(2,901)	(6,305)	(397,424)
Labor supply	6,642	4,428	−23,432
	(2,405)	(1,541)	(70,270)
Output	17,121	99,592	2,040,690
	(5,786)	(34,711)	(1,952,181)
Utility	−30,435	2,725	681,467
	(2,443)	(13,428)	(672,048)

Present discounted value of equivalent variations:

556,851
(179,582)

Note: The short run is the impact effect, the medium run is 15 years, the long run is the new resulting steady state. The numbers in parentheses are approximate standard deviations. Group-1 elasticities include: saving, labor supply, the growth rate, and substitution between labor and capital in each production sector.

Table 5.6   **Expectations and Standard Errors of the General Equilibrium Output in the Short, Medium, and Long Run Using Group-1 Elasticities (in millions of dollars)**

	Second-Order Approximation, Optimistic Standard Errors		
	Short Run	Medium Run	Long Run
Saving	32,195	46,416	616,886
	(2,904)	(6,331)	(471,912)
Labor supply	6,640	4,545	−32,643
	(2,407)	(1,561)	(72,134)
Output	17,128	102,788	2,912,719
	(5,790)	(34,872)	(2,307,385)
Utility	−30,536	4,312	978,938
	(2,446)	(13,510)	(793,121)

Present discounted value of equivalent variations

617,385
(198,328)

Note: The short run is the impact effect, the medium run is 15 years, the long run is the new resulting steady state. The numbers in parentheses are approximate standard deviations. Group-1 elasticities include: saving, labor supply, the growth rate, and substitution parameter between labor and capital in each production sector.

that all of the impact (short-run) effects are estimated very precisely. The same is true for the medium-run effects, with the exception of utility. All precision vanishes in the long run. Nevertheless, the total welfare effect is calculated with a good deal of precision. One can be highly confident about the direction of the effect on total welfare, and, in addition, one can get a fairly good sense for the magnitude of this effect.

Table 5.6 is the second-order counterpart to table 5.5. A quick comparison of these two tables reveals that the use of second-order approximations changes nothing of substance.

While continuing to restrict our attention to group-1 parameters, we move to pessimistic assumptions about parameter variances. Calculations based upon first-order approximations are presented in table 5.7. Relative to table 5.5 (which is the comparable table for optimistic assumptions), precision declines dramatically. One can still be confident about the direction of effects of consumption taxation on saving and utility in the short run and saving in the medium run (the result for output in the medium run is marginal). Once again, uncertainty about parameters essentially implies that nothing is tied down with any precision in the long run. The total impact on welfare is also calculated with a good deal of variance—while one can be fairly confident that consumption taxation is beneficial, our calculations imply that little can be said about the magnitude of this effect.

Table 5.8 is the second-order counterpart to table 5.7. Essentially the same patterns emerge, except that one can have somewhat greater confidence in the

Table 5.7   **Expectations and Standard Errors of the General Equilibrium Output in the Short, Medium, and Long Run Using Group-1 Elasticities (in millions of dollars)**

	First-Order Approximation, Pessimistic Standard Errors		
	Short Run	Medium Run	Long Run
Saving	32,114	46,303	437,258
	(15,951)	(16,357)	(468,240)
Labor supply	6,642	4,428	−23,432
	(8,777)	(5,113)	(180,850)
Output	17,121	99,592	2,040,690
	(21,625)	(61,133)	(2,345,637)
Utility	−30,435	2,725	681,467
	(13,088)	(17,145)	(801,190)

Present discounted value of equivalent variations

556,851
(293,298)

Note: The short run is the impact effect, the medium run is 15 years, the long run is the new resulting steady state. The numbers in parentheses are approximate standard deviations. Group-1 elasticities include: saving, labor supply, the growth rate, and substitution between labor and capital in each production sector.

Table 5.8   Expectations and Standard Errors of the General Equilibrium
                   Output in the Short, Medium, and Long Run Using Group-1
                   Elasticities (in millions of dollars)

	Second-Order Approximation, Pessimistic Standard Errors		
	Short Run	Medium Run	Long Run
Saving	33,736	42,298	669,435
	(16,384)	(16,615)	(581,997)
Labor supply	7,668	6,209	−36,888
	(8,990)	(5,712)	(184,682)
Output	19,963	118,674	3,146,050
	(22,163)	(62,529)	(2,883,600)
Utility	−32,633	17,293	1,051,295
	(13,415)	(19,341)	(985,517)

Present discounted value of equivalent variations

635,487
(317,499)

Note: The short run is the impact effect, the medium run is 15 years, the long run is the new resulting steady state. The numbers in parentheses are approximate standard deviations. Group-1 elasticities include: saving, labor supply, the growth rate, and substitution between labor and capital in each production sector.

directions of the medium-run impact on output and of the total impact on welfare.

We now turn to results that reflect uncertainty concerning the values of all parameters considered in section 5.4. We discuss these results in the same order as for group-1 parameters. Table 5.9 contains standard errors based upon first-order approximations under optimistic assumptions. Note that, relative to table 5.5 (the counterpart for our group-1 calculations), there are substantial increases in the variance of all policy effects. Nevertheless, this does not alter the set of variables for which the direction of the effect is known with substantial confidence. Table 5.10 provides the second-order counterpart to table 5.9. Not surprisingly, the results are substantively unchanged.

Table 5.11 provides first-order results based on pessimistic assumptions concerning the full set of parameters. Relative to table 5.7 (in which only group-1 parameters are treated as uncertain), precision declines substantially. The impacts on saving in the short run and output in the medium run are no longer known with much confidence. More importantly, the total welfare effect is now less than 1.5 times the size of its standard error.

Table 5.12 is the second-order counterpart to table 5.11. Similar patterns appear in this table, except that all three of the effects mentioned in the preceding paragraph appear to be tied down a bit more precisely. In particular, the total welfare effect is now slightly greater than 1.6 times its estimated standard error. One can therefore have a fair degree of confidence about the desirability

Table 5.9   **Expectations and Standard Errors of the General Equilibrium Output in the Short, Medium, and Long Run Using All Parameters (in millions of dollars)**

| | First-Order Approximation, Optimistic Standard Errors | | |
	Short Run	Medium Run	Long Run
Saving	32,119	46,303	437,258
	(5,302)	(9,363)	(410,127)
Labor supply	6,641	4,428	−23,432
	(2,634)	(1,787)	(71,709)
Output	17,121	99,592	2,040,690
	(6,331)	(38,731)	(2,012,521)
Utility	−30,435	2,725	681,467
	(4,777)	(13,593)	(690,486)

Present discounted value of equivalent variations

556,851
(216,504)

Note: The short run is the impact effect, the medium run is 15 years, the long run is the new resulting steady state. The numbers in parentheses are approximate standard deviations. The parameters are listed in the appendix.

Table 5.10   **Expectations and Standard Errors of the General Equilibrium Output in the Short, Medium, and Long Run Using All Parameters (in millions of dollars)**

| | Second-Order Approximations, Optimistic Standard Errors | | |
	Short Run	Medium Run	Long Run
Saving	32,291	46,704	627,260
	(5,308)	(9,392)	(482,855)
Labor supply	6,728	4,961	−24,621
	(2,637)	(1,862)	(74,017)
Output	16,872	104,187	2,981,068
	(6,379)	(38,925)	(2,359,806)
Utility	−30,515	4,474	992,724
	(4,795)	(13,682)	(809,107)

Present discounted value of equivalent variations

623,347
(233,142)

Note: The short run is the impact effect, the medium run is 15 years, the long run is the new resulting steady state. The numbers in parentheses are approximate standard deviations. The parameters are listed in the appendix.

Table 5.11   Expectations and Standard Errors of the General Equilibrium Output in the Short, Medium, and Long Run Using All Parameters (in millions of dollars)

	First-Order Approximation, Pessimistic Standard Errors		
	Short Run	Medium Run	Long Run
Saving	32,114	46,303	437,258
	(18,254)	(21,430)	(510,186)
Labor supply	6,642	4,428	−23,432
	(9,077)	(5,443)	(183,182)
Output	17,121	99,592	2,040,690
	(22,321)	(70,145)	(2,541,446)
Utility	−30,435	2,725	681,467
	(15,452)	(17,661)	(861,621)

Present discounted value of equivalent variations

556,851
(380,177)

Note: The short run is the impact effect, the medium run is 15 years, the long run is the new resulting steady state. The numbers in parentheses are approximate standard deviations. The parameters are listed in the appendix.

Table 5.12   Expectations and Standard Errors of the General Equilibrium Output in the Short, Medium, and Long Run Using All Parameters (in millions of dollars)

	Second-Order Approximations, Pessimistic Standard Errors		
	Short Run	Medium Run	Long Run
Saving	35,113	43,429	710,651
	(18,658)	(21,710)	(618,703)
Labor supply	7,961	7,829	−4,698
	(9,293)	(6,285)	(189,973)
Output	18,794	124,148	3,418,549
	(23,042)	(71,801)	(3,059,247)
Utility	−32,572	17,929	1,106,222
	(15,812)	(19,883)	(1,039,031)

Present discounted value of equivalent variations

658,847
(407,035)

Note: The short run is the impact effect, the medium run is 15 years, the long run is the new resulting steady state. The numbers in parentheses are approximate standard deviations. The parameters are listed in the appendix.

of consumption taxation, but very little can be said about the magnitude of this effect.

As mentioned in section 5.2, one of the advantages of the Pagan and Shannon (1985) approximation approach to sensitivity analysis is that the results can easily be altered to accommodate alternative sets of beliefs. Accordingly, we present first and second derivatives of the total welfare effect with respect to the full set of parameters in the appendix. The reader can use these derivatives to compute standard errors for the welfare effect under any alternative set of beliefs. To conserve space, we omit derivatives for the other effects discussed above. Tables of these derivatives are available from the authors upon request.

To summarize, we find that, under optimistic beliefs, we know enough about the underlying economic parameters to tie down the short- and medium-run effects of consumption taxation, as well as the total welfare effect, quite precisely. Under pessimistic beliefs, precision is much lower, but one can still be fairly confident that the overall effect on welfare is positive. Our analysis also indicates that differences between first- and second-order approximations are generally small, but in some cases these differences prove to be qualitatively important.

5.6 Conclusion

We have addressed two issues in this paper. First, following the approach of Pagan and Shannon (1985), we have shown that there is a practical way to calculate approximate standard errors for the output of a nonlinearized computational general equilibrium tax model. The method is not demanding computationally and should prove to be a useful methodology for many other applications. Second, we have found that the welfare gains promised by a consumption tax are quite robust to the uncertainty in the underlying parameters of the general equilibrium model. Even in our pessimistic case regarding the uncertainty about key parameters, the existence of a positive welfare enhancement in making the policy switch can be predicted with a reasonable degree of confidence.

Appendix
Numeric First and Second Derivatives of Total Welfare Effect with Respect to Parameters Considered in the Analysis[3]

Parameter	First Derivative	Second Derivative
After-tax rate of return	− 13,425,919.3485	716,430,459.7397
Saving elasticity	261,000.5700	− 109,256.2500
Labor supply elasticity	384,003.0431	415,114.1869
Substitution elasticity for Cobb-Douglas Industries	102,059.8390	− 22,455.2000
Substitution elasticity for agriculture	− 13,944.3443	− 21,885.2459
Substitution elasticity for food and tobacco	14,157.7873	18,573.8941
Substitution elasticity for textiles	6,808.2220	− 9,577.7811
Substitution elasticity for paper and printing	8,702.8299	1,476.8089
Substitution elasticity for petroleum refining	− 3,428.8203	− 7,913.0752
Substitution elasticity for chemicals and rubber	13,865.8614	24,675.4246
Substitution elasticity for lumber and furniture	14,567.9304	27,237.4619
Substitution elasticity for metals and machinery	38,282.0029	41,636.2457
Substitution elasticity for transportation equipment	2,495.0757	− 1,813.0612
Substitution elasticity for motor vehicles	8,131.6317	− 608.5663
Elasticity of export demand	1,394.8829	− 1,557.9082
External sector closing parameter	3,467.3317	− 41.4100
Endowment & time divided by labor hours	25,427.9806	− 43,128.0980
Minimum required purchases	− 17.3404	− .0101
Marginal tax rates	1,118,829.5500	2,077,134.6000
Proportion of capital income taxable under the individual income tax	443,966.2890	− 689,933.2000
LES preference parameter for food	23,627.6617	− 8,319,927.6386
LES preference parameter for alcohol	283,606.9259	− 1,050,396,021.9478
LES preference parameter for tobacco	284,805.7143	− 57,132,653.0575
LES preference parameter for utilities	17,538.7586	170,208,917.9550
LES preference parameter for housing	98,297.2276	− 9,439,698.5921
LES preference parameter for furnishings	− 58,239.7500	− 10,482,142.8570
LES preference parameter for appliances	− 42,034.8750	2,946,239,062.4985
LES preference parameter for clothing	− 100,611.8889	124,212,208.5048
LES preference parameter for transportation	91,798.2000	− 853,319,111.1113
LES preference parameter for motor vehicles	− 12,186.5068	− 57,081,478.7014
LES preference parameter for services	− 91,888.8704	− 6,312,787.6848
LES preference parameter for financial services	83,230.6883	− 81,242,486.0853
LES preference parameter for reading and recreation	− 87,047.8261	151,643,310.2290
LES preference parameter for nonfood, nondurable household consumption	− 128,441.5714	890,871,655.3291
LES preference parameter for gasoline and fuels	2,511,688.1429	− 15,081,887.7549

Notes

1. As reported in Harrison, Jones, Kimbell, and Wigle (1989), 10 parameters and a discrete approximation characterized by seven values of the parameter would require 282,475,250 model solutions. Harrison and Vinod (1989) demonstrate that it is possible to approximate the USSA result through formal statistical methods.

2. Wigle (1988) used a variant of the Pagan-Shannon approximation on a nonlinear CGE trade model and found this approximation to generate essentially equivalent results to those generated by a sequentially selected unconditional systematic sensitivity analysis of the model investigated.

3. Derivatives are calculated as the change in the revised-case minus base-case simulations generated by a perturbation of the parameter in question. Numbers are given in millions. Complete tables of derivatives are available from the authors upon request. The first 14 derivatives correspond to "group 1."

References

Auerbach, Alan J., and Laurence J. Kotlikoff. 1983. National Savings, Economic Welfare, and the Structure of Taxation. In *Behavioral Simulation Methods in Tax Policy Analysis,* ed. Martin Feldstein, 459–98. Chicago: University of Chicago Press.

Ballard, Charles L., Don Fullerton, John B. Shoven, and John Whalley. 1985. *A General Equilibrium Model for Tax Policy Analysis*. Chicago: University of Chicago Press.

Boskin, Michael J. 1978. Taxation, Saving, and the Rate of Interest. *Journal of Political Economy* 86, pt. 2: S3–S37.

Caddy, Vern. 1976. Empirical Estimation of the Elasticity of Substitution: A Review. Preliminary Working Paper OP-09. Impact Project, Industrial Assistance Commission, Melbourne, Australia.

Denison, Edward F. 1958. A Note on Private Saving. *Review of Economics and Statistics* 40 (August): 261–67.

Feldstein, Martin, and Joosung Jun. 1987. The Effect of Tax Rules on Nonresidential Fixed Investment: Some Preliminary Evidence from the 1980s. In *The Effects of Taxation on Capital Accumulation,* ed. Martin Feldstein, 101–62. Chicago: University of Chicago Press.

Fullerton, Don, John B. Shoven and John Whalley. 1983. Replacing the U.S. Income Tax With a Progressive Consumption Tax. *Journal of Public Economics* 20 (February): 3–23.

Harrison, Glenn W., Richard Jones, Larry J. Kimbell, and Randall Wigle. 1989. How Robust Is Applied General Equilibrium Analysis? Typescript. University of New Mexico, Albuquerque, September.

Harrison, Glenn W., and Larry J. Kimbell. 1985. Economic Interdependence in the Pacific Basin: A General Equilibrium Approach. In *New Developments in Applied General Equilibrium Analysis,* ed. John Piggott and John Whalley, 143–74. Cambridge: Cambridge University Press.

Harrison, Glenn W., and H. D. Vinod. 1989. The Sensitivity Analysis of Applied General Equilibrium Models: Completely Randomized Factorial Sampling Designs. Typescript. University of New Mexico, Albuquerque, July.

Kehoe, Timothy. 1983. Regularity and Index Theory for Economies with Smooth Production Technologies. *Econometrica* 51(4):895–919.

Kimbell, Larry J., and Glenn W. Harrison. 1986. On the Solution of General Equilibrium Models. *Economic Modelling* 3:197–212.

MaCurdy, Thomas. 1981. An Empirical Model of Labor Supply in a Life-Cycle Setting. *Journal of Political Economy* 89(6):1059–85.

Mroz, Thomas A. 1985. The Sensitivity of an Empirical Model of Married Women's Hours of Work to Economic and Statistical Assumptions. Typescript. Department of Economics, University of Chicago.

Pagan, Adrian R., and J. H. Shannon. 1985. Sensitivity Analysis for Linearized Computable General Equilibrium Models. In *New Developments in Applied General Equilibrium Analysis,* ed. John Piggott and John Whalley, 104–18. Cambridge: Cambridge University Press.

Summers, Lawrence H. 1981. Capital Taxation and Accumulation in a Life Cycle Growth Model. *American Economic Review* 71 (September): 533–44.

Wigle, Randall. 1988. The Pagan-Shannon Approximation: Unconditional Systemic Sensitivity in Minutes. Typescript. Wilfrid Laurier University, Waterloo, Ontario, July.

Comment   Joel Slemrod

Let me begin by stating my conclusion about this paper—that the methodology it proposes and executes represents a major contribution to the tool kit of builders of computable general equilibrium (CGE) models, but that it teaches us little, if anything, about the effect of taxation of saving. I make this pessimistic judgment in spite of the compelling kind of reassurance offered by this and other papers of this sort—that, in the face of swirling controversy among the economics profession about the determinants of saving, it can provide an estimate carried out to six significant digits of the long-run impact of eliminating the taxation of capital income in the United States, a tax change unprecedented in the fundamental economic changes it would generate.

To support my conclusions, I will begin with the trees and then move to the forest. I will first discuss the methodological advancement offered in this paper, and then come back to assess its relevance to understanding saving and how taxation affects it.

Questions about robustness have plagued CGE analysis ever since it has been applied to real policy alternatives and used as a guide to policy formulation. After all, the point estimate of the response of some variable to a policy change depends on the constellation of assumptions about model specification, including parameter values, initial conditions, and the form of the decision rules used by the model's agents.

The principal response among CGE modelers has been to resort to sensitiv-

Joel Slemrod is professor of economics, professor of business economics and public policy, and director of the Office of Tax Policy Research at the University of Michigan and a research associate at the National Bureau of Economic Research.

ity analyses, with the goal of ascertaining the robustness of key model results to certain aspects of model specification. The most popular approach (undoubtedly because it is the easiest) has been to vary key parameters within a reasonable range and observe whether the principal model results are much affected. Doing this for each parameter separately is what Harrison et al. (1985) refer to as "conditional" sensitivity analysis, conditional because each parameter is perturbed conditional on all other parameters being set only to their point estimate value. Harrison et al. prefer and perform an "unconditional" analysis, in which each parameter is perturbed conditional on all other parameters being perturbed, although they note with concern the large number of simulations that are required for this approach.

Pagan and Shannon (1985) suggest a method similar to the one employed by Bernheim, Scholz, and Shoven, where a covariance matrix of the parameters and a matrix of first and second derivatives of output variables with respect to the parameters are combined to produce estimates of the variance corresponding to model forecasts. They also suggest as an alternative determining the "extreme" bounds for the output vector. The problem is to find the maximal variation in a particular output variable given that the parameters are constrained to be selected from a given confidence interval.

The sensitivity analysis proposed by Bernheim et al. follows from the first suggestion of Pagan and Shannon. The procedure has three steps. First, a covariance matrix for the distribution of key parameters is constructed, using as inputs the reported standard errors of the underlying econometric studies, the good judgment of the authors, and assumptions that the distribution is normal and the parameter estimates are distributed independently. Two distributions are considered: an "optimistic" one where the standard errors are closely related to those estimated in the econometric studies, and a "pessimistic" one where the standard errors are increased to reflect uncertainty about the idiosyncratic bias that any individual econometric study inevitably has.

In the second step certain output variables of interest are selected—saving, labor supply, utility. How these change when a consumption tax is implemented under the base-case parameters is calculated. Then the first and second derivatives of these changes with respect to each parameter are numerically calculated. Finally, the covariance matrix of the parameter estimates is combined with the information about the derivatives of the policy impact with respect to the parameters to obtain an approximate covariance matrix for the estimate of the policy's impact.

Along the way, the authors are faced with several modeling choices. I applaud them for the ingenuity and care that they bring to this task. In almost every case, theirs seems a reasonable way to proceed. The end result is a clear improvement over the kind of unsystematic or systematic but conditional sensitivity analysis that has characterized the great majority of CGE research.

What, though, have they gained versus Monte Carlo simulation or unconditional systematic sensitivity analysis? As they note, much less calculation is required, but with the cost of making assumptions about the behavior of the model out of the neighborhood of the base-case parameters and assuming the independence of parameter estimates. Another advantage is that while the sole output of a Monte Carlo simulation is the distribution of result parameters, this procedure also generates an intermediate output of the first and second derivatives of results with respect to parameters, so that alternative assumptions about the parameters can be inserted to produce different estimates of the covariance matrix of results. Note, though, that these individual parameter derivatives are valuable only because of the independence assumption.

I do have one bone to pick, though, about the relationship between the recalibration procedure employed and the sensitivity analyses. The procedure requires that any set of parameters must be consistent with the base-case equilibrium data. Thus when any given parameter is changed, some other parameter or set of parameters must also be changed to reestablish that consistency. In the paper this recalibration procedure is denoted as the g function. First, note that there is no unique way to specify this function; it is essentially arbitrary. For example, when the parameter of interest is an elasticity of substitution, it is usually a share parameter that will be altered at the same time to restore the consistency of the base-case data set with an equilibrium. Thus when Bernheim et al. speak of a derivative of an output with respect to a particular parameter, in fact they mean the total derivative with respect to at least two parameters, the one of interest and the one (or ones) that had to be changed in the recalibration procedure. Because the model aspects altered in the recalibration procedure vary from one parameter to another, it is not clear exactly how to interpret these derivatives.

At a minimum the authors ought to report, for each parameter whose sensitivity is being studied, what other parameter(s) is changed to restore an equilibrium with base-case data, and by how much it is changed relative to the original parameter. This is important information because, although the parameters of interest are assumed to be independent, there is an implicit assumption of a strong correlation between any given parameter of interest and some unnamed other parameter. A more ambitious approach would be to investigate, for each parameter of interest, alternative recalibration procedures and also doing no recalibration at all (allowing the base-case equilibrium to change when the parameter is changed). A set of such simulations may help to isolate the sensitivity of the model results to a given parameter.

Let me now speak to what this paper tells us about saving and its tax treatment. The main problem with applying this tool kit, improved as it might be, to the problem at hand is recognized by the authors, and here I quote: "We have made no attempt to account for any uncertainty that one might have about the correspondence between the model and the real world. As a result, our estimates of variance reflect uncertainty concerning the impact of policy in the model, and not in the actual economy." Unfortunately, when the subject is saving there is tremendous uncertainty about what the true model is. The model used by Bernheim et al. makes heroic, dare I say incredible, assumptions about absolutely crucial elements of the saving decision. For example, what is the nature of intergenerational transfers, do individuals pierce the corporate veil, are many individuals liquidity constrained, do they consider the balance sheet of the government?

A final example is the subject of an earlier paper by John Shoven and two other coauthors. The conclusion of that paper (Goulder, Shoven, and Whalley 1983) is that the economic effects and welfare implications of switching to a consumption tax depend in a critical way on how the foreign sector is modeled, in particular the degree of international capital mobility that is assumed. In fact the paper concludes that when international capital flows are recognized, the consumption tax is no longer a very attractive policy, causing very substantial welfare losses. It would not significantly increase the U.S. capital stock, and the intertemporal efficiency gains are more than offset by the misallocation of capital between the domestic and foreign economies. Because of the foreign tax credit system, the capital outflows caused by the tax change imply that the U.S. forgoes the gross-of-tax return to capital but only receives the net-of-tax return.

I have mentioned what the model does not contain. Let me take a moment to summarize what it does contain. First of all, let me stress that this is a very complex model. The discussion of it in the paper is by necessity very brief—there is much more to it than this discussion suggests. It is worth emphasizing some of its aspects that are critical to this simulation. Consumers make saving decisions based on a utility function that includes present and future consumption. Come next period, with wealth augmented depending on previous saving decisions, they again decide on the balance between present and future consumption. Consumers are myopic, not liquidity constrained, and have no life-cycle aspect to their decisions. As I have already mentioned, there are no international capital flows allowed, so saving equals investment every period. The welfare measure calculates a present value of the current consumption choice made each period.

Obviously we can argue about each of these assumptions, and others I have not mentioned, at length. My point is that the estimate of the impact of a consumption tax that this model generates is already subject to tremendous uncertainty due to these large number of modeling choices.

Let me summarize. I believe that the authors have succeeded admirably in developing a methodology to assess the sensitivity of CGE-based simulations. I expect that this will be a widely cited paper and a widely used methodology in the CGE field. However, although this is a very valuable addition to the CGE tool kit, I believe this is the wrong set of tools for learning about saving. We are too far from a consensus about so many basic issues that predictions with six significant digits, even when they come with standard errors with six significant digits, are not that helpful. In most cases, the parameters are not yet the key issues in this field.

CGE analysis is more valuable, and has already proven its value, in applications where the basic model structure is less controversial. This points us back in the direction of its original use—analysis of policies whose effects are primarily intersectoral rather than intertemporal.

References

Goulder, Lawrence H., John Shoven, and John Whalley. 1983. Domestic Tax Policy and the Foreign Sector: The Importance of Alternative Foreign Sector Formulations to Results From a General Equilibrium Tax Analysis Model. In *Behavioral Simulation Methods in Tax Policy Analysis,* ed. M. Feldstein. Chicago: University of Chicago Press.

Harrison, Glenn W., Richard Jones, Larry J. Kimbell, and Randall Wigle. 1985. How Robust Is Applied General Equilibrium Analysis? Centre for the Study of International Economic Relations Working Paper no. 8501. University of Western Ontario, London, January.

Pagan, Adrian, and John Shannon. 1985. Sensitivity Analysis for Linearized Computable General Equilibrium Models. In *New Developments in Applied General Equilibrium Analysis,* ed. J. Piggott and J. Whalley. Cambridge: Cambridge University Press.

6 Taxes and Capital Formation: How Important Is Human Capital?

James Davies and John Whalley

6.1 Introduction

Work on how taxes affect both capital formation and welfare has produced a wide variety of conclusions spanning the range from little or no effect (Harberger 1964, Wright 1969), to large effects (Summers 1981), to intermediate (Ballard, Fullerton, Shoven, and Whalley 1983, Auerbach, Kotlikoff, and Skinner 1983 [AKS]), to random (King and Fullerton 1984). Despite, or perhaps because of this wide variety of conclusions, the study of tax effects on capital formation has been one of the most active areas of public finance research over the last ten or so years.

In this paper, we reevaluate some of this work in light of the fact that little of it explicitly considers how tax factors enter when accumulation of both human and nonhuman capital occurs. We motivate the paper by recognizing the potential quantitative dominance of human relative to nonhuman capital, and build on a limited but still important taxation and human capital literature. This begins with Boskin (1975) who argues that human capital is taxed on a consumption tax basis and is tax preferred relative to nonhuman capital; and Kotlikoff and Summers (1979) (KS) who show how interasset (human/nonhuman) substitution effects in a growth model can change the way taxes affect steady-state behavior. It also includes Driffill and Rosen (1983) (DR) who analyze the effects of taxes for a single consumer life-cycle optimization prob-

James Davies is associate professor of Economics at the University of Western Ontario, Canada. John Whalley is William G. Davis Professor of International Trade, and director of the Centre for the Study of International Economic Relations at the University of Western Ontario, Canada, and a research associate of the National Bureau of Economic Research.

An earlier version of this paper was presented at the NBER Conference on Taxation of Capital Income in Maui, Hawaii, January 6–7, 1989. The authors are grateful to Paul Storer for research assistance, and to Douglas Bernheim, John Burbidge, Sherwin Rosen, participants in the conference, and participants in an earlier seminar at Western Ontario for their very helpful comments. The authors claim responsibility for any errors or omissions.

lem with both human and nonhuman capital. Their simulation results show that in a partial equilibrium setting welfare costs of income taxes rise when human capital is also taken into account.[1]

Our analysis departs from this work both in considering a full dynamic model in which human and nonhuman capital substitution effects on the production side and trading in nonhuman assets among overlapping generations occur, and in computing transition paths following tax changes as well as steady states. We also develop clear intuition as to the ways in which the presence of human capital affects tax analysis. We stress both the sequential nature of asset accumulation over the life-cycle and the implications that follow for assessments of the effects of taxes on capital formation.

Compared to models that do not separately identify human and nonhuman capital, there is an additional welfare cost associated with taxes on the return to financial assets since they not only change the time profile of consumption over the lifetime as in a one-asset model, but in addition affect asset accumulation decisions. The resulting welfare losses are in addition to those emphasized in existing single asset work. Furthermore, taxes on the income return to savings affect the composition of savings, with substitution out of nonhuman capital into human capital. Therefore, two substitution margins affect financial savings rather than one as in a traditional life-cycle model. Savings in aggregate falls, in the presence of an income tax, but savings in the form of human capital rises.

We use a numerical simulation model based on earlier joint work (Davies, Hamilton, and Whalley 1989) into which we incorporate human capital to analyze how these effects interact. Human capital is incorporated into a 50-period lifetime, overlapping generations equilibrium structure. Simple, and familiar, functional forms are used: consumers have constant relative risk aversion (CRRA) utility functions, and the aggregate production function is Cobb-Douglas. A constant elasticity human capital production function is also used. The model is calibrated to a stylized data set for the U.S. economy in the mid-1970s, closely related to that used by Summers (1980, 1981). Sensitivity of the results to alternative parameter values is also examined.

Our central-case results indicate that, in a dynamic one-sector economy of the Summers type, unlike the partial equilibrium analysis of Driffill and Rosen, incorporating human capital may not change the full dynamic welfare impact of alternative tax experiments markedly. For a move from an income to either a consumption or wage tax there is almost no change in long-run welfare effects from incorporating human capital. On the other hand, *impact* effects on savings are larger, and the transition to a new balanced growth path with endogenous human capital is more rapid since stocks of both factors can adjust. We therefore find ourselves in disagreement with the partial equilibrium conclusion that welfare costs of income taxes are larger with endogenous human capital. This conclusion is, in part, a reflection of the well-known result that in full dynamic equilibrium analysis the importance of distortionary tax wedges tends to be eclipsed by gains due to movement toward the golden rule capital intensity. However, it also reflects the fact that *in steady-state comparisons* we find that there is little distortion in the pattern of human capital investment.

The paper is organized as follows. The next section reviews the effects of taxes on human capital accumulation in a 2-period framework, and discusses how insights from partial equilibrium analysis need to be modified in light of full dynamic equilibrium analysis. Section 6.3 then lays out the formal structure of a multiperiod life-cycle model of consumption, leisure, and human capital accumulation. The implementation of this general structure in our simulations, which for computational simplicity endogenize human capital but take leisure as fixed, is explained in section 6.4. Results of the simulations are presented in section 6.5.

The conclusion to the paper emphasizes how a number of features that potentially complicate tax analysis are not captured in the simulation model presented here. Especially important is the omission of endogenous labor—leisure choice since there is an important mutual interaction between labor supply and human capital investment plans. Also important is progressivity in the income tax, which for computational reasons we do not incorporate. Liquidity constraints have also not been modeled, and we assume that all human capital reflects accumulation of general rather than job-specific training. Alternative models of the educational process, such as screening, in which education has only redistributive effects rather than increasing the productivity of workers either by enhancing their skills or producing information of value in job-worker matching (both of which are captured by the human capital approach), are not considered. Also, we have not estimated the possible effect of rationing of access to either publicly funded or prestige maximizing educational institutions, under which tax effects on human capital formation have a lump-sum element. Finally, we have not examined the role of intergenerational links within the family in helping to determine patterns of human capital formation. Our analysis is, therefore, a first foray into an area of investigation from which most public finance economists have generally kept their distance. Further work may therefore alter the thrust of the results presented here, although we believe our insights on both partial equilibrium effects and differences between partial and full dynamic equilibrium analysis will endure.

6.2   Human Capital and the Analysis of Tax Treatment of Capital Income

Human capital is best thought of as the accumulation of a future income stream through the investment of time to provide for higher income in the future. As an asset, it is different from real capital. In the absence of slavery, individuals cannot purchase others' human capital or sell any which they accumulate themselves. Adjustments to the stock can only occur at a limited rate—in the case of additions sometimes at a fairly quick rate, but in the opposite direction only at the rate of depreciation. Being individual specific, human capital can also not be bequeathed or given away.[2]

Analyzing the ways in which human capital affects the standard literature analysis of the tax treatment of capital is complicated by the fact that human capital occurs in both "general" and "specific" form. General human capital consists of skills that are portable across firms, whereas specific human capital consists of skills that are only useful while working for a particular employer. While it is relatively easy to model the accumulation of human capital when all skills are general, this is not the case where skills are job-specific to some degree. Human capital theory merely predicts that the costs of and returns to investment in specific human capital (usually acquired on the job) will be shared between worker and employer, with the precise outcome being determined by implicit bargaining between the two.[3]

To the extent that firms bear some of the costs of specific training, human capital accumulation may also be directly affected by business taxes, and in particular the corporate income tax. Under the latter, training costs are fully deductible and the returns to the firm fully taxable. Neglecting the imperfect utilization of tax losses, this means that the employer's portion of investment in specific training receives cash-flow tax treatment at the corporate level. Unfortunately, there is no consensus on the determinants of how employers and employees share the costs of specific training. The result is that the present study, like previous work incorporating human capital in the public finance literature, is mostly confined to the analysis of general human capital.

There are also complex issues concerning the relationship between schooling and screening (see, e.g., Spence 1973). In the extreme, if education represents entirely unproductive signaling it is a wasteful activity and ought to be discouraged.[4] More sophisticated models, recognizing that signals may either represent useful skills or play a useful role in job matching, have less draconian policy implications. However, to the extent that education represents signaling there is usually an argument that private markets generate "too much" education. Tax systems that encourage human capital investment therefore appear especially inappropriate. In the remainder of this paper, for the most part we put these complications on one side, treating human capital as general rather than specific and rejecting the pure screening interpretation of schooling.

As pointed out by Boskin (1975), in his notes on the tax treatment of human capital, human capital basically receives consumption tax treatment. Investors in human capital forgo other uses of time when investing, which is equivalent to forgoing gross of tax income to save in the form of human capital. Supplying labor and changing consumption between periods via human capital accumulation, therefore, only involves single taxation as under a consumption tax, rather than double taxation as under an income tax. Investment in the asset is treated much like a tax shelter, with investment implicitly yielding a tax break. Taxes only apply to the income return to the asset.[5]

In the traditional 2-period consumption diagram commonly used to show how taxes influence capital accumulation and savings, human capital can be seen to complicate the analysis and, if anything, amplify the welfare cost of intertemporal tax distortions. How this occurs is shown in figures 6.1 and 6.2. In figure 6.1 (the no-tax case), the individual is endowed with an "unimproved" earnings stream E lying on the 45° line. By forgoing consumption in period 1 (C_1), the individual can transform consumption opportunities between periods according to the transformation frontier AD. The curvature of this frontier reflects the diminishing marginal rate of return to human capital investment.[6]

Given the interest rate the individual faces, optimizing behavior involves moving from the endowment point A to the tangency B (which maximizes lifetime wealth) through human capital investment. Utility maximization implies moving from point B to consumption point C by accumulating financial assets in period 1 (saving) and then reselling them in period 2. Note that the horizontal intercept of the effective budget constraint, ZZ, gives the discounted present value of lifetime earnings; that is, it is a measure of *human*

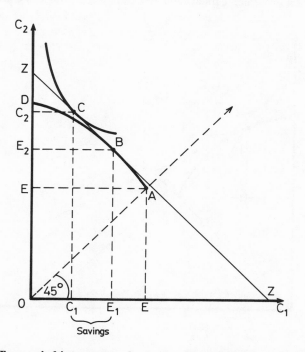

Fig. 6.1 Two-period intertemporal consumption smoothing in the no-tax case

wealth. It is important to distinguish the latter, which is a value, from *human capital,* which is a physical stock.

Optimizing behavior thus implies a two-stage process. Human capital accumulation occurs up to the point where the rate of return on human capital equals the interest rate, r. Accumulation or decumulation of financial assets then occurs, as needed, to smooth the modified earnings stream, B, into the desired consumption stream, C. Although figure 6.1 illustrates a case with positive saving, an outcome where positive accumulation of human capital occurs in the early years of the life-cycle, but there is net borrowing, could also occur.[7]

The effects of an interest income tax that applies only to the return to financial assets in this framework are shown in figure 6.2. The budget constraint ZZ from figure 6.1 becomes more shallowly sloped in the presence of the tax, as represented by $Z'Z'$ in figure 6.2 This results in more accumulation of human capital (represented by the movement from B to B' for wealth-maximizing human capital accumulation), smaller total savings, and considerably smaller financial savings because of the substitution effect. The inter-asset distortion created by the tax yields an additional welfare cost beyond that recognized in existing dynamic tax analyses (i.e., the tax-induced over-accumulation of human capital) and acts to reduce savings as conventionally

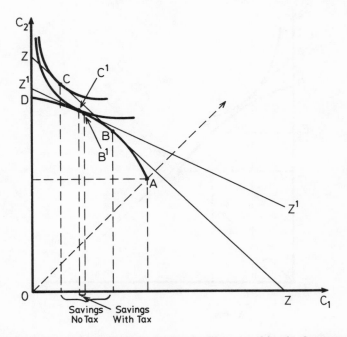

Fig. 6.2   Two-period intertemporal consumption smoothing in the presence of an interest income tax

measured, that is, in the form of accumulation of financial assets. This additional effect of taxes on saving is not widely recognized in the literature.

Diagrams of this type can also be used to illustrate the impact of wage or consumption taxes (see Davies and St-Hilaire 1987, 77–82). Either a proportional wage or consumption tax will radially shift the earnings transformation frontier, *AD*, inward. Although savings in the form of nonhuman capital will be reduced, the optimal human capital investment plan will be unchanged, and if revenues are returned to the individual via lump-sum transfers, the budget constraint will revert to its pretax position, *ZZ*. Savings in nonhuman form may, however, still differ from their pretax value if the transfer payments alter the timing of income receipts over the lifetime. A proportional wage tax used to finance social security payments in the second period, for example, would leave human capital investment unchanged but would reduce private saving.

Progressivity of either wage or consumption taxes would also alter this simple picture. With smoothly increasing marginal tax rates under a wage tax, the slope of the *AD* locus in figure 6.1 would be lower in absolute value at all points (except *A*). The result would be reduced human capital investment. Human capital investment would also be distorted somewhat under a simple progressive annual expenditure tax, but there would be no distortion under a *Blueprints*—style lifetime consumption tax (see again Davies and St.-Hilaire 1987, 79–82).

Note that if human capital is considerably larger in value terms than real capital, as many believe, and if there is significant substitution between the two, then in percentage terms, the differential impact of taxes on savings from either including or not including human capital in the analysis will be correspondingly larger.[8] Also, as one moves outside of the partial equilibrium analysis represented by figures 6.1 and 6.2, one might expect that the rate of return on the smaller real capital stock from the production side of the economy would be largely dictated by the rate of return on the larger human capital stock. Thus, the rate of return on real capital might be dictated largely by the rate of return on human capital, and changes in the tax treatment of financial assets would have relatively little impact on its own net of tax rate of return since human capital is the dominant factor of production. In a dynamic context, if the elasticity of substitution in production between human and nonhuman capital were high and intertemporal consumption elasticities were small, then changes in the tax treatment of real capital would largely affect the composition of wealth rather than its size. Thus, arguments that current tax treatment of real capital substantially increases consumption and reduces capital accumulation need revision once endogeneity of gross of tax rates of return on real assets is included.

As we stress above, despite the various effects of income taxes on intertemporal behavior and resource allocation in the presence of human capital, there has been relatively little work analyzing them. Kotlikoff and Summers (1979) (KS) and Driffill and Rosen (1983) (DR) have made the most important contributions. KS analyze steady-state tax incidence in an overlapping generations growth model with a schooling choice for young people and a labor-leisure (i.e., "retirement") choice for old people. They show that capital income taxes are partly shifted onto labor by induced increases in human capital accumulation. On the other hand, if wage taxes reduce labor supply (i.e., induce earlier retirement), they are partly shifted onto capital since labor supply declines and the capital stock increases as a result of increased saving for the now-longer retirement period. KS do not analyze the welfare costs of alternative taxes. Our paper extends their work by moving beyond steady-state comparisons to include the transition between steady states, by using a multiperiod framework, and by using specific functional forms to simulate both tax incidence and welfare costs in a growth model incorporating human capital.

DR explicitly investigate the welfare effects of capital income taxes with endogenous leisure choice and human capital formation, but in a partial equilibrium single consumer setting. They use the continuous-time human capital life-cycle analysis of Blinder and Weiss (1976) but utilize specific functional forms. Several points emerge from their work. Proportional income taxes increase human capital accumulation. An increase in income taxes reduces net of tax earnings, which reduces consumption of leisure and increases time devoted to training. Also, an income tax reduces the net of tax interest rate, which increases human capital accumulation. Their results suggest that the excess burden of income taxes is lower if human capital formation is (incorrectly) treated as exogenous. A failure to explicitly model human capital accumulation decisions leads to an overestimate of tax revenues because increased human capital investment implies a smaller income tax base. DR also find that consumption taxes have a lower excess burden than proportional income taxes, and a failure to take human capital explicitly into account downward biases estimates of efficiency gains from moving from an income to a consumption tax.[9]

Ideally, analyses of the tax treatment of human capital should also take into account progressivity in the income tax and the effects of public subsidies covering the direct costs of formal education. Individuals typically invest in human capital in years in which they are in low marginal brackets but generate a higher return to labor in years when they are in higher brackets. Although such progressivity effects have been substantially weakened by recent tax reforms in the United States and elsewhere, they nonetheless ought to discourage human capital formation. One cannot be sure whether the result of adding more "realism" would be to show that taxes and transfers are less encouraging to human capital formation than the proportional tax analysis would suggest, however, since there are very heavy public subsidies to educational institutions.[10] These likely imply a rate of subsidy to the direct costs of formal education exceeding significantly the relevant marginal tax rate for young people. The extent to which such subsidies offset the discouraging effect of progressivity in the tax system is unclear.

All the above analysis is, however, dependent both on partial equilibrium assumptions and, implicitly, the assumed perfect substitution between human and physical capital in production. The questions we address are how significant all these effects are in dynamic general equilibrium. How large are the additional welfare costs of tax distortions of savings when we move to a more standard formulation with imperfect substitution of factors in production? How much do induced changes in the rental rate on human and nonhuman capital tend to dampen behavioral responses? How serious a problem is the mismeasurement of the effects of taxes on savings?

6.3   A Life-Cycle Growth Model with Endogenous Human Capital Formation

The model we use to investigate the effects of incorporating human capital into analysis of taxes on capital formation is an extension of the overlapping generations life-cycle simulation models that, following Summers (1980, 1981) and Auerbach, Kotlikoff, and Skinner (1983) (AKS), are now widely used in the literature. In order to achieve comparability across models we adopt the same structure as Summers, even to the point of largely using the same set of base parameters in model simulations. We simulate the effects of various tax changes, and present both transitional and steady-state results. As in Summers (1980), for simplicity we assume myopic expectations along the transitional path. We differ in allowing endogenous investment in (general) human capital.

In this section we set out the structure of the now-standard model of consumption, leisure and human capital choice for an isolated individual, and indicate how it would, ideally, be embedded in a life-cycle growth model. This allows us to discuss some of the theoretical background behind the consequences of alternative taxes for capital formation and welfare that are captured in the simulations reported later, as well as effects that are not possible in our fixed-leisure simulations. The approach we describe can be used in alternative variants in which human capital and/or leisure can be fixed. Human capital fixed but leisure variable is the AKS case; in Summers's case both are fixed. Our numerical simulations reported in section 6.5 are only for the fixed-leisure case, since this is the simplest to compute.

6.3.1   Life-Cycle Optimizing Behavior

In a more general model with leisure endogenous, individuals each seek to maximize an intertemporal utility function:

(1) $$U(C_1, \ldots, C_T; \ell_1, \ldots, \ell_T),$$

where C_t and ℓ_t represent consumption and the fraction of time spent in leisure in period t, respectively.[11] Without taxes, the lifetime budget constraint is given by:

$$(2) \qquad \sum_{t=1}^{T} \frac{C_t}{(1+r)^{t-1}} \leq \sum_{t=1}^{T} \frac{E_t}{(1+r)^{t-1}},$$

where E_t is earned income in year t, and r is the interest rate. Each household assumes r is time invariant (under the assumed myopic expectations) and, additionally, implicitly assumes that the price of consumption goods does not change over time. In order to introduce taxes, let E_t be net of wage or income taxes, replace r by the net of tax interest rate r_n, allow a proportional consumption tax at rate u, and assume revenues are redistributed as lump-sum transfers R_t. The budget constraint then becomes:

$$(2') \qquad \sum_{t=1}^{T} \frac{C_t(1+u)}{(1+r_n)^{t-1}} \leq \sum_{t=1}^{T} \frac{E_t + R_t}{(1+r_n)^{t-1}}.$$

Earnings are proportional to the stock of human capital, H_t, and the time available for earning:

$$(3) \qquad E_t = W_t^n H_t (1 - s_t - \ell_t) \quad t = 1, \ldots, T,$$

where W_t^n is the net of tax rental rate on human capital in period t, and s_t is the proportion of time spent in human capital accumulation via schooling or on-the-job training. Here H_t is the (depreciated) sum of endowed human capital, H_1, and all additions to the human capital stock made in the past, h_τ:

$$(4) \qquad H_t = \begin{cases} H_1 & t = 1 \\ \dfrac{H_1}{(1+\delta)^{t-1}} + \sum_{\tau=1}^{t-1} \dfrac{h_\tau(s_\tau H_\tau)}{(1+\delta)^{t-\tau}} & t = 2, \ldots, T, \end{cases}$$

where δ is the depreciation rate. For convenience, we assume δ to be constant over time.

To understand how life-cycle optimizing behavior operates in this framework, it is helpful to first consider how any household would solve the above problem if the time path of ℓ_t were fixed at the optimal level ℓ_t^*, since if ℓ_t is fixed, the human capital investment problem and the intertemporal utility maximizing problem decompose.

With fixed leisure, optimal human capital investment is simply that which maximizes the value of lifetime earnings. Given optimal human capital investment, the individual then maximizes $U(C_1, \ldots, C_T; \ell_1^*, \ldots, \ell_T^*)$ subject to (2) where the E_ts are now fixed, that is, finding the optimal consumption path reduces to a familiar (and simple) problem.

Neglecting the possibility of corner solutions, and taking the special case where, for simplicity, H_t does not affect h_t, the solution to the wealth-maximizing human capital investment problem is characterized by the first-order conditions:

$$(5) \qquad \frac{\partial h_t}{\partial s_t} \sum_{\tau=\tau+1}^{T} \frac{W_\tau^n(1-s_\tau-\ell_\tau^*)}{[(1+r_n)(1+\delta)]^{\tau-t}} = W_t^n H_t, \quad t = 1, \ldots, T,$$

which imply that the marginal benefit of spending additional time in schooling (the left-hand side) must equal forgone earnings (the wage rate, $W_t^n H_t$) at each time t.

In equation (5) depreciation plays the same analytical role as r_n; that is, both affect the discounted present value of the returns to human capital investment in the same way. Also, we can see that by reducing r_n, interest income taxes raise the (private) marginal benefit of human capital investment and thereby distort human capital investment decisions (see Heckman 1976, S27). We also note that a proportional wage tax would have no effect on human capital investment in the absence of any change in the optimal ℓ_t, since equal proportional changes in the values of W_t^n leave (5) unchanged. Heavier wage taxes later in life under a progressive tax reduce investment in human capital, however, since they lower W_t^n early in life less than later in life in the left-hand side of (5).

The wealth-maximizing human capital investment plan tends to produce large but falling investment in human capital in early years. At some point before retirement (or the end of the life if there is not a fixed retirement age), human capital reaches a peak, where gross investment in human capital has declined to annual depreciation. Beyond this peak there is a decline in the human capital stock, but despite the fact that there is no scrap value, the stock typically remains large at the retirement point since decumulation is limited by the rate of depreciation. (This typical pattern appears in our simulation results discussed below.)

The age profile of earnings produced by this optimal human capital plan differs considerably from that assumed in some previous work in the public finance literature. Summers (1980, 1981), for example, has all workers paid the same amount at a particular date, irrespective of age. The only reason for earnings growth over the life-cycle is that there is labor-augmenting technical progress. In contrast, earnings growth due to human capital investment generates a concave age profile of earnings. Given a particular age profile of desired consumption, and holding the present value of lifetime earnings constant, such a concave profile is less conducive to saving in early years and just before retirement. Aggregate saving will therefore generally differ between models where wage growth is generated solely by technical progress and those where human capital investment enters.

Changes in taxation may alter the age profile of earnings due to induced changes in human capital investment. An interest income tax, for example, encourages human capital investment and makes the age profile of earnings steeper. Holding the consumption profile constant, this tends to reduce saving in nonhuman form.[12]

In order to see how the labor-leisure choice is determined over time in this model, assume that the human capital investment plan has been fixed on an initially optimal path, $H_1^*, \ldots, H_T^*$. Associated with $H_1^*, \ldots, H_T^*$ are optimal values of $s_1^*, \ldots s_T^*$, which we will also treat as fixed for the moment. Given these, one can maximize (1) subject to (2'), where the E_ts are given by:

(3') $\qquad E_t = W_t^n H_t^* (1 - s_t^* - \ell_t) \quad t = 1, \ldots, T.$

Assuming an interior solution, the first-order conditions are given by:

(6) $\qquad \begin{cases} \text{(a) } U_{1t} + \dfrac{\lambda(1+u)}{(1+r_n)^{t-1}} = 0 \\[3mm] \text{(b) } U_{2t} + \dfrac{\lambda W_t^n H_t^*}{(1+r_n)^{t-1}} = 0 \end{cases} \Bigg\} \ t = 1, \ldots, T,$

where U_{1t} and U_{2t} indicate partials with respect to consumption and leisure respectively in year t. If the optimal solution for any period were that $\ell_t = 1$ for that period, (6b) would become the inequality:

(6b') $\qquad\qquad\qquad U_{2t} > \dfrac{\lambda W_t^n H_t^*}{(1+r_n)^{t-1}}.$

The first-order conditions yield the following set of relationships:

(7) $\qquad \begin{cases} \text{(i) } \dfrac{U_{2t}}{U_{1t}} = W_t^n H_t^*/(1+u) \\[3mm] \text{(ii) } \dfrac{U_{1t}}{U_{1t'}} = (1+r_n)^{(t'-t)} \\[3mm] \text{(iii) } \dfrac{U_{2t}}{U_{2t'}} = (1+r_n)^{(t'-t)} \dfrac{W_t^n H_t^*}{W_{t'}^n H_{t'}^*} \end{cases} \Bigg\} \ t = 1, \ldots, T.$

Here (7i) indicates that the marginal rate of substitution (MRS) between goods and leisure in any period equals the net wage rate deflated by the rate of consumption taxation. The Euler relationship, (7ii), indicates that the marginal utility of consumption must decline at a rate equal to r_n, and (7iii) indicates that the MRS between leisure in different time periods is related to r_n in the same way as the MRS for consumption, except that changes in the wage rate alter the opportunity cost of leisure as well and need to be taken into account.

In general, the greater the amount of leisure taken over the lifetime, the less is the inducement to human capital accumulation, as can be seen in (5). Thus in models like KS, where both leisure and human capital are endogenous, taxes that tend to reduce labor supply are likely to also reduce investment in human capital, producing a second-round decline in the effective supply of labor. The age profile of earnings becomes less steep, leading to increased saving. Thus there is a tendency for the capital-labor ratio to rise a fortiori, so that, for example, a wage tax may end up largely shifted onto capital (see KS).

On the other hand, from (6) and (7) human capital investment has a major impact on the time path of leisure, via its influence on the wage rate. Thus, features of the tax or education systems that encourage human capital investment, such as interest income taxes or subsidies to higher education, produce substitution away from leisure toward consumption of goods, as well as leisure substitution between periods to the extent that the age profile of net wage rates is altered. By making the age profile of earnings steeper, they also lead to reduced saving.

There are also potentially important interactions between leisure and consumption of goods. Taking the household production view, home time and goods may be regarded as inputs in a home production function, where the output is a bundle of *commodities*. A rising price of time (i.e., a higher wage rate) leads to substitution in household production away from time toward goods within a period (7i), but also to substitution away from consumption of commodities in periods when they are made relatively more expensive by the higher wage (7iii). It appears that the latter influence tends to dominate, since it is widely observed that both expenditures on goods and wage rates are hump shaped over the life-cycle, but leisure time has a U-shaped profile.

The simulation model, whose results are reported later in this paper, has so far only been implemented with exogenous leisure. One implication is that we are unfortunately not able to examine computationally the consequences of the interaction between tax effects on labor supply and human capital investment, some of which we have outlined above. In addition, with CRRA preferences the model generates constant proportional desired growth of consumption over the lifetime, which differs both from the observed pattern, and what would be expected on the basis of the full model sketched above. Given a particular age profile of earnings, quite a different pattern of savings is likely to be generated. Also, tax experiments can only affect the *level* of the consumption profile and not its shape, so that, for example, the rich consequences of interactions between goods and leisure cannot be captured.

6.3.2 The Production Side and the Aggregate Economy

As in Summers (1981) and AKS (1983) we assume a constant rate of substitution (CRS) aggregate production function that produces a single commodity that can be used for either consumption or capital accumulation. However, inputs are no longer labor and capital, but instead are human and physical capital:

$$(8) \qquad\qquad Y_t = F(H_t^m, K_t).$$

Note that the stock of human capital employed in production, H_t^m, is only part of the overall stock, $\bar{H}_t$, since the latter can also be employed in leisure or training.

Aggregate use of these factors in any period must equal the economy's endowment, $\bar{K}_t$ and $\bar{H}_t$. In the simple case of constant population the latter evolve according to the equations of motion:

(9)
$$
\begin{cases}
\text{(i) } \bar{K}_t = \bar{K}_{t-1} + \sum_{j=1}^{T+1} (K_t^j - K_{t-1}^{j-1}) \\[2mm]
\text{(ii) } \bar{H}_t = \bar{H}_{t-1} + \sum_{j=1}^{T+1} (H_t^j - H_{t-1}^{j-1}),
\end{cases}
$$

where K_t^j and H_t^j represent the physical and human capital held by the generation of age j in period t. For each of the 50 overlapping generations identified in the model, if $(K_t^j - K_{t-1}^{j-1})$ is positive, generation j is a saver in period t, if negative a dissaver. The term $H_t^j - H_{t-1}^{j-1}$ is bounded from below since dissaving in any period can only occur through depreciation. We define $K_t^0 = H_t^0 = H_t^{T+1} = 0$. $K_t^{T+1} = 0$ is a consequence of nonsatiation in a life-cycle context.

The full employment conditions in this economy are somewhat more complex than in one-asset growth models, since time can be devoted to two nonmarket uses (schooling and leisure). Effective units of human capital available to the labor market are

(10)
$$
\bar{H}_t^m = \sum_{j=1}^{T} (H_t^j)(1 - s_t^j - \ell_t^j),
$$

where the j superscript again indicates the values for members of the various age groups. Full employment conditions are thus

(11)
$$
\begin{cases}
\text{(i) } K_t = \bar{K}_t \\
\text{(ii) } H_t^m = \bar{H}_t^m
\end{cases}.
$$

We allow technical progress at rate g, and population grows at rate n. Thus, in a steady-state solution the rental rate on human capital will be constant, but aggregate stocks will grow at rate $(n + g)$.

In equilibrium, a zero-profit condition for the aggregate production function must be satisfied:

(12)
$$
Y_t = W_t H_t^m + r_t K_t,
$$

where Y_t is aggregate output, and W_t and r_t are *gross* of tax rates of return to human and nonhuman capital. Output is the numeraire. An equilibrium in period t, finally, is given by values of the rental rates W_t and r_t, such that (11) and (12) are satisfied. Furthermore if

(13)
$$
W_{t+1} = (1+g)W_t; \quad r_{t+1} = r_t,
$$

then such an equilibrium lies on a balanced growth path.[13] Revenues raised through taxes are redistributed in lump-sum form to each of the 50 generations paying taxes.

6.4 Implementing the Model Approach

In order to use the structure outlined above for capital income tax simulation analysis, we have made some simplifying assumptions and have chosen specific functional forms. As explained earlier, in the simulations reported in this paper we have ignored leisure. Like Summers (1981) we assume that all individuals work for 40 years and retire for 10. The first 40 years of the lifetime can be used for earning or learning. The extra leisure in retirement is not assumed to affect utility. Using the constant relative risk aversion (CRRA) utility function we therefore have the simple (and familiar) preferences:

$$(1') \qquad U = \sum_{t=1}^{T} \left[\frac{C_t^{1-\alpha}}{1-\alpha} \right] \frac{1}{(1+\rho)^{t-1}},$$

where α is the inverse of the intertemporal elasticity of substitution, σ. With this choice (7) reduces to:

$$(7') \qquad \frac{C_{t'}}{C_t} = \left[\frac{1+r_n}{1+\rho} \right]^{(t'-t)/\alpha} \qquad t = 1, \ldots, T,$$

so that C_t simply grows at a constant proportional rate that rises with r_n, and falls with ρ and α.[14]

The choice of a human capital investment function, h_t, is also critical in the model. In general h_t would depend on the inputs s_t and H_t:

$$(14) \qquad h_t = h(s_t, H_t).$$

However, important special cases are provided by

$$(14') \qquad h_t = h(s_t),$$

and

$$(14'') \qquad h_t = h(s_t H_t).$$

The latter formulation embodies the "neutrality" hypothesis of Ben-Porath (1967).[15] On the other hand, (14') provides the computationally helpful simplification of making $\partial h_t / \partial s_t$ independent of H_t. In the simulations reported here we use the constant elasticity form:

$$(15) \qquad h_t = As_t^\theta.$$

Although constant elasticity is typically assumed in the empirical literature on the human capital production function,[16] (15) is, of course, a simplified formulation.

Although available empirical evidence is limited (see, e.g., Heckman 1975; and Haley 1976), there are strong a priori grounds for expecting the stock of general human capital to enter the human capital production function. It has been suggested, for example, that learning skills are likely one of the most important forms of general human capital. If H_t enters (14), tax effects on human capital investment will compound through time. Despite the absence of such compounding, (15) turns out to produce realistic age profiles of training time, human capital, and earnings, as discussed in the next section. The partial equilibrium impact of tax changes on human capital investment also turn out to be large, so that the absence of compounding in (15) does not lead to insensitivity of s_t with respect to taxes.

Finally, on the production side we use the Cobb-Douglas production function:

$$(16) \qquad Y_t = H_t^{m^\gamma} K_t^{1-\gamma}.$$

6.4.1   Parameterization

To implement the model approach described above, we choose particular values for the parameters appearing in all the functions given above by calibrating the model to a base-case balanced growth path. This growth path is much the same as used by Summers (1981), and, by extension, Davies, Hamilton, and Whalley (1989).

The basic parameter set is displayed in table 6.1, where taste, technology, and tax parameters are reported. Following Summers, we use a unitary intertemporal elasticity of substitution, σ, and rate of time preference, $\rho = .03$. While our share parameter of labor in the aggregate production function, γ, and population growth rate, n, are also set at Summers's values (.75 and .015, respectively), we have used a lower productivity growth rate, g (.01). Sum-

Table 6.1   **Base-Case Parameter Values**

Parameter		Value
Tastes:		
Intertemporal elasticity of substitution	(σ)	1.000
Rate of time preference	(ρ)	.030
Technology:		
Share parameter of labor in production function	(γ)	.750
Human capital production function:	(θ)	.500
	(δ)	.010
Population growth rate	(n)	.015
Productivity growth rate	(g)	.010
Taxes:		
Capital income tax		.500
Labor income tax		.200

mers used $g = .02$, but we found that we could not calibrate the human capital production function successfully unless a lower value was chosen for g.[17]

Our calibration of the human capital production function proceeds as follows. First, we choose arbitrary values of δ and θ. Next we iterate until we find a value of the scale parameter, A, in the human capital production function which produces a steady state with the base-case parameter values in which the ratio of rental rates, r/w, and the capital-labor ratio, K/H^m, are the same as in the one-commodity version of Davies, Hamilton, and Whalley (1989), which is similar to Summers's base case. Thus the human capital production function is calibrated by requiring that the rental rates and capital-labor ratio should be the same in the base case as in previous work, which ignores human capital. Finally, we look at the age profiles of human capital, training time, and earnings produced by the model in order to confirm that these are realistic. In principle, if the profiles were not realistic we would experiment with alternative values of δ and θ until they were. However, our initial choice, $\delta = .01$ and $\theta = .5$, proved satisfactory and further rounds of the process were unnecessary.[18]

The age profiles of human capital, training time, and earnings produced by the model are shown in figures 6.3 and 6.4. Figure 6.3 indicates that new labor-market entrants (aged, say, 20 biologically) spend about 32% of their time in human capital investment. This fraction declines at a falling rate. About halfway through the working lifetime only about 10% of available time is being spent in training. (This pattern is fairly similar to that estimated, e.g., by Heckman 1975.) The age profiles of both human capital and earnings display a shape that is familiar from both the theoretical and empirical human capital literature going back at least to Mincer (1974) (see also Weiss 1986, and Willis 1986).

Labor and capital income tax rates in the base case are set at 20% and 50%, respectively, as in Summers (1980, 1981). Following the methodology of Shoven and Whalley (1973), and unlike Summers, the revenues collected are returned to the taxpayers as lump-sum transfers. For simplicity the distribution scheme is assumed to be uniform and unrelated to age.[19]

The tax experiments we perform involve replacing initial taxes by wage and consumption taxes alternatively. The government's revenue requirement, and therefore transfer payments, are maintained on a period-by-period basis in all experiments. Tax rates adjust to yield the required revenue, with a balanced budget in every period.

In order to perform tax replacement experiments, we need to specify how expectations of future prices, tax rates, and transfer payments are formed. Like Summers (1980), we have adopted the computationally simple assumption of myopic expectations. Everyone expects that the current period rental and tax rates and transfer payments will continue unchanged indefinitely. (Note that for transfer payments, this myopic expectation always turns out to

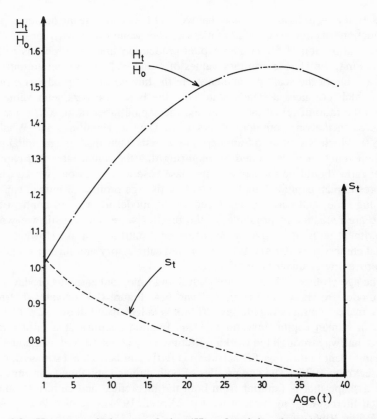

Fig. 6.3   Human capital accumulation (*H*) and training time (*s*) in base-case steady state

have been correct.) This assumption contrasts with the perfect foresight approach used, for example, by AKS and Auerbach and Kotlikoff (1983, 1987).

The main effect of using myopic expectations in the simulations performed here is that the economy converges more rapidly to the new steady state than with perfect foresight. This is because when capital income taxes are reduced, households do not anticipate that the gross rate of return on capital will decline in the future. Not surprisingly, the capital stock converges to its new, higher, steady-state level more rapidly than it would if households could foresee perfectly the declining gross rate of return.

There is some evidence on the quantitative significance of using myopic expectations for results from models such as we use. In their simulations of capital income tax reforms, based on a model similar to Summers's, but with perfect foresight, Auerbach and Kotlikoff (1983) find that the capital stock has adjusted halfway to its new steady-state level between 10 and 15 years after the policy change. In contrast, we find here that the same degree of con-

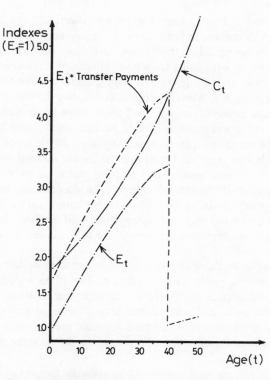

Fig. 6.4 **Earnings (E), transfer payments, and consumption over the life-cycle in the base case**

vergence has occurred after just five or six years. The latter result is similar to the findings of Summers (1980).

Our simulations thus yield base-case balanced growth scenarios for the economy and alternative time paths of behavior under changed policies. This allows for full welfare comparisons between base and revise cases, including both transitional as well as long-run effects.

6.5   Results

We have used the model described in the previous sections in two alternative modes, which we then use to evaluate the effects of alternative capital income tax changes. One is a move to a wage tax, in which the tax on interest income is removed and labor tax rates are revised upward to preserve revenues. The other is a move to a consumption tax, in which taxes on both labor income and interest income are set equal to zero and replaced by an equal-yield sales tax. As in Summers, yield equality applies on a period-by-period basis. The two alternative model analyses have human capital endogenously determined in one and exogenous in the other (effectively, the Summers case of labor growth at rate n). In both cases, an endogenous labor-leisure choice is excluded from the modeling framework for reasons of simplicity.

In table 6.2 we report results from comparisons of sequences of equilibria under a move from an income tax to a wage tax and a move from an income tax to a consumption tax. Most of the results describe the change between the base and the new steady states achieved under wage and consumption taxes. For example, we report the steady-state welfare gains, with human capital alternatively assumed endogenous and exogenous, in the second line of both panels A and B (for wage and consumption taxes, respectively). The most striking aspect of these steady-state welfare gains, as of the steady-state changes in capital intensity, rate of return, per capita consumption, and human capital stock, is the similarity of results whether human capital is endogenous or exogenous. Under the wage tax, steady-state welfare rises a little *less* when human capital is endogenous, apparently due to the operation of Summers's postponement effect.[20]

While steady-state characteristics are of interest, more important are the full dynamic welfare gains shown in the first line of each part of table 6.2. These capture the impact effects, the effects along a transitional path to a new balanced growth path, and comparisons across balanced growth paths. Welfare effects are reported in terms of the discounted present value of the period-by-period change in consumption plus the change in the value of the terminal

Table 6.2	Equilibrium Sequence Comparisons for Capital Income Tax Changes	
	Changes Relative to Base Case (%)	
	Human Capital Endogenous	Human Capital Exogenous
A. Wage Tax:		
Present value of consumption and terminal capital stock	5.2	5.7
Steady state:		
Welfare	5.1	5.3
K/H^m	92.2	87.9
r	−38.7	−37.7
Consumption	11.7	12.6
Human capital stock	−3.2	.0
B. Consumption tax:		
Present value of consumption and terminal capital stock	6.2	6.3
Steady state:		
Welfare	9.8	9.8
K/H^m	111.7	107.7
r	−45.0	−42.5
Consumption	14.0	14.5
Human capital stock	−2.1	.0

capital stock. Adding transitional effects reduces the gains under the consumption tax, reflecting the considerable losses of the old in the early transition years previously identified, for example, by AKS. In addition, transitional welfare changes are slightly more favorable with human capital exogenous under both tax experiments.[21]

These results are very different than those obtained using partial equilibrium assumptions by Driffill and Rosen (1983) (DR). However, they are not *inconsistent* with the DR results. The partial equilibrium welfare gains from either the wage or consumption tax experiment here, as measured by the equivalent variation (EV), are 4.4% greater here when human capital is made endogenous.[22] (Gains are the same under wage and consumption taxes since they are equivalent in the partial equilibrium context.) This difference is smaller than obtained by DR with their quite different functional forms, but it is still substantial—in fact, of the same order of magnitude as the full dynamic welfare gains in our model. Alternative parameterizations increase the partial equilibrium differential markedly without altering the conclusion suggested by the full dynamic results. For example, in the $\theta = .75$ run reported in table 6.5 partial equilibrium gains are 9.1% higher when human capital is made endogenous, but the full dynamic welfare gains are again little affected.

The reason for these results can be seen from tables 6.3 and 6.4. The impact effect under either change in tax treatment is to increase savings, as predicted by traditional analysis. In long-run dynamic equilibrium, with a move to a new balanced growth path, the rate of return on nonhuman capital reverts to approximately its original net of tax value in both experiments. Thus, with a 50% tax rate on capital income, a 10.6% gross of tax rate of return, r, in the original base case implies a net of tax value of 5.3%, which is not too much lower than the new long-run balanced growth values of 6.5% and 6.0% in the wage and consumption tax case, respectively (with endogenous human capital). In long-run balanced growth the net of tax rate of return on assets is largely unchanged, and there is, therefore, little long-run effect on human capital formation.

Thus, the effects which results by DR highlight, from including human capital in tax analysis of saving behavior, including the interasset substitution effect between human and nonhuman capital and the larger effect on savings that we describe in the earlier part of this paper, turn out to be transitional rather than long-run effects. Also, in the long run the impacts on welfare are largely unchanged.

The feature that the gross of tax rate of return on nonhuman capital falls to approximately the net of tax rate of return in the new balanced growth path is a property common to both our model and the Summers (1981) model without endogenous human capital, which uses a similar parameterization. The similarity of outcomes is hardly an accident. We have calibrated our human capital production function to produce an optimal age-earnings profile in the base case that will generate aggregate saving equal to that obtained with the

Table 6.3   Transitional Effects of a Move from an Income Tax to a Wage Tax

Year	K/H^m	r	C/C_{BC}	$\overline{H}/\overline{H}_{BC}$	S/Y
A. Human capital endogenous:					
0	3.140	.106	1.0	1.0	.059
1	2.887	.113	.700	1.0	.382
2	3.357	.101	.765	.993	.339
3	3.779	.092	.820	.987	.301
4	4.150	.086	.866	.982	.270
5	4.471	.081	.904	.978	.243
10	5.512	.070	1.021	.967	.161
20	6.162	.064	1.098	.963	.108
50	5.988	.065	1.118	.968	.096
100	6.035	.065	1.117	.968	.097
B. Human capital exogenous:					
0	3.140	.106	1.0	1.0	.059
1	3.140	.106	.710	1.0	.333
2	3.492	.098	.764	1.0	.301
3	3.808	.087	.810	1.0	.275
4	4.088	.083	.850	1.0	.252
5	4.338	.080	.885	1.0	.233
10	5.219	.072	1.002	1.0	.169
20	5.954	.066	1.103	1.0	.116
50	5.857	.066	1.127	1.0	.093
100	5.901	.066	1.126	1.0	.095

Note: In part A, it takes six years for K/H^m to converge halfway to its new steady-state value. The comparable figure for part B is 7 years. C/C_{BC} = ratio of aggregate consumption to that which would be observed if the base case had continued undisturbed. $\overline{H}/\overline{H}_{BC}$ = ratio of aggregate human capital stock to that which would be observed if the base case had continued undisturbed. S/Y = ratio of aggregate savings (i.e., in physical capital) to national income.

Summers-type exponential age-earnings profile. Suppose that in the Summers-type model the steady-state gross of tax rate of return fell exactly to the base-case net rate of return under either the wage or consumption tax experiment. Would we expect a similar drop in the steady-state gross rate of return in *our* model? The same drop in the gross rate of return would give a human capital investment plan under the wage or consumption tax exactly the same as in the base case. The shape of the steady-state age-earnings profile would not be affected by the tax regime. Now, would such an unchanged age-earnings profile allow the same capital deepening and, therefore, the same change in rate of return as simulated by Summers? If so, our wage or consumption tax steady-states *would* feature the gross rate of return falling to the net. Given that our age-earnings profile has been chosen to give a base-case saving pattern similar to that in the Summers model, it would not be surprising if it also gave a saving pattern similar to the Summers model under the wage or consumption taxes. Thus, the fact that in our model wage and consumption tax experiments produce similar capital deepening, and a similar drop in the gross rate of return as in Summers' model, is not unintuitive.

Table 6.4   **Transitional Effects of a Move from an Income Tax to a
Consumption Tax**

Year	K/H^m	r	C/C_{BC}	$\overline{H}/\overline{H}_{BC}$	S/Y
A. Human capital endogenous:					
0	3.140	.106	1.0	1.0	.059
1	2.887	.113	.532	1.0	.531
2	3.567	.096	.641	.993	.452
3	4.157	.086	.729	.987	.389
4	4.663	.079	.801	.983	.338
5	5.090	.074	.859	.980	.291
10	6.366	.062	1.032	.973	.177
20	6.885	.059	1.135	.974	.108
50	6.598	.061	1.138	.980	.106
100	6.646	.060	1.140	.979	.104
B. Human capital exogenous:					
0	3.140	.106	1.0	1.0	.059
1	3.140	.106	.558	1.0	.476
2	3.677	.094	.649	1.0	.414
3	4.146	.086	.725	1.0	.365
4	4.553	.080	.788	1.0	.325
5	4.904	.076	.841	1.0	.292
10	6.055	.065	1.016	1.0	.189
20	6.739	.060	1.141	1.0	.113
50	6.463	.062	1.142	1.0	.103
100	6.523	.061	1.145	1.0	.103

Note: C/C_{BC} = ratio of aggregate consumption to that which would be observed if the base case had continued undisturbed. $\overline{H}/\overline{H}_{BC}$ = ratio of aggregate human capital stock to that which would be observed if the base case had continued undisturbed. S/Y = ratio of aggregate savings (i.e., in physical capital) to national income.

Thus, the result here that the new steady-state human capital investment plan is not much different from the initial plan under the income tax reflects those aspects of a Summers-type model that make savings increase sufficiently under wage or consumption tax experiments to bring the steady-state gross of tax rate of return down to about its initial net-of-tax value. There are no doubt many alternative models in which savings would be less sensitive to tax changes, with the result that the gross of tax rate of return would not fall to the net, and effects on human capital investment would persist in steady state.

Tables 6.3 and 6.4 provide more details on the transitional paths for the human capital endogenous and exogenous models under the two alternative tax changes. They suggest a more rapid transitional process when human capital is endogenous. In both wage tax and consumption tax experiments, the short-run stimulus to saving in nonhuman form is larger when human capital is endogenous. Savings ratios in the impact year are .333 and .476 in the wage and consumption tax experiments with human capital exogenous, but are .382 and .531 when human capital is endogenous. This reflects a very substantial accompanying decline in human capital investment, which shows up in a

0.7% depletion of the human capital stock after just one year under both of the new tax regimes.[23] The result of the larger savings response is that the capital-labor ratio converges much closer to its new long-run value after five years when human capital is endogenous than when it is exogenous.

Intercohort redistributive effects follow a familiar pattern in our simulations. As in AKS, under the wage tax the most substantial gains go to those who are old in the impact year, and under the consumption tax the reverse is true. These redistributive effects show only a small amount of sensitivity to the endogeneity of human capital. The largest effect is in the wage tax case where those aged 40 and above experience welfare gains up to 0.7% more when human capital is endogenous, and younger cohorts experience up to 0.7% smaller gains. The additional benefit for older workers and retirees can be traced to the slower decline of the interest rate in the initial years of transition with endogenous human capital, while the reduced gain for younger workers appears to reflect the harm done to their lifetime optimization by myopic expectations and the emerging postponement effect.

Table 6.5 reports some of the sensitivity analysis we have done with the model. The first three rows show changes with respect to which our central-case results on welfare gains from the various tax experiments are highly robust. The first change raises the θ parameter in the human capital production function to .75. By itself, a move to $\theta = .75$ leads to a solution with almost no human capital investment taking place. Recall that we calibrated the base-case model by finding a value for the scale parameter, A, in the human capital production function, that would give human capital investment plans that would generate an overall capital-labor ratio, and gross of tax rate of return r, equal to those in the base case of Davies, Hamilton, and Whalley (1989). We have recalibrated in the $\theta = .75$ run, choosing a new value of the parameter A to once again have $r = .106$ in the base case. The second and third changes also (necessarily) involve a recalibration of the model. Here we find new values of A that generate initial steady states with the gross interest rate 2.0 percentage points below and above the central-case value of 10.6% alternatively.

The last three rows of table 6.5 display more sensitivity, although none of these experiments disturbs the similarity of results with human capital endogenous versus exogenous. Using a lower value of σ (.5), which many would now consider more "realistic" than $\sigma = 1$, reduces the full dynamic welfare gains somewhat. Setting the Cobb-Douglas share parameter in the aggregate production function, γ, equal to 0.6, instead of the central-case value of 0.75, produces an approximate doubling in welfare gains. Behind this is a somewhat greater increase in the capital-labor ratio under the various tax experiments than observed in the central-case runs. With human capital endogenous, the capital-labor ratio rises 102% when the income tax is replaced by a wage tax and 138% under the consumption tax replacement. The corresponding figures in the central case were 92% and 112%. An interesting feature of the $\gamma = 0.6$ results is that human wealth bulks significantly smaller as a proportion of overall wealth. Now human wealth in the initial steady state is

Table 6.5   **Dynamic Welfare Gains from Tax Experiments with Altered Parameter Values (% changes relative to base case)**

	Replacing Income Tax by			
	Wage Tax		Consumption Tax	
	Human Capital Endogenous	Human Capital Exogenous	Human Capital Endogenous	Human Capital Exogenous
Central case	5.2	5.7	6.2	6.3
Parameter changes:				
$\theta = .75$	5.3	5.6	6.1	6.3
$r = .086$	5.3	5.3	6.3	6.3
$r = .126$	5.5	5.8	6.2	6.3
$\gamma = .6$	9.8	10.2	12.2	12.4
$\sigma = .5$	4.3	4.6	5.4	5.6
Tax rates $= 28$	1.3	1.0	1.6	1.5

Note: In the $\theta = .75$ run and the $r = .086$ and $.126$ runs, the human capital production function is recalibrated. With $\theta = .75$ the parameter A is chosen so that initial $r = .106$, as in the base case. The $r = .086$ and $r = .126$ runs necessitate a new choice of A given the calibration procedure described in section 6.4 of the text.

about 72% of total wealth, in contrast to the figure of 80% in the central-case runs. This may represent confirmation of the intuition about the impact of the relative size of the human capital stock (discussed in app. A) on the results of intertemporal tax analysis which we briefly outlined in section 6.2.

Finally, the last row of table 6.5 indicates how our results would have differed if we had assumed equal tax rates of 28% on labor and capital income in the base case. This run is motivated by recent U.S. tax reform. Reducing the assumed rate of tax on capital income from the 50% of the central case dramatically reduces the percentage of welfare gains from wage or consumption tax experiments. However, it is interesting to note that even in this case the annual welfare gains from the move to wage or consumption taxes would equal about $63 billion and $77 billion, respectively, in current U.S. terms. (For comparison, in the second quarter of 1988 U.S. GDP was running at an annual rate of $4.8 trillion.)

6.6   Conclusion

This paper discusses how the analysis of the effects of taxes on capital formation is changed by the explicit incorporation of human capital. While there has been much discussion in recent public finance literature of the effects of intertemporal tax distortions on capital formation and welfare, little of this has explicitly incorporated human capital. In the paper we show how the impact effects of incorporating human capital suggest important and neglected tax induced interasset effects and larger effects on savings (as conventionally measured), consistent with earlier partial equilibrium analysis of Driffill and

Rosen (1983). We also present a framework for dynamic long-run equilibrium analysis in the tradition of Summers (1980, 1981), but with endogenous human capital formation.

Using this framework, we perform numerical simulation analyses designed to explore how incorporating human capital affects the welfare analysis of tax distortions of savings. For the numerical specification we use, estimates of intertemporal distorting costs of taxes are little affected by including human capital, in contrast to the conclusion offered by Driffill and Rosen from their partial equilibrium analysis. While the impact effect of removing these tax distortions is to increase savings by more in the human capital endogenous case for a move from an income tax to a consumption or wage tax and to generate an additional interasset effect, in the long run the net of tax rate of return on nonhuman capital is largely unchanged because of interasset substitution effects between human and nonhuman capital. As a result, long-run welfare analysis produces values for the discounted present value of consumption plus change in the value of terminal capital, which are similar. Our paper therefore suggests that static partial equilibrium analysis focusing on how human capital changes the analysis of tax distortions of savings can be misleading when compared to full dynamic equilibrium analysis, which captures endogenous effects on interest rates through interasset substitution effects.

These findings must, however, be qualified by the fact that some potentially important features of human capital formation and its tax treatment are neglected in our analysis. Our simulation model has exogenous leisure and does not incorporate liquidity constraints, progressivity in the income tax, or job-specific human capital. We have also not modeled rationing of access to educational institutions, and the lump-sum effects that taxes on the associated pure rents would create. Intergenerational links within the family that may affect human capital formation are also not incorporated. A further qualification is that, as in all such work, our results are contingent on specific functional forms and parameter values. Work with more general production functions for both aggregate output and human capital is an important avenue for future research. Thus, although we feel that our paper takes an important step in clarifying the impact of incorporating human capital in life-cycle simulations of tax effects in dynamic equilibrium, it should be regarded as a first foray in this area.

Appendix
Estimates of the Size of the Human Capital Stock

There are two approaches commonly used to measure the stock of human capital in the literature, and they yield different results. One uses cumulated past investments of time to measure the value of the current stock of human capital. The other calculates the present value of the stream of future incremental earnings attributable to human capital. In principle, as we argue below, the latter research (used, e.g., by Bowman 1974) is superior.

If the first approach is used, results are sensitive to a number of differences in procedure. These include the calculation of a depreciation factor for invested funds and the classification of expenditures that are allocated to human capital accumulation. Examples of papers that use this approach are Kendrick (1976) and Schultz (1960).

To us, the second approach seems analytically superior. In the absence of an explicit market, the value of human capital must equal the discounted present value of the earnings stream that it generates. In general, this is likely to differ from the accumulated cost of inputs into human capital investment because the rate of return on inframarginal investments exceeds the discount rate.

A series of factors also affects estimates generated by the second approach, however. These include the method used to approximate the profile of future earnings for workers, the choice of discount rate used to compute the present value of earnings streams, and the choice of the wage rate of "nonimproved labor." An attractive feature of work in this group of studies, however, is that calculations can be related to explicit models of the human capital accumulation process. For example, previous work on earnings functions has been used to develop models explaining earnings that can then be estimated and subsequently simulated to produce a sequence of future earning returns to workers of different type. Incremental earnings returns can then be discounted back to compute the net present value. Examples of papers that use this approach are Graham and Webb (1979) and Kroch and Sjoblom (1986).

The earliest attempt to value the stock of human capital is by Schultz (1960). Schultz's motivation for calculating the size of the human capital stock was to evaluate the contribution of education to economic growth. He wished to be able to compare the value of investments in human and nonhuman capital, the stocks of human and physical capital, and the relative rates of return to these two investment vehicles.

Schultz calculated the human capital stock by cumulating educational expenditures. Direct costs and forgone earnings vary between elementary, secondary, and higher education. Forgone earnings were calculated by determining the number of weeks per year that a student is voluntarily out of the labor market, and multiplying this by the current average weekly wage in manufacturing (forgone earnings are typically at least 50% of the costs of education). Schultz determined the educational capital stock by summing together the product of total numbers of years of each type of education and its estimated cost. Schultz calculated that in 1957 the educational capital stock for the labor force aged over 14 was approximately 30% of the total capital stock; a relatively small number.

Kendrick (1976) also provided estimates of capital investment and cumulated stocks for various types of capital, including human capital. Human capital was separated into two categories: tangible and intangible human wealth. The former includes costs such as "rearing costs" incurred in raising children to working age (14 years). Only direct costs (i.e., not the opportunity cost of parent's time) is included. Intangible investments include expenditure on education, employee training, medical, health, safety, and mobility. Of the categories of human wealth considered by Kendrick, expenditures on education and employee training are of a discretionary nature and subject to tax effects.

Various sources, such as surveys and published data, were used by Kendrick to determine expenditures, and deflators were obtained to derive real expenditure. For educational expenditures, the procedure was to first estimate the average real expenditures per head by single age groups up to age 95, then cumulate per capita lifetime expenditures for each cohort for each year covered in the calculation. This is then multiplied by the number of persons in each age group each year and summed across age groups. A depreciation adjustment was applied to education investments beginning at age 28.

While it is not possible to compare exactly the calculations of Kendrick and Schultz, the estimates appear to be close since, according to Kendrick, the ratio of human to total wealth is approximately 28% in 1957.

Unlike the calculations of Kendrick and Schultz, Graham and Webb (1979) estimate the size of the stock of human wealth by capitalizing the flow of returns to human capital. The use of this approach is motivated by the observation that the services of human capital are priced in labor markets, in contrast to the services of physical capital goods.

The basis for their calculation is 1970 Public Use Survey data, collected from detailed census questionnaires. Their methodology involves assuming that all agents in the same age cohort with the same number of years of education are the same. Agents are assumed to engage in no postschool investment in human capital. To calculate lifetime expected earnings, a secular earnings growth rate is applied to earnings of workers currently possessing t years of schooling. This means that a younger person will have a higher earnings profile than an older person with the same level of education. Their earnings streams are based on expected earnings, which are weighted by probabilities of being alive at various ages derived from life tables. Present values of earnings for a representative agent of alternative ages and with various years of schooling are calculated. These are then multiplied by the number of agents and then summed over all values of age and schooling to find the aggregate human capital stock.

Graham and Webb present numerous graphs displaying the behavior of the human capital stock over time. The pattern of lifetime human wealth increases initially, followed by a decline to zero at retirement. The peak in the wealth series generally occurs at around age 40. The point at which depreciation begins depends on the number of years of schooling.

The size of the males-only capital stock is calculated by the authors for 1969, using a discount rate of 7.5%. Their estimates of $7.2 trillion compare to Kendrick's total nonhuman capital stock figure of $3.7 trillion. A 20% discount rate, however, lowers the figure to $2.9 trillion. Using the $7.2 trillion figure for human capital means that their estimate of the male human capital stock would be roughly twice the nonhuman capital stock reported by Kendrick.

A further paper by Kroch and Sjoblom (1986) also uses a present discounted earnings approach similar to that employed by Graham and Webb. Under their approach, the stream of earnings for a representative agent with given characteristics is constructed by first fitting an earnings function model of the type suggested by Mincer (1974) to longitudinal earnings data. Their earnings function depends on years of schooling, time worked, experience, vintage effects for persons, and various interaction terms (e.g., the product of experience and schooling, to allow for different effects of experience given different levels of schooling). This earnings function is then simulated to produce earnings profiles for given types of individuals. The resulting earnings streams provide a measure of returns to human capital, and these can then be aggregated over all individuals. An attractive feature of this work is that it focuses on schooling wealth, that is, the capitalized value of improvements made to labor. A separate estimate is reported for human wealth, which is schooling wealth plus the present value of the return to unimproved labour (the wage with zero years of schooling).

Using a discount rate of 4%, the authors report values of schooling wealth that are dramatically larger than the educational wealth estimates of Kendrick and Schultz. For 1980, the stock of human wealth is calculated to be $26.5 trillion, while schooling wealth is $18 trillion. For comparison, the Federal Reserve Board measure of the aggregate value of real capital was approximately $9.6 trillion. They suggest the gap between these measures has widened markedly since the early 1970s.

Finally, Jorgenson and Pachon (1983) obtain much higher values for the human capital stock by making an allowance for the value of home production. Their conclusion is that human capital may represent as much as 96% of the total capital stock of the United States. While one may wish to discount such a high figure, it is nonetheless clear that one underestimates considerably the value of the flow of services produced by human capital if one ignores household outputs.

The literature, therefore, exhibits considerable variability as to estimates of the value of the human capital stock. The divergence in results between the first approach (cumulating costs of investment) and the second (discounting future earnings) is explicable in terms of the latter capturing the impact of high inframarginal returns to human capital investment. We prefer the second approach on theoretical grounds, and therefore conclude that the literature supports the view that human capital is substantially larger in aggregate value than the physical capital stock. Some might feel that this is evident from the national accounts, which show that the return to human capital in the form of earnings is about three times capital income. The issue, however, is how much of the return to labor one attributes as a return to human capital.

Notes

1. A review of the literature should also mention Lord (1989), which uses a model in many ways similar to ours. Lord's paper came to our attention after this paper was completed. While our analysis focuses on the impact of income taxes relative to wage or consumption taxes, Lord is concerned only with the differences between wage and consumption taxes. Thus his paper is complementary to ours.

2. There has been considerable work, largely by Gary Becker and Nigel Tomes, on the importance of intergenerational links in human capital formation. Although parents cannot bequeath *their* human capital, they typically find it efficient to achieve much, if not all, of their desired transfers to offspring via investment in the *child's* human capital. In this context, estate and gift taxes, in addition to income taxes, can distort human capital investment. Further differences vis à vis the pure life-cycle model considered in this paper arise if capital market imperfections are taken into account. See Becker and Tomes (1986), Davies (1986), and Davies and St-Hilaire (1987).

3. See the original discussion in Becker (1975, 26–37), as well as Hashimoto (1981) and Carmichael (1983) for a more recent treatment.

4. Signaling models have been leant some attraction by the frequent observation that much formal education does not impart job-relevant skills. However, models of investment in person-specific information provide an alternative, and productive, explanation of the earnings payoff to forms of education that do not provide skills (see MacDonald 1980; and Davies and MacDonald 1984). The accumulation of information in these models is in fact a form of human capital investment.

5. In human capital theory an important distinction is made between "gross" or "potential" earnings, which represent the maximum that could be earned, holding leisure constant, and "net" earnings, which correspond to the observed labor income. (The difference between potential and net earnings represents the income forgone for the sake of human capital formation.) Taxes are, of course, levied on net earnings, that is, the portion of full labor income that is currently available for consumption. The treatment therefore corresponds to that given to a "qualified" or "registered" asset in the consumption tax literature (see U.S. Treasury 1977).

6. The diminishing rate of return to investment in human capital here is due solely to diminishing productivity of time and other inputs in human capital production. In an N-period model (Ben-Porath 1967) there will usually also be a decline in the marginal rate of return to a given amount of human capital investment as the individual ages, due to the ever-receding remaining length of the working life.

7. There has recently been considerable interest in the impact of liquidity constraints in intertemporal tax analysis (see Hubbard and Judd 1986; and Browning and Burbidge 1988). It would clearly be very simple to address the implications in figures 6.1 and 6.2. One important implication is that, to the extent that such a borrowing constraint is effective, the distorting effects on human capital investment of interest income taxation discussed below are absent.

8. This is an interesting point since, as outlined in app. A, recent estimates of the value of the human capital stock suggest that it exceeds that of the physical capital stock by a ratio of about three to one.

9. Partial equilibrium welfare calculations can be generated as a by-product of the full dynamic simulations we perform later in the paper. As discussed below, the results of these calculations are not inconsistent with the DR partial equilibrium results.

10. Also, as pointed out by Sherwin Rosen in his comments on this paper, to the extent that human capital increases productivity in nonmarket activities ("leisure"), which produce untaxed income in kind, *any* subsidy to schooling, implicit or otherwise, tends to encourage overinvestment in human capital.

11. A still more general model would incorporate married couples, differentiating between the labor supplied by, and leisure consumed by, the two spouses. There are of course many possible tax effects on the division of labor between husbands and wives. Also, men and women still exhibit marked differences in patterns of human capital investment. It would be interesting to consider the impacts of alternative forms of taxation on these patterns, but that is beyond the scope of this paper.

12. Recently, a variety of alternative explanations for personal wage growth over the life-cycle have emerged. Lazear (1979) has suggested, for example, that positively sloped age-earnings profiles would be observed even if workers' marginal productivity did not vary over the life-cycle in an equilibrium where an incentive mechanism was required to discourage shirking. More recent literature confirms that a rising wage profile may be an important element in such equilibrium mechanisms (see, e.g., Kuhn 1986). To the extent that such factors, rather than human capital investment, explain the shape of the age-earnings profile, interest income taxes might have quite different effects on age-earnings profiles than they do here, with differing consequences for saving.

13. Along a balanced growth path each generation makes the same investment in human capital and provides the same labor supply. Aggregate labour supply, H_t^m, therefore grows at the rate n. Given our specification of (1), such an outcome is only possible with Cobb-Douglas preferences if $g > 0$. Otherwise succeeding cohorts will have differing labor-supply plans. In order to use a more general form of (1), AKS set $g = 0$.

14. Although this specification is widely used in the literature, the implied age profile of consumption departs markedly from what is observed. As is well known, actual age profiles of consumption are hump shaped. The implications for intertemporal tax analysis are discussed in Davies (1988) and Browning and Burbidge (1988).

15. Under Ben-Porath neutrality, an increase in H_t raises the productivity of time in the labor market and in the production of human capital equiproportionally.

16. In fact, (15) is the basic functional form estimated by Heckman (1975), whose results reject the hypothesis that H_t should appear in (14). (In contrast, some other contributions to the empirical literature, e.g., Haley 1976, adopt [14″] as a maintained hypothesis.)

17. In a Summers-type model, g governs the age profile of earnings, which is of course exponential, as well as secular wage growth. Investment in human capital increases the steepness of the age profile of earnings. With any "reasonable" amount of such investment, $g = .02$ would give an extremely steep earnings trajectory, making it impossible to generate sufficient aggregate saving to get the desired steady-state stock of physical capital, given Summers's values for the taste parameters.

18. Our choices of δ and θ are not inconsistent with available empirical evidence (which is, however, limited). Estimates of δ vary widely, from about 0.2% (Heckman 1975), to 1.2% (Mincer 1974), to 3%–4% (Haley 1976). Heckman's (1975) estimate of θ was 0.67.

19. This assumption turns out to produce only a small deviation in the results from

those obtained with Summers's approach. Each individual expects (correctly) that transfers will grow at the rate g in future. If this rate corresponded to the desired growth rate of consumption, paying out the revenues as lump-sum transfers unrelated to age would produce no change in saving (as compared to not paying any transfers). In fact, in the runs reported here the desired growth rate of consumption exceeds g, so that paying out transfers in this way generates some additional saving. The effect on the results is not marked, however.

20. The postponement effect was identified by Summers (1981, 539). With an exogenously growing revenue requirement and year-by-year budget balance, any given cohort will bear a lower present value of lifetime taxes the later it tends to pay its taxes in the life-cycle. Here, when human capital is endogenous the new steady state under the wage tax features somewhat reduced human capital investment. This tilts the age profile of earnings toward the present, resulting in earlier payment of taxes over the life-cycle under a wage tax (but *not* under a consumption tax). This appears to explain the difference here in steady-state welfare gains with exogenous vs. endogenous human capital in the wage tax experiment.

21. That the wage and consumption tax experiments produce slightly better results here in transition when human capital is exogenous may partly reflect the impact of myopic expectations. As shown in tables 6.3 and 6.4, there is a rapid decline in the rate of return on physical capital in the first 10–20 years of transition. Both human capital investment and saving decisions made in the earliest transition years under the expectation of continued high interest rates turn out ex post to have been quite wrong. In particular it turns out *not* to have been a good idea to largely cease all human capital investment, as occurs in the first few transition years with human capital endogenous. If unchanged human capital investment is closer to the perfect foresight policy in these years, one would expect that welfare in transition would be higher with exogenous rather than endogenous human capital, which is what we obtain.

22. The *levels* of the partial equilibrium gains are very sensitive to the parameterization of the utility function. In contrast, the exogenous-endogenous differential in EVs is primarily determined by the shape of the human capital production function. This is because the only difference between the two cases in partial equilibrium analysis is that the distortion in human capital investment is removed by wage or consumption taxes if human capital is endogenous, but not if it is exogenous. The severity of the distortion does not depend on preferences, since the human capital plan here is wealth maximizing.

23. Since we have set the depreciation rate of human capital at 1%, this 0.7% depletion is close to the maximum possible in a single year and reflects a radical short-run change in the allocation of time. There is almost a complete collapse of training activity in the impact year, and it takes several periods before training returns to levels close to those of the base-case steady state. An immediate result of the decline in training time is a substantial increase in labor supply. This is the sole reason for the 8.1% first-period decline in the capital-labor ratio under both wage and consumption tax experiments.

References

Ashenfelter, O. C., and R. Layard, eds. 1986. *Handbook of Labor Economics*. Amsterdam: North-Holland.

Auerbach, A. J., and L. J. Kotlikoff. 1983. National Savings, Economic Welfare, and the Structure of Taxation. In *Behavioral Simulation Methods in Tax Policy Analysis*, ed. M. Feldstein. Chicago: University of Chicago Press.

———. 1987. *Dynamic Fiscal Policy*. Cambridge: Cambridge University Press.

Auerbach, A. J., L. J. Kotlikoff, and J. Skinner. 1983. The Efficiency Gains from Dynamic Tax Reforms. *International Economic Review*, 24:81–100.

Ballard, C. L., D. Fullerton, J. B. Shoven, and J. Whalley. 1985. *A General Equilibrium Model for Tax Policy Analysis*. Chicago: University of Chicago Press.

Becker, G. S. 1975. *Human Capital*, 2d ed. New York: Columbia University Press.

Becker, G. S., and N. Tomes. 1986. Human Capital and the Rise and Fall of Families. *Journal of Labor Economics* 4 (3):S1–S39.

Ben-Porath, Y. 1967. The Production of Human Capital and the Life Cycle of Earnings. *Journal of Political Economy* 75 (supp.): 352–65.

Blinder, A. S., and Y. Weiss. 1976. Human Capital and Labor Supply: A Synthesis. *Journal of Political Economy* 84: 449–72.

Boskin, M. J. 1975. Notes on the Tax Treatment of Human Capital. In *Conference on Tax Research*. Office of Tax Analysis, Department of the Treasury, Washington, D.C.

Bowman, M. J. 1974. Postschool Learning and Human Resource Accounting. *Review of Income and Wealth*, (December): 48–99.

Browning, M., and J. Burbidge. 1988. Consumption and Income Taxation. McMaster University, September. Mimeograph.

Carmichael, L. 1983. Firm-specific Human Capital and Promotion Ladders. *Bell Journal of Economics* 14, no. 1 (Spring): 251–58.

Chamley, C. 1981. The Welfare Cost of Capital Income Taxation in a Growing Economy. *Journal of Political Economy* 89 (3): 468–96.

Davies, J. B. 1986. Does Redistribution Reduce Inequality? *Journal of Labor Economics* 4, no. 4 (October): 538–59.

———. 1988. Family Size, Household Production, and Life Cycle Saving. *Annales d'Economie et de Statistique*, no. 9, 141–65.

Davies, J. B., B. Hamilton, and J. Whalley. 1989. Capital Income Taxation in a Two-Commodity Life Cycle Model: The Role of Factor Intensity and Asset Capitalization Effects. *Journal of Public Economics* 39:109–26.

Davies, J. B., and G. M. MacDonald. 1984. *Information in the Labour Market: Job-Worker Matching and Its Implications for Education in Ontario*. Toronto: University of Toronto Press.

Davies, J. B., and F. St-Hilaire. 1987. *Reforming Capital Income Taxation in Canada*. Ottawa: Economic Council of Canada.

Davies, J. B., F. St-Hilaire, and J. Whalley. 1984. Some Calculations of Lifetime Tax Incidence. *American Economic Review* 74, no. 4 (September): 633–49.

Driffill, E. J., and H. S. Rosen. 1983. Taxation and Excess Burden: A Life-Cycle Perspective. *International Economic Review* 24, no. 3 (October): 671–83.

Eaton, J., and H. S. Rosen. 1980. Taxation, Human Capital, and Uncertainty. *American Economic Review* 70, no. 4 (September): 705–15.

Graham, J. W., and R. H. Webb. 1979. Stocks and Depreciation of Human Capital: New Evidence from a Present-Value Perspective. *Review of Income and Wealth* (June): 209–24.

Haley, W. J. 1976. Estimation of the Earnings Profile from Optimal Human Capital Accumulation. *Econometrica* 44, no. 6 (November): 1223–38.

Hamilton, J. H. 1987. Optimal Wage and Income Taxation with Wage Uncertainty. *International Economic Review* 28:373–88.

Harberger, A. C. 1964. Taxation, Resource Allocation and Welfare. In *The Role of Direct and Indirect Taxes in the Federal Reserve System*. Princeton, N.J.: Princeton University Press.

Hashimoto, M. 1981. Firm-specific Human Capital as a Shared Investment. *American Economic Review* 71 (June): 475–82.

Heckman, J. J. 1975. Estimates of a Human Capital Production Function Embedded in a Life-Cycle Model of Labor Supply. In *Household Production and Consumption*, ed. N. Terlekyj. NBER Studies in Income and Wealth, vol. 40. New York: Columbia University Press.

———. 1976. A Life Cycle Model of Earnings, Learning and Consumption," *Journal of Political Economy* 84 (August): 511–44.

Hines, F., L. Tweeten, and M. Redfern. 1970. Social and Private Rates of Return to Investment in Schooling, by Race-Sex Groups and Regions. *The Journal of Human Resources* 5(3):318–40.

Hubbard, R. G., and K. L. Judd. 1986. Liquidity Constraints, Fiscal Policy and Consumption. *Brookings Papers, on Economic Activity*, no. 1, 1–50.

Jorgenson, D. W., and A. Pachon. 1983. The Accumulation of Human/Non-Human Capital. In *The Determinants of National Saving and Wealth*, ed. F. Modigliani and R. Hemmings. Proceedings of a conference held by the International Economic Association at Bergamo, Italy. New York: St. Martin's.

Kendrick, J. 1976. *The Formation and Stocks of Total Capital*. New York: Columbia University Press.

King, M. A., and D. Fullerton, eds. 1984. *The Taxation of Income from Capital: A Comparative Study of the United States, the United Kingdom, Sweden, and West Germany*. Chicago: University of Chicago Press.

Kotlikoff, L. J., and L. H. Summers. 1979. Tax Incidence in a Life Cycle Model with Variable Labor Supply. *Quarterly Journal of Economics* 93, no. 4 (November): 705–18.

Kroch, E., and K. Sjoblom. 1986. Education and the National Wealth of the United States. *Review of Income and Wealth* (March): 87–106.

Kuhn, P. 1986. Wages, Effort, and Incentive Compatibility in Life-Cycle Employment Contracts. *Journal of Labor Economics* 4, no. 1 (January): 28–49.

Lazear, E. 1979. Why Is There Mandatory Retirement? *Journal of Political Economy* 87, no. 6 (December): 1261–84.

Lord, William. 1989. The Transition from Payroll to Consumption Receipts with Endogenous Human Capital. *Journal of Public Economics* 38 (February): 53–74.

MacDonald, G. M. 1980. Person-Specific Information in the Labor Market. *Journal of Political Economy* 88, no. 3 (June): 578–97.

Mincer, J. 1974. *Schooling, Experience and Earnings*. New York: Columbia University Press.

Schultz, T. W. 1960. Capital Formation by Education. *Journal of Political Economy* 68 (December): 571–83.

Shoven, J., and J. Whalley. 1973. General Equilibrium with Taxes: A Computational Procedure and an Existence Proof. *Review of Economic Studies* 40: 475–89.

Spence, A. M. 1973. Job Market Signalling. *Quarterly Journal of Economics* 87: 353–74.

Summers, L. H. 1980. Capital Taxation and Accumulation in a Life Cycle Growth Model. Paper presented at NBER conference on the Taxation of Capital, November 16 and 17. Mimeograph.

———. 1981. Capital Taxation and Accumulation in a Life Cycle Growth Model. *American Economic Review* 71 (4): 533–44.

U.S. Treasury. 1977. *Blueprints for Basic Tax Reform*. Washington, D.C.: Government Printing Office.

Weiss, Y. M. 1986. The Determination of Life-Cycle Earnings: A Survey. In *Handbook of Labor Economics*, ed. O. C. Ashenfelter and R. Layard. Amsterdam: North Holland.

Willis, R. J. 1986. Wage Determinants: A Survey and Reinterpretation of Human Capital Earnings Functions. In *Handbook of Labor Economics,* ed. O. C. Ashenfelter and R. Layard. Amsterdam: North Holland.

Wright, C. 1969. Saving and the Rate of Interest. In *The Taxation of Income from Capital,* ed. A. C. Harberger and Martin J. Bailey. Washington, D.C.: Brookings.

Comment   Sherwin Rosen

This is an excellent paper. It is the most complete analysis available on how human capital considerations affect income and expenditure tax distortions. The principal finding that human capital does not affect welfare calculations very much is compelling and consistent with what is known about this problem from a partial equilibrium perspective.

The most important fact about tax distortions on human capital investment is that most investment costs consist of forgone earnings and are fully "expensed" for tax purposes (Becker 1975). Accelerated depreciation of human capital eliminates most direct tax distortions. The easiest way to see this is in a school-stopping model. A person with labor-market experience x has a gross of tax earning stream of $y(x, S)$ upon completing S years of school, with y increasing S. For an income tax at rate t and out-of-pocket (tuition, books) flow expense $c(S)$, human wealth is

$$(1) \qquad W(S) = e^{-rs} \int_0^N (1 - t)y(v, S)e^{-rv}dv - \int_0^S c(z)e^{-rz}dz,$$

because $c(S)$ is not tax deductible. Thus S is chosen to maximize $W(S)$: this occurs where the marginal after-tax internal rate of return equals the after-tax interest rate. Now if $c(S)$ is small then $(1 - t)$ multiplies both marginal costs and marginal returns and cancels out. Progressive taxation is necessary to get some effect. If $c(S)$ is not small, then even proportionate taxation discourages investment. It is generally thought that forgone earnings account for three-fourths of total school expenditure. Rising costs of college tuition and related expenses in the past decade may have decreased the proportion recently, but probably not by much. There is also evidence that the return to schooling is discontinuous in degree attainment. This "sheepskin effect" gives an extra return for actually completing a degree. Both factors suggest that proportional income taxation has little direct effect on schooling choices.

The authors concentrate on on-the-job training and do not consider school investments. Taxes could affect human capital investment indirectly by affecting the composition, stability, and division of labor within families and the

Sherwin Rosen is the Edwin A. and Betty L. Bergman Professor in the department of economics at the University of Chicago and a research associate of the National Bureau of Economic Research.

labor-force participation of women. Youth dependency amounts to something like one-fourth to one-third of one's life and a nontrivial fraction of human capital investment takes place in the home in those years. Household production is tax exempt and is encouraged by both income and expenditure taxation, but this never gets counted in the calculations. Of course marital instability, declining fertility, and increasing labor-force participation of women have all affected human capital formation in recent decades, but few of these large social changes are thought to be closely associated with income or expenditure tax policy.

Davies and Whalley's simulations are based on the standard utilitarian calculus without explicit intergenerational linkages in preferences. Their analysis can be simplified by solving the time allocation variable s out of the general model and specifying earnings as a function of skills, learning, and work time instead. Thus write $y = g(H, \dot{H}, L)$, where H is human capital stock and $\dot{H}$ is investment, with $g_1 > 0$, $g_2 < 0$, and $g_3 < 0$. If A is financial assets, r the rate of interest, t the rate of income taxation, and t^* the rate of expenditure taxation, then the flow constraint on the intertemporal problem amounts to

$$(2) \qquad \dot{A} = (1-t)[rA + g(H, \dot{H}, L)] - C/(1-t^*),$$

assuming that all human capital investments are fully expensed for tax purposes.

Adding constraint (2) to their preference structure and examining the Euler equations shows the following:

(i) Both t and t^* enter the marginal condition for leisure in the same way and have identical distortions on labor supply.

(ii) The expenditure tax t^* multiplies both sides of the intertemporal consumption decision and cancels out. It is nondistorting on saving. The income tax does not factor out and has a distorting effect on saving and nonhuman investment.

(iii) Both t and t^* drop out of the marginal condition for human capital investment and have no direct effects. There is an indirect effect, because income taxes distort the valuation of future money relative to present money and taxes affect labor supply decisions. Both enter the human capital investment decision.

The main point is that introducing human capital does not add any direct distortions. All of the calculations depend on indirect effects and these turn out to be small. In fact introducing a substitute for nonhuman capital makes things better from the welfare point of view. In the simulations reported in the paper, the labor margin is suppressed and hours are fixed. Allowing hours to adjust would increase the calculated distortion, but the effect would be small for men because their compensated labor-supply elasticity is small. Expanding the model to include women would be more interesting because their wage elasticity of participation is larger, but even so the resulting welfare loss depends on the degree of substitution between market and nonmarket production, and little is known about that.

The simulations are built upon the important unstated assumption that human capital has no value outside of the market sector. Suppose the opposite, that human capital has as much value in nonmarket production as in market production. Then even hours worked in the market do not directly affect the return on human capital. However, since human capital used in household production is not taxed, both income and consumption taxes encourage its utilization there and this stimulates excess investment from the social point of view. In this case there is a *direct* distortion on the human capital margin and eliminating another investment distortion through consumption over income taxation might have much larger welfare effects than are calculated here.

Davies and Whalley point out that their analysis only covers worker-financed investments. However, firm-financed investments are similar because most firm-specific human capital investment costs are wage payments and these are fully expensed in tax accounting of firms: accelerated depreciation of human capital applies to firms as well as individuals, and most of what remains are only indirect effects.

While it probably does not affect the central conclusion, there is a conceptual objection to the form of the investment production function chosen for analysis that is obscured by the way in which the model is presented. The slope $-dy/dH = -g_2$ in the earnings function defined above is the marginal cost of investment. On their assumption that the investment production function only depends on s, direct calculation reveals that the marginal cost of investing is increasing in H. This implies that more able people whose endowments of capital are larger invest less than less able people; and that aggregate investment should fall over time, as labor augmenting technical change increases effective endowments. Neither is true. Specifying marginal cost as decreasing in embodied knowledge is preferable on these grounds. Models with that kind of increasing return do exist (Rosen 1976) and could be worked into the analysis with no greater effort than the form now used. Whatever that may be, the analysis makes no reference to changes over time in the social knowledge available for people to invest in, except insofar as it appears in exogenous technical change. This follows the human capital literature, but who is so sure that tax treatments of human capital do not have anything to do with the invention of new knowledge?

Finally, we have here another all-too-familiar instance where the pure economic case for expenditure taxation is firmly established, but where it is not much used. In this sense income taxation is related to such policies as tariffs and quotas, minimum wages, rent controls and price supports—all cases where economists' overwhelming consensus is hardly reflected in actual public policy. Could it be that political considerations enter the determination of which instruments are used? Income taxes seem to have agency-like virtues of clarifying the amounts actually paid by taxpayers and thereby serve as some limit, however small, to the size of the public sector. Value-added taxes are hard to count and do not have these virtues.

References

Becker, Gary S. 1975. *Human Capital,* 2d ed. New York: Columbia University Press for the National Bureau of Economic Research.
Rosen, Sherwin. 1976. A Theory of Life Earnings. *Journal of Political Economy,* 84, no. 4, pt. 2: S45–S67.

7 National Saving and International Investment

Martin Feldstein and Philippe Bacchetta

7.1 Introduction

Do tax policies that stimulate a nation's private saving rate increase its domestic capital stock or do the extra savings flow abroad? Does an increase in the corporate tax rate cause an outflow of capital that shifts the burden of that tax increase to labor and land?

These were the two key questions that motivated the 1980 Feldstein-Horioka (FH) study of the relation between domestic saving rates and domestic investment. FH reasoned that, if domestic saving were added to a world saving pool and domestic investment competed for funds in that same world saving pool, there would be no correlation between a nation's saving rate and its rate of investment. The statistical evidence showed that, on the contrary, the long-term saving and investment rates of the individual industrialized countries in the OECD are highly correlated. The data were consistent with the view that a sustained one-percentage-point increase in the saving rate induced nearly a one-percentage-point increase in the investment rate.

Much has happened in the international capital markets during the decade since the Feldstein-Horioka study was done. The 1980s saw an unprecedented increase in the international flow of capital to the United States. Capital market barriers in Japan and Europe have been lowered or eliminated. This experience raises the question of whether the empirical regularity observed for the 1960s and 1970s continued through the 1980s. Even those studies that followed Feldstein-Horioka were limited to data for the 1970s or the early 1980s.[1] One purpose of the present study is to examine the experience for the

Martin Feldstein is professor of economics at Harvard University and president of the National Bureau of Economic Research, Cambridge, Massachusetts. Philippe Bacchetta is assistant professor of economics at the Escuela Superior de Administración y Dirección de Empresas, Barcelona, Spain, and this research was conducted while he was an assistant professor at Brandeis University. The authors are grateful to Rudiger Dornbusch, Jeffrey Frankel, and Maurice Obstfeld.

period 1980 through 1986 and to compare the results with the analysis for earlier years.

7.1.1   International Capital Mobility and Risk Aversion

The initial FH paper created confusion about the interpretation of the results by discussing them as evidence about international capital mobility. Economists who believe that the evidence on interest arbitrage implies that there is perfect capital mobility were therefore inclined to reject the FH findings. Fortunately, Jeffrey Frankel (1986) clarified the issue by reminding everyone that perfect capital mobility does not imply the international equalization of *real* interest rates.[2]

More specifically, as Frankel pointed out, the interest arbitrage condition of integrated capital markets refers to nominal interest rates only. Perfect capital mobility implies equal ex ante real interest rates only for time periods for which the expected change in the exchange rate equals the difference in the expected inflation rates. As Frankel stresses, since ex ante purchasing power parity may not hold even for periods as long as a decade, the existence of perfect capital markets (in the sense that the interest differential between two countries is equal to the expected change in the nominal exchange rate) does not imply a continuing equality of expected real interest rates. An increase in saving in one country that gives rise to an equal increase in its investment need not violate the nominal interest arbitrage condition even though it causes a decline in the real interest rate.

Purchasing power parity does not appear to hold, even in the long run that is relevant for the tax policy questions that motivated this research. But even if it did, in that very long run the difference between the nominal interest rates in each pair of countries may no longer equal the expected change in the exchange rate because of investor risk aversion. An investor looking ahead for 10 years or more must be concerned about risks of changes in tax rules on foreign source income or even in political institutions that can affect the value of his international investments. Opportunities to hedge the interest rate or exchange rate risk on long-term positions are far more limited than for short-term positions, or at least have been until quite recently. For such long horizons, investor risk aversion may induce portfolio investors to prefer investments in their own currency. As a result, expected real interest rates may also differ internationally in the long run.

In a riskless world, long-term nominal interest rate arbitrage could be achieved even though international investors only took net positions in the short-term market if domestic investors arbitraged short-term and long-term domestic interest rates. Once risk is introduced, however, arbitrage by hedged international short-term investors and the equilibrium of risk-averse domestic investors who hold both long-term and short-term securities is not enough to provide international equality of long-term rates.

As an example, a mean-variance investor will allocate his wealth among assets in proportions that vary positively with yield and inversely with risk. An investor who has a high degree of risk aversion or who attributes a large subjective variance to long-term investments in foreign assets may want to invest a large share of his portfolio in domestic assets (depending on asset yield covariances) even when a substantial expected yield difference exists in favor of the foreign assets. Since the mean-variance investor's optimal proportional allocation of the assets is independent of the total value, an increase in saving that raises the total pool of funds will be invested primarily in the domestic economy.

In short, there is no presumption that real long-term yields would be equalized even if all investors were completely free to invest wherever in the world they want. Moreover, broad classes of financial institutions (and, in some countries, nonfinancial corporations as well) are in fact not permitted by regulatory authorities to take net positions in foreign currences. Many nonfinancial corporations also choose to avoid net foreign exchange exposure as a matter of policy rather than to evaluate the opportunities available at each point in time. The absence of these substantial pools of funds from the potential pool of arbitrage funds would not be important if other investors were risk neutral. However, if the remaining investors are risk averse, the limited size of the mobile pool of unhedged funds increases the potential importance of risk aversion and, therefore, the scope for expected real rates of return to remain unequal.

7.1.2 Government Policies and the Current Account

Although the lack of ex ante purchasing power parity and the risk aversion of international investors are sufficient to permit domestic saving rates to influence substantially the rate of domestic investment, the observed link between saving and investment may also reflect explicit government policy decisions.

It is easy to understand why governments would want to restrict the size of trade imbalances in general and of changes in trade imbalances in particular. Since an increase in the merchandise trade deficit means a loss of exports and the substitution of imports for domestic production, the affected domestic industries are likely to seek government actions to shrink the trade deficit. A decrease in the merchandise trade deficit caused by a spontaneous increase in the demand for the country's exports may be welcome if there is excess capacity in the economy but would be resisted by the government as a source of inflation if there is not excess capacity. Since a rise in exports in a fully employed economy also means a fall in the production of other goods and services, the industries producing for the domestic market are likely to seek policies to reverse the rise in exports.

These arguments refer to changes in the trade balance rather than to its level. Why should a government resist a long-run current account deficit or surplus? One answer is that an economy that starts in trade balance will not want to shift to a long-run imbalance because of its reluctance to accept the dislocations involved in changing the pattern of production from trade balance to trade imbalance. But there are also reasons why a government would resist a long-term trade and current account imbalance in addition to the problems of transition.

Because of capital income taxes, a persistent capital outflow diverts domestic savings to investment abroad that has a lower return to the originating nation. Each government therefore has an incentive to seek a capital inflow and to resist the outflow of its own capital.

A country with a trade surplus and a capital outflow also has the opportunity to trade a reduction in the trade surplus for a higher level of real income (through an improvement in the terms of trade) and a temporarily lower level of inflation (through the favorable "supply shock" of an increase in the level of the currency).

There are a variety of policies that governments can use to shift the economy toward trade and current account balance. In the short run, monetary policy can be used to influence the exchange rate and the level of economic activity. Summers (1988) has suggested that governments may tailor the size of the budget deficit to offset differences between private saving and investment. Other possibilities include the use of targeted tax policies designed to increase or decrease the level of investment or private saving: the investment tax credit, the schedule of depreciation allowances, the availability of special tax preferred savings accounts, a difference in the tax rates on capital and labor income, and so on.

7.1.3   Implication for the Effects of Fiscal Policies

The reason that saving and investment are closely correlated is important for answering the questions that motivated the original study.

Consider the Summers (1988) hypothesis that the close correlation between investment and saving reflects the response of government deficit policy to shifts in private investment and saving. If a tax change that encourages private saving is offset by an increase in the government budget deficit, there is no rise in capital formation. If however the close correlation between saving and investment reflects either the reluctance of private risk-averse investors to move capital abroad (so that private investment rises automatically) or a government tax policy to stimulate private investment until it absorbs all of the increase in domestic saving (rather than permit a capital outflow or a contraction of national income), the tax-induced rise in saving does get converted into greater domestic capital formation.

The reason for the observed saving-investment correlation is also important for assessing whether a tax on investment income causes a capital outflow that permits the incidence of the tax to be shifted to labor. If the observed saving-investment correlation reflects the unwillingness of risk-averse domestic investors to shift capital abroad, the increase in the capital tax causes a fall in the net of tax rate of return and thus no shifting of the tax burden. In contrast, if the saving-investment equality occurs because of a government decision to increase the budget deficit to absorb the capital that would otherwise go abroad, leaving just enough domestic saving to finance a level of investment at which the after-tax return is equal to the after-tax return abroad, the tax is fully shifted.

In support of the "endogenous deficit policy" hypothesis, Summers (1988) presents a regression for a cross-section of industrialized countries of the average deficit-GNP ratio for the period of 1973–80 on the average private saving-investment gap (the difference between net private saving and net private investment) for those same years. He finds a coefficient of 0.72 and concludes that it implies that 72 percent of the net savings gap may be offset by an explicit budget deficit policy.

There is however a quite different interpretation of the Summers deficit regression. If the long-run level of the budget deficit is thought of as exogenous (reflecting political considerations in the county rather than an attempt to offset the saving-investment gap), then the regression may only reflect the impact of the budget deficit on the level of investment. This would be the traditional crowding out of private investment by government deficits. Summers presents no evidence or reason to think that his regression should be interpreted as a policy response function rather than as a description of the crowding out of private investment by government deficits. We return to this in section 7.5 below.

7.1.4   Statistical Estimates

First, however we will turn to the evidence on the link between saving and investment in the most recently available data. We also take this opportunity to consider whether the correlation between saving and investment is equally strong for different subsets of countries within the OECD, including separate analyses for the European Economic Community (EEC) and non-EEC countries.

Previous comments on the FH regressions raised the issue of the possible endogeneity of national saving rates. This was actually discussed in the original FH paper and estimates using instrumental variables provided as a check on the possible bias from this source. The instrumental variables were demographic and social security variables. The resulting coefficient confirmed the ordinary least squares results. Since this issue has been explored rather thoroughly in the earlier paper, we will not present such instrumental variable estimates in the current analysis.

We will however examine two other issues in some detail. The first is the suggestion by Obstfeld (1986) that the observed correlation may reflect the common influence of economic growth on both saving and investment. We replicate the Obstfeld analysis in section 7.3 and show that, although it can in theory explain the observed saving-investment correlation, the actual data are not consistent with the Obstfeld hypothesis.

The second is an analysis of the dynamic adjustment process by which saving and investment adjust to changes in the saving-investment gap. We show in section 7.6 that the process can be described as an adjustment of investment to close the gap and not an adjustment of saving. We also present some evidence that suggests that the desired gap is not zero in all countries but that countries adjust investment to close the difference between the actual saving-investment gap and a preferred gap.

7.2   Is Capital Market Integration Increasing?

The reduction in government barriers to international capital flows, the creation of extensive new hedging markets, and the growing sophistication of financial institutions around the world have increased the likelihood of net capital flows. The sharp fall in the U.S. national saving rate in the 1980s (due to both the increased budget deficit and the decline in private saving) also provided a major incentive for the shift of capital to the United States.

The evidence in this section indicates that there has in fact been a substantial decline in the correlation between the rates of gross domestic saving and gross domestic investment. However, the effect of additional domestic saving on domestic investment remains quite substantial. Even in the 1980s, each dollar of additional saving is associated with an increase in investment of more than 50 cents.

The analysis is based on the regression equation

$$(1) \qquad\qquad I_t/Y_t = a_0 + a_1 S_t/Y_t,$$

where I_t is gross investment (as defined by the OECD and including inventory investment), Y_t is gross domestic product, and S_t is gross saving. The estimates use data for 23 OECD countries (excluding Luxembourg). The unit of observation is a single country and the data for that country has been averaged over a group of years. The coefficient a_1 that indicates the proportion of the incremental savings that is invested domestically will be referred to as the "savings retention coefficient."

Consider first the estimates for gross investment presented in column 1 of table 7.1. In the decade of the 1960s, each extra dollar of domestic saving increased domestic investment 91.4 cents with a standard error of 6.3 cents. For the next decade this had declined to 80.5 cents with a standard error of 12.1 cents. The decline of 10.9 cents is, however, less than the 13.6 cent standard error of the difference. The seven available years of the 1980s shows a further decline to 60.7 cents with a standard error of 12.6 cents. Although the 19.8 cents decline from the 1970s is only slightly larger than the associated standard error of 17.5 cents, the pattern of continuing decline from the

Table 7.1   **The Changing Impact of Domestic Savings on Domestic Investment**

Period	23 OECD Countries		9 EEC Countries		14 Non-EEC OECD Countries		17 OECD European Countries		8 Non-EEC OECD European Countries	
	Gross (1)	Net (2)	Gross (3)	Net (4)	Gross (5)	Net (6)	Gross (7)	Net (8)	Gross (9)	Net (10)
1960–69	.848	.914	.913	.742	.884	.962	.940	.835	.877	.870
	(.063)	(.081)	(.109)	(.173)	(.072)	(.091)	(.082)	(.111)	(.166)	(.146)
1970–79	.671	.805	.864	.652	.956	.810	.831	.770	.810	.636
	(.121)	(.122)	(.302)	(.282)	(.141)	(.140)	(.204)	(.173)	(.399)	(.239)
1980–86	.863	.607	.792	.356	.509	.578	.807	.581	.792	.555
	(.126)	(.136)	(.342)	(.461)	(.134)	(.145)	(.156)	(.180)	(.203)	(.224)
1960–73	.718	.911	.894	.725	.961	.951	.878	.832	.837	.906
	(.066)	(.077)	(.152)	(.211)	(.071)	(.076)	(.105)	(.114)	(.232)	(.105)
1974–86	.868	.669	.878	.462	.804	.628	.868	.641	.874	.521
	(.145)	(.154)	(.383)	(.431)	(.161)	(.172)	(.202)	(.221)	(.303)	(.308)
1960–86	.833	.791	.865	.524	.830	.816	.867	.717	.847	.668
	(.094)	(.111)	(.243)	(.318)	(.098)	(.111)	(.140)	(.158)	(.218)	(.185)

1960s implies a more significant relation. From the 1960s to the 1980s the decline of 30.7 cents is more than twice the standard error associated with this difference.

Another way of comparing the earlier and later parts of the 27-year sample period is to contrast the earlier fixed exchange rate years (1960–73) with the later floating rate years (1974–86). During the earlier 14 years the savings retention coefficient was 0.911 (standard error 0.066), barely different from the result for the decade of the 1960s. The coefficient for the later 13 years was, however, 0.669, much more similar to the coefficient for the 1980s. The difference of 0.242 is approximately 1.5 times it standard error.

The final row of column 1 in table 7.1 shows that, for the 27-year period as a whole, the savings retention coefficient was 0.791 with a standard error of 0.094. A potentially interesting line of analysis that we have not pursued would be to test whether the investment-savings relation has changed at a constant rate during this period or has had significant step changes after the beginning of the floating rate period or in the decade of the 1980s.

The net saving and investment relations (shown in col. 2 of table 7.1) do not indicate a fall over time similar to the corresponding gross saving-investment coefficients. The key savings retention coefficient only declines from 0.913 in the 1960s to 0.864 in the 1970s and 0.792 in 1980–86; none of the difference, including the difference between the 1960s and the 1980s, is as large as its standard error.

This difference between the gross and net saving-investment relations masks a more complex difference between the changes over time in the countries and among the non-EEC industrial countries of the OECD. The differences in experience among different groups of countries is the subject of the next section of this paper.

7.3 Capital Flows and the EEC

Although capital might in principle flow with equal ease among all countries or at least all industrial countries, the availability of market information, the existence of institutional relationships, and the perception of risk might make capital flows greater among some pairs of countries than among others. More specifically, in the current context, each extra dollar of saving in one country may be divided between the home capital market (which gets the largest share) and other individual national capital markets in a way that depends on a variety of institutional and other country-specific factors.

We have explored this possibility by looking separately at the investment-saving equation for nine of the EEC countries (excluding the new entrants, Spain and Portugal, as well as Luxembourg) and the investment-saving equation for the remaining 14 OECD countries. It should be emphasized that the EEC savings retention coefficient does not reflect the extent of the capital flow among the EEC countries but rather the extent to which individual EEC countries retain their national savings within the saving country.

Consider first the behavior of the investment-saving relation in the nine EEC countries shown in columns 3 and 4 of table 7.1. The gross savings retention coefficients, shown in column 3, are lower among the EEC countries than for the entire OECD group and decline much more rapidly between the 1970s and the 1980s. The decline from 0.742 in the 1960s to 0.652 in the 1970s was not large, but this was followed by a sharp decline to only 0.356 in the 1980–86 period. By comparison, the coefficients of the 14 non-EEC members of the OECD was 0.962 in the 1960s, 0.810 in the 1970s, and 0.578 in the 1980s.

We should caution, however, that the standard errors of the coefficients for the EEC countries are quite large since each is based on only nine observations. Thus the sharp decline from 0.652 in the 1970s to 0.356 in the 1980s is only two-thirds as large as its standard error of 0.456. We cannot reject the hypothesis that there was no change. Even the fall from 0.742 in the 1960s to 0.356 in the 1980s is only slightly greater than its standard error of 0.359; the hypothesis of no change cannot be formally rejected with this small sample. The test, however, is of low power because of the small sample size, and we would emphasize the large decline rather than its statistical "insignificance."

When we shift from gross to net saving and investment, the pattern of the savings retention coefficients differs even more sharply between the EEC and non-EEC countries. As already noted, among the OECD as a whole, the net saving-investment relation shows virtually no change between the early and later periods (see col. 2). In contrast, column 4 shows that the net saving-investment coefficients declined sharply within the EEC between the 1970s and 1980s. This contrast is seen most clearly when the EEC coefficients of column 4 are compared with the non-EEC coefficients of column 6.

Although the small sample of EEC countries makes it difficult to draw any firm conclusions, these data appear to indicate that there have been greater capital flows out of the individual EEC countries (i.e., a smaller share of incremental savings is retained with the saving country) than among the non-EEC countries and that the extent of this capital mobility increased in the 1980s.

We have also examined the saving-investment behavior in the wider group of all 17 European OECD countries (col. 7 and 8 of table 7.1) and in the non-EEC European OECD countries (col. 9 and 10). The results shows that the non-EEC European countries behaved more like the EEC countries than like the non-European members of the OECD.

These results are not only interesting in themselves as an indication of the increasing integration of the European capital markets but also suggest that the reason why the savings retention coefficients are generally much greater than zero reflects the extent of informational and institutional links among the capital markets. The coefficient is lower for the EEC countries despite formal barriers on capital exports in some countries because of the strength of institutional links. Even when capital is completely mobile in principle, actual capital flows are retarded by ignorance and risk aversion.

7.4 The "Missing" Growth Variable

The surprising strength of the savings retention coefficient in the original FH study led subsequent researchers to postulate that the strength of the coefficient may reflect the impact of some missing variables that influence investment and are correlated with savings. Obstfeld (1986) has developed the idea that the missing variable may be the growth rate of GDP or a combination of the GDP growth rate and of labor's share of national income.

Life-cycle theory implies that these two variables determine the long-term behavior of a country's saving rate. Obstfeld posits a model in which the rate of output growth is also an important determinant of the country's rate of investment; although demand-determined variations in output growth may have an important influence on the timing of investment, in the current context of comparing long-term differences in national investment rates we would be more inclined to regard output growth as the result of previous capital investment than to look upon output growth as an exogenous determination of investment. Obstfeld (1986) used data on GDP growth and on the ratio of employee compensation to national income in individual OECD countries to simulate the saving-GDP ratios and investment-GDP ratios for those countries that would result in a simple theoretical model. He then used these simulated investment and saving ratios to estimate statistically the basic investment-saving ratio.

The Obstfeld model assumes complete world capital mobility; that is, the only link between saving and investment in each country is that they depend on common variables. Nevertheless, a regression of the simulated investment-GDP ratio on the simulated saving-GDP ratio produces coefficients that are approximately equal to one, with the precise coefficient depending on the group of countries selected.

Although we regard this as an ingenious demonstration of how the observed investment-saving relation might in principle be just a spurious reflection of the missing growth and income distribution variables, we do not find it convincing. The real test of whether the savings variables is just a proxy for the growth and distribution variables is whether the inclusion of growth and distribution causes a significant change in the savings retention coefficient in a regression using the actual saving and investment variables instead of the simulated ones.

To test this in a way that makes it strictly comparable to Obstfeld's analysis, we began by following his procedure to create synthetic saving and investment variables. We used observations for the same countries and years as Obstfeld. Despite the usual OECD data revisions, we found that we were able to reproduce his results quite closely. For example, with a sample of 17 countries for the period 1970–79, Obstfeld found a savings retention coefficient of 0.86 (with a standard error of 0.81) and we found a coefficient of 1.01 with a standard error of 0.78. Adding the product of the growth and income distribution variables to the Obstfeld synthetic equation caused the savings absorption coefficient to become −0.75 with a standard error of 0.10 while the other variable "explained" the variation in the synthetic investment series.

However, when we replaced the synthetic variables with the actual saving and investment variables, the estimated savings retention coefficient was little affected by adding the growth and distribution variables to the equation. More specifically, with the same Obstfeld sample of countries and years, but using the actual saving and investment data rather than the synthetic ones, the estimated coefficient of the savings variable was 0.88 (with a standard error of 0.12) in the basic regression. When the growth and distribution variables were added to the equation, the coefficient of the saving variable because 0.87 (with standard error of 0.13).

Similar results were obtained with other combinations of growth rates and income. In no case did the inclusion of the growth and distribution variables substitute for the effect of the savings variable as a determinant of domestic saving.

The implication of this is clear. Although the estimated savings retention coefficient could in theory reflect only the indirect effect of omitted growth and distribution variables, the evidence indicates that this is not so.

7.5 Budget Deficits

As we wrote in section 7.1, Summers (1988) has noted that there is an alternative possible explanation for the observed relation between investment and savings rates. Summers suggests that if governments do not like capital outflows or inflows, they might adjust their budget deficits to offset the gap between investment and private saving.

As evidence of this possibility, Summers presents a regression of the ratio of the budget deficit to GDP on the difference between the private savings ratio (i.e., the ratio of domestic savings plus the budget deficit to GDP) and the investment-GDP ratio:

(2) $DEF/Y = b_0 + b_1 (PS - I)/Y,$

where DEF is the general government budget deficit (i.e, the OECD measure of general government saving with the sign changed), PS is private saving (i.e, saving as previously defined plus the budget deficit) and I and Y are investment and gross domestic product as previously defined.

For a sample of 14 countries for the period 1973–80, Summers obtained a coefficient of 0.72.[3] Taken at face value, this would imply that each dollar of the private saving-investment gap induces governments to increase their budget deficit by 72 cents. Since the precise sample used by Summers is not known, we reestimated his equation ([2] above) with data for 13 OECD countries for which data are available for the period 1973 through 1980. The estimated coefficient of 0.68 with a standard error of 0.15 is quite close to the original estimate by Summers.

There are, however, serious problems of interpretation of equation (2). Although such a model of deficit adjustment may have merit as a description of short-term stabilization policy, we find it very implausible as an explanation of why long-term differences in budget deficit ratios persist among countries. A more likely explanation of the correlation between budget deficits and net saving ratios is that budget deficit ratios are "exogenous" (reflecting political and historical characteristics) and that high deficit ratios crowd out private investment in the traditional way. Similarly, countries with budget surpluses may "crowd in" more private investment.

To assess the plausibility of this alternative specification, we reorder the variables of equation (2) and estimate the equation:

(3) $I/Y = c_0 + c_1 DEF/Y + c_2 PS/Y$

This is a natural generalization of the basic equation (1) that divides domestic saving into two components: private saving (PS) and government saving ($-DEF$). The original basic model implies that the coefficients c_1 and c_2 are equal in absolute value but opposite in sign with private saving having a positive effect and the budget deficit a negative effect.

The results, presented in table 7.2, are generally consistent with this gen-

Table 7.2   **Investment and the Components of Domestic Saving**

Period	Number of Countries	Deficit	Private Saving
1970–85	13	−.865	.699
		(.150)	(.112)
1965–84	9	−.948	.747
		(.153)	(.124)

eralization of the original basic model. For example, with the largest possible sample (13 countries for 1970–85) the coefficient of net private savings is 0.699 with a standard error of 0.112 while the coefficient of the budget deficit is −0.865 with a standard error of 0.150. Taken at face value, these coefficients imply that each dollar of gross private saving adds 70 cents to gross investment while each dollar of the budget deficit crowds out 0.87 cents of investment.

The higher absolute coefficient on government deficits than on private saving is what would be expected if governments are likely to invest less when they face a budget deficit and to invest more when tax receipts are large relative to current spending. To see this, note that total investment includes government sector investment (I_g) as well as private sector investment (I_p), while the government deficit is defined as the difference between government current outlays and taxes. Assume that private investment depends on the total pool of national savings net of government borrowing for both current and investment outlays:

(4) $$I_p/Y = \alpha + \beta \, (T - G - I_g + PS)/Y + \varepsilon,$$

where T is total tax revenue of the government. Note that this implies that government investment does not directly reduce (or increase) private investment but does so only through the domestic availability of funds.

Adding government investment to both sides of the equation and regrouping terms yields:

(5) $$I_p/Y + I_g/Y = \alpha + \beta \, (T - G)/Y + \beta PS/Y + (1-\beta) I_g/Y + \varepsilon.$$

A regression in the form of equation (3) is thus equivalent to estimating the "true" equation (5) with the last term omitted. The relation between the estimated coefficients c_1 and c_2 of equation (3) and the parameter β of equation (5) depends on the relation between government investment and the other two variables. If government investment does not depend on the level of private saving but does respond positively to government current budget surpluses, the estimated coefficient of the government surplus variable $(T - G)/Y$ will equal the true coefficient (β) plus the product of $(1 - \beta)$ and the regression of I_g/Y and $(T - G)/Y$. This implies that the coefficient of the government surplus variable ($-c_1$ of eq. [3]) will exceed the coefficient of the private saving variable (c_2 of eq. [3]). The bias is, however, relatively small. If the "true" coefficient β is 0.75 and the long-run propensity of the government to spend current surpluses on government investment is as large as 0.4, the estimated value of $-c_1$ will be 0.85 instead of 0.75.

In practice, the difference between the estimates of $-c_1$ and c_2 is not statistically significant with a sample of only 13 observations. Estimating the constrained equation for this sample produces a coefficient of 0.76 on domestic saving with a standard error of 0.09. Comparing the sums of squared residuals for the constrained and unconstrained specifications implies an F-statistic of 0.81 with 1 and 10 degrees of freedom. Since the critical value for 5 percent significance is 4.96, we cannot reject the simple original specification.

Note that the estimate of c_2 is an unbiased estimate of the true parameter β regardless of the size of β and of the government's propensity to do public investment as a function of the government's current surplus as long as the government investment is not influenced by the private saving rate.

The problem of distinguishing between the "deficit reaction function approach" of equation (2) and the "components of domestic saving" approach of equation (3) cannot be definitively resolved by these estimates since the statistical problem is one of identification and, more fundamentally, of providing the theoretically correct specification. It is helpful in this to look at the underlying raw data in the context of what we know about the particular economies.

Table 7.3 presents data on the deficit, net private saving, and net investment for the decade of the 1970s and the period 1980–84. Such data are only available for 13 countries.

It is noteworthy that in the 1970s the "deficits" were negative in all of the

Table 7.3   **Budget Deficits, Private Saving, and Investments**

	1970–79			1980–84		
	Deficit	Saving	Investment	Deficit	Saving	Investment
Germany	−.03	.10	.13	−.01	.08	.09
Austria	−.05	.11	.17	−.02	.09	.12
Switzerland	−.04	.14	.16	−.03	.14	.14
Netherlands	−.03	.13	.15	.01	.12	.09
Sweden	−.07	.05	.12	.01	.06	.07
Finland	−.07	.06	.15	−.03	.07	.11
Belgium	.00	.14	.13	.07	.13	.08
Spain	−.03	.12	.16	.01	.09	.10
United Kingdom	−.01	.07	.10	.02	.08	.04
Australia	−.05	.11	.17	.01	.04	.09
Canada	−.01	.10	.13	.03	.12	.10
United States	.01	.09	.08	.03	.08	.05
Japan	−.04	.18	.22	−.03	.14	.17

Note: All figures are expressed as ratios to gross domestic product. Investment and private saving are net variables.

countries except the United States and Belgium. The other countries had surpluses ranging from 1 percent of GDP to 7 percent of GDP. By the 1980s, most of these countries were experiencing actual deficits. It would be very interesting but beyond our capability to examine the historic reasons for these shifts country by country.

Consider, however, the case of the United States, which went from a deficit of 1 percent of GNP in the 1970s to 3 percent in the first half of the 1980s. For the 1970s, the U.S. deficit was the largest of all 13 countries; indeed, none of the others had a deficit. It is hard to argue, however, that this represented a fiscal policy decision aimed at supporting aggregate demand since inflation was a serious problem during most of this decade and there was a general feeling that national saving was too low. While it might in theory be argued that the shift to a larger deficit in the 1980s was a way of dealing with the large recession in 1980–82, the actual historic record shows that the recession was the unintended consequence of a political inability to obtain sufficient domestic spending cuts to pay for the combination of tax cuts, defense spending increases, and higher interest payments on the national debt.

One caveat should be indicated about this analysis. Government deficits reflect payments of interest on the national debt because such interest payments are part of current government outlay. Since inflation differences among the countries influence the interest rates on the government debt, the deficits reflect to differing degrees the inflation erosion of the government debt and are in this sense not "true" deficits. This is likely to be more important in the international context than over time in individual countries.

To examine the sensitivity of our conclusions to the failure to adjust for inflation, we have repeated the analysis using inflation-adjusted government deficits and private savings using data constructed by Muller and Price (1984) (as given by Roubini and Sachs 1989). The inflation-adjusted results are very similar to the unadjusted estimates. Using data for the largest available sample (13 countries for the period 1971 through 1986), the disaggregated savings coefficients are almost exactly equal in absolute value:

$$(6) \qquad I/Y = \underset{(0.012)}{0.019} - \underset{(0.14)}{0.89 \, DEF^*/Y} + \underset{(0.10)}{0.88 PS^*/Y}$$

where DEF^* and PS^* are both inflation adjusted. The evidence clearly supports the view that either source of variation in national saving has the same effect on domestic investment.

7.6 Dynamic Adjustment

As Feldstein (1983) and Feldstein-Horioka (1980) emphasized, the close relationship between domestic saving and domestic investment is a long-term characteristic and does not hold from year to year. With time-series data, the savings retention coefficients are much lower than in cross-section analyses.

It is possible however to examine the dynamic adjustment process by which the close association between domestic investment and domestic saving is maintained. The evidence presented in this section supports the view that it is domestic investment that responds to changes in domestic saving. The evidence is not consistent with a view that domestic saving (either private alone or the combination of private and public) responds to shifts in investment.

Consider therefore the simple adjustment process by which the change in the investment ratio from year to year ($I_t/Y_t - I_{t-1}/Y_{t-1}$) varies inversely with the previous year's investment-savings gap ($(I_{t-1} - S_{t-1})/Y_{t-1}$:

(7) $$I_t/Y_t - I_{t-1}/Y_{t-1} = d_0 + d_1 (I_{t-1} - S_{t-1})/Y_{t-1}$$

If an increase in the gap between investment and saving causes investment to decline, d_1 is negative. Such a decline could be caused by a rise in interest rates induced by the "shortage" of savings in year $t - 1$. The evidence presented below shows that d_1 is in fact negative, supporting the view that investment responds to shifts in saving.

A similar regression shows that the saving rate does not respond to the gap between investment and savings. For this purpose, we estimate the equation

(8) $$S_t/Y_t - S_{t-1}/Y_{t-1} = e_0 + e_1 (I_{t-1} - S_{t-1})/Y_{t-1}.$$

Although a shortage of savings could raise saving by increasing the interest rate or inducing an increase in the government surplus, the evidence suggest that this does not occur. Of course, this is quite consistent with much previous evidence that investment is more sensitive to interest rates than saving.

The results are presented in table 7.4. Equation (1) presents the results cor-

Table 7.4   **Dynamic Adjustment of Investment and Saving in 23 OECD Countries**

Equation	Dependent Variable	Coefficient Constrained?	Period	Coefficient of Lagged Investment	Coefficient of Lagged Saving
(1)	Investment	yes	1961–86	−.227 (.026)	.227 (.026)
(2)	Saving	yes	1961–86	−.036 (.026)	.036 (.026)
(3)	Investment	no	1961–86	−.275 (.028)	.198 (.027)
(4)	Saving	no	1961–86	−.014 (.025)	−.068 (.024)
(5)	Investment	no	1961–73	−.344 (.048)	.262 (.045)
(6)	Saving	no	1961–73	.034 (.039)	−.083 (.037)
(7)	Investment	no	1974–86	−.240 (.037)	.140 (.036)
(8)	Saving	no	1974–86	−.025 (.036)	−.132 (.033)

responding to equation (8) for the 23 OECD countries (i.e., all OECD countries except Luxembourg) for the period 1961–86. The coefficient of -0.227 (with a standard error of 0.026) implies that an investment-savings gap of one percentage point of GDP causes the investment-GDP ratio to fall by approximately a quarter of a percentage point in the following year. After three years the adjustment of investment alone would reduce the gap to less than one-half a percent of GDP; after six years, 80 percent of the gap would be eliminated.

The corresponding saving equation is presented as equation 2 of table 7.4. The coefficient of -0.036 is small both absolutely and relative to its standard error of 0.024 and of the wrong sign. The data thus imply no response of the saving rate to the saving-investment gap.

Disaggregating the adjustment coefficient into separate coefficients for lagged investment and lagged saving supports this interpretation of the evidence. In the unconstrained investment equation (eq. [3] of table 7.4), the coefficients of the lagged investment ratio is -0.275 with a standard error of 0.028 while the coefficient of the lagged saving variable is 0.198 with a standard error of 0.027. The coefficients are close enough in magnitude to be equal for practical purposes. But if the point estimates are taken literally, the evidence implies that a rise in the savings ratios induces a slightly smaller rise in subsequent investment than a fall in the investment ratio. This is just what might be expected if the stochastic disturbance contains a serially correlated determinant of investment.

Dividing the sample into the fixed-rate first half (1961–73) and the floating-rate second half (1974–86) shows that the results are similar in both subperiods, with some indication of a slower response in the second half than in the earlier period. These results are shown in equations (5)-(8) of table 7.4. This confirms the results presented in section 7.2.

The constant terms in equations (7) and (8) in this text imply that the investment and saving ratios would adjust monotonically over time even if there were no investment-savings gap. Since there is no justification for such a trend, we have also estimated the equations of table 7.4 with the constraint that there is no constant term. The results are very similar to the coefficients of table 7.4 and are not presented to save space.

We have also repeated this dynamic analysis for the nine EEC countries alone. The basic results, presented in table 7.5, are very similar to the result for the entire OECD. Investment adjusts to the lagged investment-savings gap while saving does not adjust. The coefficients for the EEC also imply a small savings retention, confirming the results in section 7.3. The other principal difference between the two sets of results is that the unconstrained coefficients suggest that the effect of an increase in saving is smaller than the effect of an increase in investment. This may reflect only the bias referred to above that results if the disturbance is serially correlated.

It would be worthwhile to examine the adjustment process more extensively, considerably more general adjustment dynamics and using estimation

Table 7.5   **Dynamic Adjustment of Investment and Saving in Nine EEC Countries**

Equation	Dependent Variable	Coefficient Constant?	Period	Coefficient of Lagged	
				Investment	Saving
(1)	Investment	yes	1961–86	−.159	.159
				(.042)	(.042)
(2)	Saving	yes	1961–86	−.015	.015
				(.037)	(.037)
(3)	Investment	no	1961–86	−.225	.123
				(.045)	(.042)
(4)	Saving	no	1961–81	−.059	−.055
				(.040)	(.037)
(5)	Investment	no	1961–73	−.222	.083
				(.087)	(.078)
(6)	Saving	no	1961–73	.064	−.160
				(.065)	(.058)
(7)	Investment	no	1974–86	−.216	.071
				(.055)	(.055)
(8)	Saving	no	1974–86	−.090	−.115
				(.051)	(.050)

Note: The nine EEC countries exclude Spain, Portugal, and Luxemborg.

methods that are consistent in the presence of serial correlation, although that may provide little reassurance with such small samples.

7.6.1 Persistent Current Account Imbalances

The specification of equation (7) implies that each country will adjust its investment to eliminate eventually the entire investment-saving gap. A more general specification would recognize that countries may instead have a "normal" nonzero level of current account surplus or deficit to which they adjust.

We consider therefore the following generalization of equation (7):

$$(9) \qquad I_t/Y_t - I_{t-1}/Y_{t-1} = f_0 + f_1 [(I_{t-1}\text{-}S_{t-1})/Y_{t-1}\text{-GAP}],$$

where GAP is the desired or normal investment-saving gap. Equation (9) is only distinguishable from equation (7) when the GAP is permitted to vary among countries.

Equation (9) has therefore been estimated with individual constant terms for each of the 23 OECD countries using data for 1961–86. Separate estimates for the subperiods 1961–73 and 1974–86 have also been calculated. The results are presented in table 7.6.

Equation (1) of table 7.6 corresponds to equation (9) for the entire period 1961–86. Equations (2) and (3) correspond to the two subperiods.

The individual constant terms correspond to substantial positive "normal" or "target" investment-saving gaps in several countries including Australia,

Table 7.6   Normal Investment-Saving Gaps in OECD Countries

Equation:	(1)	(2)	(3)
Time Period:	1961–86	1961–73	1974–86
Lagged Investment	−.335	−.422	−.349
Coefficient:	(.030)	(.049)	(.044)
Lagged Savings	.335	.422	.349
Coefficient:	(.030)	(.049)	(.044)
	Normal Gap (%)		
United States	−.21	−.31	−.14
United Kingdom	−.03	.55	−.75
Japan	−.54	1.64	−2.84
Germany	−1.64	−1.07	−2.07
France	−.28	−.26	−1.55
Italy	.12	.14	.20
Canada	1.37	2.11	.63
Australia	2.33	1.52	3.24
New Zealand	4.21	3.35	4.91
Switzerland	−2.09	.50	−4.73
Spain	.30	.69	−.37
Portugal	2.74	.76	4.50
Belgium	−.33	−.33	−.37
Netherlands	−1.94	−.83	−2.90
Greece	3.16	5.95	−.32
Turkey	3.22	2.25	3.90
Sweden	−.21	−.69	.49
Denmark	2.15	1.97	2.38
Finland	.89	1.23	.63
Norway	1.97	1.99	1.92
Iceland	1.85	2.41	1.29
Austria	−.03	.45	−.55
Ireland	5.28	4.13	6.02

New Zealand, Portugal, Greece, Turkey, Denmark, and Ireland. There were fewer countries with negative target investment-saving balances, but these included Germany, France, Switzerland, the Netherlands and, since 1974, Japan. It is clear that these "normal" or "target" investment-saving balances do correspond generally to the economic situations of the countries with the lower income, countries more likely to seek capital inflows while the high saving and older industrial countries correspond to a target excess of saving over investment.

7.7 Conclusion

The basic conclusion of the present analysis is that an increase in domestic saving has a substantial effect on the level of domestic investment although a smaller effect than would have been observed in the 1960s and 1970s. The more closely integrated economies of the EEC also appear to have more outward capital mobility (i.e, a lower savings retention coefficient) than other OECD countries.

There is no support for the view that the estimated saving-investment relation reflects a spurious impact of an omitted economic growth variable. Although budget deficits are inversely related to the difference between private investment and private saving, we reject the view that this reflects an endogenous response of fiscal policy in favor of the alternative interpretation that the negative relation is evidence of the crowding out of private investment by budget deficits. This interpretation is supported by the evidence that domestic investment responds equally to private saving and budget deficits.

The dynamic adjustment analysis supports the view that domestic investment adjusts rather quickly when there is an unwanted investment-saving gap while domestic saving shows little tendency to adjust.

The implication of the analysis thus supports the original Feldstein-Horioka conclusions that increases in domestic saving do raise a nation's capital stock and thereby the productivity of its work force. Similarly, a tax on capital income is not likely to be shifted to labor and land by the outflow of enough domestic capital to maintain the real rate of return unchanged.

Notes

1. These include Feldstein (1983), Caprio and Howard (1984), Murphy (1984), Penati and Dooley (1984), Sachs (1983), and Summers (1988). See Dooley, Frankel, and Mathieson (1987) for a summary of these results.
2. For a more complete discussion of these issues, see the essay by Frankel in this volume.
3. The text of Summer's paper does not specify the sample of countries or years for which his regression was estimated, but elsewhere in his paper he indicates that an equation using the deficit variable as an instrumental variable is limited to this sample of countries and years because of data limitations.

References

Caprio, Gerard, and David Howard. 1984. Domestic saving, current account, and international capital mobility. International Finance Discussion Papers no. 244. Federal Reserve Board, Washington, D.C.

Dooley, Michael, Jeffrey Frankel, and Donald Mathieson. 1987. International capital mobility: What do saving-investment correlations tell us? International Monetary Fund *Staff Papers* 34:503–30.

Feldstein, Martin. 1983. Domestic saving and international capital movements in the long run and the short run. *European Economic Review* 21:129–51.

Feldstein, Martin, and Charles Horioka. 1980. Domestic saving and international capital flows. *Economic Journal* 90: 314–29.

Frankel, Jeffrey. 1985. The implications of mean-variance analysis for four questions in international macroeconomics. *Journal of International Money and Finance*.

———. 1986. International capital mobility and crowding out in the U.S. economy: Imperfect integration of financial markets or of goods markets? In *How Open Is The U.S. Economy?* ed. R. Hafer. Federal Reserve Bank of St. Louis. Lexington, Mass.: Lexington Book.

Muller, Patrice, and Robert Price. 1984. Structural budget deficits and fiscal stance. OECD Working Paper no. 15.

Murphy, Robert. 1984. Capital mobility and the relationship between saving and investment in OECD countries. *Journal of International Money and Finance* 3:327–342.

Obstfeld, Maurice. 1986. Capital mobility in the world economy: Theory and measurement. *Carnegie-Rochester Conference Series on Public Policy.* Amsterdam: North-Holland.

Penati, Alessandro, and Michael Dooley. 1984. Current account imbalances and capital formation in industrial countries, 1949–1981. International Monetary Fund *Staff Papers* 31:1–24.

Roubini, Nouriel, and Jeffrey Sachs. 1989. Government spending and budget deficits in industrial economies. NBER Working Paper no. 2919.

Sachs, Jeffrey. 1983. Aspects of the current account behavior of OECD economies. In *Recent Issues in the Theory of Flexible Exchange Rates: Fifth Paris-Dauphine Conference on Money and International Money Problems,* ed. E. Claassen and P. Salin. Amsterdam: Elsevier.

Summers, Lawrence. 1988. Tax policy and international competitiveness. In *International Aspects of Fiscal Policies,* ed. Jacob Frenkel. Chicago: University of Chicago Press.

Comment   Rudiger Dornbusch

Feldstein's discovery of the tight link between national saving and investment rates continues to baffle the profession. Ample research over the past few years has failed to reject the basic finding: if a country raises the national saving rate by a percentage point, most of the increase in saving is retained in the form of increased investment.[1] The Feldstein finding runs counter to the spirit of the open economy literature in which, under conditions of perfect capital mobility, changes in national saving rates are primarily reflected in the current account, *not* in investment.[2]

Figure 7C.1 shows the basic evidence: using averages for the 1960–86 period, saving and investment rates for 23 OECD countries obey a very high positive correlation.

Rudiger Dornbusch is the Ford International Professor of Economics at the Massachusetts Institute of Technology and a research associate of the National Bureau of Economic Research.

1. For a review see esp. Dooley et al. (1987).
2. An earlier theory, popular in the United Kingdom, argued that budget deficits and external deficits were highly correlated because of a tendency for private investment to match saving. See Godley and Cripps (1983).

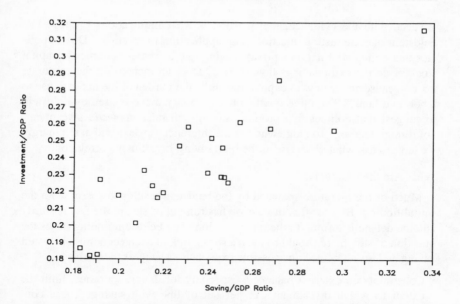

Figure 7C.1   Investment and saving 1960–86, averages for 23 OECD members

Table 7C.1   The Effect of Saving on Investment (23 OECD countries, 1960–86)

	Constant	S	R^2
Gross fixed investment	5.89	.75	.74
	(2.67)	(8.05)	
Construction:	2.51	.49	.53
	(1.09)	(5.07)	
Residential	1.99	.15	.24
	(1.54)	(2.85)	
Nonresidential	.53	.34	.38
	(.25)	(3.82)	
Machinery and equipment	3.37	.26	.23
	(1.53)	(2.78)	

Note: Saving and investment are measured as a fraction of GDP. Each observation is the 1960–86 period average for a country.

The corresponding regression, using OLS on the cross-section period averages is shown in table 7C.1 below. This evidence suggests that economies are three-quarters closed: of an extra percentage point saving only one quarter will be reflected in an improvement of the external balance while three quarters find their way into increased investment. Table 7C.1 also shows the breakdown of investment by component.

Table 7C.1 shows that the systematic effect of investment on saving extends to the components of investment; for each category of investment the coefficient is statistically significant. Half of an extra percentage point saving goes into construction and a quarter into machinery and equipment.

Faced with the evidence, the question is what implications to draw. For Feldstein one interesting question is an application to taxation: "Do tax policies that stimulate a nation's private saving rate increase its domestic capital stock or do the extra savings flow abroad? Does an increase in the corporate tax rate cause an outflow of capital that shifts the burden of the tax increase to labor, and land?" The three-quarters result shown above is used by Feldstein to suggest that policies that promote saving will raise *domestic* investment, not foreign lending. To judge whether the inference is warranted at the margin we have to ask what gives rise to the high saving-investment correlation.

What Are the Channels?

Much of the literature spawned by the Feldstein result takes issue with the initial finding. By now that discussion has run out of steam; the fact is sturdy and the debate is turning to the interpretation. The Feldstein finding raises the question of why there should be such a strong link in open economies between saving and investment. Four possible explanations suggest themselves:

- Constraints on external balances, especially for deficit countries, limit the extent to which investment can get out of line with saving. These constraints may take the form of limitations on external financing or of a government reaction function, as proposed by Summers (1988). In this analysis governments raise public-sector saving in response to incipient external deficits and thus contain the size of net foreign lending.
- There is imperfect capital mobility within economies so that many, if not most, firms have to rely on internal financing of investment. As a result investment cannot deviate substantially from saving. While there is capital mobility in respect to public-sector debt and finance of large corporations, the brunt of firms are constrained in that they do not have access to world markets. Murphy's (1984) evidence on the high saving retention by major corporations suggests that this effect may be operative.
- Internationally there is imperfect capital mobility because of investors' risk aversion. Regulatory treatment of financial institutions reinforces the cross-border reluctance of capital flows.
- The correlation reflects an economic structure that induces simultaneously *both* high saving and high investment. This contrasts with the Feldstein interpretation that structural factors (demographics, social security arrangements, taxation, etc.) determine saving and lead to a crowding in, by channels that remain unidentified, of investment.

Among the competing explanations Feldstein emphasizes imperfect capital mobility: the cross-border obstacles are sufficiently large, especially for longer maturities, that investment is crowded in domestically whenever saving rises. The mechanism for crowding in is not clear, however. If domestic capital markets are open and competitive we should expect *systematic* relationships between the cost of capital across countries. Other things equal, high saving countries should have a low cost of capital and low saving countries a high cost of capital. The cross-border reluctance of capital would allow these cost of capital differentials to persist. I am not aware of a direct test of the imperfect capital mobility hypothesis in this form.

It might be argued, of course, that crowding in takes place not only via the cost of capital but also and perhaps primarily via relaxation of credit rationing. In this view the explicit cost of capital, for moral hazard reasons, does little of the work and less obviously observable variations in credit constraints provide the mechanism. The ready availability of credit thus induces investment to fall in line with saving.

If imperfect international capital mobility is in fact the basis for the observed correlations we would expect increasingly organizations to develop means of overcoming the risks that stand in the way of capital flows. It may be risky to borrow for 30 years in dollars in the United States in order to make yen loans in Japan. But multinational corporations who operate in multiple markets are natural agents for diversifying away the risks and thus exploit cost-of-capital differences. Direct foreign investment, which is becoming very sizable, may then be a reflection of the cost of capital differentials arising from cross-border reluctance of portfolio capital flows.

Feldstein is certainly right in emphasizing the international immobility, until very recently, of most saving done via financial institutions such as pension funds or life insurance companies. Once again, their increasing perception of a *world* capital market should work in the direction of reducing the local crowding in tendency observed in the past.

Beyond the perfect capital mobility argument it is certainly the case that there is some correlation between saving and investment as a result of common determinants. For example, if the age structure of the population is such as to favor a high saving rate the same age structure induces an expansion of investment in nontraded goods industries and construction to supply the large "internal market." Conversely, if the transition to an aging population reduces the national saving rate it is likely that investment in such an economy will also decline, not only because of a reduced availability of domestic financing but also because the opportunities for profitable domestic investment decline with a shrinking of the market. Indeed, the falloff in domestic investment may even precede the decline in the savings rate.

Table 7C.2 shows the projections of aging trends in industrialized countries. The steep increase in Japanese age would suggest, on the above argument, an increasing tendency for Japanese foreign lending in the coming decades.

The view that investment is determined by the available supply of saving is suggestive for high saving countries. In high saving countries an inordinately large share of saving (by comparison with a world of unrestricted capital flows, full information and little risk aversion) is retained nationally. But how does this thinking apply to deficit countries? What is the process by which

Table 7C.2   **Changing Age Structure in OECD Countries (percentage of population age 65 and over)**

	Japan	United States	Germany	OECD
1980	9.1	11.3	15.5	12.2
2000	15.2	12.2	17.1	13.9
2020	20.9	16.2	21.7	17.9

Source: OECD.

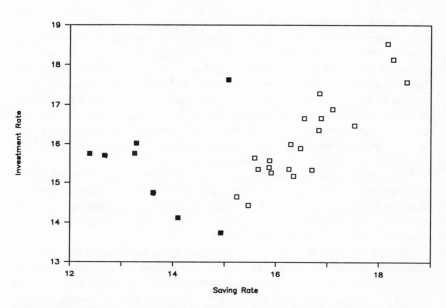

Figure 7C.2   U.S. saving and investment ratios (percentage of GNP)

investment is high relative to saving? Specifically, why is investment not more fully crowded out by the lack of domestic saving? In part the answer to this question may have to do with the question whose deficit is being financed.

Whose Deficit?

Figure 7C.2 shows the U.S. saving and investment rates in the 1960–86 period. We note the striking discrepancy between the 1980s (marked as black dots) and the earlier period. It is clear that the general positive correlation observed in the period averages in 1960–86 broke down in the U.S. in recent years. Current account deficits have become large as the decline in the national saving rate was not matched by a corresponding decline in the investment rate.

It is interesting to speculate whether this new development reflects a worldwide breaking down of reluctance to cross-border lending or whether it is peculiar to the U.S. case. The latter could be argued if foreign investors care which country they finance. It may make a difference whether the decline in saving occurs in a large country with a developed financial market or in a small country with little scope for uncomplicated cross-border investment. Moreover, it may make an important difference whether the decline in saving arises in the private sector or in the public sector. With a developed market in government debt there may be scope for easy cross-border financing while a decline in private saving may require more complicated intermediation.

To support the argument that government deficits are more "financeable" and hence have more significant foreign lending effects we can look at less-developed countries LDCs. Would Brazil, Mexico or Korea have been able to run very large persistent external deficits if the private sector had been the borrower rather than the government through state enterprises? No doubt, the private sector can borrow some, but it is doubtful that lending would have reached the proportions it did in the 1970s in that case.

Two Disagreements

In concluding I wish to comment on two conclusions in the Feldstein-Bacchetta paper that I do not share. The first concerns the evidence on a special EEC effect. Table 7C.3 shows the results of the investment equation with an EEC dummy added. It is clear that there is no special effect for EEC membership. That is not really surprising since capital mobility between Switzerland and Germany, for example, is certainly higher than that between Germany and France. In fact, there were tighter capital controls among EEC members than outside the EEC group.

My other disagreement concerns the calculation of "normal gaps" reported in the paper. These plainly do not make much sense. The gap is determined by structural factors on the saving side and by investment opportunities. There is no presumption that these factors remain invariant over extended periods of time. Table 7C.4 shows examples for several countries. For the case of Japan and Korea there is a trend toward "structural surpluses," for the United States there is presumably a short-lived deterioration and only for Germany is there any tendency for stable, long-run surpluses.

Table 7C.3   **EEC Effects in the Saving Retention**

	Constant	S	EEC*S	R^2
Gross investment	6.79	.73	−0.05	.76
	(3.05)	(7.92)	(−1.50)	
Net investment	4.57	.79	−.07	.70
	(2.99)	(7.20)	(−1.28)	

Note: EEC denotes a dummy for EEC membership, excluding, however, Greece, Portugal, and Spain.

Table 7C.4   Net Exports (percentage of GDP, national income account basis)

	1960–69	1970–79	1980–86
Japan	.2	.8	2.3
Germany	2.1	2.6	2.5
United States	.2	− .5	− 1.8
Korea	− 10.1	− 5.9	− 1.6

Source: IMF.

Concluding Remarks

The Feldstein thesis of unusually high savings retention is now well-established as a fact; perhaps just as it is established it is also going away as a result of sharply increased international financial intermediation. The reason for the finding remains undiscovered and presumably there need not be a single one. Unless we understand why savings retention is so high, or in what particular situations, we certainly should not use the observed relations to make strong inferences about the investment response to saving policies. The U.S. example in the 1980s offers a strong reminder that much of the change in saving can easily find its way into changed foreign lending rather than changes in investment.

References

Dooley, M., J. Frankel, and D. Mathieson. 1987. International Capital Mobility: What Do Saving-Investment Correlations Tell Us? *International Monetary Fund Staff Papers* 34, no. 3 (September): 503–30.

Godley, W., and F. Cripps. 1983. *Macroeconomics*. London: Fontana.

Murphy, R. 1984. Capital Mobility and the Relationship between Saving and Investment in OECD Countries. *Journal of International Money and Finance* 3 (December): 327–42.

Summers, L. 1988. Tax Policy and International Competitiveness. In *International Aspects of Fiscal Policy*, ed. J. Frenkel. Chicago: University of Chicago Press.

8 Quantifying International Capital Mobility in the 1980s

Jeffrey A. Frankel

Feldstein and Horioka upset conventional wisdom in 1980 when they concluded that changes in countries' rates of national saving had a very large effect on their rates of investment, and interpreted this finding as evidence of low capital mobility. Although their regressions have been subject to a great variety of criticisms, their basic finding seems to hold up. But does it imply imperfect capital mobility?

Let us begin by asking why we would ever expect a shortfall in one country's national saving *not* to reduce the overall availability of funds and thereby crowd out investment projects that might otherwise be undertaken in that country. After all, national saving and investment are linked through an identity. (The variable that completes the identity is, of course, the current account balance.)

The aggregation together of all forms of "capital" has caused more than the usual amount of confusion in the literature on international capital mobility. Nobody ever claimed that international flows of foreign direct investment were large enough that a typical investment project in the domestic country would costlessly be undertaken directly by a foreign company when there was a shortfall in domestic saving.[1] Rather, the argument was that the typical American corporation could borrow at the going interest rate in order to finance its investment projects and, if the degree of capital mobility was sufficiently high, the going interest rate would be tied down to the world interest rate by international flows of *portfolio* capital. If portfolio capital were a perfect substitute for physical capital, then the difference would be immaterial; but the two types of capital probably are not in fact perfect substitutes.

This paper examines a number of alternative ways of quantifying the degree

Jeffrey Frankel is professor of economics, University of California, Berkeley, and research associate, National Bureau of Economic Research.

of international capital mobility. One conclusion is that the barriers to cross-border flows are sufficiently low that, by 1989, financial markets can be said to be virtually completely integrated among the large industrial countries (and among some smaller countries as well). But this is a different proposition from saying that real interest rates are equalized across countries, which is still different from saying that investment projects in a country are unaffected by a shortfall in national saving. We will see that there are several crucial links that can, and probably do, fail to hold.

In many cases, notably the United Kingdom and Japan (and perhaps now Italy and France as well), the finding of high integration with world financial markets is a relatively new one, attributable to liberalization programs over the last 10 years. Even in the case of financial markets in the United States, integration with the Euromarkets appears to have been incomplete as recently as 1982.[2] An important conclusion of this paper for the United States is that the current account deficits of the 1980s have been large enough, and by now have lasted long enough, to reduce significantly estimates of the correlation between saving and investment. The increased degree of worldwide financial integration since 1979 is identified as one likely factor that has allowed such large capital flows to take place over the past decade. But even if U.S. interest rates are now viewed as tied to world interest rates,[3] there are still other weak links in the chain. The implication is that crowding out of domestic investment can still take place.

8.1 Four Alternative Definitions of International Capital Mobility

By the second half of the 1970s, international economists had come to speak of the world financial system as characterized by perfect capital mobility. In many ways, this was "jumping the gun." It is true that financial integration had been greatly enhanced after 1973 by the removal of capital controls on the part of the United States, Germany, Canada, Switzerland, and the Netherlands; by the steady process of technical and institutional innovation, particularly in the Euromarkets; and by the recycling of OPEC surpluses to developing countries. But almost all developing countries retained extensive restrictions on international capital flows, as did a majority of industrialized countries. Even among the five major countries without capital controls, capital was not perfectly mobile by some definitions.

There are at least four distinct definitions of perfect capital mobility that are in widespread use. (1) The *Feldstein-Horioka definition:* exogenous changes in national saving (i.e., in either private savings or government budgets) can be easily financed by borrowing from abroad at the going real interest rate, and thus need not crowd out investment in the originating country (except perhaps to the extent that the country is large in world financial markets). (2) *Real interest parity:* International capital flows equalize real interest rates across countries. (3) *Uncovered interest parity:* Capital flows equalize expected rates of return on countries' bonds, despite exposure to exchange risk. (4) *Closed interest parity:* Capital flows equalize interest rates across countries when contracted in a common currency. These four possible definitions are in ascending order of specificity. Only the last condition is an unalloyed criterion for capital mobility in the sense of the degree of financial market integration across national boundaries.[4]

As we will see, each of the first three conditions, if it is to hold, requires an auxiliary assumption in addition to the condition that follows it. Uncovered interest parity requires not only closed (or covered) interest parity, but also the condition that the exchange risk premium is zero. Real interest parity requires not only uncovered interest parity, but also the condition that expected real depreciation is zero. The Feldstein-Horioka condition requires not only real interest parity, but also a certain condition on the determinants of investment. But even though the relevance to the degree of integration of financial markets decreases as auxiliary conditions are added, the relevance to questions regarding the origin of international payments imbalances increases. We begin our consideration of the various criteria of capital mobility with the Feldstein-Horioka definition.

8.2   Feldstein-Horioka Tests

The Feldstein-Horioka definition requires that the country's real interest rate is tied to the world real interest rate by criterion 2; it is, after all, the real interest rather than the nominal on which saving and investment in theory depend. But for criterion 1 to hold, it is also necessary that any and all determinants of a country's rate of investment *other* than its real interest rate be uncorrelated with its rate of national saving. Let the investment rate be given by

$$(1) \qquad\qquad (I/Y)_i = a - br_i + u_i,$$

where I is the level of capital formation, Y is national output, r is the domestic real interest rate, and u represents all other factors, whether quantifiable or not, that determine the rate of investment. Feldstein and Horioka (1980) regressed the investment rate against the national saving rate,

$$(1') \qquad\qquad (I/Y)_i = A + B(NS/Y)_i + v_i,$$

where NS is private saving minus the budget deficit. To get the zero coefficient B that they were looking for requires not only real interest parity:

$$(2) \qquad\qquad r_i - r^* = 0$$

(with the world interest rate r^* exogenous or in any other way uncorrelated with $[NS/Y]_i$) but also a zero correlation between u_i and $(NS/Y)_i$.

8.2.1 The Saving-Investment literature

Feldstein and Horioka's finding that the coefficient B is in fact closer to one than to zero has been reproduced many times. Most authors have not been willing, however, to follow them in drawing the inference that financial markets are not highly integrated. There have been many econometric critiques, falling into two general categories.

Most commonly made is the point that national saving is endogenous or, in our terms, is correlated with u_i. This will be the case if national saving and investment are both procyclical, as they are in fact known to be, or if they both respond to the population or productivity growth rates.[5] It will also be the case if governments respond endogenously to incipient current account imbalances with policies to change public (or private) saving in such a way as to reduce the imbalances. This "policy reaction" argument has been made by Fieleke (1982), Tobin (1983), Westphal (1983), Caprio and Howard (1984), Summers (1988), Roubini (1988) and Bayoumi (1989). But Feldstein and Horioka made an effort to handle the econometric endogenity of national saving, more so than have some of their critics. To handle the cyclical endogeneity, they computed averages over a long enough period of time that business cycles could be argued to wash out. To handle other sources of endogeneity, they used demographic variables as instrumental variables for the saving rate.

The other econometric critique is that if the domestic country is large in world financial markets, r^* will not be exogenous with respect to $(NS/Y)_i$, and therefore even if $r = r^*$, r and in turn $(I/Y)_i$ will be correlated with $(NS/Y)_i$. In other words, a shortfall in domestic savings will drive up the world interest rate, and thus crowd out investment in the domestic country as well as abroad. This "large-country" argument has been made by Murphy (1984) and Tobin (1983). An insufficiently appreciated point is that the large-country argument does not create a problem in cross-section studies, because all countries share the same world interest rate r^*. Since r^* simply goes into the constant term in a cross-section regression, it cannot be the source of any correlation with the right-hand-side variable. The large-country problem cannot explain why the countries that are high-saving relative to the average tend to coincide with the countries that are high-investing relative to the average.[6]

If the regressions of saving and investment rates were a good test for barriers to financial market integration, one would expect to see the coefficient falling over time. Until now, the evidence has if anything showed the coefficient rising over time rather than falling. This finding has emerged both from cross-section studies, which typically report pre- and post-1973 results— Feldstein (1983), Penati and Dooley (1984), and Dooley, Frankel and Mathieson (1987)—and from pure time-series studies—Obstfeld (1986, 1989)[7] and Frankel (1986) for the United States. The econometric endogeneity of national saving does not appear to be the explanation for this finding, because it holds equally well when instrumental variables are used.[8]

The easy explanation for the finding is that, econometric problems aside, real interest parity—criterion 2 above—has not held any better in recent years than it did in the past. Mishkin (1984a, 1352), for example, found even more significant rejections of real interest parity among major industrialized countries for the floating rate period after the second quarter of 1973 (1973/II) than he did for his entire 1967/II to 1979/II sample period. Caramazza et al. (1986, 43–47) also found that some of the major industrialized countries in the 1980s (January 1980 through June 1985) moved farther from real interest parity than they had been in the 1970s (July 1973 through December 1979).[9] In the early 1980s, the real interest rate in the United States, in particular, rose far above the real interest rate of its major trading partners, by any of a variety of measures.[10] If the domestic real interest rate is not tied to the foreign real interest rate, then there is no reason to expect a zero coefficient in the saving-investment regression. We discuss in a later section the factors underlying real interest differentials.

8.2.2   The U.S. Saving-Investment Regression Updated

Since 1980 the massive fiscal experiment carried out under the Reagan administration has been rapidly undermining the statistical finding of a high saving-investment correlation for the case of the United States. The increase in the structural budget deficit, which was neither accommodated by monetary policy nor financed by an increase in private saving, reduced the national saving rate by 3 percent of GNP, relative to the 1970s. The investment rate—which at first, like the saving rate, fell in the 1981–82 recession—in the late 1980s approximately reattained its 1980 level at best.[11] The saving shortfall was made up, necessarily, by a flood of borrowing from abroad equal to more than 3 percent of GNP. Hence the current account deficit of $161 billion in 1987. By contrast, the U.S. current account balance was on average equal to zero in the 1970s.

By now, the divergence between U.S. national saving and investment has been sufficiently large and long lasting to show up in longer-term regressions of the Feldstein-Horioka type. If one seeks to isolate the degree of capital mobility or crowding out for the United States in particular, and how it has changed over time, then time-series regression is necessary (whereas if one is concerned with such measures worldwide, then cross-section regressions of the sort performed by Feldstein and Horioka are better). Table 8.1 reports instrumental variables regressions of investment against national saving for the United States from 1870 to 1987.[12] Decade averages are used for each variable, which removes some of the cyclical variation but gives us only 12 observations. (Yearly data are not in any case available before 1930.) That is one more observation than was available in Frankel (1986, table 2.2), which went only through the 1970s.

As before, the coefficient is statistically greater than zero and is not statistically different from one, suggesting a high degree of crowding out (or a low

Table 8.1   **The "Feldstein-Horioka Coefficient" by Decades, 1869–1987; Instrumental Variables Regression of U.S. Investment against National Saving (as shares of GNP)**

	Constant	Coefficient	Time Trend in Coefficient	Durbin-Watson Statistic	Autoregressive Parameter	R^2
1.	.411	.976		1.45		.96
	(1.340)	(.086)				
2.	3.324	.785			.46	.97
	(1.842)	(.118)			(.33)	
3.	3.291	.854	−.011	.73		.92
	(6.176)	(.279)	(.21)			
4.	1.061	.924	.001		.03	.96
	(1.507)	(.093)	(.005)		(.08)	

Note: Instrumental variables are dependency ratio and military expenditure/GNP.

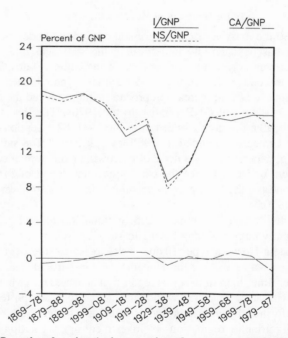

Fig. 8.1   U.S. national saving (private saving plus government budget surplus), investment, and current account: 10-year averages

degree of capital mobility, in Feldstein and Horioka's terms). But the point estimate of the coefficient (when correcting for possible serial correlation) drops from .91 in the earlier study to .79. We can allow for a time trend in the coefficient; it drops from *plus* .01 a year in the earlier study to *minus* .01 a year (or plus .001, when correcting for serial correlation) in the longer sample. Thus the additional years 1980–87 do show up as anticipated: as exhibiting a lower U.S. degree of crowding out, even if the change is small. (The trend is not statistically significant, but this is not surprising given the small number of observations.)

A date set that begins later would seem more promising than the 12 decade averages. Table 8.2 reports regressions for yearly data beginning in 1930. Much of the variation in the yearly data is cyclical, so table 8.3 uses saving and investment rates that have been cyclically adjusted, for a sample period

Table 8.2   The "Feldstein-Horioka Coefficient" by Years, 1929–87; Instrumental Variables Regression of U.S. Investment against National Saving (as shares of GNP), Comparing Regressions Before and After 1980

	Constant	Coefficient	Durbin-Watson Statistic	Autoregressive Parameter	R^2
1929–87	2.99	.79	.64		.94
	(.88)	(.06)			
1930–87	4.85	.67		.77	.89
	(2.61)	(.19)		(.09)	
1929–79	1.89	.86	1.31		.97
	(.61)	(.04)			
1930–79	2.00	.85		.38	.95
	(.66)	(.05)		(.13)	
1980–87	13.73	.15	2.09		
	(3.85)	(.27)			
1981–87	−.36	.03		−.37	.00
	(.56)	(.02)		Not Converged	

Table 8.3   The "Feldstein-Horioka Coefficient" by Years, 1955–87: Instrumental Variables Regression of U.S. Investment against National Saving (as shares of GNP and cyclically adjusted)

	Constant	Coefficient	Durbin-Watson Statistic	Autoregressive Parameter	R^2
1929–87	[a]	−.06	.96		.25
		(.25)			
1930–87	[a]	.03		.50	.42
		(.26)		(.15)	
1929–79	−.68	1.37	1.61		.73
	(.17)	(.23)			
1930–79	−.57	1.05		.35	.70
	(.18)	(.19)		(.20)	
1980–87	.39	.13	2.46		.30
	(.36)	(.17)			
1981–87	.58	.22		−.13	.34
	(.37)	(.16)		(.41)	

[a]Constant term is automaticallly zero because cyclically adjusted rates are residuals from a 1955–87 regression against the GNP gap.

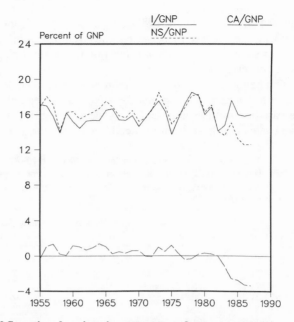

Fig. 8.2   U.S. national saving, investment, and current account

that begins in 1955. The cyclical adjustment of each is accomplished by first regressing it on the GNP gap, defined as the percentage deviation from the Bureau of Economic Analysis's "middle expansion trend" of GNP, and taking the residuals.

In previous work with a sample period of 1956–84, the coefficient in a regression of cyclically adjusted saving and investment rates was estimated at .80, statistically indistinguishable from 1 (Frankel 1986, 43–44). But now the coefficient has dropped essentially to zero, suggesting a zero degree of crowding out, or a zero degree of "saving retention" (or, in the Feldstein-Horioka terminology, "perfect capital mobility"). This finding is the result of the addition to the sample of another three years of record current account deficits, 1985–87, a period also in which the cyclically adjusted national saving rate was historically low. When the equation is estimated with an allowance for a time trend in the coefficient, the trend is negative (though statistically insignificant), whereas the earlier sample that stopped in 1984 showed a time trend that was positive (and insignificant).

To verify that the 1980s experience is indeed the source of the precipitous fall in the saving-investment coefficient,[13] the sample period is split at 1980. For the period 1955–79, not only is the coefficient statistically indistinguishable from one, but the point estimate is slightly *over* one.[14] It is clearly the unprecedented developments of the present decade that have overturned the hitherto-robust saving-investment relationship for the case of the United

States. It is likely that financial liberalization in Japan, the United Kingdom, and other countries, and continued innovation in the Euromarkets (and perhaps the 1984 repeal of the U.S. withholding tax on borrowing from abroad), have resulted in a higher degree of capital mobility and thereby facilitated the record flow of capital to the United States in the 1980s. But the magnitude of the inflow is in the first instance attributable to the unprecedented magnitude of the decline in national saving.[15]

8.3 Differentials in Expected Rates of Return, and Expected Real Depreciation

If the goal is to measure the degree of integration of capital markets, rather than the degree to which decreases in national saving have crowded out investment, then it is better to look at differences in rates of return across countries rather than looking at saving-investment correlations.[16] But measuring *real* interest differentials will not do the trick. An international investor, when deciding what country's assets to buy, will not compare the interest rates in different countries each expressed in terms of expected purchasing power over that country's goods. When he or she thinks to evaluate assets in terms of purchasing power, all assets will be evaluated in terms of the same basket, the one consumed by that particular investor. The expected inflation rate then drops out of differentials in expected rates of return among assets.

The differential in expected rates of return on two countries' bonds is the uncovered interest differential, the nominal interest differential minus the expected change in the exchange rate: $i - i* - (\Delta s^e)$. If asset demands are highly sensitive to expected rates of return, then the differential will be zero, which gives us uncovered interest parity:

$$(3) \qquad i - i* - (\Delta s^e) = 0.$$

To distinguish this parity condition, which is criterion 3 above, from the other definitions, it has often been designated "perfect substitutability": not only is there little in the manner of transactions costs or government-imposed controls to separate national markets, but also domestic currency and foreign currency bonds are perfect substitutes in investors' portfolios.

Just as criterion 1 is considerably stronger than criterion 2, so is criterion 2 considerably stronger than criterion 3. For real interest parity to hold, one must have not only uncovered interest parity, but an additional condition as well, which is sometimes called ex ante relative purchasing power parity:

$$(2') \qquad \Delta s^e = \Delta p^e - \Delta p^{e*}.$$

Equation (2') and equation (3) together imply equation (2). If goods markets are perfectly integrated, meaning not only that there is little in the manner of transportation costs or government-imposed barriers to separate national markets, but also that domestic and foreign goods are perfect substitutes in con-

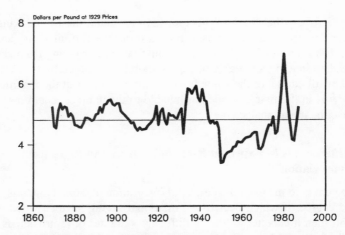

Fig. 8.3   Dollar/pound real exchange rate, 1869–1987, with period average

sumers' utility functions, then purchasing power parity holds. Purchasing power parity (PPP) in turn implies (2'). But as is by now well known, goods markets are not in fact perfectly integrated. Because of the possibility of expected real depreciation, real interest parity can fail even if criterion (3) holds perfectly. The remainder of this section considers the question of whether ex ante relative PPP, equation (2'), holds.

The enormous real appreciation of the dollar in the early 1980s and subsequent real depreciation have by now convinced the remaining doubters, but abundant statistical evidence against PPP was there all along. Krugman (1978, 406), for example, computed for the floating rate period July 1973 through December 1976 standard deviations of the (logarithmic) real exchange rate equal to 6.0 percent for the pound/dollar rate and 8.4 percent for the mark/dollar rate. He also computed serial correlation coefficients for PPP deviations of .897 and .854, respectively, on a monthly basis, equal to .271 and .150 on an annual basis. The serial correlation coefficient is of interest because it is equal to one minus the speed of adjustment to PPP. It may be best not to rely exclusively on the standard deviation of the real exchange rate as a summary statistic for the degree of integration of goods markets, because it in part reflects the magnitude of monetary disturbances during the period.[17]

Table 8.4 shows updated annual statistics on the real exchange rate between the United States and Great Britain. During the floating rate period 1973–87, though there is no significant time trend, there is a large standard error of 15.6 percent. The serial correlation in the deviations from PPP is estimated at .687, with a standard error of .208. (The equation estimated is $[er_{t+1} - \overline{er}_{t+1}) = AR[er_t - \overline{er}_t]\varepsilon_{t+1}$, where er is the real exchange rate, $\overline{er}$ is the long-run equilibrium level, alternatively estimated as the sample mean or a time trend, and AR is the autoregressive coefficient.) This means

Table 8.4   **Purchasing Power Parity between the United States and the United Kingdom**

Statistics on Percentage Deviation from Mean	1973–87	1945–72	1945–87	1869–1987
Mean absolute deviation	.120	.074	.110	.093
Standard deviation	.156	.091	.156	.121
Time trend	.001	−.001	.006*	−.001*
	(.010)	(.002)	(.002)	(.001)
Regressions of Real Exchange Rate				
Autoregressions				
Deviation from mean	.687*	.722*	.830*	.844*
	(.208)	(.130)	(.092)	(.050)
Deviation from trend	.688*	.730*	.741*	.838*
	(.208)	(.131)	(.101)	(.052)
Regression Against Nominal Exchange Rate				
Coefficient[a]	2.516*	1.220*	1.687*	.916*
	(.417)	(.103)	(.186)	(.093)
Autocorrelation Coefficient	.959*	.989*	.992	.988*
	(.054)	(.015)	(.011)	(.014)

Note: Standard errors are reported in parentheses.
[a]With constant term and correction for autocorrelation.
*Significant at the 95 percent level.

that the estimated speed of adjustment to PPP is .313 per year, and that one can easily reject the hypothesis of instantaneous adjustment.

From the ashes of absolute PPP, a phoenix has risen. In response to findings such as those reported here, some authors have swung from one extreme, the proposition that the tendency of the real exchange rate to return to a constant is complete and instantaneous, to the opposite extreme that there is no such tendency at all. The hypothesis that the real exchange rate follows a random walk is just as good as the hypothesis of absolute PPP for implying ex ante relative PPP. But there is even less of an a priori case why PPP should hold in rate-of-change form than in the level form.

Even though ex ante relative PPP has little basis in theory, it does appear to have some empirical support. Typically, the estimated speeds of adjustment during the floating rate period, .31 in table 8.4 (1973–87), while not so low as to be implausible as point estimates, are nevertheless so low that one statistically cannot reject the hypothesis that they are zero. In other words one cannot reject the random walk hypothesis that the autoregression coefficient is 1.0.

A 95 percent confidence interval on the autoregressive coefficient covers the range 0.27–1.10. If the null hypothesis is an autoregressive coefficient of 1.0, one cannot legitimately use the standard t-test derived from a regression where the right-hand-side variable is the level of the real exchange rate, because under the null hypothesis the variance is infinite. (This does not invalidate the t-test just reported of the null hypothesis that the tendency to return to PPP was 100 percent, that is, $AR = 0$). There are a number of ways of dealing with this nonstationarity problem. Here one simply applies the corrected Dickey-Fuller 95 percent significance level, 3.00. The .31 estimate for the floating-rate period is insignificantly different from zero.

This failure to reject a random walk in the real exchange rate is the same result found by Roll (1979), Frenkel (1981, 699), Adler and Lehman (1983), Darby (1981), Mishkin (1984a, 1351–53) and Pigott and Sweeney (1985). Most of these studies used monthly data. On the one hand, the greater abundance of data reduces the standard error of the estimate but, on the other hand, one is no longer testing whether $AR = .69$ is different from 1.0, but rather whether $.97(= AR^{1/12})$ is different from 1.0, so that it may not be much easier to reject. Another problem is that one does not know that the nature of the true autoregressive process is truly first order on a monthly (or continuous-time) basis. In any case, the monthly date in the studies cited were generally not powerful enough to reject the random walk.[18]

A more promising alternative is to choose a longer time sample to get a more powerful estimate. Table 8.4 also reports statistics for the entire postwar period, 1945–87. PPP held better for the Bretton Woods years than it did after 1973, as measured either by the mean absolute deviation and standard deviation of the real exchange rate or by the ability to reject the hypothesis of zero autocorrelation. But, despite the longer time sample, one is only at the borderline of being able to reject the random walk. The 95 percent confidence interval for AR runs from 0.64 to 1.02 (or 0.52 to 0.96, when allowing for a trend in the long-run equilibrium), and the t-ratio of 1.85 (or 2.56, when allowing for the trend) falls short of the Dickey-Fuller 95 percent significance level of 2.93.

The asymptotic standard error of an estimate of AR is approximately the square root of $(1 - AR^2)/N$. So if the true speed of adjustment is on the order of 30 percent a year ($AR = .7$), a simple calculation suggests that we might require at least 49 years of data ($2.93^2[1 - .7^2]/[1 - .7]^2 = 48.6$) to be able to reject the null hypothesis of $AR = 1$. It is not very surprising that 43 years of data is not enough, much less the 15 years of data used in most studies.[19] Econometricians consider the asymptotic standard error on which this calculation is based to be a bad approximation in small samples. But the correct power calculation suggests that, if anything, the sample required to reject a random walk would be even larger than 49.[20]

The last column of table 8.4 presents an entire 119 years of U.S.–U.K. data. With this long a time sample, the standard error is reduced considerably.

The rejection of no serial correlation in the real exchange rate is even stronger than in the shorter time samples. More important, one is finally able to detect a statistically significant tendency for the real exchange rate to regress to PPP, at a rate of 16 percent a year. The confidence interval for AR runs from 0.75 to 0.94, safely less than unity, and the t-ratio of 3.12 exceeds the Dickey-Fuller significance level of 2.89.[21]

The last row of the table reports regressions of the real exchange rate against the nominal exchange rate. The coefficient is highly significant for all time samples. The figures suggest that changes in the nominal rate (due, for example, to devaluations under fixed exchange rates or monetary disturbances under floating exchange rates) in the presence of sticky goods prices cause transitory changes in the real exchange rate. Such results specifically rule out the possibility, which has been occasionally suggested in the past, that apparent deviations from PPP might be attributed to (random) measurement errors in the price data.

The motivation for looking at PPP in this section has been to obtain insight into the expected rate of real depreciation, because that is the variable that can give rise to real interest differentials even in the presence of uncovered interest parity.[22] In rejecting the random walk description of the real exchange rate, one has rejected the claim that the rationally expected rate of real depreciation is zero.[23] To take an example, in 1983–84, when the dollar had appreciated some 30 percent above its PPP value, survey data show expected future real depreciation of 4.3 percent per year. It is thus not difficult to explain the existence of the U.S. real interest differential, even without appealing to any sort of risk premium. There is little excuse for authors such as Koraczyk (1985, 350) and Darby (1985, 420) ruling out the possibility of expected real depreciation a priori and thereby concluding that real interest differentials *necessarily* constitute risk premiums.

If the failure of ex ante relative purchasing power parity could, in itself, explain the failure of real interest parity, then it could also, by itself, explain the failure of saving and investment to be uncorrelated. In the recent U.S. context, a fall in national saving could cause an increase in the real interest differential and therefore a fall in investment, even if financial markets are perfectly integrated and even if the fall in saving is truly exogenous, provided the real interest differential is associated with expected real depreciation of the dollar.

Demonstrating that the failure of ex ante relative purchasing power parity is *capable* of producing a correlation between saving and investment is, of course, not the same thing as asserting that this in fact is the explanation for the observed correlation. There are plenty of other competing explanations that have been proposed. But some support for the idea that the existence of expected real depreciation *is* key to the observed correlation comes from Cardia (1988). She simulates saving and investment rates in a sequence of models featuring shocks to fiscal spending, money growth, and productivity, in order to see which models are capable, for empirically-relevant magnitudes of the parameters, of producing saving-investment correlations as high as those observed. To get at some of the explanations that have been most prominently proposed, she constructs models both with and without PPP, both with and without endogenous response of fiscal policy to current account imbalances, and both with and without the small-country assumption. The finding is that the model that allows for deviations from PPP is able to explain saving-investment correlations as high as one, while the various models that impose PPP are generally not able to do so.[24]

Further empirical support for the idea that the Feldstein-Horioka results may in fact be due to imperfect integration of goods markets, rather than imperfect integration of financial markets, is provided by a test by Bayoumi and Rose (1989). They compute the correlation of saving and investment across regions within the United Kingdom, reasoning that these regions—unlike nations—are highly integrated with respect to their goods markets, and find no positive correlation.

8.4   A Decomposition of Real Interest Differentials for 25 Countries

Because there are so many competing definitions of the degree of international capital mobility, it would be worth knowing if the sort of countries that register high by one criterion are also the sort that register high by the others. In this section we look at rates of return in the 1980s across a sample of 25 countries. We begin with the broadest measure of barriers to international capital mobility, the differential in real interest rates, defined as:

$$(4) \qquad r - r^* = (i - \Delta p^e) - (i^* - \Delta p^{e*}).$$

Subsequently we will decompose the real interest differential into a component due to "political" or country factors and a component due to currency factors:

$$(5) \qquad r - r^* = (i - i^* - fd) - (fd - \Delta p^e + \Delta p^{e*}),$$

where i is the domestic nominal interest rate, i^* is the foreign nominal interest rate, and fd is the forward discount on the domestic currency. The first term $(i - i^* - fd)$ is the covered interest differential. We call it the political or country premium because it captures all barriers to integration of financial markets across national boundaries: transactions costs, information costs, capital controls, tax laws that discriminate by country of residence, default risk, and risk of future capital controls. The second term could be described as the real forward discount. We call it the currency premium because it captures differences in assets according to the currency in which they are denominated, rather than in terms of the political jurisdiction in which they are issued. As we will see, the currency premium can in turn be decomposed into two factors, the exchange risk premium and expected real depreciation.

The decomposition of the real interest differential would not be possible without the use of data on forward exchange rates. Many previous studies have used forward rate data to test covered interest parity, but only for a few countries. The present study uses forward rate data for panel of 25 countries, which so far as I know is the largest set ever examined. The set of 25 includes countries both large and small, industrialized and developing, Atlantic and Pacific. The forward rate data for most of the countries come from Barclay's Bank in London, via Data Resources, Inc.[25]

8.4.1   Real Interest Differentials

Table 8.5 reports statistics on three-month real interest differentials for the 25 countries, in each case expressed as the local interest rate measured relative to the Eurodollar interest rate. For local interest rates we use the interbank market rate or, where no market rate exists, the most flexibly determined interest rate available.[26] We use, to begin with, the realized inflation rates during the ex post three-month period. Column 2 of table 8.5 reports the mean real interest differential during the sample period, September 1982 to January 1988. (In this and subsequent tables, because the ex post data run three months behind the ex ante expectations, they go up to April 1988.) The numbers are negative for a majority of countries, averaging −1.74 across all 25, which reflects the high level of real dollar interest rates during this period.

The countries are classified into five groups chosen on a priori grounds. The group with real interest rates the farthest below the world rate is Bahrain, Greece, Mexico, Portugal, and South Africa. These five (very diverse) countries bear the burden of representing a wide class of LDCs in our sample. Altogether there are eight countries classified as LDCs that happen to have forward rate data available and thereby appear in our sample; three of these are East Asian countries that are thought to have open financial markets in the 1980s (Hong Kong, Singapore, and Malaysia) and so are here classified separately.

One might object that the large negative real interest differentials in the group of five reflect administered local interest rates that are kept artificially low by "financial repression." But countries cannot maintain artificially low interest rates without barriers to capital outflow. These statistics reflect a low degree of capital mobility precisely as we want them to. In this respect our group of five is typical of LDCs. A number of studies, including much larger LDC samples than available here, have shown the extremes to which real interest rates can go, particularly some very negative levels in the 1970s.

As with the other measures of interest rate differentials that we will be considering below, the mean is not always the most useful statistic. A small mean over a particular sample period may hide fluctuations in both directions. Even if a mean is statistically significant,[27] it is useful to know in addition the variability of the differential. The standard deviation is reported in table 8.5, column 4. We also report the root mean squared error in column 5. (This would

Table 8.5   **Real Interest Differentials (local minus Eurodollar; three-month rates): Interest Differential Less Realized Inflation Differential, September 1982 to January 1988**

	Number of Observations (1)	Mean (2)	Standard Error of Mean (3)	Series Standard Deviation (4)	Root Mean Squared Error (5)	95 Percent Band (6)
Open Atlantic developed countries:						
Canada	63	.09	.38	2.09	2.09	3.96
Germany	63	−1.29	.65	2.77	3.06	5.95
Netherlands	62	−.71	.86	3.91	3.97	7.63
Switzerland	62	−2.72	.81	3.39	4.36	8.43
United Kingdom	63	.46	.79	3.45	3.48	5.69
Group	313	−.83	.66	3.16	3.46	
Liberalizing Pacific:						
Hong Kong	62	−2.89	.94	4.80	5.62	11.61
Malaysia	62	.83	1.00	4.61	4.68	8.19
Singapore	61	.08	.68	3.33	3.34	6.71
Group	185	−.67	.82	4.28	4.62	
Closed less-developed countries:						
Bahrain	60	2.19	1.46	7.10	7.44	12.93
Greece	56	−9.22	1.91	9.36	13.19	21.77
Mexico	62	−20.28	9.43	21.19	29.45	52.13
Portugal	61	−3.90	2.97	11.28	11.95	23.62
South Africa	61	−4.84	1.17	4.85	6.88	11.16
Group	300	−7.25	1.30	12.16	16.06	
Closed European developed countries:						
Austria	64	−2.20	.83	3.84	4.43	7.32
Belgium	63	.53	.68	2.90	2.95	4.99
Denmark	61	−3.42	.90	4.34	5.54	9.64
France	64	−.48	.72	2.94	2.98	5.54
Ireland	61	1.53	1.03	3.95	4.24	7.13
Italy	61	1.01	.86	3.62	3.76	5.83
Norway	50	−.64	.84	3.23	3.29	6.83
Spain	63	.53	1.44	5.92	5.95	11.90
Sweden	63	−.21	1.07	4.52	4.53	8.28
Group	550	−.37	.81	4.00	4.29	
Liberalizing Pacific developed countries:						
Australia	60	1.16	.90	3.69	3.87	7.43
Japan	63	−.58	.62	3.41	3.46	6.03
New Zealand	60	1.04	1.83	7.15	7.23	11.36
Group	183	.52	.73	5.00	5.09	
All countries	1,531	−1.74		6.47	8.07	

be a superior measure of how closely the rates are tied together if, for example, we are worried about the possibility of a large differential that is fairly constant over time because of government administration of interest rates.) Finally, we report in column 6 how big a band would be needed to encompass 95 percent of the deviations from real interest parity.

Country-group comparisons of the measures of real interest differential variability in some respects suit a priori expectations: the five closed LDCs constitute the group with the highest variability, and the five open Atlantic countries the group with the lowest.[28] But there are some results that are anomalous if the real interest differential is taken as a measure of financial market integration. France, for example, had stringent capital controls in place during our sample period (at least until the latter part of the period) and yet appears to have a *higher* degree of capital mobility by the criterion of real interest differential variability than Japan, which announced liberalization of its capital controls before our sample period (1979–80). One might conceivably argue that the Japanese liberalization must not have been genuine. But the French real interest differential is smaller and less variable even than those of the Netherlands and Switzerland, major countries that are known to be virtually free of capital controls. Only Canada shows a smaller and less variable real interest differential than France.

Because the realized inflation rates could not have been precisely known a priori, it is necessary to project them onto contemporaneously known variables. Three such variables were used: the forward discount, nominal interest differential, and lagged inflation differential. (The results are reported in NBER Working Paper no. 2856, but are omitted here to save space.) In a majority of cases, a statistically significant amount of the variation in the real interest differential turned out to be forecastable.[29] The standard deviation of the projected differential gives us our final measure of variability. The results for the ex ante real interest differential are mostly similar to those for the ex post. France, for example, still shows a lower degree of variability than the Netherlands.

8.4.2 Covered Interest Differentials: The Country Premium

We now use the Barclay's forward rate data to decompose the real interest differential into one part due to country factors and another due to currency factors, as in equation (5). The first component, the covered interest differential, encompasses all factors related to the political jurisdiction in which the asset is issued. Its size and variability measures barriers to international capital mobility most narrowly and properly defined.

Column 2 of table 8.6 reports the mean of the covered interest differential for each of our 25 countries. A good rule of thumb, when the absolute magnitude of the mean or the variability of the differential indicates the existence of significant barriers, is as follows: a negative differential vis-à-vis the Eurocurrency market indicates that, to the extent that barriers exist, they are capital

Table 8.6   "Country Premia" or Covered Interest Differentials (local minus Eurodollar; three-months rates): Interest Differential Less Forward Discount, September 1982 to April 1988

	Number of Observations (1)	Mean (2)	Standard Error of Mean (3)	Series Standard Deviation (4)	Root Mean Squared Error (5)	95 Percent Band (6)
Open Atlantic developed countries:						
Canada	68	−.10	.03	.21	.24	.44
Germany	68	.35	.03	.24	.42	.75
Netherlands	68	.21	.02	.13	.25	.45
Switzerland	68	.42	.03	.23	.48	.79
United Kingdom	68	−.14	.02	.20	.25	.41
Group	340	.14	.01	.21	.34	
Liberalizing Pacific:						
Hong Kong	68	.13	.03	.28	.31	.60
Malaysia	63	−1.46	.16	1.28	1.95	3.73
Singapore	64	−.30	.04	.31	.43	.73
Group	195	−.52	.05	.76	1.14	
Closed less-developed countries:						
Bahrain	64	−2.15	.13	1.06	2.41	4.17
Greece	58	−9.39	.80	6.08	11.26	20.39
Mexico	43	−16.47	1.83	12.01	20.54	28.86
Portugal	61	−7.93	1.23	9.59	12.49	27.83
South Africa	67	−1.07	1.17	9.55	9.61	2.68
Group	293	−6.64	.48	8.23	11.82	
Closed European developed countires:						
Austria	65	.13	.05	.39	.41	.39
Belgium	68	.12	.03	.26	.29	.59
Denmark	68	−3.53	.19	1.57	3.89	6.63
France	68	−1.74	.32	2.68	3.20	7.18
Ireland	66	−.79	.51	4.17	4.24	7.80
Italy	68	−.40	.23	1.92	1.96	4.11
Norway	50	−1.03	.11	.76	1.29	2.10
Spain	67	−2.40	.45	3.66	4.39	7.95
Sweden	68	−.23	.06	.45	.51	.81
Group	588	−1.10	.09	2.25	2.77	
Liberalizing Pacific developed countries:						
Australia	68	−.75	.23	1.94	2.08	2.59
Japan	68	.09	.03	.21	.23	.43
New Zealand	68	−1.63	.29	2.42	2.92	5.24
Group	204	−.76	.12	1.78	2.06	
All countries	1,620	−1.73	.09	3.81	5.36	

controls or transactions costs currently operating to discourage capital from flowing *out* of the country. Investors would not settle for a lower return domestically if they were free to earn abroad the higher return covered to eliminate exchange risk. This is the case for all the LDCs in the sample, with the exception of Hong Kong, and for all of the traditionally "closed" European countries, with the exceptions of Austria and Belgium (which should by now probably be classified with the "open" countries). The negative differential that existed for the United Kingdom before Margaret Thatcher removed capital controls in 1979 is now extremely small.[30] Similarly, Canada's differential is effectively zero.[31]

Column 6 of table 8.6, the size of the band wide enough to encompass 95 percent of deviations from international covered interest parity, can be compared with the approach of Frenkel and Levich (1977). They tested a larger band meant to represent transactions costs between pound and dollar securities. They found, for the case of the United Kingdom, that a smaller percentage of deviations (87.6–89.7 percent; Frenkel and Levich 1977, 1217) fell within the band. This confirms that capital mobility has increased since the 1970s.

Germany and several other neighboring European countries (Switzerland, the Netherlands, Austria, and Belgium) show higher interest rates locally than offshore, which suggests some barriers discouraging capital *inflow:* investors would not settle for a lower mark return in the Euromarket if they were free to get the higher return in Germany. But the magnitude is quite small, as it has been observed to be ever since Germany removed most of its controls on capital inflow in 1974 (Dooley and Isard 1980; and Giavazzi and Pagano 1985, 27).

Japan has a covered differential that by all measures is smaller and less variable than those of Switzerland and Germany, let alone France and most of the other countries. This might come as a surprise to those accustomed to thinking of Japanese financial markets in terms of the large barriers to capital inflow that were in place in the 1970s. The liberalization of Japanese markets, which has been documented elsewhere, continued during our sample period.[32] Australia and New Zealand, while lagging well behind Japan, also show signs of liberalization during the course of our sample period.[33]

The covered interest differential for France is much larger and more variable than that for the other major industrialized countries known to be free of capital controls. This is the reverse of the finding from the criterion of real interest differentials in table 8.5. It supports the value of the criterion of covered interest differentials as the proper test of financial market integration. The differential, with its negative sign signifying controls on French capital outflows, has been previously studied, especially its tendency to shoot up shortly before devaluations of the franc.[34] Our data indicate that the last major occurrence of this phenomenon was February 1986; since then the differential has been close to zero.

Similarly, the same phenomenon for Italy, which has also been previously studied (e.g., Giavazzi and Pagano 1985), appears to have ended after the February 1986 realignment. France and Italy dismantled their capital controls quickly enough to meet a 1990 deadline for liberalization recently set by the EEC Twelve.[35] Of four countries that required a later deadline, Spain and Portugal have by our measures already been liberalizing (plots show that the magnitude of the covered interest differential fell sharply in 1987 for these two countries), but Greece and Ireland have not. Sweden is one non-EEC European country that appears to have moved toward liberalization during our sample period, while Norway does not. All of these European countries show up with negative mean differentials, which implies that the remaining controls act to discourage capital outflow rather than inflow. For the EEC countries, this finding supports records of the European Commission, which reports more freedom for short-term inflows than short-term outflows.[36]

Registering impressively open financial markets are our three East Asian LDCs (which, especially in the case of Singapore, have rapidly outgrown the appellation "less developed"). Hong Kong and Singapore show smaller covered differentials even than some open European countries like Germany. Malaysia's differential has been considerably higher, particularly in 1986, but still compares favorably with some European countries.

Not surprisingly, our remaining LDCs (Mexico, Greece, Portugal, Bahrain, and South Africa) show by far the largest and most variable covered interest differentials.[37] Again, the results are precisely what one would expect if covered interest differentials are the proper criterion for capital mobility, but the reverse of what the saving-investment criterion shows.

Why does the covered differential criterion give such different answers from the saving-investment criterion, which shows a high degree of saving retention among industrialized countries? Feldstein and Horioka (1980, 315) argue that financial markets are less well integrated at longer-term maturities, as compared to the three-month maturities used in tests of covered interest parity such as those reported above: "It is clear from the yields on short-term securities in the Eurocurrency market and the forward prices of those currencies that liquid financial capital moves very rapidly to arbitrage such short-term differentials. . . . There are however reasons to be sceptical about the extent of such long-term arbitrage."

Studies of international interest parity have been restricted by a lack of forward exchange rates at horizons going out much further than one year.[38] But even without the use of forward rate data, there are ways of getting around the problem of exchange risk. Data on currency swap rates can be used in place of forward exchange rates to test the long-term version of interest rate parity. Popper (1990) finds that the swap-covered return differential on five-year U.S. government bonds versus Japanese bonds averaged only 1.7 basis points from October 3, 1985 to July 10, 1986, and that the differential on seven-year bonds averaged only 5.3 basis points. The means mask some variation in the differential. But a band of 46 basis points is large enough to encompass 95 percent of the observations for the five-year bonds. The band is 34 basis points for the seven-year bonds. The means on five-year bonds for some other major countries are as follows: Canada 15.9, Switzerland 18.7, United Kingdom 51.1, and Germany 28.4.

The magnitude of these long-term differentials compares favorably with the magnitude of the short-term differentials. The implication is that Feldstein and Horioka are wrong in their conjecture that there is a term-structure wedge separating national capital markets.[39] The most relevant distinction appears to be, not long-term versus short-term, but rather real versus nominal.

8.4.3 "Real Forward Discounts": The Currency Premium

Even for those countries that exhibit no substantial country premium, as reflected in covered interest parity ($fd - [i - i^*] = 0$), there may still be a substantial currency premium that drives real interest differentials ($[i - \Delta p^e] - [i^* - \Delta p^{e*}]$) away from zero. If real interest differentials are not arbitraged to zero, then there is in turn no reason to expect saving-investment correlations to be zero. Table 8.7 reports the statistics for the currency premium, as measured by the "real forward discount":

$$fd - (\Delta p^e - \Delta p^{e*}).$$

Germany, Switzerland, the Netherlands, Austria, and Japan, for example, all have substantial real forward discounts (or—more precisely—real forward premia), which constitute approximately the entirety of their real interest differentials. These are countries with currencies that have experienced a lot of exchange rate variability, both nominal and real, vis-à-vis the dollar since 1973, and especially since 1980. As a consequence, some combination of exchange risk premiums and expected real depreciation—factors pertaining to the currency, not to the political jurisdiction—produces the gap in real interest rates. For these five financially open industrialized countries, and for Hong Kong as well, the currency factors produce a *negative* real interest differential, while the covered interest differential (though small) is *positive:* the small regulations or frictions that remain in these countries are, if anything, working to resist capital inflow (at least at the short end of the maturity spectrum), not outflow as one would mistakenly conclude from the real interest differential criterion. The other countries all have highly variable currency premiums as well. Indeed the real forward discount (currency premium) is more variable than the covered interest differential (country premium) for all but three of our 25 countries (Greece, Mexico, and France). The last rows of tables 8.6 and 8.7 show that the average variability across all countries is higher for the currency premium than for the country premium.

We can project the real forward discount on the same three variables as we did for the real interest differential (the forward discount, nominal interest differential, and lagged inflation differential) to get an ex ante measure.[40] Its

Table 8.7   **"Currency Premia" or Real Forward Discounts: Forward Discount Less Realized Inflation Differential, September 1982 to January 1988**

	Number of Observations (1)	Mean (2)	Standard Error of Mean (3)	Series Standard Deviation (4)	Root Mean Squared Error (5)	95 Percent Band (6)
Open Atlantic developed countries:						
Canada	63	.18	.38	2.08	2.09	4.02
Germany	63	− 1.66	.69	2.89	3.34	6.57
Netherlands	62	− .92	.88	3.98	4.09	7.52
Switzerland	62	− 3.15	.84	3.49	4.72	8.79
United Kingdom	63	.61	.83	3.56	3.61	5.97
Group	313	− .98	.69	3.24	3.65	
Liberalizing Pacific:						
Hong Kong	62	− 2.99	.93	4.79	5.66	11.76
Malaysia	62	2.29	1.14	5.06	5.56	10.17
Singapore	62	.40	.67	.32	3.35	6.86
Group	186	− .10	.82	4.43	4.95	
Closed less-developed countries:						
Bahrain	60	4.37	1.52	7.27	8.51	16.18
Greece	60	.83	1.67	9.98	10.01	18.77
Mexico	43	.03	3.58	15.23	15.23	22.08
Portugal	59	4.94	2.13	11.73	12.74	21.56
South Africa	62	− 3.82	1.81	11.36	11.99	14.75
Group	284	1.29	1.37	11.05	11.60	
Closed European developed countries:						
Austria	62	− 2.25	.88	3.94	4.55	7.68
Belgium	63	.42	.69	2.95	2.98	5.05
Denmark	61	.14	1.01	4.63	4.63	7.13
France	64	1.35	.54	2.50	2.85	4.82
Ireland	59	2.14	1.40	6.41	6.76	13.85
Italy	61	1.42	.72	3.15	3.46	5.52
Norway	64	1.07	.75	3.25	3.43	5.91
Spain	63	3.12	1.26	5.53	6.36	11.08
Sweden	63	.04	1.07	4.57	4.57	8.29
Group	560	.83	.67	4.23	4.54	
Liberalizing Pacific developed countries:						
Australia	60	1.97	.88	4.06	4.52	7.85
Japan	63	− .69	.64	3.48	3.55	6.32
New Zealand	60	2.82	1.98	7.96	8.46	14.11
Group	183	1.33	.79	5.48	5.84	
All countries	1,526	.49		6.11	6.50	

standard deviation now shows six countries for whom the currency premium is less variable than the country premium (Greece, Mexico, Portugal, France, Italy, and Spain). But the currency premium remains the major obstacle to real interest parity for most countries.

8.4.4 Further Decomposition into Exchange Risk Premium and Expected Real Depreciation

Our decomposition so far has lumped two terms, the exchange risk premium and expected real depreciation, together into the currency premium:

$$fd - \Delta p^e + \Delta p^{e*} = (fd - \Delta s^e) + (\Delta s^e - \Delta p^e + \Delta p^{e*}).$$

In this section we attempt to complete the decomposition by separating these two terms. To do so requires a measure or model of expected depreciation. The usual approach is to use the ex post changes in the spot rate (Δs) as a measure of ex ante expectations (Δs^e), and to argue that under rational expectations the expectational error ($e \equiv \Delta s - \Delta s^e$) should be random (uncorrelated with information currently available at time t).

Column 2 of table 8.8 reports the mean value of ($fd - \Delta s$) for each of our countries. Most of the means are positive, showing that the weak-dollar period (1985–88) dominates over the strong-dollar period (1982–1985).[41] But only three currencies have mean risk premiums, of either sign, that are statistically significant.[42] Furthermore, in a majority of cases (16/25), the sign of the mean return differential is the *opposite* of the sign of the mean real interest differential during the same period (table 8.5, col. 2). So this measure of the exchange risk premium does not explain any positive part of the real interest differential.

The measures of variability of ($fd - \Delta s$) show up very large in columns 4, 5, and 6. These are measures of the variability of ex post return differentials, not ex ante. They tell us little about the variability of the exchange risk premium. But the high variability of the exchange rate does tell us two things. First, it provides an obvious explanation—low power—why the first moments might not be statistically significant. On the other hand, the existence of substantial uncertainty regarding the future spot rate suggests, via the theory of optimal portfolio diversification, that a nonzero exchange risk premium must exist, to reward risk-averse investors for holding currencies that are perceived as risky or that are in oversupply.

To estimate the ex ante exchange risk premium, we can project ($fd - \Delta s$) onto our same three variables: the forward discount, interest differential, and inflation differential.[43] The regression is statistically significant for a majority of currencies, as many others have found.[44] The standard deviation shows the most variable exchange risk premiums belong to Mexico and New Zealand, but the United Kingdom, Netherlands, Austria, Germany, and Switzerland follow close behind.

In table 8.9 we report the statistics for the other component of the currency

Table 8.8   **Return to Forward Exchange Speculation: Forward Discount Less Realized Exchange Depreciation, September 1982 to January 1988**

	Number of Observations (1)	Mean (2)	Standard Error of Mean (3)	Series Standard Deviation (4)	Root Mean Squared Error (5)	95 Percent Band (6)
Open Atlantic developed countries:						
Canada	65	1.04	2.03	9.15	9.21	16.95
Germany	65	4.11	5.92	25.85	26.18	44.23
Netherlands	65	4.35	6.09	26.32	26.68	44.91
Switzerland	65	3.98	6.22	27.74	28.02	46.77
United Kingdom	65	3.77	6.21	27.72	27.98	42.95
Group	325	3.45	5.36	24.27	24.55	
Liberalizing Pacific:						
Hong Kong	65	−3.78	2.22	10.76	11.41	24.43
Malaysia	65	−.74	2.31	10.31	10.34	18.92
Singapore	65	−.35	2.01	9.64	9.65	18.07
Group	195	−1.62	1.71	10.19	10.44	
Closed less-developed countries:						
Greece	65	3.64	5.32	25.84	25.10	46.22
Mexico	43	6.04	12.29	50.74	51.10	89.44
Portugal	61	11.27	5.07	22.53	25.23	41.80
Saudi Arabia	65	−1.49	0.52	2.82	3.19	5.55
South Africa	65	−4.83	9.19	42.50	42.77	83.90
Group	299	2.59	3.83	31.59	32.21	
Closed European developed countries:						
Austria	63	5.38	6.00	26.27	26.82	46.00
Belgium	65	7.51	5.40	23.77	24.94	44.75
Denmark	65	5.50	5.51	24.27	25.42	43.91
France	65	7.47	5.54	24.23	25.37	42.98
Ireland	63	7.27	5.75	24.67	25.73	45.05
Italy	65	8.77	5.33	23.20	24.82	40.91
Norway	65	7.20	4.73	21.10	22.31	38.55
Spain	65	8.98	5.04	22.28	24.05	45.08
Sweden	65	6.20	4.47	20.21	21.15	39.05
Group	581	7.37	5.82	23.22	24.39	
Liberalizing Pacific developed countries:						
Australia	65	1.09	6.55	32.41	32.43	61.46
Japan	65	10.98	5.27	25.12	27.45	53.50
New Zealand	65	8.81	8.42	36.98	38.03	73.92
Group	195	6.96	5.59	31.72	32.75	
All countries	1,595	4.53		25.25	26.01	

Table 8.9   **Realized Exchange Depreciation Less Realized Inflation Differential, September 1982 to January 1988**

	Number of Observations (1)	Mean (2)	Standard Error of Mean (3)	Series Standard Deviation (4)	Root Mean Squared Error (5)	95 Percent Band (6)
Open Atlantic developed countries:						
Canada	63	−.27	1.81	8.45	8.46	15.17
Germany	63	−6.35	5.75	25.10	25.90	44.21
Netherlands	62	−6.11	5.90	25.14	25.88	43.78
Switzerland	62	−8.35	6.11	26.78	28.07	45.67
United Kingdom	63	−2.84	6.06	27.29	27.44	47.88
Group	313	−4.77	5.24	23.48	24.13	
Liberalizing Pacific:						
Hong Kong	62	.62	2.23	10.61	10.63	22.57
Malaysia	62	2.44	2.46	10.60	10.88	19.74
Singapore	62	.63	2.39	10.86	10.88	19.23
Group	186	1.23	2.11	10.63	10.74	
Closed less-developed countries:						
Bahrain	60	5.92	1.62	7.94	9.94	21.24
Greece	60	−1.82	4.99	25.08	25.15	46.41
Mexico	62	−3.32	9.31	47.96	48.96	89.57
Portugal	57	−8.12	4.73	22.63	24.06	46.25
South Africa	62	−.27	10.74	47.16	47.16	78.62
Group	301	−1.46	4.27	33.93	34.26	
Closed European developed countires:						
Austria	64	−7.30	5.64	25.16	26.21	44.92
Belgium	63	−7.69	5.09	22.61	23.90	44.90
Denmark	61	−7.94	5.60	24.05	25.35	41.85
France	64	−6.26	5.39	24.87	24.87	42.24
Ireland	61	−5.85	5.56	24.12	24.84	43.47
Italy	61	−8.01	5.44	23.24	24.60	41.38
Norway	64	−5.92	4.64	21.05	21.88	37.90
Spain	63	−6.01	5.25	22.67	23.47	39.51
Sweden	63	−6.23	3.95	18.36	19.41	33.17
Group	564	−6.79	5.76	22.73	23.74	
Liberalizing Pacific						
Australia	60	2.38	6.78	33.00	33.09	70.90
Japan	63	−12.13	5.63	25.30	28.10	52.98
New Zealand	60	−4.77	8.49	37.00	37.31	82.32
Group	183	−4.96	5.63	31.86	32.79	
All countries	1,547	−4.16		25.61	26.28	

premium, expected real depreciation. As noted earlier, given the widely accepted failure of purchasing power parity on levels, there is no theoretical reason to expect it necessarily to hold in terms of expected rates of change, the hypothesis sometimes known as ex ante relative purchasing power parity. Table 8.9 reports the statistics for ex post real depreciation. The means in column 2 are negative, indicating real appreciation of the currency against the dollar, for all European countries and for most others as well. The only five exceptions, countries that experienced real depreciation against the dollar, were our three East Asian developing countries, Australia, and Bahrain. This last was the only one, of either sign, that was statistically significant.

We already know, from the results reported above for the 119 years of U.S.-U.K. data, that we cannot expect to reject ex ante relative PPP on just a few years of data: new disturbances to the real exchange rate are so large that one needs a much longer time sample to find evidence of systematic movement. But the signs of the mean real depreciations are usually the same as the signs of the mean real interest differentials in Table 8.5 (20/25), suggesting a high correlation of the real interest differential and expected real depreciation across countries.[45]

To estimate ex ante real depreciation, we project ex post real depreciation, again, on the same three contemporaneous variables.[46] The standard deviations for the various currencies are quite similar to those for the projected exchange risk premium.[47] In most cases (18/25) the projected exchange risk premium is slightly more variable than projected real depreciation.

8.5   Conclusion

We can sum up with four conclusions.

1. Capital controls and other barriers to the movement of capital across national borders remained for such countries as the United Kingdom and Japan as recently as 1979, and France and Italy as recently as 1986. But a continuing worldwide trend of integration of financial markets in the 1980s had all but eliminated short-term interest differentials for major industrialized countries by 1988.

2. Only the *country premium* has been eliminated; this means that only *covered* interest differentials are small. Real and nominal exchange rate variability remain, and indeed were larger in the 1980s than in the 1970s.[48] The result is that a *currency premium* remains, consisting of an exchange risk premium plus expected real currency depreciation. This means that, even with the equalization of covered interest rates, large differentials in *real* interest rates remain.

3. The United States in the 1980s began to borrow on such a massive scale internationally that the traditional "Feldstein-Horioka" finding of a near-unit correlation between national saving and investment has broken down. The

process of liberalization in Japan and other major countries was probably one factor behind this massive flow of capital to the United States.

4. In addition to the gaps that distinguish covered interest parity from real interest parity, there is a further gap that separates real interest parity from the proposition that changes in national saving do not crowd out investment because they are readily financed by borrowing from abroad. Bonds are not perfect substitutes for equities, and equities are not perfect substitutes for plant and equipment. Thus at each stage, there are good reasons to think that shortfalls in national saving continue to be capable of crowding out investment, even if to a smaller extent than before 1980.

Notes

1. Despite the increased attention to inward foreign direct investment in the United States in recent years, it continues to be a smaller component of the capital inflow than portfolio investment. As of the end of 1987, foreign direct investment accounted for only 17 percent of the total stock of foreign-held assets in the United States.

2. There were relatively large differentials separating U.S. interest rates from the Eurodollar rates; at the long-term end of the spectrum, well-known U.S. corporations could borrow more cheaply in the Euromarket than domestically. These differentials fell steadily toward zero between 1982 and 1986, probably as the outcome of innovation that occurred in the Euromarkets—partly in response to these differentials—making it easier for U.S. corporations to borrow there. Much of this innovation went under the name of securitization. See Frankel (1988a) for documentation and further references. (It appears that the securitization trend suffered a setback in 1987 and 1988, in part associated with the October 1987 stockmarket crash; it is now said to be slightly *more* costly for U.S. corporations to issue bonds in the Euromarket than domestically. It remains to be seen whether this reversal of the trend toward perfect integration is serious or lasting.)

3. Even if this relationship does not break down in the future under pressure from fears of international creditors that U.S. indebtedness is becoming excessive.

4. There is a fifth possible—yet more narrowly defined—criterion for the degree of integration of financial markets: the size of transactions costs as measured directly by the bid-ask spread in, for example, the foreign exchange market. Surprisingly, the covered interest differential does not appear to be statistically related to the bid-ask spread (MacArthur 1988).

5. Obstfeld (1986) and Summers (1988) argue that the saving-investment correlation may be due to the common influence of growth rates.

6. Obstfeld (1986, 1989) makes the large-country point in a time-series context, where it properly belongs. But even in a time-series regression for a single country such as the United States, one can correct for the large-country problem by expressing saving and investment rates as deviations from the *rest-of-world* rates of saving and investment, respectively. Under the null hypothesis, an exogenous fall in the U.S. saving rate may drive up the world real interest rate and crowd out investment, but there is no evident reason for the crowding-out to be reflected in U.S. investment *to any greater extent* than in rest-of-the-world investment. In Frankel (1986, 44–45), I

found that the close correspondence between U.S. saving and investment for 1970–85 remains, even with this adjustment.

7. Obstfeld (1986a) finds that the coefficient fell after 1973, in time-series correlations for most of his countries, but Obstfeld (1989) finds that it has risen over time (1967–84 vs. 1956–66), with the United States showing the highest correlation of any.

8. In a U.S. time-series context, Frankel (1986) used two instrumental variables: the fraction of the population over 65 years of age and the ratio of military expenditure to GNP. The former is considered a determinant of private saving and the latter of public saving, and both have some claim to exogeneity. In the context of cross-sections of developing and industrialized countries, Dooley, Frankel, and Mathieson (1987) used the dependency ratio and, again, the military expenditure variable.

9. Other studies that reject real interest parity for major industrialized countries include Mishkin (1984a, 1984b), Cumby and Obstfeld (1984), Mark (1985), and Cumby and Mishkin (1986). Glick (1987) examines real interest differentials for six Pacific Basin countries vis-à-vis the United States.

10. The 10-year real interest differential vis-à-vis a weighted average of G-5 countries was about 3 percent in 1984, whether expected inflation is measured by a distributed lag, by OECD forecasts, or by Data Resources, Inc. (DRI) forecasts. In 1980, by contrast, the differential was about -2 percent. Frankel (1986, 35–36).

11. Gross investment was 16.0 percent of GNP in 1980, which was itself considered a low number (down 0.5 percent from 1971–80).

12. The instrumental variables used are the dependency ratio (the sum of those older than 64 and those younger than 21, divided by the working-age population in between), which is a determinant of private saving, and military expenditure as a share of GNP, which is a determinant of the federal budget deficit. A data appendix is available for details on these and the other variables.

13. There are two other potential sources of differences from the results in Frankel (1986): the Commerce Department released revised national accounts data for the entire period in 1986, and we now use the dependency ratio as the demographic instrumental variable in place of the ratio of the over-65 to the over-20 population. But the years 1985–87 are indeed the source of the fall in the coefficient; when these three years are omitted the coefficient is over 1 (as when the 1980s are omitted in table 8.3).

14. If the 1956–87 sample is split at 1974, when the United States and Germany removed capital controls, rather than at 1979, there is still a precipitous decline in the cyclically adjusted saving-investment coefficient over time: from .87 (statistically, no difference from 1) to .31 (borderline difference from 0). (See table 3a in the working paper version.) If the 1930–87 sample is split at 1958, when many European countries restored currency convertibility, there is a small increase in the coefficient over time: from .83 (statistically different from 1) to 1.14 (no difference from 1). (See table 2a in the working paper version.) But this is no doubt because the saving and investment rates are not cyclically adjusted for this period (the BEA series is not available back to 1930). Only when expressed on a cyclically adjusted basis is the U.S. national saving rate of 1985–1987 especially low.

15. Feldstein and Bacchetta (in this volume) find a similar drop in the saving-investment coefficient in the 1980s, for a cross-section of industrialized countries (though they do not use instrumental variables, and are thus liable to the econometric criticisms that others have raised concerning the endogeneity of national saving).

16. Measuring barriers to integration by differences in rates of return has the problem that a given degree of integration can appear smaller or larger depending on the disturbances to saving (or to other variables) during the sample period in question. For example, the greater degree of variability in the U.S. real interest differential in the 1980s, as compared to the 1970s or 1960s, could be attributed to the greater swings in variables such as the structural budget deficit, rather than to a lower degree of capital

mobility. (In any case, the degree of variability in *covered* interest differentials is very low in the 1980s, as we will see below.) All we can say for sure is that if the barriers to integration are essentially zero (the degree of capital mobility is essentially perfect), then differentials in rates of return should be essentially zero.

17. For example, Krugman (1978) found that the standard deviation for the real mark/dollar exchange rate during the German hyperinflation, February 1920 through December 1923, was much larger (20.8 percent) than during the 1970s, even though the serial correlation was no higher (.765).

18. Cumby and Obstfeld (1984, 146) used a Q-statistic to test for higher-order serial correlation in monthly real exchange rate changes and found none. However they also found that expected inflation differentials were unrelated to expected exchange rate changes, rejecting the random walk characterization of the real exchange rate. Huizinga (1986) was also able to reject the random walk in some cases.

19. As already noted, an AR coefficient of .7 on a yearly basis corresponds to an AR of .97 on a monthly basis ($.97^{12} = .70$). Thus it might take 564 months of data ($2.93^2[1 - .97^2]/[1 - .97]^2 = 563.7$) to be able to reject the null hypothesis of $AR = 1$. This is 47 years, very little gain in efficiency over the test on yearly data. Summers (1986) demonstrates the low power of random walk tests in the context of stock market prices.

20. DeJong, Nankervis, Savin, and Whiteman (1988, table 2) offer power tables for the Dickey-Fuller test that show that when the true AR parameter is .8, even a sample size of 100 is sufficient to reject a random walk only about 65 percent of the time.

21. As the sample period covers a number of changes in exchange rate regime, it would be desirable to allow for shifts in the coefficient (and in the variance of the disturbance term). But many of the proponents of a random walk in the real exchange rate claim it as evidence in favor of an "equilibrium" hypothesis, under which fluctuations in the real exchange rate are caused only by real, as opposed to monetary, factors. Under this null hypothesis, changes in regime should not matter for the real exchange rate. Thus our statistical test is a valid rejection of the null hypothesis, even though it lumps together all the 119 years of observations.

22. Sticky goods prices are only one of a number of possible sources of deviations from ex ante relative PPP. Another is the existence of the prices of nontraded goods in the relevant price index. Dornbusch (1983) shows how movement in the relative price of nontraded goods affects the real interest rate, saving, and borrowing from abroad, while Engel and Kletzer (1989) show specifically how such movement can give rise to the Feldstein-Horioka finding. Bovenberg (1989) too shows how imperfect substitutability of goods can give rise to the finding.

23. The rationally expected rate of real depreciation estimated from a specific time-series process is not necessarily the same as the actual expectation of real depreciation held by investors. Frankel (1986, 58–59) used survey data on expectations of exchange rate changes (collected by the *Economist*-affiliated *Financial Report*) and forecasts of price level changes (by DRI) to compute a direct measure of expected real depreciation for the dollar against five currencies. The numbers showed an expectation that the real exchange rate tends to regress back toward PPP at a statistically significant rate of 8–12 percent a year. (The expected speed of *nominal* depreciation back toward PPP is estimated more sharply at 12–16 percent a year in Frankel and Froot 1987). For a thorough rejection of the view that investors' expected exchange rate changes are zero, see Froot and Frankel 1989.)

24. Obstfeld (1986a) shows, in a life-cycle model of saving with actual OECD data on the functional distribution of income and on population growth, that the coefficient in an investment regression can be similar to those estimated by Feldstein and Horioka. (Similar claims based on models of intertemporal optimization are made by Ghosh 1988; Roubini 1988; Tesar 1988; and Leiderman and Razin 1989.) But Feldstein and

Bacchetta (1989) argue that the growth rate is not in fact responsible for the observed coefficient.

25. Some of these data were also analyzed in Frankel and MacArthur (1988). Some forward rate observations for Italy, Austria, and Belgium in the Barclay's data looked suspicious. In addition, Barclay's does not quote a rate for Portugal. For this study, forward exchange rates for Italy and Belgium are taken from the Bank of America (also obtained via DRI) and for Austria and Portugal from the *Financial Times*. The Barclay's data for Ireland also appear suspect (1986–88).

26. The data appendix to NBER Working Paper no. 2309 gives details.

27. The standard errors for individual country means are usable, indeed are conservative, despite the use of overlapping observations, because they are calculated as if there were $T/3$ observations rather than the actual T observations used.

28. Saving-investment regressions, by contrast, show the counterintuitive result: coefficients for LDCs that are lower (suggesting higher capital mobility, in Feldstein and Horioka's terms) than for industrialized countries. See Fieleke (1982), Dooley, Frankel and Mathieson (1987), and Summers (1988).

29. It is possible that, for some countries, seasonal variation constitutes one forecastable component.

30. The British liberalization of 1979 is explained and analyzed in Artis and Taylor (1989).

31. As shown, e.g., by Boothe, et al. (1985, 112).

32. For example, Otani (1983) and Frankel (1984).

33. The frequently large negative covered differential that had been observed for Australia up to mid-1983 (see, e.g., Argy 1987) largely vanished thereafter.

34. Claassen and Wyplosz (1982), Giavazzi and Pagano (1985, 27–28), Frankel (1982), and Wyplosz (1986), among others.

35. "Capitalism," *The Economist* (21 May, 1988): 95.

36. For France, Italy, Ireland, Spain, and Greece (as reported in *World Financial Markets,* 9 September 1988, 5). Denmark's covered differential remains quite high in our sample. The country has been reported to have no capital controls left (see *Economist* article in n. 35), but this evidently applies only to securities: the European Commission reports that deposits and other short-term transactions remain subject to authorization in Denmark as of 1988.

37. Bahrain shows a smaller differential than the others, and even than some of the European countries with controls, like Spain and Ireland. (It should be noted that the forward rate quoted by Barclay's applies to the Saudi riyal; we match it up with the Bahraini interest rate because no local interest rate is available for Saudi Arabia and the two countries are said to be closely tied financially. The riyal is classified by the IMF under the same exchange rate arrangement as Bahrain's currency, the dinar, which would suggest that the same forward rate could be applied to both. But the riyal exchange rate does in fact vary somewhat, so that our measured covered interest differential is not entirely legitimate.)

38. Taylor (1988) is one of the most recent of many studies of covered interest parity *within the London Euromarket.* Such studies do not get at the degree of financial market integration *across national boundaries.* When authors find deviations from covered interest parity in such data (e.g., Mishkin 1984a, 1350), it is often due to low quality of the data, e.g., inexact timing. With high-quality data, Taylor finds that covered interest parity held extremely well in 1985, that it held less well in the 1970s, particularly during "turbulent" periods, that the differential had mostly vanished by 1979, and that the differentials that do exist are slightly larger at the longer-term than shorter-term maturities. But, like other studies, Taylor has no data on maturities longer than one year.

39. It is still quite likely, however, that there is a wedge in each country separating

the long-term interest rate from the after-tax cost of capital facing firms. Such a wedge could be due either to the corporate income tax system or to imperfect substitutability between bonds and capital. Hatsopoulos, Krugman, and Summers (1988) argue that the cost of capital facing U.S. corporation is higher than that facing Japanese corporations, even when real interest rates are equal, because U.S. companies rely more heavily on equity financing, which is more expensive than debt financing. See also papers in Feldstein (1987).

40. The results are reported in NBER Working Paper no. 2856, but are omitted here to save space.

41. The five exceptions, currencies that depreciated against the dollar at a rate more rapid than predicted by the forward discount, were the Hong Kong dollar, Malaysian ringgit, Singapore dollar, Saudi Arabian riyal, and South African rand.

42. The currencies are the Saudi Arabian riyal, and two that appreciated strongly against the dollar relative to the forward rate: the Japanese yen and the Portuguese escudo.

43. Again, the results are reported in a working paper but are omitted here.

44. Many others have found a highly significant predictable component of $(fd - \Delta s^e)$, often when regressing against fd, and particularly in sample. It is possible that such findings are not due to a time-varying premium, as the rational expectations approach would have it, but rather to a time-varying model of spot rate determination (together with insufficiently long sample periods), and learning by investors. Such speculations go outside the scope of this paper. (See Frankel and Froot 1990; and Froot and Frankel 1989.)

45. Columns (4–6) show very high variability in real depreciation, but again this tells us little about the variation of *ex ante* expected depreciation, beyond the observation that the high level of variability implies low power in our tests of ex ante relative purchasing power parity.

46. Once again, the results are reported in a working paper, but are omitted here.

47. It seems that in both cases an apparently predictable component of the spot rate changes constitutes most of the variation (as opposed to variation in the forward discount or inflation differential, respectively): the significant coefficients on the forward discount, interest differential, and ex post inflation differential when $(\Delta s - \Delta p - \Delta p^*)$ is the dependent variable are always of opposite sign and similar magnitude as the coefficients when $(fd - \Delta s)$ is the dependent variable.

48. One view is that the high degree of integration of financial markets is one of the *causes* of the high degree of volatility of exchange rates. The issue is discussed, and further references given, in Frankel (1988b).

References

Adler, Michael, and Bruce Lehman. 1983. Deviations from Purchasing Power Parity in the Long Run. *Journal of Finance* 39, no. 5: 1471–78.

Argy, Victor. 1987. International Financial Liberalisation—The Australian and Japanese Experiences Compared. *Bank of Japan Monetary and Economic Studies* 5, no. 1: 105–68.

Artis, Michael, and Mark Taylor. 1989. Abolishing Exchange Control: The U.K. Experience. Centre for Economic Policy Research Discussion Paper no. 294. London, February.

Bayoumi, Tamim. 1989. Saving Investment Correlations: Immobile Capital, Government Policy or Endogenous Behavior? International Monetary Fund Working Paper no. 89/66. Washington, D.C., August.

Bayoumi, Tamim, and Andrew Rose. 1989. Domestic Savings and Intra-National Capital Flows. Typescript. University of California, Berkeley, December.

Boothe, P., K. Clinton, A. Cote, and D. Longworth. 1985. International Asset Substitutability: Theory and Evidence for Canada. Ottawa: Bank of Canada.

Bovenberg, A. Lans. 1989. The Effects of Capital Income Taxation on International Competitiveness and Trade Flows. *American Economic Review* 79, no. 5: 1045–64.

Caprio, G., and D. Howard. 1984. Domestic Saving, Current Accounts, and International Capital Mobility. International Finance Discussion Papers no. 244. Federal Reserve Board, Washington, D.C.

Caramazza, F., K. Clinton, A. Cote, and D. Longworth. 1986. International Capital Mobility and Asset Substitutability: Some Theory and Evidence on Recent Structural Changes. Technical Report no. 44. Bank of Canada, Ottawa.

Cardia, Emanuela. 1988. Crowding Out in Open Economies. Cahier no. 8823. Université de Montreal, June.

Claassen, Emil, and Charles Wyplosz. 1982. Capital Controls: Some Principles and the French Experience. *Annales de l'INSEE* 47–48: 237–67.

Cumby, R., and F. Mishkin. 1986. The International Linkage of Real Interest Rates: The European-U.S. Connection. *Journal of International Money and Finance* 5:5–24.

Cumby, R., and M. Obstfeld. 1984. International Interest Rate and Price Level Linkages under Flexible Exchange Rates: A Review of Recent Evidence. In *Exchange Rate Theory and Practice,* ed. J. Bilson and R. Marston. Chicago: University of Chicago Press.

Darby, Michael. 1981. Does Purchasing Power Parity Work? *Proceedings of the Fifth West Coast Academic/Federal Reserve Economic Research Seminar.* Federal Reserve Bank of San Francisco.

———. 1986. The Internationalization of American Banking and Finance: Structure, Risk and World Interest Rates. *Journal of International Money and Finance* 5, no. 4:403–28.

DeJong, David, John Nankervis, N. E. Savin, and Charles Whiteman. 1988. Integration versus Trend-Stationarity in Macroeconomic Time Series. Department of Economics Working Paper no. 88–27a. University of Iowa, December.

Dominguez, Kathryn. 1986. Expectations Formation in the Foreign Exchange Market: New Evidence from Survey Data. *Economic Letters* 21: 277–82.

Dooley, Michael, Jeffrey Frankel, and Donald Mathieson. 1987. International Capital Mobility: What Do Saving-Investment Correlations Tell Us? *International Monetary Fund Staff Papers* 34, no. 3: 503–30.

Dooley, M., and P. Isard. 1980. Capital Controls, Political Risk and Deviations from Interest-Rate Parity. *Journal of Political Economy* 88, no. 2:370–84.

Dornbusch, Rudiger. 1983. Real Interest Rates, Home Goods and Optimal External Borrowing. *Journal of Political Economy* 91.

Engel, Charles, and Kenneth Kletzer. 1989. Saving and Investment in an Open Economy with Non-traded Goods. *International Economic Review* 30 (November): 735–52.

Feldstein, M. 1983. Domestic Saving and International Capital Movements in the Long Run and the Short Run. *European Economic Review* 21:139–51.

———. 1987. *The Effects of Taxation on Capital Accumulation.* Chicago: University of Chicago Press.

Feldstein, M., and C. Horioka. 1980. Domestic Saving and International Capital Flows. *Economic Journal* 90:314–29.

Fieleke, Norman. 1982. National Saving and International Investment. In *Saving and Government Policy.* Conference Series no. 25. Federal Reserve Bank of Boston.

Frankel, Jeffrey. 1982. On the Franc. *Annales de l'INSEE* 47–48: 185–221.

———. 1984. The Yen/Dollar Agreement: Liberalizing Japanese Capital Markets. *Policy Analyses in International Economics,* no. 9. Washington, D.C.: Institute for International Economics.

———. 1986. International Capital Mobility and Crowding-out in the U.S. Economy: Imperfect Integration of Financial Markets or of Goods Markets? In *How Open is the U.S. Economy?* ed. R. Hafer, 33–67. Lexington, Mass.: Lexington Books.

———. 1988a. International Capital Flows and Domestic Economic Policies. In *The United States in the World Economy,* ed. M. Feldstein. Chicago: University of Chicago Press.

———. 1988b. International Capital Mobility and Exchange Rate Variability. In *International Payments Imbalances in the 1980s,* ed. N. Fieleke. Boston: Federal Reserve Bank of Boston.

Frankel, Jeffrey, and Kenneth Froot. 1987. Using Survey Data to Test Standard Propositions Regarding Exchange Rate Expectations. *American Economic Review* 77, no. 1 (March).

———. 1990. Chartists, Fundamentalists, and the Demand for Dollars. In *Private Behavior and Government Policy in Interdependent Economies,* ed. A. Courakis and M. Taylor, 73–126. Oxford: Oxford University Press.

Frankel, Jeffrey, and Alan MacArthur. 1988. Political vs. Currency Premia in International Real Interest Differentials: A Study of Forward Rates for 24 Countries. *European Economic Review* 32.

Frenkel, Jacob. 1981. Flexible Exchange Rates, Prices and the Role of "News": Lessons from the 1970s. *Journal of Political Economy* 89, no. 4: 665–705.

Frenkel, J., and R. Levich. 1977. Transaction Costs and Interest Arbitrage: Tranquil versus Turbulent Periods. *Journal of Political Economy* 85, no. 6: 1209–26.

Froot, Kenneth, and Jeffrey Frankel. 1989. Forward Discount Bias: Is It an Exchange Risk Premium? *Quarterly Journal of Economics* 104:139–61.

Ghosh, Atish R. 1988. How Mobile is Capital? Some Simple Tests. Typescript. Harvard University.

Giavazzi, Francesco, and Marco Pagano. 1985. Capital Controls and the European Monetary System. In *Capital Controls and Foreign Exchange Legislation,* Occastional Paper. Milan: Euromobiliare.

Glick, Reuven. 1987. Interest Rate Linkages in the Pacific Basin. *Economic Review,* no. 3, 31–42.

Harberger, Arnold C. 1980. Vignettes on the World Capital Market. *American Economic Review* 70: 331–37.

Hatsopoulos, George, Paul Krugman, and Larry Summers. 1988. U.S. Competitiveness: Beyond the Trade Deficit. *Science* 24 (July 15): 299–307.

Huizinga, John. 1987. An Empirical Investigation of the Long Run Behavior of Real Exchange Rates. *Carnegie-Rochester Conference Series on Public Policy,* vol. 27.

Koraczyk, Robert. 1985. The Pricing of Forward Contracts for Foreign Exchange. *Journal of Political Economy* 93, no. 2: 346–68.

Krugman, Paul. 1978. Purchasing Power Parity and Exchange Rates: Another Look at the Evidence. *Journal of International Economics* 8, no. 3, 397–407.

Leiderman, Leo, and Assaf Razin, 1989. The Saving-Investment Balance: An Empirical Investigation. Typescript. International Monetary Fund, Washington, D.C., June.

MacArthur, Alan. 1988. International Financial Market Integration: Empirical Analysis with Data from Forward and Futures Currency Markets. Ph.D. thesis, University of California, Berkeley.

Mark, Nelson. 1985. Some Evidence on the International Inequality of Real Interest Rates. *Journal of International Money and Finance* 4: 189–208.

Mishkin, Frederic. 1984a. Are Real Interest Rates Equal Across Countries? An Empirical Investigation of International Parity Conditions. *Journal of Finance* 39: 1345–58.

Mishkin, Frederic. 1984b. The Real Interest Rate: A Multi-country Empirical Study. *Canadian Journal of Economics* 17, no. 2: 283–311.

Morgan Guaranty Trust Company. 1988. Financial Markets in Europe: Toward 1992. *World Financial Markets* 5, (September 9): 1–15.

Murphy, Robert. 1984. Capital Mobility and the Relationship between Saving and Investment in OECD Countries. *Journal of International Money and Finance* 3: 327–342.

Obstfeld, Maurice. 1986. Capital Mobility in the World Economy: Theory and Measurement. *Carnegie-Rochester Conference Series on Public Policy*, 24:55–104.

Obstfeld, Maurice. 1989. How Integrated are World Capital Markets? Some New Tests. In *Debt, Stabilization and Development: Essays in Memory of Carlos Diaz-Alejandro*, ed. G. Calvo, R. Findlay, and J. de Macedo, 134–55. Oxford: Basil Blackwell.

Otani, Ichiro. 1983. Exchange Rate Instability and Capital Controls: The Japanese Experience, 1978–81. In *Exchange Rate and Trade Instability: Causes, Consequences and Remedies*, ed. D. Bigman and T. Taya. Cambridge, Mass.: Ballinger.

Penati, A., and M. Dooley. 1984. Current Account Imbalances and Capital Formation in Industrial Countries, 1949–1981. *IMF Staff Papers* 31: 1–24.

Pigott, Charles, and Richard Sweeney. 1985. In *Exchange Rates, Trade and the U.S. Economy*, ed. S. Arndt, R. Sweeney, and T. Willett. Washington, D.C.: American Enterprise Institute.

Popper, Helen. 1990. International Capital Mobility: Direct Evidence from Long-Term Currency Swaps. International Finance Discussion Paper no. 386. Federal Reserve Board, Washington, D.C., September.

Roll, Richard. 1979. Violations of Purchasing Power Parity and Their Implications for Efficient International Commodity Markets. In *International Finance and Trade*, vol. 1, ed. M. Sarnat and G. Szego. Cambridge, Mass.: Ballinger.

Roubini, Nouriel. 1988. Current Account and Budget Deficits in an Intertemporal Model of Consumption and Taxation Smoothing: A Solution to the "Feldstein-Horioka Puzzle"? Typescript. Yale University, October 1988.

Summers, L. 1986. Does the Stock Market Rationally Reflect Fundamental Values? *Journal of Finance* 41 (July): 591–601.

———. 1988. Tax Policy and International Competitiveness. In *International Aspects of Fiscal Policies*, ed. Jacob Frenkel. Chicago: University of Chicago Press.

Taylor, Mark. 1988. Covered Interest Arbitrage and Market Turbulence: An Empirical Analysis. Centre for Economic Policy Research Discussion Paper no. 236. London.

Tesar, Linda. 1988. Savings, Investment and International Capital Flows. University of Rochester Working Paper no. 154. August.

Tobin, James. 1983. Comment on Domestic Saving and International Capital Movements in the Long Run and the Short Run," by M. Feldstein. *European Economic Review* 21:153–56.

Westphal, Uwe. 1983. Comments on Domestic Saving and International Capital Movements in the Long Run and the Short Run. *European Economic Review* 21:157–59.

Wyplosz, Charles. 1986. Capital Flows Liberalization and the EMS: A French Perspective. INSEAD Working Paper no. 86/40. *European Economy*, European Economic Community, June.

Comment   Maurice Obstfeld

This paper covers a broad area in its attempt to define and measure the real-world counterpart of a concept central to open-economy economic models, capital mobility. At the simplest level, one might say that capital is freely mobile between two regions when at least some residents of each are free to engage in cross-border asset trades. The potential for such trades should equalize the prices residents of the two regions are willing to pay for identical assets; but in the real world this equalization need not occur. Even within a country, for example, investors in different marginal income tax brackets may place differing values on the same asset. While such discrepancies certainly imply deviations from Pareto optimality, they may have little to do with the concept of capital mobility relevant for assessing, say, the impact of New York Fed open-market operations on California's money supply. Nor does the absence of asset-valuation discrepancies imply that physical capital will always generate the same marginal value product throughout the world.

Quantifying Capital Mobility in an Idealized Economy

Despite the questionable policy relevance of defining capital mobility in terms of an asset-valuation criterion, it is useful to start out by considering an idealized world, free of government interventions, in which contracts contingent on any state of nature can be written and costlessly enforced. Following Arrow and Debreu, one might define an asset as follows. Let there be C commodities and monies, L locations, and S states of nature. Then an asset is an infinite sequence of three-dimensional arrays $\{p(\kappa, \lambda, \sigma; t)\}$—where t runs from tomorrow to the infinite future—in which $p(\kappa, \lambda, \sigma; t)$ specifies the payoff κ of a particular commodity or money to be made in location λ in state σ on date t. Under perfect capital mobility, residents of two regions should end up (in equilibrium) placing the same value on any asset. Interregional valuation discrepancies would therefore be evidence of barriers to capital movement—barriers whose origins are, perhaps, bureaucratic, cultural, or informational.

Stepping away from this rarefied setting, it is easy to see how government interventions, actual or prospective, can lead to cross-border differences in asset valuations. Take as an example of an asset a one-deutschemark deposit in Frankfurt maturing in six months. If i_{DM} is the six-month nominal interest rate, and if bank failure is temporarily ruled out, this asset is a promise to pay $1 + i_{DM}$ deutschemarks into a Frankfurt account in all states of nature six

Maurice Obstfeld is professor of economics at the University of California, Berkeley, and a research associate of the National Bureau of Economic Research.

The present written version of this comment was prepared while the author was a visiting scholar in the External Adjustment Division of the Research Department, International Monetary Fund. Research support from the Olin Foundation and the National Science Foundation is acknowledged with thanks.

months from the deposit date. Imagine that there is some possibility that the German government will impose a regulation preventing foreigners from repatriating their interest earnings, but leaving them free to spend the interest within Germany. In general, this possibility will cause the value of Frankfurt deposits carrying a given interest rate to be lower for foreigners than for Germans. The result might be asset-market segmentation.

Frankel offers four possible definitions of perfect capital mobility, but none of them, not even covered interest parity, corresponds to the asset-valuation criterion described above. Covered interest parity between New York dollar deposits and London sterling deposits, with cover purchased in London, predicts that promises to deliver a dollar on a given date in the future in New York should sell for the same price as promises to do the same in London. This equality may or may not hold true, and its validity may or may not be related to the degree of capital mobility between New York and London. Large dollar deposits in New York and Eurodollar deposits in London may offer different payoffs in different states of nature because of more stringent prudential regulation in New York and the consequent relative instability of the Eurocurrency system. Yet an equilibrium in which investors, regardless of country of residence, attach a common value to New York deposits of a currency and attach a distinct but still common value to London deposits of the same currency is perfectly consistent with free international asset trade.[1]

Alternatively, however, a covered interest differential may indicate genuine barriers to capital movement, as Frankel assumes. In a country imposing significant costs on cross-border financial flows, domestic residents' valuation of any state-contingent money payment will generally differ from that of foreigners, and, as a result, onshore and offshore interest rates will generally differ as well.

Frankel's covered interest parity calculations are motivated by the desire to compare the prices of assets that are as similar as possible, except for their locations. The reasoning underlying this comparison is that, absent locality-specific risks and regulations that affect foreign and domestic residents equally, the answer one gets is close to what one would get from a comparison of different investors' valuation of the same asset. Despite the reservations just expressed, I agree with Frankel that the approach of comparing onshore with

1. Frankel's use of covered interest parity is really a roundabout way of comparing interest rates on (hopefully) similar assets that pay off in the *same* currency but in different locations. His tests rely on the fact that Euromarket deposits of one currency can be easily transformed into another through the forward market. As a result, one can in principle measure the interest differential between London yen and Tokyo yen, say, by comparing the London Eurodollar rate (after covering in the London dollar/yen forward market) with the Gensaki rate. The practical problem with Frankel's method is that it introduces additional measurement errors when the forward premium and interest rates are measured at different times, as is apparently the case in this study. I would therefore prefer, when possible, to work directly with Euroyen rather than covered Eurodollar interest rates.

offshore interest rates is the most reliable method available for quantifying impediments to capital movement. I adopted essentially the same approach in my 1986 paper (Obstfeld 1986), and also reached the conclusion that the degree of financial integration among industrial countries is now very high. But I hope the present discussion makes clear how approximate an answer interest-rate comparisons yield.

Capital Mobility and Economic Policy: The Case of Crowding Out

While the asset-valuation measure of capital mobility offered above may be useful for a detailed theoretical analysis of economic efficiency, it is less useful for addressing many questions of macroeconomic interest. The problem is that to analyze the effects of policies, it is not enough to know only that investors in different countries value some identical assets differently. One usually needs to know, in addition, *why* investors' valuations of the assets differ.

A simple example focuses on the question of crowding out, which motivated the Feldstein-Horioka (1980) study. Feldstein and Horioka reasoned that, under perfect capital mobility, changes in a country's saving rate should not affect its investment rate. Because investment projects can be financed out of a global pool of internationally mobile savings, saving shifts within a particular country should not crowd out (or crowd in) domestic investment.

Consider a small country that would be a capital importer under laisser-faire.[2] The assumption that this country would run a deficit on current account under free asset trade means that, in the presence of restrictions on foreign borrowing, its interest rate exceeds the world interest rate. The observation that the interest rate its residents face differs from that faced by foreigners is not enough to determine whether a fall in national saving would crowd out domestic investment. Two possible situations are (1) the country's government has imposed a nonprohibitive tariff on capital imports and (2) the government has placed a binding quantitative limit on capital imports. In either of these cases, the domestic interest rate is above the world interest rate. But in case 1, a small fall in national saving has no crowding out effect at all; in a certain sense, capital remains fully mobile at the margin despite the international interest differential. In contrast, a decline in saving crowds out investment point for point in case 2.

Even if potential interest-arbitrage opportunities are absent, or if the causes generating them are known, policy effects obviously may still depend on the economy's structure. An economy large enough to affect the world interest rate will show a different degree of crowding out than a small economy. As

2. For the purpose of this example, think of a world with one commodity on each date. Then "the" real interest rate is just the price of present output in terms of future output, less one. (International real interest differentials, to be discussed below, can arise in this setting only as a result of impediments to international asset trade.) The underlying model I have in mind here is Irving Fisher's two-period model of investment and saving under conditions of full employment.

Frankel notes, an economy where the expected real interest rate varies with goods-market prices may behave differently from one in which purchasing power parity holds ex ante.

In attempts to determine empirically such parameters as the degree of crowding out in an open economy, asset-valuation comparisons can therefore be beside the point, if not misleading. In most cases, a direct econometric attack on the problem of interest is preferable. As Frankel's own analysis of crowding out indicates, however, the design of appropriate estimation strategies may not be easy.

Feldstein and Horioka (1980) were the first to attempt to measure the degree of crowding out by regressions of investment rates on saving rates. Their finding of near-unit coefficients (a result weakened by more recent data) reflected a stylized fact that calls out for explanation, the typically small sizes of current-account imbalances in the postwar period through the early 1980s. Their interpretation of the finding, that imperfect capital mobility causes most of a change in saving to be reflected in the home capital stock, has been widely criticized. My 1986 paper made the theoretical argument that even under capital mobility, high saving-investment correlations could result from common factors affecting both saving and investment at the same time. Later on I evaluate Frankel's claim that the most important common factor is the domestic real interest rate.

Frankel apparently rejects the view that investment-saving regressions measure capital mobility, but he accepts them as a valid way to measure the effect of exogenous shifts in saving on investment, provided instrumental variables are used to correct for the endogeneity of saving.[3] He interprets time-series regressions based on U.S. saving and investment data as evidence that for the United States, the crowding out effect has become dramatically smaller over the past decade.

A Model of Saving and Investment

It is difficult to evaluate Frankel's interpretation of the regression results outside the context of a specific model. One standard model shows quite easily that Frankel's estimated coefficients need *not* consistently measure the degree of crowding out, despite the use of exogenous instrumental variables correlated with saving. Further, the coefficients estimated are vulnerable to the Lucas critique: they change with changes in the stochastic processes driving the model's exogenous variables. This vulnerability makes the estimates potentially unstable and thus particularly misleading as guides to policy.

My exemplary full-employment model is a variant of one used for a similar purpose by Feldstein (1983), though the original source is probably Metzler

---

3. This procedure was proposed in Frankel (1986). Frankel also attempts to adjust for cyclical factors that simultaneously affect saving and investment.

(1960). If r is the domestic real interest rate and u an exogenous disturbance, then the share of saving in output is given by

(1) $$S_t/Y_t = ax_t + br_t + u_t,$$

where all variables are deviations from (unconditional) means and coefficients are positive. In equation (1), the variable x is Frankel's instrumental variable, which influences saving but is uncorrelated with all the model's disturbances. The investment rate depends on r plus an investment shock v,

(2) $$I_t/Y_t = -dr_t + v_t.$$

Capital inflows are modeled so as to reflect the possibility of imperfect mobility. Let r^* be an exogenously varying world real interest rate, expressed in terms of *foreign* output. If q is the relevant real exchange rate (the price of foreign output in terms of domestic, expressed as a natural logarithm), then desired net capital inflows (scaled by output) should depend on the difference between the domestic real interest rate r and the expected rate of return on foreign investment *expressed in terms of domestic output,*

(3) $$K_t/Y_t = f[r_t - r_t^* - E_t(q_{t+1} - q_t)] + w_t,$$

where w is an exogenous disturbance to capital inflows. As f grows arbitrarily large, the condition

$$r_t = r_t^* + E_t(q_{t+1} - q_t),$$

which defines perfect capital mobility in this model, is approached.

Finally, the current-account surplus is modeled as a function of the contemporaneous real exchange rate and an international-trade shock z,

(4) $$CA_t/Y_t = eq_t + z_t.$$

In equilibrium, any current account imbalance must be financed by net capital flows, so

(5) $$CA_t + K_t = 0.$$

To close the model, one supplements this requirement of flow consistency in the balance of payments with the output-market equilibrium condition:

(6) $$S_t - I_t = CA_t.$$

The foregoing model neglects some important dynamic elements, such as the intrinsic dynamics due to cumulating asset stocks or possible lagged current-account adjustment to real exchange-rate changes. It is nevertheless useful as kind of first-order approximation, one that hopefully captures the main factors behind medium-term comovements of interest rates, real exchange rates, and the saving-investment balance.

The Model's Solution

The equilibrium real exchange rate is found using the usual solution technique for rational-expectations models. Define the composite disturbance n_t as

(7)
$$n_t = r_t^* + (ax_t + u_t - v_t)/(b + d)$$
$$- w_t/f - (b + d + f)z_t/f(b + d),$$

and define the parameter h as $h = (b + d)/[(b + d) + (e/f)(b + d + f)]$. Then (5) and (6) imply that the real exchange rate is a convergent infinite sum,

(8) $q_t = h[n_t + hE_t(n_{t+1}) + h^2E_t(n_{t+2}) + h^3E_t(n_{t+3}) + \ldots]$.

As usual, the relation of q_t to the exogenous shocks that define the composite variable n_t depends on the serial-correlation properties of those shocks. To illustrate the pitfalls in Frankel's estimation approach, however, I assume for now that the instrumental variable x follows a martingale process, and therefore is rationally expected to remain at its current level; all other random variables on the right-hand side of (7) are assumed to be white noise. Under these assumptions,

$$q_t = (f/e)ax_t/(b + d + f) + \text{(terms in } r_t^*, \text{ etc.)},$$

and (by [5]) the domestic real interest rate is

(9) $r_t = -ax_t/(b + d + f) + \text{(terms in } r_t^*, \text{ etc.)}.$

Solution (9) may now be combined with equations (1) and (2) to find the reduced-form saving and investment equations,

(10) $S_t/Y_t = (d + f)ax_t/(b + d + f) + \text{(terms in } r_t^*, \text{ etc.)},$

(11) $I_t/Y_t = dax_t/(b + d + f) + \text{(terms in } r_t^*, \text{ etc.)}.$

Equation (11) makes transparent the effect of an *exogenous and permanent* shift in saving on the investment rate. Given the specification (1), an exogenous shift in saving can arise from a permanent shift in ax_t or in u_t. The variable ax_t, changes in which are permanent, carries the coefficient $d/(b + d + f)$ in (11), so this coefficient tells us, for example, the amount of investment crowded out by a permanent autonomous decline in the saving rate. Notice that even under complete capital immobility $(f = 0)$, crowding out is less than complete provided saving is interest sensitive $(b > 0)$. The reason is that an exogenous negative saving shift raises the home interest rate, causing equilibrium saving (and hence investment) to fall by less.[4] Under per-

---

4. This fact shows, already, that one cannot interpret a simple saving-investment correlation as measuring the extent of crowding out. Even in an economy where capital controls lead to a perfect correlation between saving and investment, the effect on investment of an exogenous saving shift is reduced by a partially offsetting change in the endogenous, interest-sensitive component of saving.

fect capital mobility (an infinite f), however, exogenous shifts in saving do not affect investment provided the shifts are permanent.

Do the Instrumental-Variable Estimates Measure Crowding Out?

We can now ask whether an instrumental-variable (IV) regression of investment on saving produces a consistent estimate of the policy coefficient of interest, $d/(b + d + f)$. Equations (10) and (11) lead to a clear negative answer for the present model.

This can be seen as follows. If the instrumental variable x is uncorrelated with all the model's disturbances, as Frankel assumes, *and* with the world interest rate r^*, then (10) shows that a first-stage regression of S/Y on x yields a consistent estimate of the coefficient $(d + f)a/(b + d + f)$. The reduced form equation for investment, (11), therefore can be rewritten as

$$(12) \qquad I_t/Y_t = [d/(d + f)](\hat{S_t}/Y_t) + \text{(terms orthogonal to } x_t\text{)},$$

where $(\hat{S_t}/Y_t)$ is the fitted value from the first-stage regression of S/Y on x.

Equation (12) is the regression that is run to obtain the IV estimate of the crowding out coefficient, $d/(b + d + f)$; however, the resulting estimate clearly converges in probability, not to $d/(b + d + f)$, but to the larger number $d/(d + f)$. The econometric pitfalls of regressing investment on saving apparently go deeper than the observation that saving needs an exogenous instrument. Here, an issue of equation specification is also involved. The "structural" equation for I/Y in which S/Y appears on the right-hand side with coefficient $d/(b + d + f)$ also involves x as a separate regressor. The implication is that x is not really a valid instrument for the purpose at hand, despite its lack of correlation with the model's disturbances.[5]

The following conclusions can be drawn from this analysis: (1) IV estimates such as those Frankel presents may overstate the degree to which exogenous saving shifts affect investment. This overstatement is large when d and f are small relative to b. (2) There are some special cases in which IV is appropriate in the above example. One occurs when saving is not interest sensitive ($b = 0$), a situation many view as plausible on empirical, if not on theoretical, grounds. (In the present model, the saving rate is an exogenous variable if $b = 0$.) The IV method is also appropriate when investment is not interest sensitive ($d = 0$), but in this case exogenous saving shifts leave investment unchanged regardless of the degree of capital mobility. Finally, the IV estimator "works" in this specific example if one wishes to test the null hypothesis of perfect capital mobility (an infinite f). But if that hypothesis is rejected, inferences about crowding out require additional information. (3) Changes over time in the IV coefficient do reflect changes in the degree of capital mobility and in the degree of crowding out—other things the same. If

---

5. Equivalently, the crowding-out coefficient is not generally identified (despite the availability of x) under the present assumptions.

f, rises, for example, both the degree of crowding out and the IV coefficient fall. (4) One should not take the calculation above too literally as an indication of the biases due to IV estimation. In reality, shocks to x may be transitory; the instrument x may be correlated with the world interest rate r^*; or some model other than the one sketched above may be relevant. Any of these departures from my simplifying assumptions would change the analysis.

As an illustration of point 4, imagine that the instrumental variable x follows the first-order autoregression $x_t = \rho x_{t-1} + \varepsilon_t$, with ρ strictly between 0 and 1 and $E_{t-1}(\varepsilon_t) = 0$. In this case, shifts in x are not perceived as permanent. The reduced-form coefficients of x in the equations explaining S/Y and I/Y therefore differ from the ones shown in (10) and (11), and can no longer be interpreted as measures of the effects of *permanent* changes in x. Instead, these coefficients reflect the actual persistence of innovations in x in the historical sample. This is just an instance of the Lucas critique: without knowledge of structural parameters, it is not generally possible to infer from the reduced-form coefficients the effects of permanent shifts in the instrumental variable x.

One might still be interested in knowing the amount of investment crowded out over the sample period by innovations to x. It is easy to show that, once again, the IV estimate overstates the true figure when $b > 0$. With x a stationary process, however, this overstatement occurs even when capital mobility is perfect. Furthermore, the IV coefficient now is *not* asymptotically zero under perfect capital mobility, so one cannot test that hypothesis by looking for a zero coefficient.[6]

The main message of the example is that the existence of exogenous "instruments" correlated with saving is no panacea in cases of underidentification. This message applies to cross-section as well as time-series estimation.

Real Interest Rates, Saving, and Investment

Regardless of one's interpretation of investment-saving regressions, their results, as noted above, point to an intriguing empirical regularity: from the end of World War II up until the early 1980s, current-account deficits tended to be quite small compared with national income. Even in the 1980s, major industrial countries' current-account imbalances have not surpassed the levels sustained by Great Britain in the decades leading up to World War I. Alternative solutions to this "Feldstein-Horioka puzzle" have sharply different implications for policy. Presumably, a good explanation should throw light on both the short-run time-series behavior of current accounts and the cross-sectional coincidence of saving and investment over longer time spans.

Frankel's favorite approach rests on the observation that real interest rates

6. Because it is unlikely that the x process would remain stable over a very long period, it is also unlikely that the IV regression coefficient would be stable. This mechanism, rather than shifts in capital mobility, could be the main factor behind the striking coefficient instability reported in this paper and in Frankel (1986).

can differ across countries even when there is uninhibited international asset trade. The undeniable fact of real interest differentials does not, however, offer an automatic explanation of the Feldstein-Horioka results. Think again about the saving-investment model set out above, and consider the case of perfect capital mobility.

The model certainly allows for real interest differentials, yet *permanent* disturbances do not give rise to them under perfect capital mobility. This result would be attenuated a bit if the model were expanded in a way that endogenized the process of asset accumulation; but it is probably not a bad approximation to say that permanent shocks have slight effects, compared with temporary ones, on the rationally expected change in the real exchange rate.

Because of their more powerful short-run effect on the real interest rate, temporary disturbances can give rise to high correlations between saving and investment. For example, if x in (1) follows a first-order autoregression with positive autoregressive coefficient ρ, the IV slope coefficient analyzed above converges to $d(1 - \rho)/[d(1 - \rho) + e]$ under perfect capital mobility. This coefficient is close to unity when e (the current-account effect of the real exchange rate) is small, and it is larger the smaller the degree of persistence ρ.

The foregoing result is still not enough to resolve the Feldstein-Horioka puzzle. While temporary shocks to x, u, or v cause saving and investment to covary positively, other temporary shocks cause negative covariation. A temporary positive shock to the trade balance (z in equation [4]) increases the domestic real interest rate and therefore causes saving to rise and investment to fall. Monetary shocks, if formally introduced into the model, could also cause saving and investment to move in opposite directions. To explain observed time-series correlations between saving and investment on the basis of real interest differentials, one must therefore argue that direct shocks to the saving and investment schedules not only display low persistence, but also are the dominant sources of fluctuations.

A solution to the Feldstein-Horioka puzzle based on temporary shocks to saving and investment is deficient in another respect. Since temporary shocks tend to offset each other over time, they cannot explain the high cross-sectional correlation between long time-averages of saving and investment rates. To apply the real-interest explanation to the cross-section findings, one would need (at the very least) an empirically significant mechanism through which persistent shifts in saving or investment rates have persistent effects on real interest rates under capital mobility. Stories can certainly be told, but a convincing case has yet to be made. I doubt that any single mechanism, out of the many that have been proposed, provides a full answer to the puzzle.

References

Feldstein, Martin. 1983. Domestic saving and international capital movements in the long run and the short run. *European Economic Review* 21: 129–51.

Feldstein, Martin, and Charles Horioka. 1980. Domestic saving and international capital flows. *Economic Journal* 90: 314–29.

Frankel, Jeffrey A. 1986. International capital mobility and crowding-out in the U.S. economy: Imperfect integration of financial markets or of goods markets? In *How open is the U.S. economy?*, ed. R. W. Hafer. Lexington, Mass.: Heath.

Metzler, Lloyd A. 1960. The process of international adjustment under conditions of full employment: A Keynesian view. Typescript. (Reprinted in *Readings in international economics,* ed. R. E. Caves and H. G. Johnson. Homewood, Ill.: Irwin, 1968.)

Obstfeld, Maurice. 1986. Capital mobility in the world economy: Theory and measurement. *Carnegie-Rochester Conference Series on Public Policy* 24: 55–103.

9   A Cross-Country Study of Growth, Saving, and Government

Robert J. Barro

Government policies have numerous effects on a country's economic performance. In this study I assess the effects of various kinds of public services and taxation on long-term rates of growth and saving. The focus of the research is an empirical investigation of the growth experiences of a large number of countries in the post–World War II period. The framework for this empirical work derives from some recent theories of endogenous economic growth. In section 9.1, I sketch a model in which public services and taxation affect an economy's long-term growth and saving. This model neglects population growth, allows no distinction between physical and human capital, and concentrates on steady-state results. Section 9.2 extends the theory to allow for choices of population growth and for distinctions between physical and human capital. Section 9.3 brings in some transitional dynamics. In this extension, increases in per capita income go along with decreases in population growth and increases in the amount invested in each person's human capital. Section 9.4 discusses the empirical findings. These results are preliminary and amount to a progress report from an ongoing project on economic growth.

9.1   Effects of Government Policies on Long-Term Growth and Saving

In this section I discuss a theory of the long-term effects of government policies on saving and economic growth. The analysis is an exposition and extension of a model developed more fully in Barro (1990), which built on work by Romer (1989), Lucas (1988), and Rebelo (1987). The aspects of government policies considered are the effects of public services on private

Robert J. Barro is professor of economics at Harvard University and a research associate of the National Bureau of Economic Research.

The author has benefited from research assistance by David Renelt. This research is being supported by the National Science Foundation and the Walker Foundation.

production and household utility, the influences of governmental activities on property rights, and the effects of taxation on private incentives to save and invest.

Assume that the representative household in a closed economy seeks to maximize

$$(1) \qquad U = \int_0^\infty u(c) \, e^{-\rho t} dt,$$

where u is the momentary utility function, c is consumption per person, and $\rho > 0$ is the constant rate of time preference. The form of the utility function is

$$(2) \qquad u(c) = \frac{c^{1-\sigma} - 1}{1 - \sigma}, \quad \sigma > 0,$$

so that marginal utility has a constant elasticity with respect to c. The case where $\sigma = 1$ corresponds to log utility. The infinite horizon in equation (1) applies naturally when parents are altruistic toward children, who are altruistic toward their children, and so on. Then the rate of time preference can be thought of as reflecting the degree of altruism toward children, rather than the influence of time, per se. I assume at this point that population (which equals the labor force) is constant, although later parts of the paper allow for population growth.

In the main analysis, the production function has the Cobb-Douglas form,

$$(3) \qquad y = Ak^{1-\alpha}g^\alpha,$$

where $0 < \alpha < 1$, y is output per person (assumed to be net of depreciation of capital), k is capital per person, and g (representing public services) corresponds to real government purchases per person. Production could be carried out directly by households or equivalently by competitive firms. I assume a one-sector production technology, so that (net) product, y, can be used either for consumption, c, (net) investment, $\dot{k}$, or government purchases, g.

I assume that the government buys only final product from the private sector, including bridge services, jet fighter services, and so on. Alternatively, the government could buy labor services and capital goods or services from the private sector and then use these inputs to carry out public production. If the technologies for the government and the private sector are the same, and if capital is mobile between the public and private sectors, the results would not change. At this point I assume that public services (provided free of charge to the users) enter into the production function, but not directly into the utility function.

The idea behind equation (3) is that some "infrastructure" activities of government are inputs to private production and also raise the marginal product of private capital. For the usual public-goods reasons, such as nonexcludability and perhaps increasing returns to scale, the private market does not sustain the "appropriate" level of these services. These considerations apply especially to activities such as the enforcement of laws and contracts, national defense, and perhaps to highways, water systems, and so on. In equation (3), output per capita, y, depends on government purchases per capita, g. When the public-goods aspect of government services is important, it may be more accurate to relate y to the total of government purchases, rather than to the amount per capita. But the general nature of the results would not change if the specification were modified along these lines.

Equation (3) assumes constant returns to scale in k and g. The variable k should be interpreted as a broad measure of private input, which is viewed as the service flow from a broad concept of private capital. Thus, k includes physical capital, human capital, and aspects of privately owned knowledge. (My analysis does not consider the free-rider problems associated with general-purpose knowledge, as analyzed by Romer 1986.) Then the idea is that constant returns apply to this broad measure of reproducible capital, as long as the public service input, g, changes in the same proportion as k.

In the initial setup the government is constrained to a balanced budget and a proportional income tax at rate τ. Hence

$$(4) \qquad g = \tau y = \tau A k^{1-\alpha} g^{\alpha}.$$

Using equation (3) to calculate the marginal product of capital, f_k (calculated when k changes with g held fixed), and substituting $g = \tau y$ leads to

$$(5) \qquad f_k = (1-\alpha) \cdot A^{1/(1-\alpha)} \cdot \tau^{\alpha/(1-\alpha)}.$$

Given the specification of the production function in equation (3), an increase in $\tau = g/y$ shifts upward the marginal product of private capital in equation (5).

Given the form of equation (1), the initial capital $k(0)$, and a proportional income tax at rate τ, the first-order condition for each household's maximization of utility leads in the usual way to a condition for the growth rate of consumption per person,

$$(6) \qquad \gamma = \dot{c}/c = (1/\sigma) \cdot [(1-\alpha) \cdot A^{1/(1-\alpha)} \cdot (1-\tau) \cdot \tau^{\alpha/(1-\alpha)} - \rho],$$

where γ denotes a per capita growth rate. The expression within the brackets and to the left of the minus sign is $(1-\tau) \cdot f_k$, which is the private rate of return to investment (and saving). I assume parameter values for A, α, and ρ so that γ is positive for some values of τ (which means that sustained per capita growth is feasible in this model), and values for A, α, ρ, and σ so that the attained utility, U, is finite for all values of τ. (The latter condition holds for sure if $\sigma \geq 1$—e.g., with log utility where $\sigma = 1$.)

In this model the economy is always in a steady state where the variables c, k, and y all grow at the rate γ shown in equation (6). The levels for the paths of c, k, and y are determined by the initial quantity of capital, $k(0)$. Using equation (3) and the condition, $g = \tau y$, the level of output can be written as

(7) $y = A^{1/(1-\alpha)} \cdot \tau^{\alpha/(1-\alpha)} \cdot k$.

Therefore, $k(0)$ determines $y(0)$ from equation (7), given the value of τ. The initial level of consumption, $c(0)$, equals $y(0)$ less initial investment, $k(0)$, and less initial government purchases, $\tau \cdot y(0)$. Using the fact that initial investment equals $\gamma \cdot k(0)$ (because the capital stock grows always at the proportionate rate γ), the initial level of consumption turns out to be

(8) $c(0) = k(0) \cdot [(1-\tau) \cdot A^{1/(1-\alpha)} \cdot \tau^{\alpha/(1-\alpha)} - \gamma]$.

Figure 9.1 (which assumes particular parameter values for α, σ, A, and ρ, and is meant only to be illustrative) shows the relation between γ and τ. The growth rate γ rises initially with τ because of the effect of public services on private productivity. As τ increases, γ eventually reaches a peak and subsequently declines because of the reduction in the term, $1 - \tau$, which is the fraction of income that an individual retains at the margin. The peak in the growth rate occurs when $\tau = \alpha$. Given the form of equation (3), this point corresponds to the natural efficiency condition, $f_g = 1$. (At this point, an increment in g by one unit generates just enough extra output to balance the resources used up by the government.) This result—that the productive efficiency condition for g holds despite the presence of a distorting income tax—depends

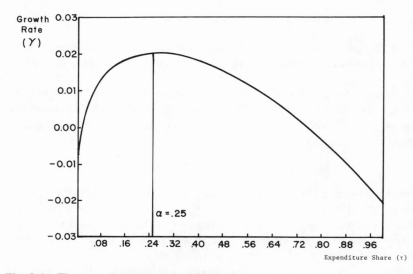

Fig. 9.1   The growth rate and size of government
Note: The curve shows the growth rate, γ, from equation (6). The parameter values are $\sigma = 1$, $\alpha = .25$, $\rho = .02$, $A^{1/\alpha} = .113$. These values imply that the maximum value of γ is .02.

on the Cobb-Douglas form of the production function. However, the general nature of the relation between γ and τ applies for other forms of production functions. The basic idea is that more government activity of the infrastructure type is good initially for growth and investment because anarchy is bad for private production. (It is not true that I learned this fact since coming to Harvard.) However, as the government expands, the rise in the tax rate, τ, deters private investment. This element dominates eventually, so that growth and the size of government are negatively related when the government is already very large.

The saving rate is given by

(9) $$s = \dot{k}/y = \gamma \cdot A^{-1/(1-\alpha)} \cdot \tau^{-\alpha/(1-\alpha)}.$$

Substituting the result for γ from equation (6) leads to the relation between s and τ that is shown in figure 9.2. The behavior is similar to that in figure 9.1, but s must peak in the region where $\tau < \alpha$.

In this type of model, where steady-state per capita growth arises because of constant returns to a broad concept of capital, the growth and saving rates, γ and s, are intimately connected. The analysis predicts that various elements, including government policies, will affect growth and saving rates in the same direction. This result differs from the predictions of models of the Solow (1956)–Cass (1965)–Koopmans (1965) type, where the steady-state per capita growth rate (reflecting exogenous technological progress) is unrelated to the

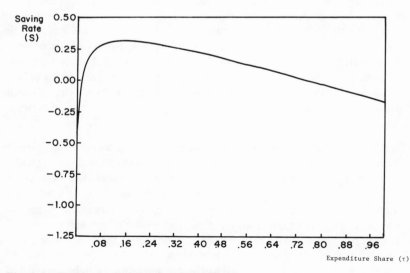

Fig. 9.2   The saving rate and the size of government
Note: The curve shows the saving rate, s, from equation (9). Parameter values are indicated in figure 9.1.

saving rate (or to parameters, such as the rate of time preference, that influence saving).

I show the following in Barro (1990):

1. With a Cobb-Douglas production technology, the choice $\tau = \alpha$, which corresponds to $f_g = 1$, maximizes the utility attained by the representative household. That is, maximizing U corresponds to maximizing γ, even though a shift in τ has implications (of ambiguous sign) for the level of c, through the impact on $c(0)$ in equation (8).

2. A command optimum also entails $\tau = \alpha$ $(f_g = 1)$, but has higher growth and saving rates than the decentralized solution. The deficiencies of growth and saving in the decentralized result reflect the distorting influence of the income tax.

3. The decentralized equilibrium corresponds to the command optimum if taxes are lump sum and if the size of government is set optimally at $g/y = \alpha$. (In the present setting, with no labor-leisure choice, a consumption tax is equivalent to a lump-sum tax.) However, if $g/y \neq \alpha$, the decentralized results with lump-sum taxes differ from the command optimum (conditioned on the specified value of g/y). The last result reflects external effects that involve the determination of aggregate government expenditures (given that the ratio, g/y, is set at a specified, nonoptimal value).

4. The results depend on how public services enter into the production function. The specification assumes that an individual producer cares about the quantity of government purchases per capita (and not—as with the space program, the Washington Monument, and not too many other governmental programs—on the aggregate of government purchases). The setup assumes also that the quantity of public services available to an individual does not depend on the amount of that individual's economic activity (represented by k and y). If an increase in an individual's production, y, leads automatically to an increase in that individual's public services (as with sewers and police services, and perhaps with national security), an income tax (or a user fee) can give better results than a lump-sum tax.

Thus far, the model views public services as entering directly into private production functions. This form applies to some aspects of highways, public transportation and communication, enforcement of contracts, and some other activities. Governments also expend resources on domestic law and order and national defense to sustain property rights. (Other governmental activities—such as regulation, expropriation, taxation, and military adventures—can reduce property rights.) Instead of entering directly into the production function, one can think of property rights as included in the $(1-\tau)$ part of the private return to capital, $(1-\tau) \cdot f_k$. That is, greater property rights amount to a larger probability that an investor will receive the marginal product, f_k (and also retain ownership to the stock of capital). Therefore, more property rights works like a reduction in τ. If the government spends resources to enhance property rights, the effects of more spending on growth and saving rates look in a general way like those shown in figures 9.1 and 9.2.

Consider now the model's predictions for the relations of the per capita growth rate, γ, and the saving (and investment) rate, s, to the government spending ratio, g/y. Here I think of g as encompassing only those activities of government that can be modeled as influencing private production or as sustaining property rights. Thus, g would not include public services that enter directly into household utility (discussed below), or transfer payments, which are difficult to model in a representative-agent framework. In practice, this means that the concept of g considered here corresponds to a relatively small fraction of government expenditures.

If governments randomized their choices of spending, the model predicts that long-term per capita growth and saving rates, γ and s, would relate to g/y as shown in figures 9.1 and 9.2. The relations would be nonmonotonic, with γ and s increasing initially with g/y, but decreasing with g/y beyond some high values.

The conclusions are different if governments optimize rather than behaving randomly. In the model, the government optimizes by setting $g/y = \alpha$, which corresponds to the productive-efficiency condition, $f_g = 1$. (Since optimization corresponds to productive efficiency for government services, the results do not depend on public officials being benevolent. Productive efficiency can be desirable even for public officials that have little concern for their constituents.) In considering long-term behavior across countries, observed differences in spending ratios, g/y, would correspond in an optimizing framework to variations in α. That is, the sizes of governments would differ only because the relative productivities of public and private services are not the same in each place. (Perhaps the differences in α relate to geography, weather, natural resources, and so on?) Whatever the reason for variations in α across countries, the covariation between g/y and γ or s that is generated by these variations does not correspond to the relations shown in figures 9.1 and 9.2.

Equation (7) shows that, for a given τ, the level of productivity, y/k, depends on the parameter, $A^{1/(1-\alpha)}$. Suppose that this parameter is held constant while α varies across countries (i.e., the variations in relative productivity of public and private services are assumed to be independent of this concept of the level of productivity). Then it can be shown from equations (6) and (9) that an increase in α—which implies an increase in g/y—goes along with decreases in γ and s. For a given level of productivity, the economy does better (and has a higher growth rate) if the relative productivity of private services is higher—that is, if α is lower. The reason is that public services require public expenditures, which have to be financed by a distorting income tax. It is only because of this effect that the model predicts a nonzero correlation between α and γ. The more general point is that, if governments optimize, they go to the point where the marginal effect of more government on growth is nil. Therefore, there would not be much cross-country relation between growth rates and the size of government if governments optimize (if we include in government spending only the activities that relate to private production).

Governments also carry out consumption expenditures, g^c, which do not affect private production functions, but do have a direct impact on the representative household's utility. With an income tax, a higher level of g^c/y implies a lower value of $1 - \tau$, but no change in the private marginal product, f_k. Therefore, an increase in g^c/y (which may be warranted in terms of maximizing the representative person's utility) leads to lower values for growth and saving rates. (In an example considered in Barro, 1990, I showed that government consumption spending would not affect the optimal share in GNP of the government's productive expenditure—this share remained at α in the case considered.)

Unlike predictions for productive government spending, the predictions for government consumption are more straightforward. In the case of consumption activities (i.e., public services that affect utility but not production), a larger share of government spending would correlate negatively with growth and saving rates.

The main difficulty of interpretation is the possibility of reverse causation from the level of income to the choice of government consumption spending as a share of GNP, g^c/y. Suppose, for example, that this spending is a luxury good in the sense that a higher level of income leads to an increase in g^c/y. (Empirically, I find that this "Wagner's law" effect applies to transfers, but not to other types of government spending that I classify below as consumption.) Given the initial level of income, $y(0)$, a higher growth rate γ means a higher average level of income over the sample, and hence, a higher sample average for g^c/y. (If the growth rate γ were anticipated, even the initial value of g^c/y would be positively correlated with the sample average of γ.) Thus, this reverse effect could generate a positive association between g^c/y and γ. In the empirical work I argue that this effect is important for transfer payments, but not for other categories of government spending.

9.2 Population Growth and Human Capital in the Model of Steady-State Growth

The model described above did not allow for population growth, and it also did not allow for distinctions between physical and human capital. Empirically, population growth appears to interact closely with the level and growth rate of income, as well as with investment in human capital. In order to incorporate these elements into the model, I use some results from the existing literature.

Becker and Barro (1988) and Barro and Becker (1989) consider the determination of population growth in a model where altruistic parents choose own consumption, the number of children, and the bequests left to children. However, these models do not allow for endogenous per capita growth. Becker, Murphy, and Tamura (1990) and Tamura (1988) have extended the model to analyze the joint determination of population growth and per capita growth. The important consideration—which makes it worthwhile to study population growth jointly with per capita growth—is that population growth influences investment, especially in human capital, and thereby affects per capita growth rates. In effect, population growth is a form of saving and investment (in number of children) that is an alternative to investment in human capital (the quality of children). Therefore, some factors, such as a decrease in the cost of raising children, that lead to higher population growth tend to reduce the growth rate of output per capita.

Building on Becker and Barro (1988), Lucas (1988), Rebelo (1987), and especially Becker et al. (1990), I have been working on the following model:

$$(10) \qquad U = \int_0^\infty u(c)e^{-\rho t}[N(t)]^{1-\varepsilon}dt,$$

$$(11) \qquad y = c + \dot{k} + nk = A\,[(1-\eta-v)h]^\beta k^{1-\beta},$$

$$(12) \qquad \dot{h} + nh = Bvh - \delta h,$$

$$(13) \qquad n = \dot{N}/N = \theta\eta - \delta,$$

For the new variables, N is the level of population, n is the growth rate of population, h is human capital per person, η is time spent raising children, v is time spent investing in human capital, $1-\eta-v$ is time spent producing goods (used either for consumables or new physical capital), B is a parameter for productivity in generating new human capital, θ is a parameter for productivity in raising children, δ is the mortality rate, and ε $(0 < \varepsilon < 1)$ is a parameter that measures diminishing marginal utility of children. Time spent at leisure is ignored (that is, is regarded as fixed). Government services and taxation can be thought of as effects on the parameters A and B. For convenience, I depart from Becker et al. in setting up the model in continuous time. The main abstraction here is that the family size, $N(t)$, has to be thought of as evolving continuously over time. For purposes of aggregate analysis, I believe that this abstraction is no problem.

This model can be used to analyze steady-state per capita growth, population growth, and saving/investment rates. The effects associated with population growth involve two main channels. First, higher population growth corresponds to a higher effective rate of time preference (through the effect of N with $0 < \varepsilon < 1$ in equation [10]). Second, given the mortality rate δ, higher population growth goes along with more time spent raising children (η), which implies a lower rate of return on human capital. (This result assumes that human capital is productive in producing goods or new human capital, but not in producing new persons.) Through both channels, forces that lead to a higher rate of population growth tend to go along with a lower rate of per capita growth and a lower rate of investment, especially in human capital.

The model can be used (as in Lucas 1988) to assess some effects from an international capital market. A perfectly functioning world credit market ensures equal rates of return on capital in all countries. (Wages on human capital would not be equated in the absence of labor mobility.) Countries may differ in terms of productivity parameters, A and B, partly because of the effects of government policies on these coefficients. But countries may be similar in their productivity for raising children, θ. Investments in physical and human capital would tend to occur in the places with high values of A and B. (In this constant-returns model, these forces are not offset by diminishing marginal productivity of capital.) In effect, countries with low values of A and B have a comparative advantage in producing bodies, and would concentrate on this activity. The existence of the international credit market means that countries with low values of A and B end up with lower values of k and h than otherwise. Hence wage rates per person tend to be even lower than otherwise in these poor countries.

Countries may differ more in the parameter A (productivity in market goods) than in B (productivity in creating human capital). Then, without an international credit market, all countries would have similar rates of return (determined mainly by the similar values of B), but wage rates per unit of human capital would be increasing in A. In this case the introduction of a world credit market has little impact on the results. The more significant element would be mobility of human capital—people would like to migrate with their human capital toward the countries with high values of A.

I hope to go further with this analysis to distinguish effects on national saving from those on domestic investment. It seems that, empirically, these two variables move closely together; in effect, national saving equals domestic investment plus noise, where the noise corresponds to the current-account balance, which is unrelated (over samples of 15–25 years) to variables that I have examined. With a well-functioning global capital market, this behavior is puzzling.

9.3 Transitional Dynamics Associated with Population Growth

One well-known empirical regularity is that population growth declines with the level of real per capita income over a broad range of incomes, both across countries and over time for a single country. This property does not emerge from the steady-state analysis considered above. Becker et al. (1990) introduced two sources of transitional dynamics, which can account for this behavior of population growth. (In the model outlined in part 9.2, the only transitional dynamics involves the relative amounts of k and h. This element seems important in recoveries from wars or other emergencies, but not in the pattern of long-term economic development.)

Becker et al.'s (1990) first element that creates dynamics is the treatment of human capital as the sum of raw labor (which comes with all bodies) and accumulated human capital. At high levels of development, the raw component is unimportant, but at low levels, this component is significant for investment and growth. In particular, Becker et al. model the rate of return on human capital investment as increasing in the amount of investment over some range. Therefore, if the amount of human capital per person is low, the low rate of return tends to discourage investment, and thereby makes it difficult to escape from underdevelopment. Becker et al.'s second dynamic element is that the cost of raising children (inversely related to θ) includes goods as well as time. As wage rates become high, the time cost dominates the goods cost. Therefore, at higher levels of per capita income it is more likely that an increase in income will lead to lower population growth (because the substitution effect from higher value of time is more important relative to the income effect). At low levels of development, it is likely that an increase in income leads (as in Malthus) to higher population growth, which makes it difficult for a country to escape from underdevelopment.

The presence of these dynamic elements in Becker et al.'s model leads to two types of steady states. Aside from the steady-state growth equilibrium (as in the model discussed before), there is a low-level underdevelopment trap. If an economy starts with low values of human capital, it may not pay to invest. Such an economy has high population growth, low investment, and low (or zero) per capita growth. If an economy starts with sufficiently high values of human capital, it tends to grow over time toward a steady state with constant per capita growth. During the transition, expansions of per capita income are accompanied by decreases in population growth and increases in each person's human capital. Over some range, the rate of investment in physical capital, and the rate of per capita growth also tend to increase.

9.4   Empirical Findings for a Cross Section of Countries

My empirical analysis uses data across countries from 1960 to 1985 to analyze the joint determination of the growth rate of real per capita GDP, the ratio of physical investment expenditure (private plus public) to GDP, a proxy for investment in human capital (the secondary school enrollment rate), and the growth rate of population. Thus far, I find that national saving rates behave similarly to the rates for domestic investment—the present results refer only to domestic investment.

I began with data from Summers and Heston (1988), and supplemented their cross-country data set with measures of government activity and other variables from various sources (see the data appendix). These additional vari-

ables, such as the breakdown of government expenditure into various components, and spending figures at the level of consolidated general government,
necessitated the reduction in the sample size from about 120 countries from
Summers and Heston to 72 countries. (In a few cases where the central government was known to account for the bulk of government spending—primarily African countries—the figures refer to central government.) After considerable effort, with the help of David Renelt, I have assembled a usable data
set for the 72 countries. (See the data appendix for a list of the countries
included.) The data include total government expenditures for overall consumption purposes, for investment purposes, and for education, defense, and
transfer payments. The data I use are, in most cases, averages over 15–25-
year periods for the variables considered. For a few countries, the averages
cover less than 15 years. This averaging over time seems appropriate for a
study of long-term effects on growth and saving.

The sample excludes the major oil-exporting countries. These countries
tend to have high values of real GDP per capita, but act more like countries
will lower values of income. This behavior can probably be explained by
thinking of these countries as receiving large amounts of income from natural
resources, but otherwise not being advanced in terms of technology, human
capital, and so on. I plan eventually to use this approach to incorporate these
countries into the analysis.

The variables that I use are the following:

$y(0)$:   Real per capita GDP for 1960 in 1980 prices (using the Summers
            and Heston data, which are designed to allow a comparison of
            levels of GDP across countries).

Δy: Average annual growth rate of real per capita GDP from 1960 to
            1985.

i/y: Ratio of real investment expenditures (private plus public) to real
            GDP. Although this variable is available from Summers and Hes-
            ton from 1960 for most countries, I have the breakdown between
            public and private components typically only since 1970. I mea-
            sured the variable i/y as an average from 1970 to 1985.

school: Fraction of relevant age group in the 1970s enrolled in secondary
            schools. This variable (from the World Bank) is a proxy for in-
            vestment in human capital.

ΔN: Average annual growth rate of population from 1960 to 1985
            (from Summers and Heston 1988).

g^c/y: Ratio to real GDP of real purchases of goods and services for
            consumption purposes by consolidated general government. The
            idea here is to obtain a proxy for the types of government spend-
            ing that enter directly into household utility rather than firms'
            production functions. I began with Summers and Heston's num-
            bers for government general consumption expenditures. These

figures include substantial components for spending on national defense and education, which I would model more like productive government spending (and which are more like public investment than public consumption). Thus, I subtracted the ratios to GDP for expenditures on defense and education from the Summers-Heston ratios for general government consumption. (However, unlike the values from Summers and Heston, the defense and education variables are ratios of nominal spending to nominal GDP, rather than real spending to real GDP.) Summers and Heston's numbers are available since 1960 for most countries, but I have the data on defense and education mainly since 1970. The variable g^c/y is, in most cases, an average from 1970 to 1985. (Fewer years are included for countries with missing data on defense or education.)

g^i/y: Ratio to real GDP of real investment expenditures by consolidated general government. I think of public investment as a proxy for the type of infrastructure activities that influence private production in the theoretical model. (It is not inevitable that public investment corresponds to spending that affects production, whereas public consumption corresponds to spending that affects utility. But, in practice, the breakdown of government spending into categories may work this way.) The variable g^i/y is, in most cases, an average from 1970 to 1985. (Fewer years are available for some countries.) I used the Summers-Heston deflators for total investment and GDP to adjust the data, which were obtained as ratios of nominal spending to nominal GDP. That is, I assumed that the deflator for total investment was appropriate for public investment.

g^d/y: Government spending for national defense as a ratio to GDP. The data are ratios of nominal spending to nominal GDP, and are in most cases averages of values from 1970 to 1985. Holding fixed a country's external threat, an increase in g^d may mean more national security and hence, more property rights. Then the effects on growth and investment are as worked out for productive government spending in the theory. However, defense outlays are highly responsive to external threats (or to domestic desires for military adventures), in which case g^d may proxy negatively for national security. Thus, it is difficult to predict the relation of defense spending to growth and investment.

g^e/y: Government expenditures for education as a ratio to GDP. The values are ratios of nominal spending to nominal GDP, and are, in most cases, averages of figures from 1970 to 1985. I anticipate that this variable would work similarly to the public investment variable.

g^s/y: Government transfers for social insurance and welfare as a ratio to GDP. The variable is, in most cases, an average of values from 1970 to 1985. At present, I have data on this variable for only 66 of the 72 countries that are in the main sample. I anticipate that this variable would work similarly to g^c/y—that is, associate with lower rates of per capita growth and investment.

Pol. rights: Ordinal index, running from 1 to 7, of political rights from Gastil (1987). (This type of variable has been used in previous studies of economic growth by Kormendi and Meguire 1985, and Scully 1988.) Figures are averages of data from 1973 to 1985, with higher values signifying fewer rights. My intention is to use this variable as a proxy for property rights; thus, a higher value of the index should be associated with lower rates of investment and growth. (One shortcoming of this variable is that, aside from its subjective nature, it pertains to political rights rather than to economic rights, per se. Although countries like Chile, Korea, and Singapore are exceptions, my conjecture is that economic and political rights are strongly positively correlated across countries.)

Soc: Dummy variable taking the value 1 for economic system primarily socialistic, and 0 otherwise. The underlying data are from Gastil (1987).

Mixed: Dummy variable taking the value 1 for economic system mixed between free enterprise and socialism, and 0 otherwise. These data are also from Gastil (1987). Countries not classified as either socialistic or mixed were in the category "free enterprise."

War: Dummy variable equal to 1 for countries that experienced violent war or revolution since 1960. (See the appendix for sources.) The expectation is that war and related aspects of political instability compromise property rights and lead thereby to less investment and economic growth. Refining the variable to measure number of years of war or revolution did not add to the explanatory value. It appears, however, that better measures of political stability are available from Arthur Banks's data bank on cross-national time series. I plan to look into these data.

Africa: Dummy variable equal to 1 for countries in Africa, and 0 otherwise.

Lat. Amer.:   Dummy variable equal to 1 for countries in Latin America (including Central America and Mexico), and 0 otherwise.

My general strategy is to consider a system of equations in which four key variables are simultaneously determined: the per capita growth rate, Δy, the physical investment ratio, i/y, the amount of investment in human capital (proxied by the variable "school"), and population growth, ΔN. I treat the measures of government expenditures and the other variables mentioned above as explanatory variables. The endogeneity of these variables affects the interpretation of the results. Some of these effects—such as the consequences of government optimization with respect to choices of productive spending and the response of defense spending to external threats—have already been mentioned. I will consider here some issues concerning the endogeneity of initial real per capita GDP, $y(0)$, and the responsiveness of government consumption spending (g^c/y and g^s/y above) to changes in income.

I want to think of cross-country differences in $y(0)$ in terms of the transitional changes in the level of income as an economy moves from a starting point of low income toward a position of steady-state per capita growth. Then, in accordance with Becker et al.'s (1990) analysis, the prediction is that higher $y(0)$ goes along with lower population growth and a greater share of national product devoted to investment in human capital. As $y(0)$ rises, the extent of these responses diminishes, and eventually vanishes when the economy reaches the steady-state growth position. There are also weaker effects on per capita growth and the physical investment ratio—but, over some range, the effect of $y(0)$ on these variables would also be positive. For countries where income levels are too low to escape the trap of underdevelopment, the predictions are reversed. That is, in this range, population growth would rise with $y(0)$, while human capital investment and the other variables would decline.

One problem is that $y(0)$ may be influenced by temporary measurement error or by temporary business fluctuations. These factors tend to generate a negative association between $y(0)$ and subsequent rates of growth per capita. For growth rates averaged over 25 years, the business-cycle effect would tend to be minor. However, measurement error for GDP can be extreme for the low-income countries. To assess this effect, I looked at an interaction between $y(0)$ and the quality of the data (as reported subjectively by Summers and Heston 1988). The results suggested no effect from data quality, which may indicate that this type of measurement error is not important.

A different effect is that $y(0)$ would be positively correlated with per capita growth in the past. To the extent that the factors that create growth are persisting (and are not separately held constant), this relation tends to generate a positive association of $y(0)$ to per capita growth and the investment variables. At this point I do not see how to gauge the magnitude of this effect.

I mentioned before that the ratios of various components of government spending to GDP could be related to the level of income and, therefore, to the per capita growth rate, γ. If the response is positive (negative), this element generates a positive (negative) correlation between the expenditure ratio and the growth rate.

Table 9.1 shows Wagner's law–type regressions for various categories of government spending. The table shows the regression coefficient on log $[y(0)]$ (where $y(0)$ is per capita GDP in 1960) for the ratio of each type of spending to GDP (averaged typically from 1970 to 1985). The results show that in two areas—education and transfers for social insurance and welfare—the ratio of spending to GDP tends to rise with the level of per capita income. Quantita-

Table 9.1   Regressions of Government Spending Ratios on the Level of Income

Category of Spending [mean]	Number of Observations	Constant	Log[y(0)]	R^2	$\hat{\sigma}$
g^c/y [.105]	74	.115 (.006)	−.027 (.006)	.19	.050
g^i/y [.033]	73	.032 (.002)	.002 (.002)	.01	.016
g^d/y [.032]	74	.031 (.005)	.001 (.005)	.00	.040
g^e/y [.042]	75	.040 (.002)	.007 (.002)	.15	.014
g^s/y [.057]	68	.038 (.005)	.047 (.005)	.58	.038

Note: The table shows a regression of each expenditure ratio (calculated as an average from 1970 to 1985) on the logarithm of $y(0)$, which is the 1960 value of real per capita GDP. Standard errors are shown in parentheses and $\hat{\sigma}$ is the standard error of estimate. g^c refers to government general consumption spending (excluding defense and education), g^i to public investment, g^d to defense spending, g^e to educational expenditures, and g^s to transfers for social insurance and welfare.

tively, the effect is particularly important for transfers, g^s/y, where an increase in $y(0)$ by 10% corresponds to a rise by one-half a percentage point in the spending ratio. In the case of government general consumption (exclusive of defense and education), the spending ratio tends to decline with the level of income. In two other areas—public investment and defense—the spending ratios bear no significant relation to the level of income. Overall, in only one of the five spending categories—transfers for social insurance and welfare— does the level of income account for a substantial fraction of the cross-country variation in the spending ratio. The R^2 here is about .6, as compared to values less than .2 in the other cases. Therefore, except for the transfers category, the bulk of the variations across countries in the spending ratios would be pre- dominantly unrelated to differences in income. Thus, when looking at the relation with economic growth, the area of transfers is the one case where important reverse causation (the positive effect of the growth rate on the ex- penditure ratio) is likely to be important.

The basic regression results appear in table 9.2. Regressions 1, 3, 5, 7 exclude dummies for Africa and Latin America, whereas regressions 2, 4, 6, 8 include these dummies.

Consider first the coefficients on the starting (1960) level of income, $y(0)$, which appears linearly and also as a squared term. The linear terms show a pronounced negative relation with population growth (regressions 7 and 8 of table 9.2) and a strong positive relation with schooling (regressions 5 and 6). (The simple correlation between $y[0]$ and ΔN is $-.71$, while that between $y[0]$ and schooling is .80—see figs. 9.3 and 9.4 for scatter plots.) The oppos- ing signs on $[y(0)]^2$ indicate that the effects of income on population growth and schooling attenuate as income rises. At the sample mean for $y(0)$ of $2,200, the coefficients in regression 7 imply that an additional $1,000 of per capita income is associated with a decline in population growth by .35 percentage points per year. This negative effect of income on population growth vanishes when income reaches $5,600 per capita. (The highest level of $y[0]$ in the sample is $7,380 for the United States.) For schooling in regression 5, the positive effect of income is gone when income reaches $6,200. (However, the use of the secondary school enrollment rate as a measure of schooling automatically tends to truncate the sample at the highest income levels.)

The results accord with the model of Becker et al. (1990), in the sense of suggesting an important trade-off between quality and quantity of children as the level of per capita income rises. That is, the transition from low to high per capita income involves lower population growth and more investment in each person's human capital. I did not, however, find any indication that the signs of the income coefficients were different for the countries with the lowest per capita incomes (say less that $500). That is, I did not see evidence of the particular kind of low-level trap of underdevelopment that Becker, Murphy, and Tamura discussed.

The relation of $y(0)$ to per capita growth, Δy, is less pronounced, although regressions 1 and 2 of table 9.2 show significantly negative effects. At the sample mean of $y(0)$, an increase in per capita income by $1,000 is associated (according to regression 1) with a decline in the per capita growth rate of .60 percentage points per year. As discussed by Romer (1989), this type of inverse relation between the per capita growth rate and the level of per capita income is present in models that predict convergence of levels of per capita income across countries (although the inverse relation is not itself sufficient to guarantee full convergence). The convergence property tends to arise when there are diminishing returns to capital, but not in the sort of constant-returns models that I discussed earlier. As Romer noted, the simple correlation between per capita growth and the starting level of per capita income is, in fact, close to zero in the kind of cross-country sample that I am using. For my sample, the simple correlation is .05—see the scatter plot in figure 9.5. Therefore, the negative coefficient on $y(0)$ in regressions 1 and 2 depends on holding constant the other variables in the equations.

For the investment ratio, i/y, the smiple correlation with $y(0)$ is positive (.43—see the scatter plot in fig. 9.6). The coefficients on $y(0)$ in regressions 3 and 4 of table 9.2 are positive, but insignificantly different from zero.

I regard the variable g^c/y (where g^c refers to government general consumption spending aside from defense and education) as a proxy for government expenditures that do not directly affect private sector productivity. It is a robust finding that g^c/y is negatively related to per capita growth (regressions 1 and 2 of table 9.2)[1] and the investment ratio, i/y (regressions 3 and 4). Figure 9.7 shows a scatter plot of per capita growth against g^c/y. In the sample, g^c/y has a mean of .107 with a standard deviation of .054. Regressions 1 and 3

Table 9.2   **Basic Regressions for 72 Countries**

Dependent Variable	Δy [.024]		i/y [.21]		School [.41]		ΔN [.018]		Δy		ΔN	
	(1)	(2)	(3)	(4)	(5)	(6)	(7)	(8)	(9)	(10)	(11)	(12)
Constant	.059	.063	.203	.215	.246	.253	.0246	.0254	.045	.052	.0308	.0316
	(.010)	(.009)	(.038)	(.038)	(.104)	(.099)	(.0041)	(.0039)	(.012)	(.012)	(.0046)	(.0049)
$y(0)$ [2.2]	−.0084	−.0107	.018	.009	.165	.181	−.0062	−.0080	−.0166	−.0183	−.0048	−.0068
	(.0041)	(.0043)	(.016)	(.018)	(.043)	(.047)	(.0017)	(.0019)	(.0037)	(.0044)	(.0018)	(.0021)
$[y(0)]^2$	.0005	.0007	−.0026	−.0017	−.0133	−.0165	.00055	.00083	.00135	.00157	.00045	.00071
	(.0006)	(.0006)	(.0022)	(.0024)	(.0059)	(.0064)	(.00023)	(.00025)	(.00047)	(.00055)	(.00022)	(.00025)
g^c/y [.108]	−.154	−.132	−.41	−.35	−.27	−.12	.008	.005	−.096	−.090	−.005	−.004
	(.034)	(.032)	(.13)	(.13)	(.37)	(.35)	(.015)	(.014)	(.030)	(.029)	(.014)	(.014)
g^i/y [.033]	.262	.255	2.22	2.21	1.55	1.31	−.068	−.054	−.068	−.026	−.065	−.057
	(.099)	(.091)	(.39)	(.38)	(1.06)	(.99)	(.042)	(.039)	(.100)	(.099)	(.044)	(.044)
g^d/y [.030]	.005	−.004	.17	1.16	−.70	−1.00	.062	.078	.032	.035	.046	.058
	(.046)	(.044)	(.18)	(.18)	(.49)	(.48)	(.019)	(.019)	(.040)	(.043)	(.017)	(.018)
War [.35]	−.0098	−.0122	−.037	−.045	.015	.013	−.0002	−.0009	−.0057	−.0081	−.0002	−.0011
	(.0037)	(.0036)	(.014)	(.015)	(.040)	(.039)	(.0016)	(.0016)	(.0032)	(.0033)	(.0015)	(.0016)

	(1)	(2)	(3)	(4)	(5)	(6)	(7)	(8)	(9)	(10)	(11)	(12)
Pol. rights [3.2]	−.0038 (.0013)	−.0020 (.0013)	−.0112 (.0050)	−.0065 (.0052)	−.041 (.014)	−.025 (.014)	.0012 (.0005)	.0008 (.0005)	−.0011 (.0011)	−.0006 (.0011)	.0003 (.0005)	.0003 (.0005)
Soc [.04]	−.0095 (.0088)	−.0141 (.0082)	.047 (.034)	.033 (.034)	.150 (.093)	.136 (.089)	−.0084 (.0037)	−.0089 (.0036)	−.0224 (.0074)	−.0243 (.0074)	−.0081 (.0034)	−.0094 (.0034)
Mixed [.47]	.0061 (.0034)	.0046 (.0031)	.006 (.013)	.002 (.013)	.071 (.036)	.056 (.034)	−.0033 (.0014)	−.0029 (.0014)	.0023 (.0029)	.0020 (.0028)	−.0015 (.0013)	−.0015 (.0013)
Africa [.22]	. . .	−.0178 (.0053)	. . .	−.049 (.022)	. . .	−.109 (.057)	. . .	.0013 (.0023)	. . .	−.0106 (.0048)	. . .	−.0013 (.0022)
Lat. Amer. [.25]	. . .	−.0117 (.0041)	. . .	−.027 (.017)	. . .	−.145 (.044)	. . .	.0056 (.0018)	. . .	−.0039 (.0039)	. . .	.0027 (.0017)
Δy	. . .	. . .	. . .	. . .	. . .	. . .	. . .	. . .	. . .	. . .	−.120 (.056)	−.120 (.058)
i/y	. . .	. . .	. . .	. . .	. . .	. . .	. . .	. . .	.120 (.027)	.106 (.027)	.026 (.014)	.024 (.014)
School	. . .	. . .	. . .	. . .	. . .	. . .	. . .	. . .	.015 (.012)	.011 (.012)	−.0176 (.0047)	−.0152 (.0048)
ΔN	. . .	. . .	. . .	. . .	. . .	. . .	. . .	. . .	−.59 (.28)	−.59 (.28)	. . .	. . .
r^2	.45	.56	.62	.66	.75	.79	.70	.74	.67	.69	.79	.81
$\hat{\sigma}$	.0131	.0119	.051	.049	.139	.129	.0055	.0052	.0104	.0102	.0047	.0046

Note: Standard errors of coefficients shown in parentheses, means of variables shown in brackets. $\hat{\sigma}$ is the standard error of estimate. See text for definitions of variables.

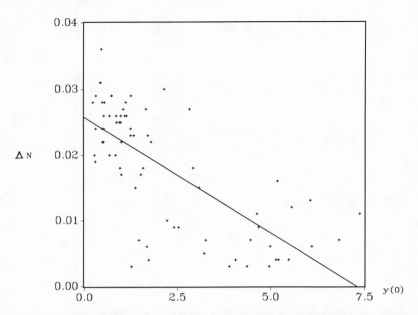

Fig. 9.3   Population growth versus the initial level of per capita GDP for 72 countries

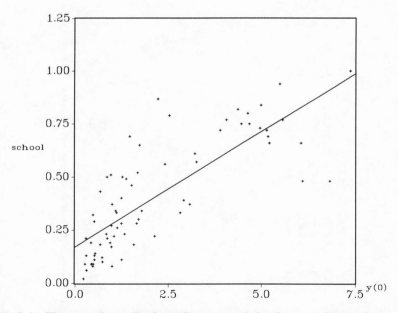

Fig. 9.4   The secondary school enrollment rate (school) versus the starting level of per capita GDP for 72 countries

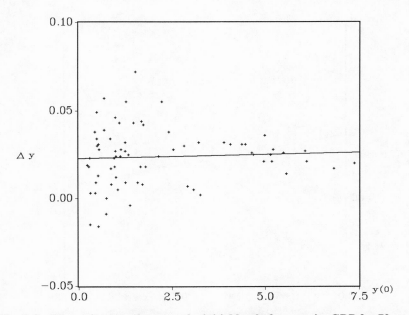

Fig. 9.5   Per capita growth versus the initial level of per capita GDP for 72 countries

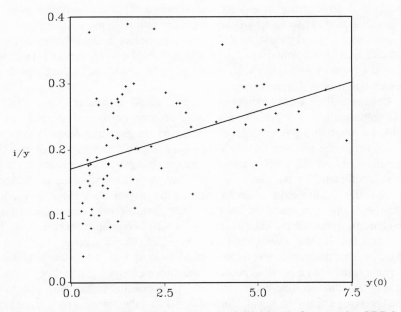

Fig. 9.6   The investment ratio (*i/y*) versus the initial level of per capita GDP for 72 countries

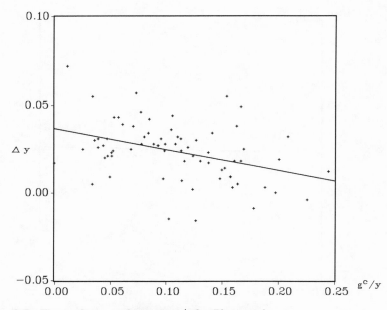

Fig. 9.7   Per capita growth versus g^c/y for 72 countries

imply that an increase in g^c/y by one standard deviation above its mean is associated with a decline by 0.8 percentage points in the annual per capita growth rate and a decrease by 2.2 percentage points in the investment ratio. (Recall that investment includes private and public components.) The estimated effects of g^c/y on schooling and population growth (regressions 5–8) are insignificantly different from zero.

Conceptually, I would expect government transfers to interact with growth and investment in a manner similar to government consumption purchases. I added the variable g^s/y to the regressions (where g^s is transfer payments for social insurance and welfare), although this addition necessitated a drop in the sample size from 72 to 66 countries. The variable g^s/y had a significantly negative coefficient for population growth, but the other estimated coefficients were insignificant (and the results for the other explanatory variables did not change much). For example, for per capita growth (with continent dummies excluded), the estimated coefficient on g^s/y was .046 (standard error = .051), whereas that for the investment ratio was − .33 (standard error = .19). It is puzzling that the transfers variables would show up with a negative coefficient for investment but a positive point estimate for per capita growth. My conjecture is that this positive coefficient reflects reverse causation from growth to the spending ratio, g^s/y. Recall from table 9.1 that the transfers ratio is, in fact, closely related to the level of income, so this type of reverse effect is likely to be important here. I plan to investigate these possibilities further.

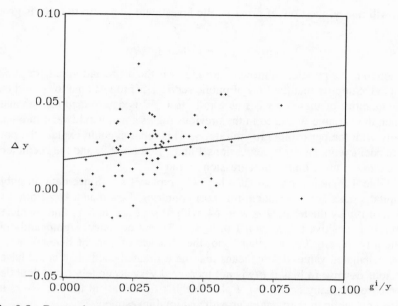

Fig. 9.8   Per capita growth versus g^i/y for 72 countries

I thought of the public investment ratio, g^i/y, as a proxy for government infrastructure type spending, which affects private-sector productivity. The estimated coefficient of this variable in the growth equation (regressions 1 and 2 of table 9.2) is significantly positive. See figure 9.8 for a scatter plot of per capita growth versus g^i/y (Aschauer 1989 gets analogous results from the U.S. time series). Abstracting from the possibility of reverse causation from growth to the public-investment variable, the results would indicate that the typical government was operating where the marginal effect of public investment spending on the per capita growth rate was positive. As indicated in the theory, this type of result is inconsistent with public-sector optimization (which dicatated the choice of public spending to maximize the per capita growth rate).

The estimated coefficients on g^i/y are also positive in the equations for the investment ratio, i/y (regressions 3 and 4 of table 9.2). Recall that investment, i, includes public, as well as private, spending—that is, g^i is a component of i. Therefore, if taken literally, the coefficient of 2.2 in the regressions for i/y means that an extra unit of public investment induces about a one-for-one *increase* in private investment.

One problem is that the flow of public investment spending does not coincide with the flow of services from public capital, which is the concept that corresponds to the public service input, g, in the theoretical analysis. If k^g is the stock of public capital per person, and if this stock grows at the per capita growth rate γ, the flow of gross public investment as a ratio to GNP is given by

(14) $i^g/y = (\gamma + n + \delta^g) \cdot k^g/y,$

where n is the population growth rate and δ^g is the depreciation rate for public capital. Suppose that the flow of public services is proportional to k^g, and that the quantity of these services as a ratio to GNP is determined exogenously. Then the variable i^g/y, used in the previous regressions, would vary automatically with the per capita growth rate, γ. This relation could explain the positive coefficients on i^g/y in regressions 1 and 2 of table 9.2, and the coefficients in excess of unity on i^g/y in regressions 3 and 4.

Table 9.3 shows regressions where k^g/y replaces i^g/y. Since data on public capital stocks are unavailable for most countries, I estimated k^g/y from division of i^g/y by the term, $\gamma + n + \delta^g$, with δ^g set equal to 0.1. The coefficient on k^g/y is positive (regression 1 of table 9.3), but no longer significantly different from zero. On the other hand, the presence of γ in the denominator of the calculated value of k^g/y means that the estimated coefficient could have a serious downward bias if i^g/y is not measured very accurately (as is doubtless the case for many countries). I plan to think further about how to assess the effect of public investment on growth and total investment.

Table 9.3	**Regressions for 72 Countries, Using Estimate of Public Capital Stock**			
Dependent	Δy	i/y	School	ΔN
Variable	(1)	(2)	(3)	(4)
Constant	.064	.235	.270	.0238
	(.010)	(.039)	(.102)	(.0040)
$y(0)$	$-.0082$	.011	.161	$-.0059$
	(.0043)	(.017)	(.045)	(.0018)
$[y(0)]^2$	.0005	$-.0022$	$-.0132$	.00053
	(.0006)	(.0023)	(.0060)	(.00024)
g^c/y	$-.154$	$-.45$	$-.29$	.010
	(.036)	(.14)	(.37)	(.015)
k^g/y	.020	$-.275$	.17	$-.0096$
[.23]	(.015)	(.059)	(.15)	(.0060)
g^d/y	.017	.24	$-.65$	.060
	(.047)	(.19)	(.49)	(.019)
War	$-.0104$	$-.043$	.011	.0000
	(.0039)	(.015)	(.040)	(.0016)
Pol. rights	$-.0040$	$-.0129$	$-.042$	.0013
	(.0013)	(.0053)	(.014)	(.0005)
Soc	$-.0104$	.028	.139	$-.0077$
	(.0092)	(.037)	(.095)	(.0038)
Mixed	.0053	.004	.068	$-.0033$
	(.0035)	(.014)	(.036)	(.0014)
R^2	.40	.57	.75	.70
$\hat{\sigma}$	.0136	.054	.140	.0055

I looked also at government spending for education, g^e/y. My expectation was that this investment in human capital would operate in a manner similar to other types of public investment. The estimated coefficients on g^e/y turn out to be insignificant for per capita growth and the investment ratio. If added to regressions 1 and 3 of table 9.2, the estimated coefficients are .12 (standard error = .56) for Δy, and .31 (standard error = 1.53) for i/y.

The defense spending variable, g^d/y, is insignificant in the equations for growth and investment (regressions 1–4 of table 9.2). There is some indication of a negative effect on schooling (regression 5 and 6) and a positive effect on population growth (regressions 7 and 8). The variable "war" enters negatively for growth and investment (regressions 1–4), as would be expected if the variable proxies for political instability. This variable is insignificant for schooling or population growth (regressions 5–8).

The political rights variable indicates that fewer rights associate with lower per capita growth (regression 1 of table 9.2), lower investment in physical and human capital (regressions 3 and 5), and higher population growth (regression 7). These effects are attenuated with the inclusion of dummies for Africa and Latin America (regressions 2, 4, 6, and 8). (That is, the African and Latin American countries tend to have fewer political rights, although the data prefer the continent dummies to the particular measure of these rights.)

There is some indication that socialistic countries have lower per capita growth rates, although the small number of these countries in the sample makes the results unreliable. Countries with mixed economic systems have slightly higher per capita growth than the free enterprise economies, but the difference is not statistically significant.

Even with the other explanatory variables held fixed, the dummy for Africa is significantly negative for per capita growth, investment, and schooling. The dummy for Latin America is significantly negative for growth and schooling, and significantly positive for population growth. (The last effect does not represent the influence of the Roman Catholic religion. A dummy variable for Catholicism as the majority religion is insignificant in the equations for population growth or the other variables.) I think that the continent dummies are proxying for aspects of political instability, which are not captured well by the other variables. Better measures of this instability, which I am presently constructing, may make the continent dummies unnecessary—that is, these other variables may explain why it matters for growth, and so on, that a country is located in Africa or Latin America.

Table 9.4 shows correlation matrices for the residuals from the equations estimated in table 9.2. One matrix applies to the regressions that omit the continent dummies and the other to the regressions that include these dummies. Although the magnitude of the correlations tends to be weaker in the latter case, the general pattern of results is similar.

The results show that the residual for per capita growth is positively related to that for physical investment (correlation in the equations without continent

Table 9.4   **Correlation Matrix for Residuals**

	Δy	i/y	School	ΔN
Δy		.52	.41	− .35
		[.46]	[.31]	[− .29]
i/y			.28	− .04
			[.21]	[.03]
School				− .50
				[− .42]

Note: The entries give the correlation of the residuals from regressions with the indicated dependent variables. The upper figure in each cell refers to regressions 1, 3, 5 and 7 from table 9.2. The lower number (in brackets) refers to regressions 2, 4, 6 and 8 from table 9.2, which include dummies for Africa and Latin America.

dummies of .52) and schooling (.41), and negatively related to the residual for population growth (− .35). These results accord with the theory discussed before in which the determination of per capita growth is directly connected to the determination of investment rates. The other striking finding is the negative relation between the residuals for schooling and population growth (correlation = − .50). This result again suggests the importance of the trade-off between the quality and quantity of children.

Another way to look at the interaction among the dependent variables is to consider regressions where the other dependent variables appear as regressors. With per capita growth as the dependent variable, regressions 9 and 10 of table 9.2 show that the estimated coefficient on the investment ratio, i/y, is significantly positive, while that on population growth is significantly negative. (See figs. 9.9 and 9.10 for scatter plots of per capita growth against i/y and population growth.) One interesting finding from the regressions is that the coefficient on the public investment ratio, i^g/y, is insignificant (with negative point estimates) when the total investment ratio, i/y, is included as a regressor. This result suggests a close linkage between growth and investment, but not a special role for the public component of investment. In any event, it would be inappropriate to argue that regressions 9 and 10 isolate a positive effect from an exogenous increase in the investment rate (or a negative effect from an exogenous increase in population growth) on per capita growth. At this point, one can just as well tell stories about causation in opposing directions—for example, Franco Modigliani has sometimes argued that the positive relation between per capita growth and the saving rate reflects the effect of growth on an economy's aggregate propensity to save.

Regressions 11 and 12 of table 9.2 use population growth as the dependent variable. The coefficients on per capita growth are significantly negative, but the most striking results are the significantly negative coefficients on the schooling variable. The scatter plot in figure 9.11 shows the striking negative correlation between population growth and the school enrollment variable.

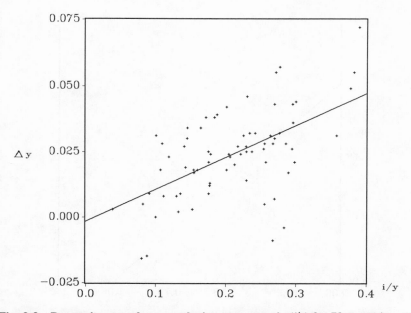

Fig. 9.9   Per capita growth versus the investment ratio (*i/y*) for 72 countries

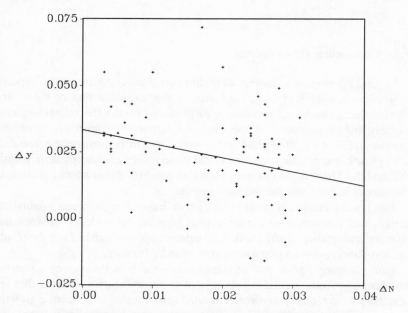

Fig. 9.10   Per capita growth versus population growth for 72 countries

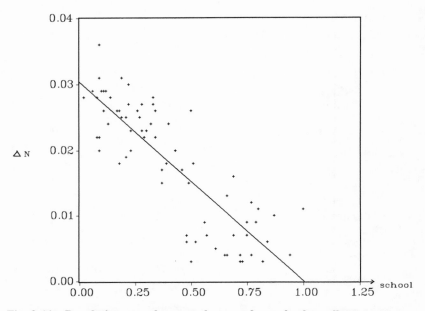

Fig. 9.11   Population growth versus the secondary school enrollment rate (school) for 72 countries.

9.5   Concluding Observations

I regard the empirical findings as preliminary, but suggestive. Some aspects of government services (and, implicitly, of the taxes that finance these services) affect growth and investment as predicted by the theoretical models. Notably, public consumption spending is systematically inversely related to growth and investment. Public investment tends to be positively correlated with growth and private investment, and these results are interpretable within the models. There is also an indication that property rights affect growth and investment in ways that the theories predict.

The results bring out a strong negative interaction between population growth and investment in human capital (that is, the trade-off between the quantity and quality of children). This relation appears partly from the residual correlation between population growth and schooling.

I am planning a good deal of additional research on theories of economic growth and of empirical analysis related to these theories. Many other researchers have recently become interested (once again) in economic growth, and much interesting work is presently under way. I am optimistic that this research will result in greater understanding about the factors that influence long-term economic growth and, especially, about the role of government in this process.

Data Appendix

Seventy-two Countries Included in Main Sample (listed alphabetically by geographical regions)

Botswana	Philippines	Barbados
Cameroon	Singapore	Canada
Egypt	Sri Lanka	Costa Rica
Ghana	Thailand	Dominican Republic
Kenya	Austria	El Salvador
Liberia	Belgium	Guatemala
Malawi	Cyprus	Mexico
Mauritius	Denmark	Nicaragua
Morocco	Finland	Panama
Senegal	France	United States
Sierra Leone	Germany (West)	Argentina
Swaziland	Greece	Bolivia
Tunisia	Iceland	Brazil
Uganda (X)	Ireland	Chile
Zaire	Italy	Colombia (X)
Zambia	Luxembourg	Ecuador (X)
Burma	Malta	Guyana
India	Netherlands	Paraguay (X)
Israel	Norway	Peru
Japan (X)	Spain	Uruguay
Jordan	Sweden	Australia
Korea (South)	Switzerland	Fiji
Malaysia	Turkey (X)	New Zealand
Pakistan	United Kingdom	Papua New Guinea

(X) indicates missing data on transfers for social insurance and welfare.

Aside from Summers and Heston (1988), the sources for data on government expenditures were International Monetary Fund, *Government Finance Statistics Yearbook,* 1987, 1983, 1978, and *International Financial Statistics; Supplement on Government Finance,* 1986; OECD, *National Accounts* (various years); United Nations, *Yearbook of National Accounts Statistics* (various years); World Bank, *World Tables,* first and second editions; and UNESCO, *Yearbook,* 1987. The series on secondary school enrollment rates was from World Bank, *World Tables.* The data on war and revolution were from R. E. Dupuy and T. N. Dupuy, *Encyclopedia of Military History* (New York: Harper and Row, 1986); G. D. Kaye, D. A. Grant, and E. J. Emond, *Major Armed Conflict: A Compendium of Interstate and Intrastate Conflict, 1720 to 1985* (Ottawa: Orbita Consultants, Ltd., 1985); and M. Small and J. D. Singer, *Resort to Arms: International and Civil Wars, 1816–1980* (Beverly Hills, Calif.: Sage, 1982).

Note

1. Landau (1983) reports analogous results using the Summers-Heston measure of government consumption. Landau's results hold constant a measure of investment in human capital (school enrollment) but not investment in physical capital. Kormendi and Meguire (1985) report no correlation between per capita growth and the average growth of a measure of g^c/y. However, the type of growth model developed in section 9.1 above (based on constant returns to a broad concept of capital) suggests that per capita growth would depend on the average level of g^c/y, rather than on the growth of g^c/y.

References

Aschauer, D. A. 1989. Is Public Expenditure Productive? *Journal of Monetary Economics* 23 (March): 177–200.

Barro, R. J. 1990. Government Spending in a Simple Model of Endogenous Growth. *Journal of Political Economy* 98 (October): S103–S125.

Barro, R. J., and G. S. Becker. 1989. Fertility Choice in a Model of Economic Growth. *Econometrica* 57 (March): 481–501.

Becker, G. S., and R. J. Barro. 1988. A Reformulation of the Economic Theory of Fertility. *Quarterly Journal of Economics* 103 (February): 1–25.

Becker, G. S., K. M. Murphy, and R. Tamura. 1990. Human Capital, Fertility, and Economic Growth. *Journal of Political Economy* 98 (October): S12–S37.

Cass, D. 1965. Optimum Growth in an Aggregative Model of Capital Accumulation. *Review of Economic Studies* 32 (July): 233–40.

Gastil, R. D. 1987. *Freedom in the World*. Westport, Conn.: Greenwood Press.

Koopmans, T. C. 1965. On the Concept of Optimal Economic Growth. In *The Econometric Approach to Development Planning*. Amsterdam: North-Holland.

Kormendi, R. C., and P. G. Meguire. 1985. Macroeconomic Determinants of Growth: Cross-Country Evidence. *Journal of Monetary Economics* 16 (September): 141–64.

Landau, D. 1983. Government Expenditure and Economic Growth: a Cross-Country Study. *Southern Economic Journal* 49 (January): 783–92.

Lucas, R. E. 1988. On the Mechanics of Development Planning. *Journal of Monetary Economics* 22 (July): 3–42.

Rebelo, S. 1990. Long Run Policy Analysis and Long Run Growth. NBER Working Paper no. 3325. Cambridge, Mass., April.

Romer, P. M. 1986. Increasing Returns and Long-Run Growth. *Journal of Political Economy* 94 (October): 1002–37.

———. 1989. Capital Accumulation in the Theory of Long-Run Growth. In *Modern Business Cycle Theory*, ed. R. J. Barro. Cambridge, Mass.: Harvard University Press.

Scully, G. W. 1988. The Institutional Framework and Economic Development. *Journal of Political Economy* 96 (June): 652–62.

Solow, R. M. 1956. A Contribution to the Theory of Economic Growth. *Quarterly Journal of Economics* 70 (February): 65–94.

Summers, R., and A. Heston. 1988. A New Set of International Comparisons of Real Product and Price Levels: Estimates for 130 Countries, 1950–1985. *Review of Income and Wealth* 34 (March): 1–25.

Tamura, R. 1988. Fertility, Human Capital and the "Wealth of Nations." Ph.D. diss., University of Chicago, June.

Comment   James Tobin

Long-term growth, the subject of Barro's paper, is a much less divisive subject for macroeconomists than business cycles and unemployment. Almost all of us recognize that, whatever may be the role of the monetary events and policies in short-run fluctuations of real output and employment, real phenomena are paramount in longer-run growth trends. The growth of productive capacity, as determined by inputs and their productivity, is generally more important in comparisons over decades and across economies than differences in utilization of capacity. To put the point another way, full employment equilibrium tends to be established and reestablished eventually, by market adjustments or macro policies or both. Although the famous (or notorious) neo-Keynesian neoclassical synthesis emphasized the demand side of short-run fluctuations, it stressed the supply side for growth and development.

Of course, some disagreements over short-run macro theories carry over to growth theory. One concerns superneutrality, how the path of real output at full employment is related to inflation. Another concerns the impact of fiscal policy, in conjunction with monetary policy, on the aggregate rate of saving and investment and thus on the growth and eventual levels of productivity. These are subjects on which Bob Barro and I have disagreed in the past, but you will be relieved to know that they are not on the table today.

As a sometime growth theorist myself, I feel some satisfaction in observing its renascence. But I think the rediscoveries go too far in dubbing it *the* paradigm of macroeconomics, and in heralding it, as Prescott is quoted as doing, as delivering the profession from IS-LM and other demand-side models. I am sure Bob Solow did not see it that way 30 years ago, and does not now. Growth theory is *not* real business-cycle theory. The issue is whether business fluctuations are to be regarded as modeled as a continuous sequence of market-clearing equilibria or as departures from an equilibrium path that growth theory describes. The latter view does not require that the equilibrium be independent of cyclical events and policies. Perhaps the biggest challenge to contemporary macroeconomics is to provide a credible integration of demand-side short-run fluctuations and long-run growth.

Barro's paper is a progress report of his research on the determinants of growth, which he hopes to detect by comparing different economies. Research of this kind has been greatly facilitated by the Penn World Model, especially

James Tobin is the Sterling Professor Emeritus of Economics at Yale University and an affiliate of the Cowles Foundation for Research in Economics.

its most recent version due to Robert Summers and Alan Heston. This enables Barro to look at 72 countries, many more than the nine industrialized economies of Europe and North America that were the data base for Ed Denison's 1967 study *Why Growth Rates Differ.* However, Summers and Heston do not provide in standardized form many of the candidate variables in which Barro is interested. He does his best to fill in the gaps.

At the beginning of the paper is a theoretical model, of which the central feature is a production function relating real GDP per worker to two factors, capital stock K and the share τ of government expenditure G in Gross Domestic Product GDP. This model has some bizarre implications: (1) the marginal productivity of capital is constant and equal to its average productivity. (2) the marginal productivity of τ is nonnegative and declining. (3) The value of τ that maximizes the quantity GDP minus government purchases, the output available for consumption and capital accumulation, is—as will be intuitively clear—equal to α, the elasticity of output with respect to τ. This is reminiscent of Phelps's Golden Rule in ancient growth theory, but it seems like a Laffer curve. (4) Labor (other than what human capital we are to understand to be included in K) makes no contribution whatever to output.

Agents considering investment calculate a private marginal productivity of capital conditional on the prevailing absolute volume of government expenditures. They do not take into account that government policy will adjust expenditures as GDP increases so as to maintain the ratio τ. The amount of investment, or, equivalently, saving, is determined by households' equating their private marginal productivity of capital to their intertemporal marginal rate of substitution in consumption. Neither of these magnitudes depends on the size of the capital stock. Thus the economy's growth rate—the saving rate times the social productivity of capital—is endogenous.

I am sympathetic to the quest for theory in which not only equilibrium capital stock but also equilibrium growth will be endogenous. But I think that assuming constant returns to capital is an exorbitant price to pay for that feature. Anyway, this model is the only theoretical structure introduced as rationalization for the cross-country calculations that follow.

In Barro's empirical calculations, four interdependent endogenous variables depend jointly on a set of "explanatory" variables. The endogenous variables are per capita GDP growth, physical investment in ratio to GDP, secondary school enrollment as a fraction of the relevant age cohorts, and population growth. The explanatory variables are of two kinds: first, the government-related variables in which Barro is particularly interested: five classes of government expenditures in ratio to GDP, for public consumption, public investment, national defense, education, social insurance and welfare; an index of political rights; dummies for socialist and mixed economies; and a dummy for violent war or revolution since 1960. Then there are sometimes two dummies, for Africa and Latin America, extraneous to the hypotheses under investigation. Finally, the regressors include the initial level of GDP.

The hypotheses are that productivity and growth are fostered by government expenditures for physical capital and for education, retarded by those for public consumption and transfers, and probably also by defense spending. Another hypothesis is that government support of property rights, contract enforcement, and free markets is good for economic performance. These are tested by the nongeographical dummies mentioned above.

Barro does not estimate or test a formal structural model, which would specify the interdependence of the endogenous variables. His equations are reduced forms of an unwritten structural model. However, his 4×4 correlation matrix of the residuals conform to his priors, and I suspect to all of ours. Population growth is negatively related to the other three variables, which are positively associated with each other.

The model is evidently a dynamic one. The Δy depend on $y(0)$, among other things, and thus a new y vector is generated. Barro does not pursue these dynamics.

I have two sets of misgivings about Barro's procedures. The first concerns the variables he does use, the second the variables he does not use.

As for the first, I am not sure that the shares of GDP of government expenditures of a given type describe the way in which government activities affect productivity and the other dependent variables. Moreover, I discern some ambiguity whether the specified variables affect the *levels* or *changes* of real GDP and of other endogenous variables. For example:

1. Services from stocks of different kinds of capital, not average flows, are inputs in production. *Changes* in the stocks are related to *changes* in real output.

2. The stock of human capital depends on the net cumulation of individual educations over long periods of time, of which the average fraction represented by "School" is a very imperfect approximation.

3. The relations of the explanatory variables to the demographics determining population growth rates are very loose and unclear. Moreover, population growth may be quite different from labor force growth.

4. Economies differ not only with respect to Barro's explanatory variable but also, and maybe more important, with respect to their relationships to the endogenous variables.

I come to my second consideration, the limited list of other explanatory variables. Note that saving and consumption choices, the topic of the conference, were important in Barro's theoretical model, but these behaviors are not involved in the empirical study.

Let us not forget that economies are not just entities with different sovereign governments. They are diverse geographic areas. They are not self-contained economically or even demographically. They are engaged in trade of commodities and assets with other areas, and in movements of labor among them.

In recent U.S. history, growth rates have differed widely across regions. Think of New England, hit by energy price shocks but then prosperous in the

1980s. Think of Texas and the Southwest, booming with high oil prices and depressed in this decade. Think of the Midwest, the Rust Belt, hit by changes in international and interregional comparative advantage, its farm sector also losing once-bountiful export markets. These changes of fortune, and of rates of economic and population growth, are not related to government policies and expenditures, although they may induce changes in these. They are related to changes in relative prices of commodities and resources, in technology and in terms of trade.

We know these same phenomena are very important throughout the world, perhaps especially the Third World, liberally represented in Barro's sample. Differential endowments of land, oil, and other natural resources are surely very important. If they are responsible for most of the observed differences, we cannot have much faith in Barro's results, even those few that appear significant, unless we have faith that his variables are orthogonal to the more important ones.

Denison had a similar objective to Barro's, namely to explain growth differences among nine industrial countries in Europe and North America, 1950–62. Denison's methodology could not be more different from Barro's. Denison does not employ reduced forms, or any regressions, or any statistical methods. He has a precise formal structure, "growth accounting," based on production functions. He accounts for output changes by changes in inputs, and changes in their productivity. He accounts for input changes by meticulously detailed studies, for example the changes in numbers, types, skills, educations, ages of workers, and in hours of work. He accounts for growth in factor productivities so far as he can by advances in knowledge, economies of scale, and reallocations of resources, (e.g., away from agriculture). Government activities and expenditures enter only indirectly, as they may affect these proximate determinants of output and its growth. I think Barro's research could benefit from a look back at Denison's.

10 Consumption Growth Parallels Income Growth: Some New Evidence

Christopher D. Carroll and Lawrence H. Summers

10.1 Introduction

The idea that consumers allocate their consumption over time so as to maximize a stable individualistic utility function provides the basis for almost all modern work on the determinants of consumption and saving decisions. The celebrated life-cycle and permanent income hypotheses represent not so much alternative theories of consumption as alternative empirical strategies for fleshing out the same basic idea. While tests of particular implementations of these theories sometimes lead to statistical rejections, life-cycle/permanent income theories succeed in unifying a wide range of diverse phenomena. It is probably fair to accept Franco Modigliani's (1980) characterization that "the Life Cycle Hypothesis has proved a very fruitful hypothesis, capable of integrating a large variety of facts concerning individual and aggregate saving behaviour."

This paper argues, however, that both permanent income and, to an only slightly lesser extent, life-cycle theories as they have come to be implemented in recent years are inconsistent with the grossest features of cross-country and cross-section data on consumption and income and income growth. There is clear evidence that consumption growth and income growth are much more closely linked than these theories predict. It appears that consumption smoothing takes place over periods of several years not several decades.

Christopher D. Carroll is an economist at the Federal Reserve Board in Washington, D.C. Lawrence H. Summers is professor of economics at Harvard University and a research associate of the National Bureau of Economic Research.

The authors gratefully acknowledge funding from the National Science Foundation. Also thanked are David Cutler, James Poterba, Greg Mankiw, Olivier Blanchard, Daniel Feenberg, and the members of the M.I.T. Public Finance Lunch, Money Lunch, and Money Workshop for constructive comments. Thanks especially to Knut Morck for generous help in obtaining data, and to Steve Zeldes for discussions on uncertainty. Remaining errors are of course the authors'. Views expressed here do not necessarily reflect those of the Federal Reserve Board or its staff.

These results confirm Milton Friedman's (1957) initial view that "the permanent income component is not to be regarded as expected lifetime earnings. . . . It is to be interpreted as the mean income at any age regarded as permanent by the consumer unit in question, which in turn depends on its horizon and foresightedness." They call into question the usefulness of standard representative consumer approaches to the analysis of saving behavior. And they call for increased emphasis on liquidity constraints and short-run precautionary saving as determinants of consumption behavior.

This paper is divided into five sections. Section 10.2 presents the rational expectations version of the permanent income hypothesis, which has been increasingly popular in empirical macroeconomics recently, and draws out the low frequency implications of this hypothesis. The principal implications on which we concentrate are, first, that (absent capital market imperfections) the anticipated rate of growth of income should be unrelated to the rate of growth of consumption and, second, that the rate of interest should be a powerful determinant of the rate of growth of consumption. We present evidence that challenges both of these propositions. We demonstrate that over periods of several years there is nearly perfect equality between rates of income growth and consumption growth. These facts hold both across countries and, within countries, across different eras when productivity increased at different rates. The prediction of the permanent income hypothesis that consumption growth and anticipated income growth are unrelated is clearly refuted. We next argue that these facts cannot be explained by imperfections in the international capital market, since there is no evidence that countries with more rapid consumption growth have higher rates of return on bonds or other assets.

Section 10.3 asks whether recognizing that consumers have finite lifetimes helps in understanding these stylized facts. This is plausible a priori. Because the gap in lifetime income between old and new generations ones is greater in rapidly growing than in slowly growing countries, the life-cycle hypothesis would predict that consumption growth should equal income growth looking across countries with permanently different productivity growth rates. We find, however, that the life-cycle story is not consistent with the data. Contrary to the predictions of the theory, individual consumers in rapidly growing countries like Japan have had more rapid consumption growth rates than consumers in the United States, where income growth is slower. Indeed, where life-cycle theory predicts that longitudinal age-consumption profiles should be similar in countries with different growth rates, the fact is much more nearly that point-in-time cross-sectional age consumption profiles are similar across countries.

The close international linkages between consumption growth and income growth could arise either because some common factor causes some countries both to defer consumption and to grow rapidly or because individual consumers display more sensitivity to current income than theory suggests they should. In Section 10.4 we seek to distinguish these alternative views by looking at the relationship between income growth and consumption growth for consumers in different occupations and educational categories. Using data from several American Consumer Expenditure Surveys, we discover that there is considerable variation in the lifetime profile of income across categories, and that the lifetime profiles of consumption track the profiles of income very closely.

Section 10.5 uses information on saving rates to confirm the inference drawn in the previous sections that consumers are not responsive to changes in their long-run future income. First, we show that there is no tendency for countries that experience reductions in their expected growth rate to experience short-run increases in saving as theory would predict. Second, we test the pure life-cycle theory's prediction, that when a country experiences a sharp productivity slowdown as the United States has in recent years, there should be a tendency for the relative saving rate of the young to increase greatly. This prediction is not borne out. Third, we document that, contrary to the theory's prediction, there is no tendency for young people in occupations where income rises rapidly to have lower saving rates than those in occupations where income rises slowly.

Section 10.6 discusses the implications of these results for consumption theory. We suggest that both our data and the available time-series evidence are consistent with Milton Friedman's view that people save to smooth consumption over several years in the face of uncertain income but, because of liquidity constraints, caution, or shortsightedness do not seek to smooth consumption over longer horizons. We follow the recent work of Deaton (1989) in arguing for a "buffer stock" view of saving as appropriate for most consumers. This view is supported by tabulations from a longitudinal data set on tax returns suggesting that about 40% of the population never earned more than $100 in dividend and interest income over a six-year period, 30% of the population earned more than $100 in every year, and 30% earned more than $100 in some but not all years. The buffer stock view of saving is attractive in another respect. If the size of the stock is proportional to income, then one would expect to observe the close relation that is actually observed between saving rates and income growth. We also present evidence, however, that suggests that even if the typical consumer may be accurately described by the buffer stock model, the typical saver may not be. This discrepancy is possible if the distribution of saving is more unequal than the distribution of consumption, so that the great majority of dollars saved are not saved by the typical consumer but rather by a small number of very wealthy consumers who have very high saving rates. We argue that the apparent importance of the distinction between the typical consumer and the typical saver is large enough to justify more attention and perhaps to justify different models for the two groups.

Section 10.7 concludes the paper. We begin by discussing the destructive implications of the results for representative consumer approaches to the study of asset pricing, economic growth, and economic fluctuations. We then suggest some constructive implications of the results for understanding international differences in saving rates, takeoffs of economic growth, and the effects of tax policies. Finally, we suggest some directions for future research.

10.2   International Evidence on Consumption and Growth

The representative agent infinite-horizon consumer model is the simplest and probably most commonly used model in studies of intertemporal issues. The Ramsey model (as we will refer to it throughout) provides the basis for the large body of work on consumption that has emanated from the seminal analysis of Hall (1978). The increasing popularity of this framework for analyzing intertemporal income and consumption behavior is suggested by the large literature surveyed in Campbell and Mankiw (1989). The focus of the research described there has been on the relationship between short-run fluctuations in consumption and income and on the nature of substitution between present and future income. Here we focus instead on long-term predictions of the theory.

In the commonly used constant relative risk-aversion formulation, solution of the model gives rise to the first-order condition for a consumer operating under certainty:

$$(1) \qquad\qquad \dot{c}/c = \sigma(r - \delta),$$

where σ is the elasticity of substitution of consumption, δ is the consumer's subjective discount rate, and r is the interest rate. Under uncertainty, it will continue to be the case that the interest rate is a sufficient statistic for predicting consumption growth. In a world with a well-functioning capital market that equates returns on the safe asset in different countries, the simple model of (1) predicts that consumption growth rates averaged over long time periods should be equalized around the world if tastes for present as opposed to future consumption do not vary across countries.[1] It certainly would not imply that consumption growth rates should bear any particular relation to income growth rates. We shall now argue that this prediction is obviously and dramatically falsified by the recent experience of industrialized economies.

We have gathered data on income and consumption for 15 OECD countries for the period 1960–85.[2] Our sample includes all the major Western European economies, Japan, the United States, and Canada as well as all of the smaller economies for which relatively complete data was available for the entire period. We study the effects of low-frequency variations by looking at differences both across countries and across different time periods in individual countries. For these comparisons, the issues of measurement and time aggregation that have been discussed in the literature on the time-series properties of consumption are not very important. In order to highlight the strength of the patterns in the data we present them graphically.

Figure 10.1, panels a–d, document a stylized fact that any theory of consumption should account for: *at low frequencies there is near perfect equality between consumption growth rates and income growth rates.* When consumption growth rates are plotted against income growth rates the result is almost precisely a 45° line. While figure 10.1a–c documents this fact looking across the entire 1960–85 period and two different subperiods, *d* compares the change in income growth with the change in consumption growth between the 1960–73 and 1980–85 periods. We choose these periods so as to avoid the difficulty of assessing when during the 1970s expectations became entrenched

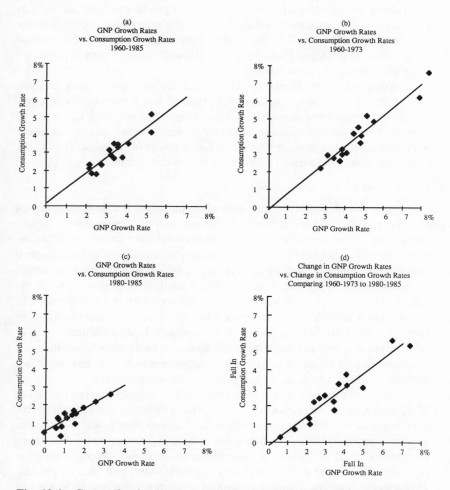

Fig. 10.1   Comparing income growth and consumption growth in the OECD countries, 1960–85
Source: OECD National Income Accounts data.

that the productivity slowdown would last. Again the result is close to a 45° line.

While we have used GDP growth in these comparisons rather than the disposable income measures that would be more appropriate on some views, this and other measurement issues cannot be important. It is easy to see that the consumption growth–income growth regularity has to hold up using almost any measure. Suppose that over a 25-year period a country's saving rate changed by 15 percentage points. This would only alter its consumption growth rate by .6 percentage points, a rather small difference compared to the spread of growth experiences illustrated in figure 10.1a–d. In fact, the striking thing about saving rates, whether measured on a private or a national basis, is their stability through time. Comparing the saving rates of the countries in our sample before and after 1973, no country experienced a change of more than 5% in either its private or its national saving rate.[3] This compares with a range of saving rates across countries of over 10%.

Returning now to the Ramsey model, figure 10.1a–d appears anomalous in light of the model's implication that the expected rate of growth of consumption should be the same across countries and should be unrelated to the rate of growth of income. We therefore consider in turn whether income surprises, imperfect capital markets, or international differences in tastes can explain the consumption/income parallel within roughly a Ramsey framework.

10.2.1 Income Growth Surprises

One possible objection to direct tests of the independence proposition arises from the possibility that differences in income growth over time were largely unexpected. If the consumer receives information about present or future income she will adjust her *level* of consumption discontinuously to be consistent with her new intertemporal budget constraint. From this new level the proposition will again apply, but if we calculate consumption growth between the period before the information arrived and the period after it arrived we will not observe a growth rate of $\sigma(r - \delta)$. Moving from the abstract to the concrete, this point would be important if, for instance, Japan's continued growth over the postwar period constituted a succession of pleasant surprises that successively caused Japanese consumers to adjust consumption upward in accordance with their new, surprisingly higher, lifetime income.

A first bit of evidence on the plausibility of this scenario is given by figure 10.2, which plots Data Resource, Inc.'s (DRI's) projected income growth for our sample of 15 countries from 1988 to 2000 against their actual growth rates over the period 1976–88. The figure illustrates that there are major differences in expected rates of growth of income across countries. Furthermore, expected future income growth is clearly correlated with past income growth. This suggests that the simplest version of a "surprise" theory, in which any deviation from the average growth rate is unanticipated, is very hard to sustain.

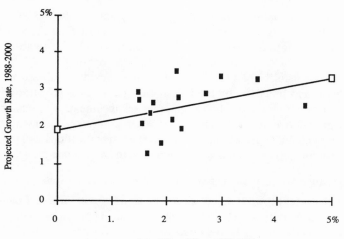

Fig. 10.2   Projected per capita income growth, 1988–2000, versus actual income growth, 1976–88
Source: DRI International Economic Model Database (workspace @INTL/MODELBANK).

Table 10.1   Regressions of Consumption Growth on Income Growth (standard errors in parentheses)

Income Growth Measure	Coefficient on Income Growth[a]	Coefficient on Lagged Income Growth[b]
Current income (OLS)	.601	.253
	(.037)	(.048)
Past 3 years	.725	1.101
	(.220)	(.388)
Past 5 years	.964	.97
	(.194)	(.237)
Past 10 years	1.000	1.14
	(.524)	(.595)

Note: These equations were run using the 15 countries described in the text. Data for 1960–85 were used, and dummies for each year (not reported) were included in all regressions. Eq. (1) runs current consumption growth on current income growth. Eq. (2) forms an expectation of current income growth using the average income growth over the past 3 years. Eq. (3) and (4) form expectations using previous 5-year and previous 10-year growth rate.
[a]This column gives the coefficient when the right-hand-side variable is as just described.
[b]This column gives the coefficient using a one-year lag of the variable just described.

Table 10.1 presents some more formal tests of the idea that the close international correlation between income growth and consumption growth reflects the effects of income surprises. We estimate an international cross section relating consumption growth to measures of expected income growth formed on the basis of past income growth. Each equation includes year dummies, so the identifying variation comes from variations across countries in consumption growth and lagged income growth. The results using measures of income growth over long past periods suggest a nearly one-to-one relationship between expected income growth and consumption growth.[4]

The results using only a single lag of income growth are less strong. However, this is accounted for by the fact that lagged income growth over a long period is a better predictor of contemporaneous income growth than is lagged income growth over a short time period. When past income growth is used as an instrument for expected income growth all specifications suggest a very strong relationship between consumption growth and income growth.

10.2.2   Imperfect Capital Markets and Different Interest Rates

Consider a set of independent closed economies with different rates of exogenous productivity growth. Then theory predicts that each would converge to a steady state with consumption growth equal to income growth. The first-order condition (1) would be satisfied in each country because of differences across countries in the steady-state real rate of interest. More rapidly growing countries would have higher real interest rates. It is possible therefore that the close correlation between consumption growth and income growth is a consequence of imperfections in the international capital market. In this case, one would expect to observe a close relationship between consumption growth rates and rates of return.

Figure 10.3a–d illustrates, however, that there is essentially no evidence, looking across countries, that differences in consumption growth rates across countries are explained by differences in real interest rates or other proxies for ex ante returns. This point may be seen most easily by comparing the United States and Japan. It is almost inconceivable that a plausible measure could be found on which ex ante returns were higher in Japan than in the United States in recent years. This evidence is reinforced by figure 10.3e which asks whether changes in consumption growth rates in different countries between the pre-1973 period and the post-1980 period are predicted by changes in real interest rates. Perhaps surprisingly, the countries with the greatest declines in consumption growth rates had the smallest increases in real interest rates.

The point that differences in average returns across countries cannot account for differences in consumption growth can be made another way. The range of consumption growth rates in our sample of countries is 3.4%. Most estimates of the intertemporal elasticity of substitution put it at below .25. Even taking the high rate of .25, and assuming that differences in consumption growth rates were perfectly explained by differences in rates of return, the range of rates of return would have to be 13.6%. Persistent differences in safe rates of return of this magnitude over a 25-year period are implausible on even strong views about world capital immobility.

In an influential paper, Mehra and Prescott (1985) have raised questions about the ability of the representative consumer model to account for the risk

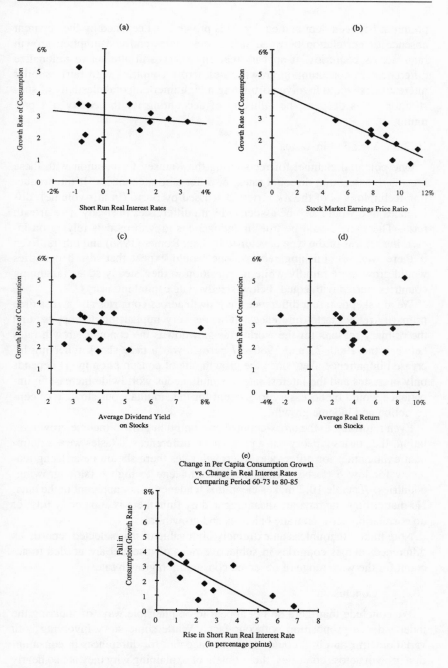

Fig. 10.3   Per capita consumption growth and real rates of return
Source: See data appendix.

premium between debt and equity. This problem is deepened by the apparent absence of correlation between safe interest rates and consumption growth rates across countries. It appears that any successful attempt to rationalize differences in consumption growth rates across countries with fairly similar interest rates would involve postulating a high intertemporal elasticity of substitution. This deepens the difficulty of accounting for the equity risk premium.

10.2.3 Variation in Tastes

One potential channel for reconciling the Ramsey formulation with these facts is to assert that discount rates, δ, differ across countries. If the production technology is of the Ak variety discussed by Barro (in this volume), differences in δ would also be associated with differences in steady state growth rates. The same would be true in endogenous growth models relying on increasing returns of the type developed by Paul Romer (1986) and others. Even if there were diminishing returns, one would expect that low δ countries would grow more rapidly while in transition to their steady states (assuming countries started with equal, below-steady-state capital intensity).

We are skeptical that differences in growth across countries and across time primarily reflect taste differences. It seems very implausible to suppose that the primary reasons for the worldwide slowdowns in economic growth rates between the 1960–73 and 1980–87 periods was a taste shock reflecting increased impatience. Yet, since the growth rate of consumption in (1) depends only on tastes and the interest rate, a simultaneous worldwide increase in impatience would be necessary to account for the simultaneous slowing of consumption and income growth.

Even returning to the cross-country consumption growth/income growth relation, the "tastes" theory has a problem. If differences in tastes were a dominant explanation for differences in growth rates there should be a strong tendency for low δ (fast-growing) countries to lend to high δ (slow-growing) countries. As table 10.2 makes clear, this tendency is not apparent in the data. No matter how the data are disaggregated by time there is apparently little or no correlation between trade balances and growth rates.

Note finally that unless an extremely high value of σ is selected, enormous differences across countries in subjective rates of discount are needed to account for the wide range of observed consumption growth rates.

10.2.4 Conclusion

We conclude that there do not appear to be plausible ways of squaring the independence proposition with our facts. While some story involving both variations in r and in δ could be used to account for differences in consumption growth across countries, the problem of explaining why they are so nearly equal to differences in income growth would remain.

Table 10.2   The Relationship between Trade Balances and Growth Rates

Sample Period	Cross-Country Correlation between Average Trade Balance and Average Growth over Sample Period
1961–85	.051
1961–73	.213
1974–85	.045
1961–65	.113
1966–70	.265
1971–75	−.116
1976–80	−.327
1981–85	.222

Sources: DRI @IMF database for trade balance; DRI @OECDNIA database for real GDP Growth. Country sample same as for table 10.1. See appendix for details.

10.3   The Life Cycle and the Consumption/Income Parallel

As a matter of logic, the life-cycle hypothesis is consistent with both the stylized fact that consumption and income growth rates are equated across a sample of countries and the fact that saving and growth rates are positively correlated. To see this, think of a very simple life-cycle model where individuals seek level consumption over their lifetimes. Even though individuals would have level consumption over their lifetimes regardless of their income growth rates, it will nonetheless be true that in steady state, total consumption will grow at the same rate as total income. This is because the gap in lifetime income between old and young generations is greater in rapidly than in slowly growing countries.

Consider the modern life-cycle hypothesis's explanation of the equality between consumption and income growth rates across countries with different growth rates. The essence of the theory (assuming common tastes worldwide and the irrelevance of rate of return differences) is that the rate of growth of consumption for all individuals is the same in all countries. (Implicitly we are assuming rational expectations rather than the myopic expectations assumed by Modigliani in some early statements of the life-cycle hypothesis.) Countries differ in their consumption growth rates only because of the differential effect of the continuous replacement of old, lifetime poor individuals by young, lifetime rich ones.

This argument has two essentially equivalent testable implications. First, tracking the consumption of a given cohort, say those who were 25 in 1950, one should find no difference across countries in the rate of growth of consumption. Second, at a point in time the age-consumption cross-section profile should be less positively sloped in a rapidly growing country than in a slowly growing country. This is because in more rapidly growing countries the old are much lifetime poorer than the young; thus consumption of the old will be much lower relative to consumption of the young. This point is illustrated graphically in figure 10.4a. This figure supposes that each individual desires a rate of growth of consumption over his lifetime of 2% annually and demonstrates what the age/consumption cross-section profile should look like in steady state across countries with different growth rates, normalizing the consumption of all individuals by the consumption of individuals at age 20.

Compound interest produces dramatic results here. The ratio of the consumption of the 65-year-olds to the consumption of 25-year-olds should be more than twice as great in countries growing at a 4% rate as in countries growing at a 2% rate. Given the large differences in growth rates illustrated in section 10.2 above, if the life-cycle hypothesis is even approximately accurate, some tendency for consumption of the elderly to be relatively low in rapidly growing countries ought to show up in the international comparisons.

In order to test this proposition, we have obtained cross-sectional point-in-time consumer expenditure profiles by age for Canada, Denmark, Japan, Norway, the United Kingdom, and the United States.[5] Our estimates of the age-consumption profiles are provided in figure 10.4b. We have carried the profiles only up to age 65 because of concern that measures of the consumption of the aged are distorted in some countries by the tendency of the poorer elderly to move in with their children.

The results are at odds with the life-cycle hypothesis, since the profiles look quite similar across countries. The similarity of these profiles means that there is no evidence that old people in the slow-growing countries have relatively higher consumption than those in the fast-growing countries. To take a specific example, the profile is more positively sloped in Japan than in the United States, exactly the opposite of what the theory would predict given Japan's much more rapid growth rate. Norway, which has also grown relatively rapidly, also has relatively higher consumption among the aged than the United States. Deaton (1989), using a sample of LDC age-consumption profiles, reaches conclusions similar to those reached here.

This comparison is very crude. But it is instructive to observe how large the differences in age-consumption profiles predicted by the theory would be. Over the 25-year period 1960–85, per capita GNP in Japan grew at 5.2% as compared with 2.1% in the United States. Suppose that we take the Japanese steady-state growth rate to be 4.0% and the U.S. steady-state growth rate to be 2.5%. Then the lifetime income of 30-year-olds in Japan should be 3.94 times the lifetime income of 65-year-olds, compared with a ratio of 2.37 in the United States. This is a difference equal to more than 150% of the income of the average 65-year-old. It is large enough that one would expect it to show up even in our crude measures of age-consumption profiles.[6]

What about the experience of individual cohorts? The longitudinal evidence that we would like to have to answer this question is not available. However,

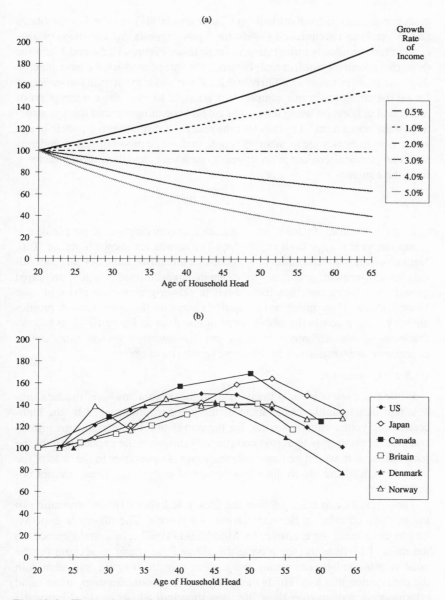

Fig. 10.4   Theoretical and empirical age-consumption cross-section profiles in countries with differing rates of income growth

Source: (*a*) Theoretical calculations described in the text, (*b*) empirical calculations described in the data appendix.

evidence discussed by Kotlikoff and Summers (1981) for the United States and by Ando and Kennickell (1986) for Japan suggests that the shape of age-expenditure profiles is quite stable through time. Figures 10.5a and 10.5b for these two countries confirm that, between the dates for which we have specific data, the profiles have been fairly stable. If we make the stability assumption for all the countries in our sample, it is possible to trace the consumption of individual cohorts by using data on aggregate consumption and the age structure of the population. If c_i indicates the relative consumption of people in age group i, p_{it} indicates the number of people in this age group in year t, and y_t is total real personal consumption in year t, then we calculate a scaling factor s_t from the equation:

$$(2) \qquad y_t = s_t \sum_i c_i p_{it}.$$

Using the scaling factor s_t we calculate real consumption of people of age group i in year t, cr_{it}, from $cr_{it} = c_i s_t$. The results are shown in figure 10.6. Not surprisingly given our results so far, this technique indicates that individuals in fast-growing countries like Japan have enjoyed much more rapid growth in consumption than individuals in slower-growing countries like the United States. How much more rapid? Given that the cross-section profiles are very similar across the whole range of countries in figure 10.4b, it follows that *none of the difference in aggregate consumption growth rates across countries can be explained by life-cycle replacement effects.*

10.3.1 Conclusion

While there are obviously many measurement problems here, the data suggest that demographic replacement of the low-consuming aged by the high-consuming young cannot account for the correlation between income growth and consumption growth across countries. If this were the explanation for the correlation there would be large differences across countries in the ratio of the consumption of the old to the consumption of the young. These are not observed.

These results call into question the life-cycle hypothesis' interpretation of the positive correlation between saving and growth. The life-cycle explanation as described, for example, by Modigliani (1967) relies on differences in the ratio of lifetime income among the old and the young to account for the positive relation between saving and income growth. It is not consistent with the observation that individuals in rapidly growing countries enjoy more rapid consumption growth over their lifetimes than individuals in slowly growing countries.

10.4   Tests Using Individual Data

Section 10.2 demonstrated that consumption growth has been very closely related to income growth across both countries and time and argued that this

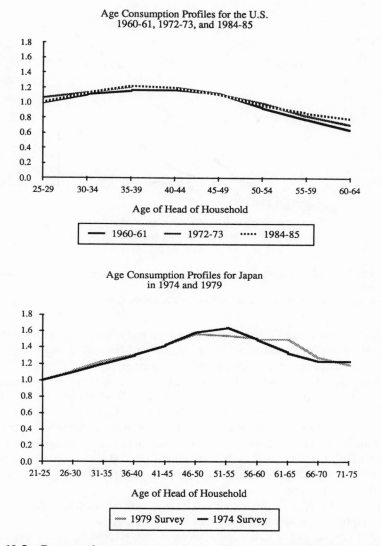

Fig. 10.5   Cross-section age-consumption profiles for the United States and Japan over time
Source: For the United States, direct calculations with the 1960–61, 1972–73, and 1985–86 CES tapes; for Japan, Ando and Kennickell (1986).

was not consistent with the standard Ramsey model. Section 10.3 argued that the consumption/income parallel could not be explained by life-cycle considerations. This leaves two classes of explanations for the apparent international association of consumption growth and income growth. A first possibility is that because consumers are myopic or liquidity constrained or operate on the

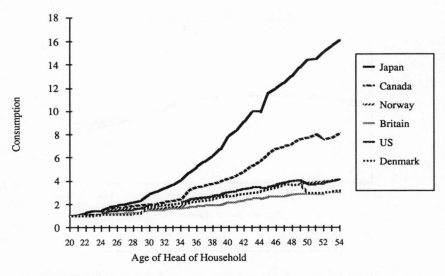

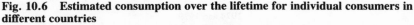

Fig. 10.6   Estimated consumption over the lifetime for individual consumers in different countries
Source: Calculations by the authors using data described in the data appendix.

basis of rules of thumb, consumption and income are strongly associated. A second possibility is that some common cause of both rapid income growth and rapid consumption growth operates across countries.

In an effort to distinguish these possibilities, this section uses information on income growth and consumption growth for individuals in different occupations and with different educational backgrounds. Liquidity constraints, myopia, or the like would be expected to create an association between age-consumption and age-income profiles across different occupations. On the other hand, theories of growth that might apply at the international level would not imply that individual age-income and age-consumption profiles should move together.

Anecdotal evidence about sports stars and medical students suggests that consumption is closely tied to current income, but for a more formal test we turned to the Bureau of Labor Statistics Consumer Expenditure Surveys (CES) of 1960–61 and 1972–73. These studies, originally done for the purpose of calculating consumer price indices, contain detailed expenditure and income accounts for a large representative sample of households (13,000 in 1960–61, 20,000 in 1972–73) and so are an ideal source for comparing income and consumption of households at different ages. For our income measure we took the total after-tax income of the household. Results were similar using several definitions of consumption and expenditure, ranging from total expenditures of the household (including payments for social security and prearranged pension plans) to just consumption of nondurable goods. The consumption measure chosen does not include payments for social security, private pensions, or home mortgages, but does include gifts and contributions to private charities and to other households, as well as insurance premia.

Figures 10.7a,b and 10.8a,b present mean income and consumption profiles for the nine occupational groups and the five educational levels that could usefully be distinguished with the CES.[7] The data's suggestion that saving for almost all groups increased between the first and second survey is almost certainly a consequence of changes in measurement procedure. What is more interesting is the figures' apparent refutation of the simple life-cycle/permanent income view that the shape of the path of income should not have an effect on the shape of the consumption path. In life-cycle terms, these graphs indicate that people in occupational or educational groups with income peaks late in life do not borrow significantly against those future earnings in order to finance higher consumption when they are young. Conversely, people with income peaks relatively early in life do not appear to save much in anticipation of lower future income. These observations appear inconsistent with life-cycle theory.

It is possible to imagine some combinations of circumstances that can explain some of the apparent correlation above while remaining roughly within a life-cycle framework. For instance, suppose that each cohort in a category consumes its permanent income and that the differences in income across categories and age groups are the result of idiosyncratic shocks to cohorts. Then we would observe the pattern that the income and consumption of households of any given age within a category would be closely related, as we see in the figures. This explanation works, however, essentially by denying any element of predictability in income profiles. But at least across educational categories there is a very strong resemblance of the age-income profiles in the 1972–73 CES to those in the 1960–61 CES—surely a strong refutation of the "no predictability" hypothesis. And, informally, we surely believe that people with college and postgraduate educations can expect higher wage growth over their lifetimes than those with only grade school educations, so that there is some degree of predictability. Although the degree of similarity of 1960–61 and 1972–73 income profiles is smaller across occupations than across educational categories, it is still the case that several occupations, particularly professionals, managers, operatives, and unskilled workers, have quite similar, and thus presumably predictable, profiles in the different years.

The calculations here do not take account of changes in family composition. By calculating consumption on an equivalence scale basis it is possible to create consumption profiles that do not follow estimated income profiles. But it is not clear what this proves, since total consumption spending does follow income. More relevant is the observation that there do not appear to be large differences in average family sizes at different ages among different edu-

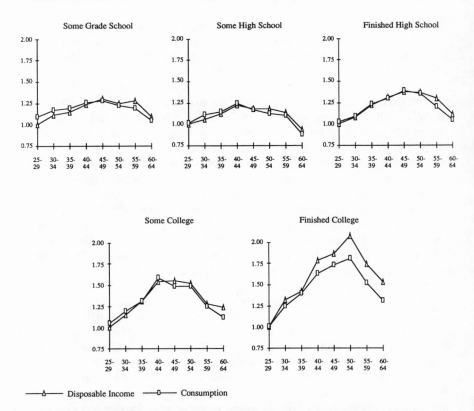

——△—— Disposable Income   ——□—— Consumption

Fig. 10.7a   Income and consumption profiles by educational group, 1960–61 CES

Source: Calculations by authors using CES tapes.

cational and occupational groups. While the issue deserves further research, our tentative conclusion is that parallel movements in income and consumption cannot be explained by family size considerations.

Another explanation of the consumption/income parallel was provided by Ghez (1975). Using the 1960 CES, Ghez prepared a figure for all consumers similar to our figures 10.7 and 10.8 for subcategories of consumers and sought to explain the observed close correlation between income and consumption using a "family production function" model of the type advocated by Becker (1965). Suppose, for example, that utility is a function both of consumption c and hours of leisure h. Suppose further that, because of the accumulation of experience or other human capital, hourly wages grow over the life cycle. Then individuals will have an incentive to work the longest hours when they are most productive, late in life. But this extra work takes away leisure time, giving the consumer an incentive to consume more time-substituting goods.

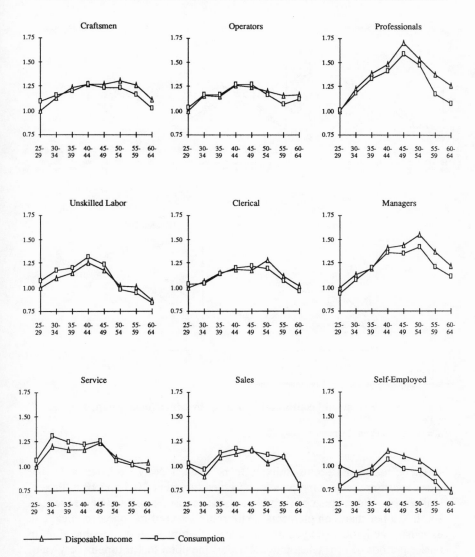

Fig. 10.7*b*   **Income and consumption profiles by occupational group, 1960–61 CES**
Source: Calculations by authors using CES tapes.

The consumer will therefore be observed consuming more during those periods of life when he works most and earns the most income. To be more specific, this model would suggest that busy executives late in life would be more likely to have a maid to do housekeeping chores and more likely to send out their laundry than young people with (presumably) more time on their hands.

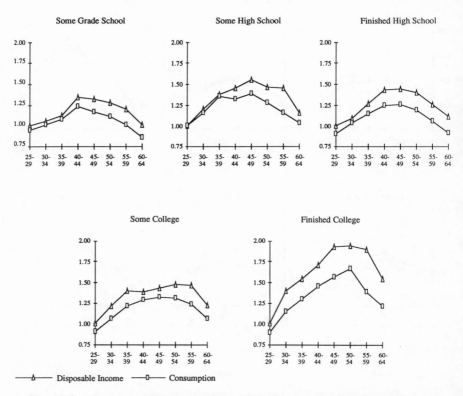

Fig. 10.8a   Income and consumption profiles by educational group, 1972–73 CES
Source: Calculations by authors using CES tapes.

The Ghez model seems unlikely to be a satisfactory explanation for the close consumption/income parallel observed in figures 10.7 and 10.8 for several reasons. First, it is not even obvious that consumption and hours are substitutes rather than complements. With more leisure time one can engage in expensive activities, such as foreign travel, that may not be possible at all in busier periods of life. Ghez himself makes the point that if time is very valuable one may eat more fast food (presumably inexpensive) and fewer elaborate meals out (presumably expensive). Further, even if we accept that consumption and hours are substitutes, the Ghez model only makes predictions about the sign of the relationship between income and consumption, not about its size. There is no reason in his model to expect that the relationship between income and consumption will be one-for-one as we observe. Finally, the Ghez explanation relies heavily on the assumption that hours and income move exactly in parallel. Figure 10.9, which is reproduced from a book by Ghez and Becker (1975), plots hours worked and hourly earnings at each age across the

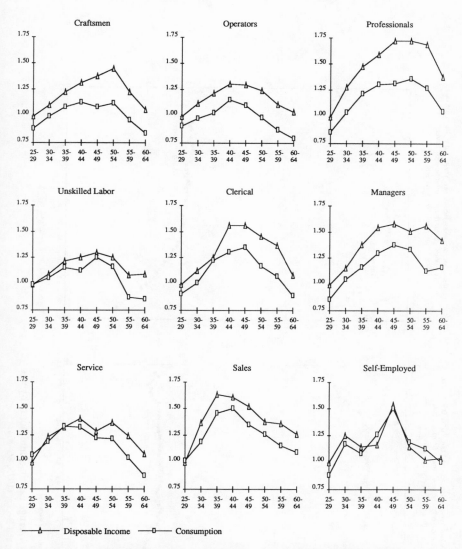

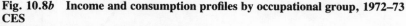
⸺△⸺ Disposable Income   ⸺▫⸺ Consumption

Fig. 10.8b Income and consumption profiles by occupational group, 1972–73 CES

Source: Calculations by authors using CES tapes.

life cycle for two educational groups using 1960 census data. It is apparent that there is very little variability in hours worked over the lifetime in either group. Furthermore, hours seem to decline after roughly age 35, while income and consumption both peak in the CES data roughly at age 50. Finally, there is no clear difference across the two educational groups in the age profile

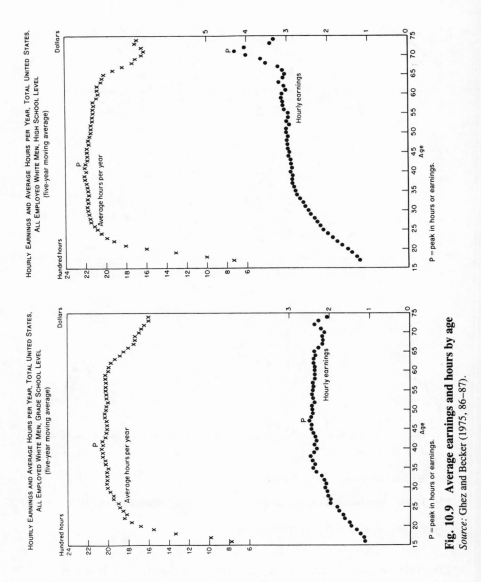

Fig. 10.9 Average earnings and hours by age
Source: Ghez and Becker (1975, 86–87).

of hours worked in spite of a noticeable difference in the profile of wages. We conclude that consumption/hours substitution is not a viable explanation for the consumption/income parallel.

10.4.1   Conclusion

This evidence on individuals suggests that explaining why consumers should allow their consumption to be heavily influenced by current income is a more plausible way to explain the international correlations with which we began the paper than is seeking an endogenous growth theory that could explain a high correlation between consumption growth and income growth. The behavior of these profiles suggests that the excess association of income and consumption is stronger at the low frequencies considered here than it is in the higher frequency contexts that have been more extensively studied.

10.5   Saving and Expected Income Growth

The analysis so far has suggested that both internationally and across individuals consumption and income growth are much more closely associated than standard theories would predict. A different way of stating the same point is to observe that saving decisions appear to be less responsive to expected long-term growth rates of income than simple theories would predict. In this section we examine the response of saving to differences in expected income growth using several different types of data.

The worldwide productivity slowdown after 1973 provides one natural test of the proposition that a decline in growth should lead to reduced human wealth and increased saving. As figure 10.10 demonstrates, the life-cycle hypothesis predicts that a two percentage point decline in expected income growth should have dramatic effects on saving, particularly for young consumers. Young consumers targeting even a 3% annual consumption growth rate are predicted to raise their saving ratio out of income by 20%. For the population as a whole the saving rate should increase by about 10% since the human wealth effect is less important for older consumers.

As figure 10.11a–d demonstrates, these predictions are not borne out. Saving rates around the world did not rise following the productivity slowdown. If anything they have fallen. Moreover, there is no tendency for the countries that have suffered the greatest declines in growth to have had greater increases in saving.

This failure of the theory might be due to other shocks that have changed saving behavior. A further test using information derived from the productivity slowdown focuses on its effects on consumers in different age groups. A decline in growth reduces expected future income by much more for young consumers than for older ones and not at all for those who have retired. Whatever happened to overall saving, one would expect to observe a tendency for the *relative* saving rate of the young to rise following the productivity slow-

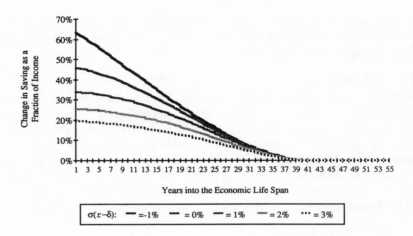

Fig. 10.10   Change in saving as a fraction of income if the expected growth rate of income changes from 3% to 1% per capita per year
Source: Calculations by the authors described in the text.
Note: The assumed growth rate of consumption $\sigma(r-\delta)$, ranges from -1% to 3% annually.
Consumers are assumed to retire 40 years into their 55-year economic life span.

down if consumers were farsighted. This tendency should have been reinforced by declining fertility. It is borne out only to a very slight extent in figure 10.12. (Again, because of changes in measurement procedures, nothing can be inferred from the position of these profiles, only their shape.) This finding is perhaps not so surprising given that the shape of the age-saving rate profiles in figure 10.12 is not really consistent with the predictions of the life-cycle theory in the first place.

Information on the shape of occupational income profiles can also be used to test the life-cycle theory. It predicts a tendency for those in occupations where income can be expected to rise rapidly to save less than those in occupations where income can be expected to rise slowly. The profiles from figures 10.7 and 10.8 can be used to calculate a ratio of future income to current income for young people in different occupational groups, and the results can then be compared with observed saving rates.

Figure 10.13 plots, for each occupation in 1960, the ratio (future income/current income) against the saving rate of young people in that occupation, where "future income" is defined as the sum of income for people age 30–65, "current income" is the sum of income for people age 25–29, and "young" refers to people in the age group 25–29. The slope of these lines should be strongly negative because high-future-income occupations should be low-saving occupations. Instead, the slope seems to be positive. This evidence is also consistent with the view that consumption is excessively sensitive to current income, though this cannot explain the positive association in the data.

Overall information on saving supports the conclusion reached in earlier

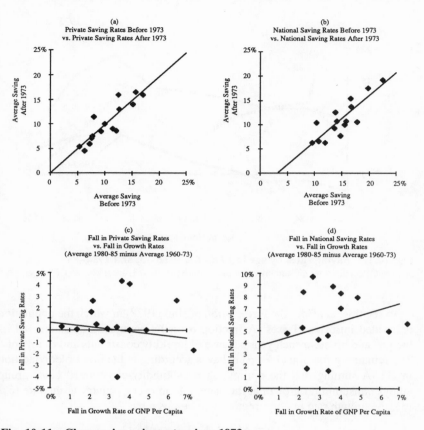

Fig. 10.11   Changes in saving rates since 1973
Source: OECD National Income Accounts.

sections that consumption is much more closely tied to current income than strong forms of the life-cycle or permanent income hypotheses would predict. While reassuring, this evidence is of course not independent of the earlier evidence on the behavior of measured consumption.

10.6   Liquidity Constraints, Myopia, and Uncertainty

One obvious interpretation of the close link between consumption growth and income growth is that consumers are liquidity constrained or myopic. This would "explain" why consumption and income growth are so closely associated. The principal difficulty with this line of thought is that in order to account for the observed equality of consumption and income growth rates one would have to assume that essentially all consumers were liquidity constrained or myopic.

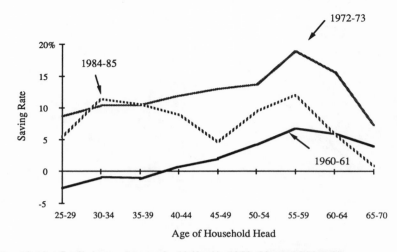

Fig. 10.12   Saving rates by age in 1960–61, 1972–73, and 1984–85
Source: Calculations by the authors using the 1960–61, 1972–73, and 1984–85 CES tapes.

To see this, consider the formulation of Hall (1978) in which the population is divided into two classes. A fraction α of the population consumes all its income and no more each year because of liquidity constraints and/or myopia. The remaining fraction $(1 - \alpha)$ behaves according to the first-order condition in (1). Assuming that the optimizing non-liquidity-constrained latter group enjoys consumption growth at the same rate in every country at the rate $(\dot{c}^*/c^*)$, the growth rate of consumption will be given by:

$$(3) \qquad \dot{c}/c = \alpha(\dot{y}/y) + (1-\alpha)(\dot{c}^*/c^*)$$

In order to account for the unit slope observed in figure 10.1, it is necessary to postulate that $\alpha = 1$ so that the entire population is liquidity constrained. This assumption robs the permanent income theory of any content. In addition, it leaves unanswered the unquestion of where savings come from. Of course it is also contradicted by all of the evidence supporting the permanent income hypothesis. The challenge is finding a theory that can account for the apparent absence of pervasive liquidity constraints or myopia in high frequency tests but can still account for our low frequency facts.

However, the possibility that most consumers act as if they were liquidity constrained or expected to be in the future should not be ruled out. Studies such as Campbell and Mankiw (1989), which seek to estimate the fraction of rule-of-thumb or liquidity-constrained consumers by applying time-series techniques, are likely to understate it for three reasons. First, the specification adopted assumes a restrictive form of liquidity-constrained behavior. It would be more difficult to demonstrate conclusively the existence of an economically significant population of myopic consumers if the myopes were assumed

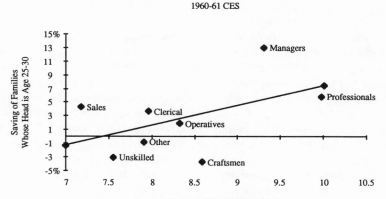

1960-61 CES

Incomes of Families Age 30-65
Divided by Current Income of Families Age 25-30

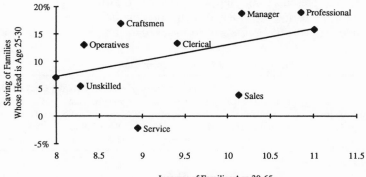

1972-73 CES

Incomes of Families Age 30-65
Divided by Current Income of Families Age 25-30

Fig. 10.13   Young families' saving as a fraction of income versus future income streams in their occupations
Source: Calculations described in the text using the income profiles of figures 10.7 and 10.8 calculated from the 1960–61 and 1972–73 CES.

to follow a rule in which consumption responded to income and its lags. Second, the assumption that liquidity constrained consumers spend a fixed fraction of their income on nondurable consumption rules out the possibility that these consumers cut durable spending disproportionately when income declines. If this is in fact the case, standard methods will understate the liquidity-constrained fraction of the population. Third, most recent research efforts have focused on the post-war period where income is close to a random walk. DeLong and Summers (1986) present evidence that in the prewar period, when income fluctuations were more transitory, the fraction of liquidity-constrained consumers was greater.

In spite of the considerable evidence that liquidity constraints are important, the assertion that people spend their incomes is not a rich enough theory of saving. We are attracted by Angus Deaton's (1989) view of savings as a "buffer stock" for contingencies. As he shows, if liquidity-constrained consumers facing risky income are both risk averse and impatient, they will maintain a small "buffer stock" of assets to insulate consumption against transitory income but will not engage in long-horizon borrowing or lending. The buffer stock view has the appeal of predicting (or at least labeling) the consumption smoothing that goes on at high frequency while not implying that consumption smoothing should go on over long horizons. It also has the potential to explain the observed correlation between saving and growth. If consumers desire (as financial planners recommend) a buffer stock equal to a certain number of months' income, saving will be greater for consumers with rapidly growing incomes than for those with slowly growing incomes. Essentially, the accelerator mechanism will create a positive growth-saving relationship.

Table 10.3 presents some empirical evidence, drawn from panel data on tax returns for the period 1979–84, that supports the buffer stock idea. For persons under and over 65, it presents estimates of the fraction of people, fraction

Table 10.3   **The Incidence of Liquidity Constraints**

Number of Years with < $100 in Interest and Dividend Income	Fraction of the Population Falling in This Category	Fraction of Total Labor Income That Goes to People in This Category	Fraction of Total Income That Goes to People Who Fall in This Category	Fraction of Total Capital Income That Goes to People in This Category
A. Total population:				
0	27.6	37.3	41.4	90.4
1	6.5	8.0	7.7	4.5
2	5.5	6.0	5.7	2.0
3	5.9	7.0	6.5	1.6
4	6.9	7.0	6.6	0.9
5	8.8	8.3	7.6	0.5
6	38.7	26.7	24.5	0.2
B. Population under age 65:				
0	35.2	39.7	47.4	92.8
1	6.2	7.8	7.1	2.8
2	5.2	6.0	5.3	1.7
3	5.3	6.3	5.8	1.0
4	6.1	6.7	5.9	.7
5	7.8	7.9	6.7	.4
6	34.2	25.6	21.8	.3

Source: Calculations by Daniel Feenberg of the National Bureau of Economic Research. See appendix for more detailed discussion of calculations.

of labor income, fraction of total income, and fraction of interest and dividend income going to persons with less than $100 in interest and dividend income in various numbers of years. The results suggest that liquidity constraints are potentially very important. More than half of total income went to persons who usually (three years or more out of six) had less than $100 of interest and dividend income. Furthermore, the fraction of total interest and dividend income received by those who do not always have such income is quite small. This suggests that even in years when such people have over $100 of interest and dividend income they do not have very large amounts of such income. Interestingly, whatever weights are used it appears that about a third of households have minimal interest and dividend income in some but not all years. This is what one expects on the buffer stock view. It suggests that "snapshot" evidence estimating the fraction of the population without assets is likely to underestimate the potential significance of borrowing constraints.

The view that borrowing constraints are important for a large fraction of consumers is also supported by the observation that a large majority of American households report that they have substantial amounts of consumer debt. The interest rate on this debt is typically considerably greater than the rate on safe assets like Treasury bills. Simultaneously borrowing at high rates and holding safe assets is difficult to square with the Ramsey model view of consumption decisions. As Julio Rotemberg and others have argued, it is rational for a consumer who believes he may be liquidity constrained in the future. Such a consumer would also tend to allow his consumption to closely follow his income.

It is also important to recall that typical consumers and typical savers may behave very differently. This point is illustrated by table 10.4. The conceptual unit in this table is the typical dollar of income rather than the typical taxpayer. If the distribution of property income is very unequal we should expect the median or mean dollar of property income to accrue to a person with a very large amount of such income. This is exactly what the table shows. Although the median dollar amount of interest and dividend income was $185, the median dollar of such income went to someone with property income of $16,100. Furthermore, although the mean amount of interest and dividend income was $2,755, the mean dollar went to a taxpayer earning $46,533 of property income. (See the appendix for details.)

The numbers become even more striking when we use assumed rates of return to convert statements about capital income into statements about liquid assets (see the appendix for details). When we do this we discover that the median dollar of (estimated) assets is held by a person holding $274,893 and that the mean dollar is held by a person with three quarters of a million dollars of assets. The general picture of extreme inequality in the distribution of wealth painted by these numbers is borne out by an analysis of some evidence from the Federal Reserve's Survey of Consumer Finances (SCF) in a recent paper by Avery and Kennickell (1988). The SCF allows a direct calculation

Table 10.4   **Sources of Dividend and Interest Income**

	Whole Population		Population Excluding Elderly	
	Mean	Median	Mean	Median
A. Interest and dividend income weighted by:				
Adjusted gross income	9,344	544	7,878	364
Taxpayers	2,755	185	1,600	113
Interest & dividend income	46,533	16,100	62,515	12,657
Estimated assets	43,840	14,930	58,401	11,457
B. Adjusted gross income weighted by:				
Adjusted gross income	62,910	38,537	63,279	38,773
Taxpayers	30,069	24,693	30,481	25,468
Interest & dividend income	101,983	45,728	150,050	56,695
Estimated assets	99,797	43,883	148,073	53,676
C. Wage income weighted by:				
Adjusted gross income	42,940	32,923	45,327	35,248
Taxpayers	25,212	20,995	27,616	23,439
Interest & dividend income	28,198	6,051	45,110	25,960
Estimated assets	27,701	6,361	44,750	26,920
D. Estimated assets weighted by:				
Adjusted gross income	162,342	9,966	137,393	6,735
Taxpayers	48,914	3,588	28,282	2,183
Interest & dividend income	778,317	287,375	1,032,177	224,299
Estimated assets	753,831	274,893	995,144	212,415

Source: Calculations by Daniel Feenberg of the NBER from IRS tax panel data.
Note: See appendix for detailed description of calculations. All figures are in 1988 dollars.

of net saving via a comparison of families' net worth in 1983 and 1986. In their table 12, the authors estimate the fraction of aggregate positive saving between 1983 and 1986 that was done by the members of each 1983 wealth decile. They estimate that nearly 70% of all the positive saving between 1983 and 1986 was done by families in the top 1983 wealth decile. Using crude smoothing techniques (see appendix), we calculated that the median dollar of saving was done by a family roughly at the 94th percentile in the wealth distribution. Smoothing again, we estimated that a person at the 94th percentile in the 1983 wealth distribution had $661,000 (1988 dollars) of net wealth. This compares with an estimated median 1983 net wealth of $46,800 (1988 dollars).[8] Again it would appear that wealth and saving are extremely unequally distributed.

Taken together, this evidence along with tables 10.3 and 10.4 suggest that there are two kinds of consumers. The great majority of consumers are liquidity constrained and have only small amounts of liquid assets, which they keep as a buffer against uncertainty. A small minority of consumers, however, have very substantial assets and are not liquidity constrained. These wealthy consumers are the source of most of the net dollars saved in the economy.

10.6.1   Conclusion

The broad picture painted above suggests that focusing separately on two different models, one for the liquidity-constrained majority of consumers who save little outside of housing equity and one for the small but wealthy minority who seem to do most of the saving, will yield more empirical success than continuing to work with a single model postulating identical unconstrained consumers. These are not new ideas: in arguing for a typically short horizon, Milton Friedman (1957) observed, "The appropriate definition of the permanent component [of income] is a period of three years or slightly longer. This is the same as the conclusion reached earlier from [different] data on urban families. It is also consistent with the time series data. It is encouraging to find such a close agreement in the precise definition of permanent components suggested by three independent bodies of data." And the idea that accumulation is chiefly an activity of the already wealthy goes back at least to Pareto.

10.7   Conclusions

Recent studies of consumption behavior have tested increasingly subtle implications of the life-cycle/permanent income hypothesis using increasingly sophisticated time-series techniques with increasingly ambiguous results. Many existing estimates suggest that at least a large fraction and possibly all of consumption is done by optimizing nonmyopic non-liquidity-constrained consumers maximizing individualistic utility functions with long or infinite horizons. We believe this conclusion is not correct. It seems to us that the wide variety of evidence presented here is much more robust to the possibility of measurement or specification error than the numerous complex econometric tests that have been performed. We regard our evidence as decisively refuting the low frequency predictions of standard intertemporal theories.

As we emphasized in the introduction, the evidence here is generally consistent with the life-cycle and permanent income hypotheses as they were originally advanced. Indeed, Milton Friedman explicitly rejected the idea that consumers had horizons as long as a lifetime in discussing the permanent income hypothesis. And Modigliani relied on myopic expectations in some early development of his theory. What is decisively rejected here is the modern representative consumer versions of these theories, not the core idea that people seek to smooth consumption.

While the evidence here does not undercut the usefulness of the life-cycle and permanent income theories in explaining some broad features of consumption behavior, it does cast serious doubt on modern uses of these theories, which take the idea of a representative forward-looking consumer very seriously. The absence of any relation between rates of return on a variety of assets and consumption growth rates across countries makes us skeptical of the use of consumption information in explaining risk premia on different capital assets. The absence of any clear tendency for consumption to respond to expectations of future income growth leads us to doubt that models that assume consumers optimize over long or infinite horizons will give very good predictions about the effects of various tax changes. And we suspect that those concerned with modeling the determinants of income growth should build in a different consumption function than the one suggested by the Ramsey model. Finally, we note that a major claim of real business-cycle theorists is that their models are calibrated on the basis of noncyclical phenomena. It does not appear that the representative consumer approach used in most real business-cycle models is consistent with low frequency evidence.

We argued in section 10.6 that Deaton's notion of the saving of the typical consumer as a buffer stock to smooth consumption over short horizons and to prepare for temporary sharp declines in income was consistent with both the evidence usually cited in favor of life-cycle permanent income theories and our low frequency evidence. We argued further, however, that although the buffer stock model may describe the typical consumer well, it may not accurately describe the typical saver because saving and wealth are extremely unequally distributed. Further research is needed to determine how the behavior of the typical consumer differs from the behavior of the typical saver.

Even though it may not apply to all consumers, we are attracted to the buffer stock model for several reasons. It provides a natural explanation for the correlation between saving and income growth both across countries and across occupational groups. If consumers desire to hold a cash reserve equal to a certain number of months of income, they will have higher saving rates the more rapid their income growth.

This notion raises a number of interesting possibilities for the growth process. If, as recent studies have argued, steady growth rates are increasing functions of saving rates, and if, as we have just suggested, saving rates are positive functions of growth rates, there is a clear possibility of multiple equilibria. This idea might be relevant to the experience of nations like Taiwan and Korea where actual and expected growth rates have increased sharply and at the same time that saving rates have soared.

The buffer stock model, if correct, also has implications for certain tax policy issues. In the United States there has been considerable controversy about the efficacy of IRAs and other saving vehicles. Critics allege that individuals transfer money from one account to another to realize tax benefits without doing any incremental saving. To the extent that, because of its illiquidity, IRA saving is not a substitute for buffer stock saving, it may be incremental even for households that have liquid assets.

Our future research in this area will proceed in two directions. First we need to refine our knowledge about the behavioral differences between the typical consumer and the typical saver. Second, we will try to develop models that can explain the differences between typical consumers and typical savers and models that are consistent both with the high frequency evidence that some consumption smoothing exists and the low frequency evidence that consumption growth tracks income growth. Although a single unified model may be desirable as an eventual goal, it may turn out to be more fruitful in the meantime to pursue separate models to explain the consumption/income parallel and the consumption/saving divergence. We hope that this multifaceted approach will eventually succeed both in explaining international differences in saving rates and in making predictions about the response of saving to policy changes.

Appendix
Data Sources and Methods

This appendix describes the sources and methods used to prepare the data charts and tables of the paper. We proceed roughly in the order in which the data appear.

OECD Data on Income, Consumption, and Interest Rates

OECD data come from the DRI @OECDNIA, @IMF, and @OECDMEI data bases. Data for most countries for most series begin in 1960. Gross Domestic Product (GDP) is given by the series VAGDPA, personal consumption is given by AGPC, real personal consumption by AGPCR. We derived the CPI deflator and hence inflation rates by dividing AGPC/AGPCR (for some reason the direct data on deflators is less complete than this indirect source). Population figures come from the @IMF database, series 199z. Trade balance data were taken from the @IMF database series 177 ac&d or the nearest existing equivalent. The 15 countries that appear in most of the figures are the United States, the United Kingdom, Austria, Belgium, France, West Germany, Italy, Norway, Switzerland, Canada, Japan, Finland, Greece, Australia, and Sweden.

For short-run interest rates we generally used the rate of return on three-month Treasury-bills, except in Italy where the only series was for six-month Treasury-bills (with a few missing observations that we filled from other interest rate series), and France and Germany where we used call money rates because there was no three-month Treasury-bill data before the early 1980s. The other rate of return data are courtesy David Cutler, who calculated them from the Morgan Stanley *Capital International Perspective*.

International Cross-Section Data on Income and Consumption

Gathering the data for figure 10.4*b* sent us far and wide. For Japan we used the profiles given in Ando and Kennickell, (1986, 194), specifically the data on mean CONSM in the working families. For Canada we used data taken from the Statistics Canada publication *Family Expenditure in Canada* (1989), kindly provided to us by Harry Champion of Statistics Canada prior to publication. For Norway we used unpublished data from government consumer surveys, graciously provided by Knut Morck. For Denmark we used data from the *Statistisk årbog* (Statistical yearbook) *1988* (Danmarks Statistik 1988, 171). Data for Great Britain were taken from Browning, Deaton, and Irish (1985, 503).

To generate figure 10.6 we used the above-described cross-section age-consumption data from all our countries, cohort population data from *Global Estimates and Projections of Population by Sex and Age* (United Nations 1987), and real personal consumption data from the DRI OECD databases mentioned above. We imputed family consumption by age of head of household by assuming that the relative magnitudes of consumption of typical families at different ages did not change over time (see eq. 2 and the description of the calculations in the text).

U.S. Cross-Section Data on Income and Consumption

All the microdata for the U.S. presented in figures 10.5*a*, 10.7, 10.8, and 10.12 were calculated from the Consumer Expenditure Survey (CES) Bureau of Labor Statistics (BLS) for the 1960–61, the 1972–73, and the 1985 and 1986 surveys. These surveys attempt to construct a complete balance sheet for the households surveyed over a one-year period, including information on changes in assets and liabilities that should balance the difference between income and consumption. Fortunately the definitions of variables have not changed much between the surveys so we are able to calculate income and consumption measures that should correspond over time. The 1960 survey, however, differed from the later surveys in at least two respects. First, each household was interviewed only once, at the end of the survey year, and asked to recall income and expenditures for the preceding year. In the later surveys each household was interviewed quarterly for five quarters in a row and asked about consumption over the preceding three months. Second, in the 1960 survey the interviewers made a greater effort to ensure that the family balance sheets actually balanced, so that if income exceeded consumption by $1,000 the interviewer tried to make sure that net assets rose by $1,000. There was less emphasis on such balance in the later surveys.

The figures result from straightforward calculations from the 1960–61, 1972–73, and 1985 CES tapes. In all years our income measure was disposable income after tax, calculated in the earlier surveys by subtracting all taxes from the total income variable; disposable income exists directly in the 1980s tapes so was not calculated. As our measure of consumption we took the variable called "current consumption expenditures" in the 1960 and 1972 surveys and added insurance premia and cash contributions and gifts. To construct the same variable from the 1980s surveys we took the "total expenditures" variable and subtracted contributions to pensions, retirement funds, and social security. The 1972–73 survey presented a particular problem because income numbers below $2,000 or above $35,000 were not reported. By comparing means of our tape sample with means in the BLS's printed summaries of the 1972–73 CES, however, we were able to calculate the average income of the bottom-coded individuals as $973.18 and the average income of the top-coded consumers as $54,942. The disposable income figures were $897.14 and $44,057, respectively. For consumers whose income was top- or bottom-coded, we assumed an income equal to the average income of their group. A final adjustment to the 1972 and 1985 samples was necessary because a small fraction of the people did not provide complete information about income; these were excluded from the sample altogether.

The basic patterns presented here were robust to the few reasonable variations in calculation technique we could think of, which consisted of excluding people from the sample for various plausible reasons and of considering different definitions of consumption and income (e.g., nondurables consumption, pretax income, wage income, etc). Detailed charts for 1985 analogous to those from 1960–61 and 1972–73 were not presented for two reasons. First, the 1985 data seemed to have much higher variability. This is partly due to a smaller sample size (about half as large) and partly (we think) due to a new processing methodology devised by the BLS. Second, CES occupational group classifications in the 1980s series are much less detailed, and occupations within each group seem less similar, than is the case with the 1960–61 and 1972–73 surveys.

Liquidity Constraints Tax Panel Data

The liquidity constraints tax panel is a random sample (based on primary taxpayer's Social Security number) of tax returns. It includes single and joint returns, but women drop from the sample when they marry and return when they divorce or widow. The sample was maintained for 1979 to 1984. Of the total set of tax returns in the data set, there were 5,997 taxpayers with positive adjusted gross income in all six years. This is the sample we used in preparing tables 10.3 and 10.4. The calculations for the tables were performed by Daniel Feenberg of the NBER.

The procedure for estimating liquid assets from capital income was simple. To estimate the market value of the stock portfolio we took dividend income and divided by the dividend/price ratio on the stock market as a whole for the appropriate year. To estimate the dollar value of interest-bearing assets we divided by the average interest rate on interest-bearing assets and cash. The latter was estimated by taking total personal interest earnings from the NIPA and dividing by the sum of cash and interest-bearing assets taken from the *Balance Sheets for the U.S. Economy* (Board of Governors of the Federal Reserve 1989). The latter figure yields interest rates in the 8%–10% range, probably much higher than the actual interest rate on the typical dollar of interest-bearing assets and cash. Overestimating the interest rate should cause us to underestimate associated wealth, however, so whatever error exists here biases our results against finding the extreme inequality in wealth that we do in fact find. A better interest rate measure should only intensify our findings about inequality.

The rates used in these calculations are given in table 10A.1. The dividend/price ratios were taken from *The Dow Jones-Irwin Business and Investment Almanac, 1986* Levine (1986).

A brief word about the interpretation of the numbers in table 10.4 is in order. Consider, for example, the part of the table concerning adjusted gross income (AGI) for everyone excluding the elderly. We claim that the median AGI weighted by AGI is $38,537. What this means is that if we were to sort all taxpayers by AGI and then to find the taxpayer such that the sum of the AGIs of the taxpayers with less AGI than his equals the sum of the AGIs of the taxpayers with more AGI than his, that taxpayer has an AGI of $38,537. This is what we mean when we say that the median dollar of AGI goes to a taxpayer with AGI $38,537. The meaning of the mean dollar of AGI weighted by AGI is less intuitive, but can be understood by analogy with calculation of mean tax rates. Suppose we knew income and total taxes paid by a set of individuals, and we wanted to calculate the average tax rate on all the dollars of income in the group. Simply taking the average of the tax rates across individuals would be inappropriate because the tax rate on individuals with high incomes clearly has more influence on the tax rate on the average dollar of income than the rate on low-income individuals. The appropriate procedure is to take a weighted mean of all the tax rates, where the weights are given by the incomes of the individuals. By analogy, the appropriate procedure to find the "typical" dollar of income in the mean sense is to take a weighted mean of income where the weights are also given by income.

Wealth Calculations from Avery and Kennickell

Avery and Kennickell (1988) present tables drawn from the 1983 and 1986 Federal Reserve *Survey of Consumer Finances,* which is virtually the only reinterview wealth survey containing a large number of high-income families. This survey allows a direct calculation of net saving via a comparison of each family's net worth in 1983 and 1986. In their table 12 the authors estimate the fraction of aggregate positive saving between 1983 and 1986 that was done by the members of each 1983 wealth decile. We used this table to generate a crude approximation to the distribution function for saving by wealth decile.

Table 10A.1   Rates of Return on Equities and on Interest-bearing Assets, 1979–84

Year	Dividend Price Ratio	Average Interest Rate
1979	5.47	7.8
1980	5.26	8.4
1981	5.20	9.4
1982	5.81	9.3
1983	4.40	8.8
1984	4.64	8.9

The technique was as follows. The graph of saving by wealth decile appeared to be close to exponential, so we assumed that the function log(saving) = f(1983 wealth decile) was exactly linear. Using two points, the saving of the first decile and the saving of the last decile, we calculated the slope and the intercept for the line passing through those two points. This technique should substantially underestimate the inequality of the wealth distribution because research (as well as the simple graph of log saving against wealth decile) suggests that wealth is even more unequally distributed in the upper income brackets than the log assumption suggests. Since the results indicate a high degree of inequality in spite of this bias we are confident that our figures do not overstate the degree of inequality.

Given a continuous function for the distribution of saving as a function of wealth, it is a simple matter of numerical integration to find the point at which saving below that point equals saving above the point. This is the point that defines the amount of saving done by what we call in the text the "median" saver. The procedure described above was repeated using Avery and Kennickell's (1988) table 10 to produce a distribution of wealth by wealth decile, and the resulting function was used to calculate the estimated wealth of someone at the 94th percentile in the wealth distribution, the point that the previous function identified as being associated with the median saver.

Notes

1. We comment below on the possibility that differences in tastes can explain our observations.
2. Because of data limitations we do not carefully distinguish durable and nondurable consumption as theory would suggest. Given that durables are a relatively stable share of consumption in the United States at least, we doubt that this has much impact on our results.
3. We use both private and national saving measures in order to avoid taking a stand in the Ricardian equivalence debate.
4. Note that this test differs from the popular Hall-style tests by focusing on low-frequency measures of income growth rates like the geometric average over the previous five years rather than very high frequency variables like previous quarter's income growth. If we believe there is long-term dependence in growth rates, then this is an appropriate variable to use as a proxy for expected current and future growth. We recognize that the previous discussion does not fully address the implications of uncertainty, because the model that produces (1) is a perfect certainty model. We address the implications of a model that incorporates important uncertainty below.
5. See the data appendix for details on data sources and methods.
6. Given the large differences in lifetime income between cohorts it is also surprising under the life-cycle theory that the consumption of 30-year-olds is not much greater than the consumption of 65-year-olds in both countries.
7. The unused occupational groups were retired people, nonresponses, and others. The unused educational group was "none, nonresponse, or other." The figures grouped by occupation are in order of increasing standard deviation of the mean level of in-

come, so more credibility should probably be ascribed to inferences drawn from figures near the top of the page than those near the bottom. The difference in variance across educational groups was substantially less (the groups are closer in size) so the figures grouped by education are ordered by increasing educational level.

8. Note that these wealth estimates include housing equity, which accounts for the discrepancy between the estimated median wealth here and in table 10.4.

References

Ando, A., and Arthur B. Kennickell. 1986. How Much (or Little) Life Cycle Is There in Micro Data? The Cases of the United States and Japan. In *Macroeconomics and Finance: Essays in Honor of Franco Modigliani*. Cambridge, Mass.: MIT Press.

Avery, Robert B., and Arthur B. Kennickell. 1988. Savings and Wealth: Evidence from the 1986 Survey of Consumer Finances. Paper presented at the 50th Anniversary Conference on Research in Income and Wealth of the National Bureau of Economic Research. Washington, D.C., May.

Becker, Gary. 1965. A Theory of the Allocation of Time. *Economic Journal* 73, no. 5 (September): 493–517.

Board of Governors of the Federal Reserve. 1989. *Balance Sheets for the U.S. Economy, 1949–88*. Washington, D.C., April.

Browning, Martin, Angus Deaton, and Margaret Irish. 1985. A Profitable Approach to Labor Supply and Commodity Demands Over the Life Cycle. *Econometrica* 53, no. 3 (May).

Campbell, John Y. and N. G. Mankiw. 1989. Consumption, Income, and Interest Rates: Reinterpreting the Time Series Evidence" NBER Working Paper no. 2924. Cambridge, Mass., March.

Danmark Statistik. 1988. *Statistisk årbog* (Statistical yearbook). Copenhagen: Danmark Statistik.

Deaton, Angus. 1989. Saving in Developing Countries: Theory and Review. Paper prepared for the First Annual World Bank Conference on Economic Growth. Washington, D.C., April.

DeLong, J. Bradford, and Lawrence H. Summers. 1986. Is Increased Price Flexibility Stabilizing? *American Economic Review* 76, no. 5 (December): 1031–44.

Friedman, Milton. 1957. *A Theory of the Consumption Function*. Princeton, N.J.: Princeton University Press.

Ghez, Gilbert. 1975. Education, the Price of Time, and Life-Cycle Consumption. In *Education, Income, and Human Behavior*, ed. F. Thomas Juster, 295–312. New York: Maple Press for the Carnegie Commission on Higher Education and the National Bureau of Economic Research.

Ghez, Gilbert, and Gary S. Becker. 1975. *The Allocation of Time and Goods Over the Life Cycle*. Studies in Human Behavior and Social Institutions, no. 6. New York: Columbia University.

Hall, Robert E. 1978. Stochastic Implications of the Life Cycle–Permanent Income Hypothesis: Theory and Evidence. *Journal of Political Economy* 86 (December): 971–87.

Kotlikoff, Laurence J., and Lawrence H. Summers. 1981. The Role of Intergenerational Transfers in Aggregate Capital Accumulation. *Journal of Political Economy* 89: 706–32.

Levine, Sumner N. 1986. *The Dow Jones-Irwin Business and Investment Almanac, 1986*. Homewood, Ill.: Dow Jones-Irwin.

Mehra, Rajnish, and Edward Prescott. 1985. The Equity Premium: A Puzzle. *Journal of Monetary Economics* 15, no. 1 (January): 145–61.

Modigliani, Franco. 1970. The Life Cycle Hypothesis of Saving and Intercountry Differences in the Saving Ratio. In *Induction, Growth, and Trade: Essays in Honour of Sir Roy Harrod*. Oxford: Clarendon Press.

———. 1980. The Life Cycle Hypothesis of Saving Twenty Years Later. In *The Collected Papers of Franco Modigliani*, vol. 2: *The Life Cycle Hypothesis of Saving*, ed. Andrew Abel. Cambridge, Mass.: MIT Press.

———. 1986. Life Cycle, Individual Thrift, and the Wealth of Nations. *American Economic Review* 76, no. 3 (June): 297–313.

Morgan Stanley. 1968 to present. *Capital International Perspective*. New York: Sladkus.

Ramsey, Frank. 1928. A Mathematical Theory of Saving. *Economic Journal* 38 (December): 543–59.

Romer, Paul. 1986. Increasing Returns and Long-Run Growth. *Journal of Political Economy* 94 (October): 1002–37.

Statistics Canada. 1989. *Family Expenditure in Canada*. Statistics Canada catalog no. 62–555. Ottawa.

United Nations, Department of International Economic and Social Affairs. 1987. *Global Estimates and Projections of Population by Sex and Age: The 1984 Assessment*. New York: United Nations.

Comment   N. Gregory Mankiw

Christopher Carroll and Lawrence Summers present us with a collage of facts about consumption and income. They give us scatter plots from aggregate cross-country data, tabulations from individual tax return data, and profiles of consumption and income from consumer survey data. Although they do not give us a model to explain all these data, the myriad pieces of evidence they present form a compelling image of how consumers behave.

Most important, the image of the consumer that arises from the paper contrasts sharply with the modern renditions of the permanent income hypothesis that pervade much of macroeconomics. According to these modern theories, consumers are rational, forward looking, and able to borrow and lend to smooth consumption over time. In the Carroll and Summers collage, we see consumers who, because of myopia or liquidity constraints, do not set their consumption on the basis of the present value of expected future income. Instead, current income exerts a larger influence on consumption than many modern theories imply.

I find myself sympathetic to many of the conclusions of this paper. In our joint work on the time-series properties of consumption and income, John Campbell and I also found that current income is a more important determinant of consumer spending than the permanent income hypothesis suggests. I

N. Gregory Mankiw is professor of economics at Harvard University and a research associate of the National Bureau of Economic Research.

think that Carroll and Summers are right that these findings call for more work on liquidity constraints and precautionary saving.

Because I agree with Carroll and Summers on the implications of these findings for the theory of the consumer, I would like to discuss the implications for another topic: the theory of economic growth. Their cross-country evidence provides as serious a challenge for those economists trying to model economic growth as it does for those trying to model consumer spending.

The Central Fact

From the standpoint of growth theory, the central fact in the paper is found in figure 10.1: countries with high growth in income have high growth in consumption. This fact is compelling because it is simple and because it is robust. Much of the paper is aimed at arguing that this fact is a problem for standard theories of the consumer, because most of the natural explanations of it do not hold up under close scrutiny.

Although I am convinced that this fact is correct, I am left somewhat skeptical of the authors' interpretation. They would like us to believe that, because they are looking at averages over long periods, the differences in mean income growth reflect differing steady-state growth rates rather than differing shocks across countries. This is probably not completely true, however. For example, much of the Japanese growth miracle was unanticipated—otherwise it would not be called a miracle.

The question Carroll and Summers do not fully answer is how much of the cross-country variation was unanticipated. If the differences in income growth across countries were mostly due to luck, the Carroll and Summers facts would be far less interesting. For example, the correlation between income and consumption growth would be explained trivially by the revision in permanent income. The distinction between anticipated and unanticipated growth is thus important for how we interpret these facts.

For now, however, I will assume that this fact will stand up to closer empirical scrutiny. Like the authors, I will assume that the observed differences in sample means reflect differences in steady-state growth rates. I want to discuss what their cross-country evidence implies for our theories of economic growth.

A Diamond Model

In order to think about this fact systematically, let us consider a couple of simple growth models. Let me begin with a standard Diamond model with some plausible and convenient functional forms. Suppose the production function is Cobb-Douglas

$$(1) \qquad\qquad Y = AK^\alpha L^{1-\alpha},$$

where Y is output, K is capital, which lasts for one period, and L is labor. Suppose that people live for two periods, supply labor inelastically when young, and consume in both periods according to the utility function

(2) $$U = \gamma \log C^y + (1-\gamma) \log C^o.$$

Suppose further that the population is constant, and that labor supply is normalized to be

(3) $$L = 1.$$

Not surprisingly, these assumptions make the model easy to solve. Log utility tells us that consumption when young is a constant fraction γ of labor income, and the Cobb-Douglas production function tells us that labor income is a constant fraction $(1-\alpha)$ of total income. In addition, consumption when old equals capital income, which is also a constant fraction α of total income. Thus, most quantity variables in this economy are simply proportional to total income.

Can this sort of model mimic the close connection between consumption growth and income growth that Carroll and Summers document? As stated, the model is not even a growth model: it reaches a steady state with fixed level of capital and income. The standard way to get steady-state growth into such a model is to assume that the technological parameter A grows exogenously over time:

(4) $$A = a(1 + g)^t.$$

Countries will have different steady-state growth rates if the parameter g varies across countries.

This model can now explain the observed relation between consumption growth and income growth. Summing the consumption of the young and old shows that the steady-state level of aggregate consumption is

(5) $$C = [\gamma(1-\alpha) + \alpha]\, Y.$$

Because aggregate consumption is proportional to aggregate income, high growth in aggregate income leads to high growth in aggregate consumption. In addition, if we look at growth in consumption over an individual's life, we obtain

(6) $$C^o/C^y = [\alpha/((1-\alpha)\gamma)]\, (Y_{+1}/Y).$$

Individual consumption also grows more quickly if aggregate income is growing quickly. Hence, the growth in aggregate consumption and the growth in individual consumption in this model appear to be in line with the Carroll and Summers findings.

This model begins to have problems when we turn to examining rates of return. The steady-state real interest rate is

(7) $$1 + r = [\alpha/((1-\alpha)(1-\gamma))]\, (Y_{+1}/Y).$$

High growth should lead to a high real interest rate. Thus, the absence of any correlation between real interest rates and growth, which Carroll and Summers document, appears to be evidence against this traditional growth model.

Finally, I should note that this growth model does not run into problems because it adopts the life-cycle theory of the consumer. If instead I had supposed that young consumers in this economy obeyed an arbitrary Keynesian consumption function according to which consumption was proportional to income, the model would be little changed—it would merely turn into a textbook Solow growth model. Again, the model would predict, counterfactually, a correlation between growth rates and real interest rates.

A Romer Model

Let us now consider a second growth model—identical to the first except for the determination of technological change. In particular, I want to replace the assumption of exogenous technological change with an assumption of endogenous technological change along the lines pioneered by Paul Romer. Suppose that total factor productivity is given by

$$(8) \qquad A = aK^{\beta}.$$

The state of technology evolves not as a function of time, but rather as a function of the level of capital.

I will not go into detail about why technology evolves in this way. The key underlying assumption is that there are externalities to capital accumulation. One possible story is that when a firm builds a factory, it thinks up good ideas that become part of the general pool of knowledge. Alternatively, there may be network externalities or external benefits to specialization and product differentiation that, because of scale economies, are only possible as the economy grows larger.

The crucial implication of these externalities is that the private and social production functions now diverge. The economy faces the aggregate production function

$$(9) \qquad Y = aK^{\alpha+\beta}L^{1-\alpha}.$$

Individual firms, however, ignore the external effects and view themselves as facing the Cobb-Douglas production function (1). It is therefore the Cobb-Douglas production function that governs the distribution of income between capital and labor.

To turn this model into one of endogenous steady-state growth, let us take Romer's suggestion and assume that $\alpha + \beta = 1$, so that the aggregate production function exhibits constant returns to scale in capital. Under these assumptions, it is straightforward to show that the steady-state growth rate is

$$(10) \qquad Y_{+1}/Y = (1-\gamma)(1-\alpha)a.$$

In contrast to traditional growth models, the steady-state growth rate in this model depends on preferences. If we view all countries as obeying this model and differing by their rate of time preference γ, we obtain different equilibrium growth rates. Impatient countries such as the United States have high γ

and thus low growth rates; patient countries such as Japan have low γ and thus high growth rates.

The appealing feature of this model is that it mimics some of the facts documented by Carroll and Summers. To see this, note first that the relation between consumption and income remains the same:

$$(5) \qquad\qquad C = [\gamma(1-\alpha) + \alpha]\, Y.$$

This implies that countries with high income growth also have high consumption growth (and also a high rate of saving). Inferring the growth in individual consumption from equations (6) and (10), we obtain

$$(11) \qquad\qquad C^o/C^y = [\alpha a(1-\gamma)/\gamma].$$

Because high growth countries have low γ, they also have high growth in individual consumption.

In addition to producing the positive correlation between income growth and consumption growth, the model also mimics the observed patterns in real interest rates. The real interest rate in this economy, which is determined by the private marginal product of capital, is easily shown to be:

$$(12) \qquad\qquad 1 + r = \alpha a.$$

Note that the real interest rate is independent of γ and thus will not vary systematically with the growth rate. In this model, the externalities associated with capital accumulation imply that higher saving causes higher growth, and they also prevent higher saving from lowering capital's rate of return.

The Real Interest Rate Puzzle

From the standpoint of the theory of economic growth, the puzzling fact in the Carroll and Summers paper is not the high correlation between consumption growth and income growth. This correlation will arise in almost any growth model. The puzzle is the absence of any correlation between growth and real interest rates. I have shown that one can explain this fact by appealing to an endogenous growth model that assumes constant returns to capital. Yet many economists (including myself) will find this assumption unappealing.

The findings in this paper therefore call for two directions of future research. First, as Carroll and Summers emphasize, economists need better models of consumer spending. Second, as I have emphasized, economists need better models of growth—in particular, models to explain why real interest rates fail to vary across countries with growth rates.

11   Saving Behavior in Ten
              Developing Countries

Susan M. Collins

11.1 Introduction

The 1987 *World Development Report* (World Bank 1987) noted that gross domestic savings, as a share of income, ranged from 31% to 33% in Korea, Malaysia, and Indonesia, while Singapore saved 42% of GDP.[1] In contrast, the highest saving rate for a Latin American developing country was 26% for Mexico. Argentina, Brazil, Colombia, and Venezuela saved 16%, 22%, 17%, and 24% respectively. For comparison, saving rates were 16% in the United States and 32% in Japan. Why do the developing countries in Asia save so much? Were Korea, Malaysia, and Indonesia outliers? Have they always had high saving rates? Did the savings come primarily from the government, corporate, or household sector?

This paper examines saving behavior in nine Asian developing countries plus Turkey since the early 1960s. The paper has two primary objectives. The first is to present a variety of facts about saving and other key variables. The times-series data used were collected for each country. Unfortunately, data problems are notorious both in measuring savings and in many developing countries. It is especially difficult to make cross-country comparisons. While the empirical findings should be interpreted with caution, they do indicate trends and differences in saving across countries and within countries over time. The findings that seem most likely to be robust to improved savings indicators concern shifts in saving behavior within particular countries over time. In fact, many of these countries have experienced striking shifts.

Section 11.2 of the paper provides a first look at the data. It highlights the

Susan M. Collins is associate professor of economics at Harvard University and a faculty research fellow of the National Bureau of Economic Research.

The author thanks Maurice Obstfeld and John Shoven for suggestions and Lisa Robinson for research assistance.

roles of economic growth rates, the standard of living, and the age distribution of the population as determinants of saving. In particular, it points to a central role for dependency ratios—the percentage of the population aged 14 or younger. In fact, the high savers tended to have high growth rates and to have experienced a dramatic decline in fertility rates, reducing their dependency ratios.

The second objective of the paper is to empirically examine the determinants of saving across these 10 countries and over time. The empirical work builds on the extensive literature on saving behavior in developing countries. A number of authors have examined the impact of demographic factors on saving in developing countries. See Hammer (1985) for a survey. Early cross-section studies (see Leff 1980 for a review and update) concluded that dependency ratios were an important determinant of differences in saving behavior. Later work (e.g., Ram 1982) took issue with these results. Empirically, saving seemed to be negatively correlated with dependency rates among developed countries, but positively correlated among developing countries.

In a series of recent papers, Mason (e.g., 1988; and Mason et al. 1986) argued that these equations are misspecified because the effect of dependency rates (and other variables) on savings depends on the economic growth rate. Declining dependency ratios should tend to lower savings in slow-growing economies but to raise savings in rapidly growing economies. His empirical estimates did show saving rates negatively related to dependency rates for four Asian countries. But these results were based on annual observations. As discussed further in sections 11.2 and 11.5 of this paper, year-to-year fluctuations in saving rates seem to be closely tied to agricultural inventories and to exhibit considerable measurement error. Therefore, it is preferable to consider time averages.

The third section of this paper sets out a version of the life-cycle model of saving behavior to illustrate the effects of growth, dependency rates, and other variables on aggregate savings. The model follows Mason (1987, 1988) in emphasizing that socioeconomic factors and the economic growth rate might influence saving interactively.

The saving equation is used in section 11.4 to econometrically examine saving in the 10 countries. Five-year time averages are used. The empirical estimates suggest that growth rates, demographic factors, and the standard of living account for a substantial portion of saving behavior across countries and over time. They also point to the importance of the interaction effects between growth and other socioeconomic characteristics, and imply that there are structural differences between low-income and middle-income countries in the determinants of savings.

Section 11.5 of the paper turns to one country, Korea, to examine some of the issues raised in more detail. In particular, the aggregate date suggests that most of the changes in aggregate savings are attributable to the household sector. However, it is difficult to interpret disaggregated national savings data.

This section presents some additional data from surveys of urban and rural households' income and expenditure in Korea.

The final section provides a summary and concluding remarks. I hope that the findings presented in this paper will be provocative and will raise a variety of interesting areas for future research.

11.2   Saving Behavior in 10 Countries

This section takes a first look at the experiences of the 10 countries. The focus is on five sets of variables for each country. The key variable is savings as a share of income. How to best measure savings raises a number of important but difficult problems even in developed economies.[2] Instead of piecing together the details for one or two countries, the objective of this paper was to draw inferences for a group of countries over time. Thus, the regressions in section 11.4 and much of the discussion in this section focus on gross national savings as a share of GNP. This variable can be interpreted as a share of total national resources available to finance investment. The data sources for each country are listed in the appendix. There are clearly shortcomings with this indicator; however, none of the alternatives available for these countries, given the data limitations, was clearly superior. A number of issues deserve mention.

First, net savings may be more appropriate than gross savings when the concern is growth rates and development, since net savings indicates domestic resources available for additions to the capital stock. However, net savings data were available for only four of the 10 countries—Korea, the Philippines, Taiwan, and Thailand. Even in these four, the capital consumption allowance seems unreliable. The definitions change frequently. Even in Korea, a country with relatively good data, different sources report different aggregate depreciation series. See Mason (1987) for further discussion of gross versus net savings measure for developing countries.

A second issue is whether to focus on aggregate savings or to disaggregate by sector. Although life-cycle theories of saving apply most directly to households, there remains an active controversy over the extent to which household saving should be treated as independent from corporate and government saving. The same issue is relevant for developing countries, with the added twist that the line between households and firms is more difficult to draw. When disaggregated data exist, the "household sector" is simply the residual once government and corporate savings are subtracted from total national savings. Accurate information on the size of the "informal" business sector is not available. Even though the precise interpretation is unclear, it is interesting to look at the trends in different components of savings where data do exist. Strong trends within countries over time are likely to be robust and do warrant some interpretation. However, differences in the composition of savings across countries may primarily reflect differences in definitions and errors in measurement. Additional data on household and firm behavior is potentially quite informative. Section 11.5 of this paper takes some steps in that direction, discussing data from surveys of Korean households.

Finally, these data do not adequately treat asset valuations (in particular, land or housing) or consumption of durables. It is difficult to tell how these omissions might bias the existing series. An interesting area for future work is to incorporate these corrections for those countries where adequate data are available.

In addition to savings, the discussion below considers four sets of variables: real economic growth rates, the age distribution of the population, per capita income, and inequality. The discussion of age distribution focuses on the share of the population below the age of fifteen ($D15$). In fact, the results change little if the "dependency ratio" is defined more broadly to include the share of the population over the age of 65 ($D15 + D65$). In this sample, most of the differences across countries and over time come from the relative importance of children. The per capita income measures come from Heston and Summers's (1988) pioneering work to obtain internationally comparable series on real income and prices. These data are measured in 1980 international prices.

Finally, an indicator of income distribution is used for seven of the countries. This indicator, from the *1987 World Development Report* gives the share of income going to the poorest 20% of the population relative to the share going to the richest 10% as a measure of income inequality. Measures of income distribution are well known to be unreliable. Nonetheless, many of the discussions about rates of saving focus on the distribution of income, and no ideal measures are available.

The remainder of this section discusses behavior of savings and other key variables for the 10 countries. I begin by comparing the "long-run" experiences across countries, and then I move to a discussion of time trends in individual countries.

11.2.1   Cross-Country Experiences

Table 11.1 shows key variables for each country. Saving rates are averaged across 1960–84 (1960–81 in a few cases). The countries are ordered from Singapore, the country with the highest average saving rate, at the top, to Indonesia, with the lowest rate, at the bottom. The table includes four additional indicators: real economic growth rates, per capita income, the dependency ratio (share of the population age 14 or younger), and the measure of inequality.

The table shows a wide variation in performance across countries. For example, savings rates range from 12% to 24%, while growth rates range from 4% to 10%. Taiwan and Korea have relatively equitable distributions of income, while in Turkey and Malaysia the poorest 20% of the population receive less than 9% of the income that goes to the richest 10%. However, it is

Table 11.1   **Key Indicators: 1960–84**

	Gross Savings (% GNP)[a]	Real Growth[a]	Dependency Ratio (<15)		Real Per Capita Income[b]	Income Distribution
			1960[b]	1980[b]		
Singapore	24.3	8.5	43.2	29.3	3,481	. . .
Taiwan	23.0	8.8	38.9	33.4	1,778	. . .
Malaysia	22.5	7.0	51.2	55.6	1,959	8.8
Korea	22.0	9.3	42.9	34.4	1,429	20.7
Philippines	21.3	4.2	44.6	44.1	1,167	13.5
Thailand	21.2	6.9	44.7	41.9	1,158	16.9
Hong Kong	19.1	10.2	40.9	28.1	3,643	17.3
Turkey	16.6	5.2	42.0	39.0	1,874	8.6
Burma	12.0	3.9	38.2	41.2	397	. . .
Indonesia	11.9	5.9	40.7	40.1	505	19.4

Note: See data appendix and text for sources and description.
[a]Period averages.
[b]End of period.

Table 11.2   **Rapid versus Slow Growth Countries**

	Real Growth	Gross Savings (% GNP)	Real Per Capita Income	Dependency	
				1960	1980
Rapid	9.2	22.1	2583	41.5	31.3
Slow	4.8	15.4	986	41.4	41.1

Source: See data appendix and text.
Note: The rapid growth countries are Hong Kong, Korea, Taiwan, and Singapore. The slow growers are Malaysia, Thailand, Burma, and the Philippines.

important to make two points at the outset. First, by world standards, these countries have grown rapidly. The group that we will identify as the slow growers had average annual growth rates of 4%-6%.

Second, most enjoy equitable income distributions. This is especially true in Korea and Taiwan which, like Japan, underwent fundamental land reforms in the 1940s and 1950s. The income share of the poorest 20% of the population is 9.5% in Taiwan, and averages 5.1% in the other seven countries. In comparison, the poorest 20% receive just 3.1% of income in a sample of eight Latin American countries.[3] In only one country, El Salvador, do they receive at least the minimum share (3.5%) that they receive in the Asian countries.

Tables 11.2–11.4 further explore the relationships between these variables and savings rates. Table 11.2 comparés performance of the four countries with growth rates above 8% and the four countries with growth rates below 6%. Not surprisingly, the high-growth countries are substantially richer than the slow growers. Also, the rapid growers save 40% more income than the slow growers.

Table 11.3   Savings and Per Capita Income

	Real Per Capita Income[a]	Gross National Savings (% GNP)
Poorest	451	12.0
Middle	1,561	20.9
(excluding Turkey)	1,498	21.7
Richest	3,562	21.7

Source: See data appendix and text for sources and description of savings data.
[a]These data are average real per capita incomes during 1980–84 (Summers and Heston 1988). The poorest countries (Burma and Indonesia) have per capita incomes < $1,000. The middle-income countries have per capita incomes between $1,000 and $2,000 and the richest (Singapore and Hong Kong) have incomes above $3,000.

Table 11.4   Income Distribution and Savings

	Income Inequality	Gross Savings (% GNP)	Real Growth	Real Per Capita Income
Equal	18.4	18.6	8.1	1,684
Equal, excluding Indonesia	18.1	20.7	8.8	2,077
Unequal	10.3	20.1	5.5	1,667

Source: See text and data appendix for sources and description.
Note: Income inequality is the share of income received by the poorest 20% relative to the share received by the richest 10%. The countries with relatively equitable income distributions are Korea, Indonesia, Hong Kong, and Thailand (labeled "Equal" above). The inequitable ones are Malaysia, Turkey, and the Philippines (labeled "Unequal").

At the beginning of the period, all of the countries had very similar age distributions. However, by the end of the period, there had been no change in the dependency ratios in the slow growers but a 25% reduction in the dependency rates of the rapid growers. In fact, each of the rapid growers experienced a significant decline (i.e., a drop in fertility rates), and these were the only countries in the sample which did. Using the broader measure of dependency that includes the share of the population over age 65, the rapid growers experienced a decline in the dependency ratio from 44.7 in 1960 to 36.1 in 1980. The comparable figures for the slow growers are 47.6 in 1960 and 49.0 in 1980.

Table 11.3 groups countries by per capita income levels. The two poorest countries had very low saving rates. However, there is no clear relationship between per capita incomes and saving rates among the middle- and upper-income groups. When Turkey is excluded from the middle-income group, the mean saving rate is 21.7%, exactly the same as for the richest countries. While it is not possible to generalize from such small samples, these data do not suggest that saving rates rise with income across countries. In the next sections we will ask whether there is a relationship between saving and the standard of living within a country over time.

Table 11.4 compares the countries with relatively equal income distributions with the less equitable ones. In the first group, the poorest 20% of individuals receive 18% of the income received by the richest 10%. The comparable number for the second group of countries is just 10%. The table shows that, on average using this measure of distribution, there is no relationship between income equality and the standard of living. Hong Kong, the richest country in the sample, and Indonesia, one of the poorest, have very similar indicators of inequality. However, the countries with less equal distributions did grow more slowly than the more equitable countries.

There is also little support for the view that saving is related to income distribution. If Indonesia, the only country with distribution data available with a per capita income below $1,000, is excluded, saving rates are almost identical across the two groups.

11.2.2   Trend Saving Behavior

Averaging saving rates over a 20-year period masks important changes in saving behavior over time. We turn next to a discussion of saving trends in individual countries. The discussion divides the 10 countries into four groups. The first group is composed of the countries that experienced trend increases in saving. The second group is made up of the low-income countries. The third includes countries in which saving declined over the sample period. Finally, one country, Turkey, does not fit neatly in any of these groups.

Where available, we also decompose savings into type: government, corporate, and household. As discussed above, there are some problems with these decompositions. In particular, the household sector is typically the residual, once government and corporate savings are subtracted from total national savings. Therefore, it includes savings of unincorporated businesses, which is likely to be important for many developing countries. Furthermore, savings exhibits strong positive correlation with real output growth rates in most of the countries. While it is not possible to explain this correlation in each country, additional data for South Korea shows that there, much of the correlation comes from rural households, where savings are closely linked to farm inventories.

Countries with Increasing Savings

In 1986, savings rates as a percentage of GDP in Singapore (fig. 11.1), Taiwan, and Korea were 46%, 37%, and 33% respectively. However, none of these countries began with a high savings rate. Each experienced a dramatic increase.[4] The real question is not why these countries save a lot now, but why they experienced significant increases in savings since the 1960s when so many other countries did not.

It is interesting to note that Hong Kong, the richest country in the sample, underwent a rapid rise in saving rates from 2% of GNP in 1960 to 34% in 1976 (see fig. 11.2). However, saving rates have declined since then to approximately 25% of income.[5]

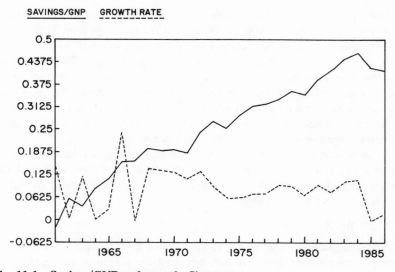

Fig. 11.1   Savings/GNP and growth: Singapore

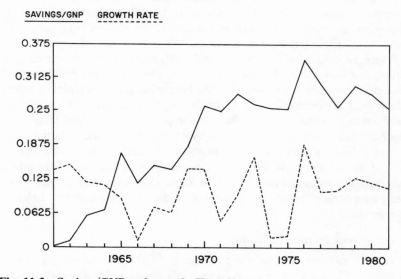

Fig. 11.2   Savings/GNP and growth: Hong Kong

Malaysia began with a higher standard of living than Korea, and with a relatively high saving rate. Malaysian saving has trended upward slightly during the period 1960–80 (fig. 11.3). It is interesting to note that Malaysia's average growth rate was 7% during this period as compared to over 9% in Korea. Like Korea, Malaysian saving is positively correlated with real growth

SAVINGS/GNP   GROWTH RATE

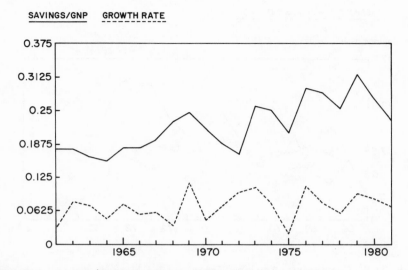

Fig. 11.3   Savings/GNP and growth: Malaysia

HOUSH/GNP   GOV'T/GNP   CORP/GNP

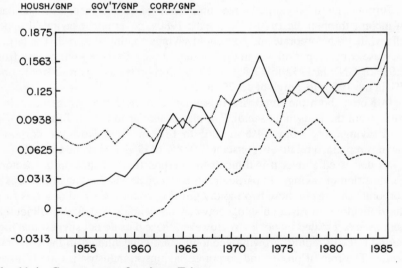

Fig. 11.4   Components of savings: Taiwan

rates. This may also be attributable to measurement problems from the treatment of agricultural inventories.

Savings decompositions are available for two of these high savers: Taiwan and Korea. Figures 11.4 and 11.5 show their savings as a percentage of GNP by the government, corporate sector, and households through 1986.

HOUSEHOLD   GOVERNMENT   CORPORATE

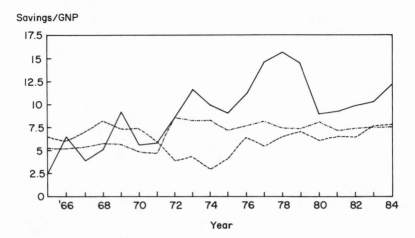

Fig. 11.5   Components of savings: Korea

Turning first to Taiwan, all three components of savings increased as a share of income through the 1970s. During the 1980s, government savings dropped off, while both corporate and household savings continued to rise. The largest increase over the period was in the household sector, where savings rose from 1.9% of GNP in 1952 to 17.8% in 1986. Corporate savings rose from about 7% in the 1950s to a high of 15.7% in 1986.

In Korea, both the trend rise in savings and the large swings in savings came from the household sector. The rise is similar to that in Taiwan: household savings rose from 2.4% in 1965 to 18% in 1986. However, corporate savings remained relatively constant (7%-8% of GNP) since the early 1970s.

As discussed above, it is difficult to interpret the evidence on the sectoral composition of savings. In particular, it is not clear whether the differences in corporate savings in these two rapidly growing countries is real or arises from the difficulties in distinguishing between households and firms, difficulties perhaps exacerbated by tax laws. However, these data do not suggest that high saving rates in rapidly growing economies are concentrated in the corporate sector. The role of profits and corporate savings in industrialization is an especially interesting area for additional analysis. See Murphy, Shleifer, and Vishny (1988) for an interesting theoretical discussion.

The Low Income Countries

Both Burma and Indonesia had extremely variable, and often negative, real growth rates during the early part of the sample. As shown in figures 11.6 and 11.7, they also had low and variable saving rates. However, in recent years, performance in both countries more closely resembled performance of the

SAVINGS/GNP   GROWTH RATE

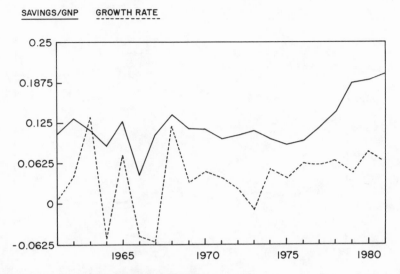

Fig. 11.6   Savings/GNP and growth: Burma

SAVINGS/GNP   GROWTH RATE

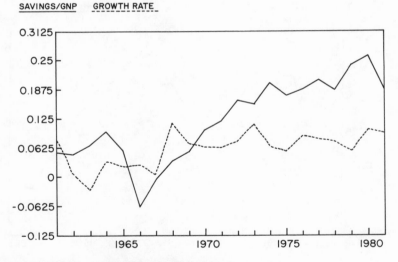

Fig. 11.7   Savings/GNP and growth: Indonesia

high savers. As real growth rates stabilized, both countries enjoyed a rapid rise in saving rates.

Declining Savers

Two countries experienced declines in savings rates. In Thailand (Fig. 11.8), savings rates were subject to large swings and a trend decline. Again, most of the movements came from the household sector.

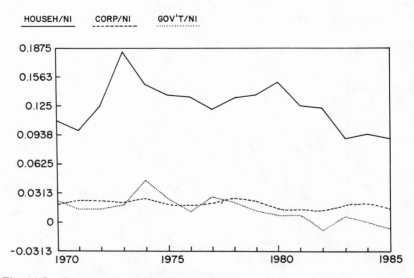

Fig. 11.8   Components of savings: Thailand

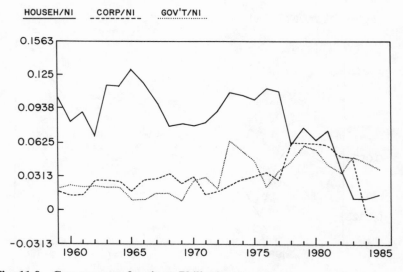

Fig. 11.9   Components of savings: Philippines

In the Philippines, saving rates were approximately constant until the mid-1970s and then declined (Fig. 11.9). The decline was concentrated in the private sector, with household savings falling from 11% of GNP in 1976 to 7% during 1979–81 and just 1% during 1984–86. Corporate savings also declined, becoming negative by 1985. The fall in savings coincided with a se-

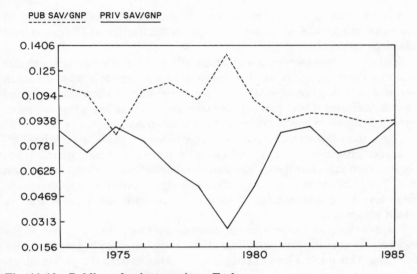

PUB SAV/GNP   PRIV SAV/GNP

Fig. 11.10   Public and private savings: Turkey

vere deterioration in economic performance. Real growth rates averaged 6.4% during 1972–80, plunging to 1.5% during 1981–82 and − 5.3% during 1983–84. See Dohner and Intal (1989) for a recent analysis of the Philippine economic crisis.

Other

Finally, Turkey did not fit any of the above categories. Turkey's saving rate rose during the 1960s and has since stabilized. As shown in figure 11.10, a decomposition of Turkish savings is interesting and unusual. Public-sector savings were strongly negatively correlated with private savings.

11.3   A Model of Saving Behavior

This section uses a simple life-cycle model of household savings to derive the equations to be estimated in section 11.4. The approach, which follows Fry and Mason (1982) and Mason (1988), emphasizes three aspects of saving behavior.

First, it clearly distinguishes between level and growth effects. In a stationary economy (with no real growth and a constant age distribution) changes in the timing of household savings will have no effect on the aggregate savings rate as long as households consume their entire lifetime earnings over their life cycle. However, there is substantial empirical evidence against this strict life-cycle assumption. In fact, households frequently leave positive wealth, whether because of uncertainty or the desire to leave bequests. Thus, the framework developed below allows for the possibility that lifetime consumption is a fraction of lifetime resources, and that the fraction may depend on economic and social environment. Changes in this fraction will be called level effects on saving.

Second, the framework shows that the effect of real growth on saving depends on the mean age at which households earn income relative to the mean age at which they consume. In two economies with identical (nonnegative) growth rates, one would expect lower saving rates in the one where the mean age of consumption was lower relative to the mean age of earnings.

Third, most factors that influence saving behavior will have both level effects and "growth-tilt" effects—effects on the mean age of earnings relative to consumption that enter the savings equation interactively with the real growth rate. These effects need not have the same sign. Furthermore, econometric estimates of the determinants of savings are misspecified if the interactive effects are omitted.

For example, an increase in the dependency rate is likely to reduce the mean age of consumption, with little effect on the mean age of earnings in the economy. This implies lower saving rates working through the growth-tilt effect, provided that there is a positive real growth rate. However, the level effect of an increase in the share of the population under age 15 is less clear. It may either raise the lifetime consumption of households, reducing savings, or raise the share of lifetime earnings the household wishes to leave to future generations. The remainder of this section develops a life-cycle model of aggregate savings.

Households are characterized by their age and by the year in which they were formed. Define $w(a,t)$ as the earnings of a household at age a which was formed at time t. We will refer to this as a household of generation t. Let $w(a)$ be the age-earnings profile of the initial household, and assume that the economy grows at a constant rate g over time. Therefore,

$$(1) \qquad w(a,t) = w(a)e^{gt}.$$

The present value of earnings for a household of generation t is

$$(2) \qquad V(t) = \int_a w(a,t)\, e^{-ra} da.$$

Therefore, in year τ, the lifetime earnings of an age a household (a household of generation $\tau - a$) is

$$(3) \qquad V(\tau - a) = V(\tau)e^{-ga}.$$

It is also useful to define $\gamma(a,t)$ as the share of lifetime income households of generation t earn at age a.

$$(4) \qquad \gamma(a,t) = w(a,t)/V(t).$$

In addition, if $n(a,t)$ is the number of age a households in year t, then GNP is:

(5) $$X(t) = e^{gt} \int_a n(a,t) \, w(a) \, e^{-ga} \, da.$$

Turning next to consumption, define $\alpha(a,t)$ as the share of lifetime income households of generation t consume at age a. As discussed above, we do not impose the strict life-cycle assumption, but allow for the possibility that the value of income exceeds the value of consumption over the life cycle. The consumption of an age a household as a share of GNP in year t is $\alpha(a,t-a)V(t-a)/X(t)$. Therefore, aggregate consumption as a share of GNP in year t is

(6) $$C(t) = \int_a \alpha(a,t-a) \frac{V(t-a)}{X(t)} n(a,t) \, da.$$

Substituting from (3), (4) and (5), (6) can be rewritten as

(7) $$C(t) = \frac{\int_a n(a,t) \, \alpha(a,t-a) \, e^{-ga} da}{\int_a n(a,t) \gamma(a,t) \, e^{-ga} da}.$$

Taking a linear approximation of (7) around $g = 0$, the following expression for aggregate savings as a share of aggregate income $s(t)$ is obtained

(8) $$-\ln C(t) = \ln\left(\frac{1}{1 - s(t)}\right) \ln(L) + g(\mu_c - \mu_y),$$

where

$$L \equiv \frac{_a\int n(a,t) \, \gamma(a,t) \, da}{_a\int n(a,t) \, \alpha(a,t-a) \, da}$$

$$\mu_y \equiv {_a}\int a \, n(a,t) \, \gamma(a,t) \, da$$

and

$$\mu_c \equiv {_a}\int a \, n(a,t) \, \alpha(a,t-a) \, da.$$

The left-hand side of (8) is approximately equal to the ratio of savings to GNP for moderate saving rates. There are two terms on the right-hand side. Here L is the level effect. A reduction in consumption relative to income, either because of a decline in the share of income consumed over the life cycle or because of a shift in the age distribution away from high-consumption households, will raise aggregate savings. The second term is the growth-tilt effect, which shows that real growth rates enter interactively with the difference between the economywide mean ages of consumption and earnings.

Finally, we assume that L and $(\mu_c - \mu_y)$ are simple functions of social and economic characteristics, W.

(9) $$L = \exp(W\beta),$$

(10) $$\mu_c - \mu_y = W\delta$$

As discussed further below, the small sample precluded the inclusion of a large number of characteristics in the regressions. The included variables (W) are a constant, the percentage of the population below the age of 15, $(D14)$ and per capita income (PCI). The results are not substantially different if the broader measure of dependency is used. The variable PCI is taken as a percentage of the per capita income for Hong Kong during 1980–84. Combining (8) with (9) and (10) gives a simple log-linear specification that is used in the estimations.

(11) $$\ln\left(\frac{1}{(1-s)}\right) = \beta_0 + \beta_1 \cdot D14 + \beta_2 \cdot PCI + \delta_0 \cdot g$$
$$+ \delta_1 \cdot g \cdot D14 + \delta_2 \cdot g \cdot PCI$$

11.4 Estimation Results

Equation (11) was estimated using data from the nine Asian economies plus Turkey from 1960 through 1984. Because disaggregated data is only available for some countries, the aggregate savings rate is used as the dependent variable. However, for most of these countries, annual savings rates are highly correlated with annual growth rates. As discussed above, additional information for Korea suggests that much of the correlation arises from fluctuations in inventories of rural households. To minimize these types of relationships, data on savings rates, per capita income, and growth were averaged over 1960–64, 1965–69, 1970–74, 1975–80, and 1980–84. In some cases, averages were taken over fewer years (e.g., 1980–82) because of missing values. The reported standard errors use the White heteroskedasticity correction, since the variance of the errors can be expected to vary with group size.

Table 11.5 reports the results from two sets of regressions. The first set includes all 10 countries. The second set excludes the two low income countries, Burma and Indonesia. There was not enough data to run separate regressions for these countries. Each set consists of two regressions—one with and one without the growth interaction terms.

A comparison of columns 1 and 3 with columns 2 and 4 in table 11.5 shows the importance of the growth interaction effects. Even though exclusion of these effects causes only a modest reduction in the overall fit, it does severely bias the parameter estimates. For example, if they are excluded, the dependency ratio does not seem to significantly influence saving rates. However, once the interaction effects are included, the dependency rates do enter significantly for the middle-income countries.

Table 11.5   **Regression Results**

$$\ln\!\left(\frac{1}{(1-s)}\right) = \beta_0 + \beta_1 \cdot D14 + \beta_2 \cdot PCI + \delta_0 \cdot g + \delta_1 \cdot g \cdot D14 + \delta_2 \cdot g \cdot PCI$$

	All Countries		Middle-Income Countries	
	1	2	3	4
Constant	.10	−.31	.15	−.71
	(2.52)	(1.31)	(2.62)	(−1.92)
D14	−.01	.74	−.06	1.40
	(−.17)	(1.29)	(−.74)	(2.09)
PCI	.23	.60	.21	.95
	(3.42)	(3.86)	(2.53)	(2.27)
g	1.01	7.25	.78	12.40
	(3.02)	(1.82)	(2.05)	(2.39)
g·D14		−11.83		−20.69
		(−1.27)		(−2.04)
g·PCI		−4.79		−8.69
		(−2.79)		(−1.98)
Adjusted R^2	.51	.56	.38	.44
Number of Observations	43	43	35	35

Source: Data sources are given in the text and the data appendix.
Note: Estimation Method: ordinary least squares, with heteroskedasticity consistent standard errors. *t*-statistics are in parentheses. Variable Definitions: s = aggregate savings/GNP; $D14$ = share of the population aged 14 or younger; PCI = real per capita income, as a share of 1980–84 income in Hong Kong; g = real economic growth rate.

For the middle-income countries, the dependency rate has a positive level effect and a negative growth-tilt effect on savings. In other words, given the standard of living and the real growth rate, increases in the population share of children tend to lower the fraction of lifetime income that a household consumes over its life cycle. This is consistent with an increased population share of children raising household bequests or increasing household precautionary savings.

The positive level effect on savings is offset by the reduction in the mean age of consumption in the economy relative to the mean age at which income is earned. The magnitude of this offset is tied to the economic growth rate. In countries where the growth rate exceeds 6.8%, the negative growth-tilt effect dominates, and the net effect of a rise in the dependency rate will be to reduce savings. From table 11.1, all of the middle-income countries except Turkey and the Philippines had average growth rates above 6.8%. It is interesting to note that Fry and Mason (1982) find both level and growth-tilt effects to be negative. The relationship between age distribution and saving seems quite sensitive to the countries and time period considered.

When the two low-income countries are included in the sample, the effects retain their signs, but the magnitudes decrease and the parameter estimates become insignificant. Interestingly, the overall fit in these equations is better than for the middle-income countries alone, because per capita income becomes a more important determinant of saving behavior. The results suggest that household consumption over the life cycle is less sensitive to the age distribution in poor countries, possibly because a larger percentage of households simply consume all of their income, regardless of the household size. Similarly, changes in the age distribution seem to have less effect on the mean age of consumption relative to income in the poor countries.

The estimates in table 11.5 also imply that the standard of living (PCI) has a positive level effect on savings but a negative growth-tilt effect. The net effect (for the middle-income countries) is positive for growth rates below 10.9%. Hong Kong, the fastest grower in the sample, averaged 10.2% over 1960–84. Thus, in this sample, countries save more as they get richer even though younger households dissave more relative to older households, because households consume a smaller share of lifetime incomes over their life cycles.

While the parameter differences are not statistically significant, including the low-income households seems to reduce the effect of per capita income on savings even though its explanatory power rises. One interpretation is that an increase in per capita income lowers the share of lifetime income consumed over the life cycle by more in the middle-income than in the poor countries.

The regressions discussed above point to the importance of growth rates, per capita incomes, and the dependency ratio as determinants of saving in developing countries. The simple equations explain only a modest portion of the differences in saving across countries and over time. The next section considers additional information about saving in Korea, to examine the rapid rise in the amount of savings between 1960 and 1986 in more detail.

11.5 Korean Saving Behavior

The previous sections used data from national income accounts to examine saving behavior in 10 countries. Disaggregation, where available, showed that most of the interesting developments in saving were concentrated in the household sector. However, the household sector is typically measured as a residual, once government and corporate savings have been subtracted out. This section discusses household savings in Korea, using data from household surveys. There are separate surveys for urban and rural households—surveys that have been conducted annually from 1965. However, there have been some changes in the sampling procedure. The surveys prior to 1975 are not strictly comparable to the more recent surveys.

Table 11.6 shows savings behavior (disposable income less consumption expenditure) for urban and rural households since 1965. As shown, urban household savings have risen dramatically to over 20% since 1978. Urban savings have been somewhat cyclical, declining during the 1974–75 and 1980–82 recessions.

Rural households seem to save substantially more than urban households.

Table 11.6   Urban and Rural Household Savings in Korea (household survey data)

	Urban	Rural	Rural Inventory Adjusted	Urban + Rural	Urban + Adjusted Rural
1965	−2.2	4.4	1.3	2.8	1.2
1966	3.2	10.5	1.1	8.6	4.4
1967	4.3	9.8	1.1	8.1	4.8
1968	2.6	16.1	.4	11.3	5.2
1969	3.4	17.8	4.3	12.5	7.6
1970	5.6	15.2	4.1	9.8	5.8
1971	9.2	29.0	7.9	16.0	7.7
1972	12.2	24.5	4.9	15.7	8.0
1973	12.6	26.2	7.8	16.6	9.4
1974	11.2	33.2	7.9	19.0	8.6
1975	9.6	26.6	7.5	14.9	7.6
1976	15.2	32.6	11.1	20.2	12.3
1977	18.9	28.9	10.4	20.4	13.7
1978	21.4	26.5	13.1	21.1	16.7
1979	22.9	21.0	7.8	21.0	17.3
1980	22.5	15.7	3.6	19.6	16.5
1981	21.2	22.7	3.3		
1982	20.5	22.5	3.7		
1983	22.9	18.3	3.1		
1984	24.2	21.8	2.4		
1985	25.3	17.6	2.8		

Source: Economic Planning Board (Korea), Annual Report on the Family Income and Expenditure Survey, 1965–86
Note: It was not possible to calculate the weighted averages of urban and rural savings ratios after 1980 because data for number of households was unavailable.

However, rural savings include increases in inventories (especially cereals). Excluding this component of savings, rural households savings has averaged just 6.5% as compared to 18.6% for urban households. During the 1960s and 1970s, rural household savings also rose significantly, from 1% to 10% of disposable income. However rural savings fell to just 3%-4% since 1979. One reason for the drop was the extremely poor performance of the agricultural sector during 1978–82, including a 20% decline in real output in 1980.

The final column of table 11.6 shows combined urban plus inventory-adjusted rural savings. The series shows a strong upward trend and is only slightly procyclical. The remainder of the discussion focuses on urban household savings.

Figure 11.11 shows saving by age of the head of the household since 1975. The plot shows that savings have increased at each age level over the past decade. This development is consistent with a strong level effect on savings— total household consumption has declined as a share of income over the life cycle. Possible explanations include the rising life expectancy or a growing bequest motive.

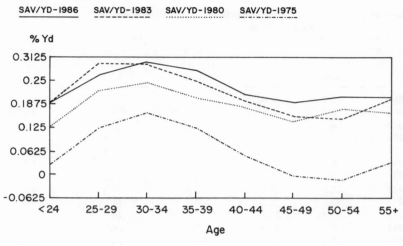

Yd: Disposable Income

Fig. 11.11   Household savings by age of head of household: Korea

The regressions in the previous section suggest that we should also observe a rise in the share of total savings accounted for by younger households if the mean age of consumption has in fact risen relative to the mean age of earnings. Instead, the plot points out a puzzle—the savings profile shows evidence of flattening out over time. In 1975, saving was quite concentrated among households with heads from 25 to 40 years of age. Households with heads aged 50–54 were dissaving slightly. By 1986, however, even older households saved nearly 18% of their incomes. In this respect, Korea is becoming more like Japan, where the saving rate seems to be independent of age.

The regressions in the previous section suggest that a rising standard of living may account for the rising savings. Real incomes have risen dramatically in Korea, and households with older heads tend to earn higher incomes. In 1986, household heads aged 50–54 earned the highest average incomes. To explore this channel further, figure 11.12 shows savings rates at a variety of real income levels (in constant 1980 won) from 1975–86. The figure was constructed by deflating the average nominal incomes of households grouped by nominal income ranges (eg. 100,000 to 149,000 won, etc.). The plot shows that low-income households have continued to save approximately the same fraction of their incomes. Thus, not all households saved more in 1986 than comparable households in 1975. Of course, the percentage of households in the low-income groups has declined over time as Korea's standard of living increased and saving rates rise steeply with household real incomes. The plot suggests that households with higher real incomes saved a greater percentage of income over time. Unfortunately, this picture may be misleading, because the 1975 data averages together all nominal incomes over 110,000 won. In

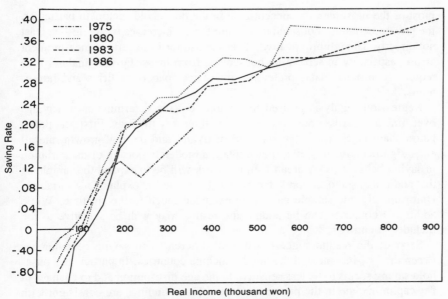

Real Income (thousand won)

Fig. 11.12   Household savings by income group: Korea

contrast, the 1980 survey divides incomes between 70,000 and 649,999 won
into 14 groups and averages incomes over 650,000 won.

11.6   Concluding Remarks

Many Asian countries do have high saving rates. However, much more interesting than the current level is the widespread and dramatic rise in saving
that has occurred since the early 1960s. The real question then is why savings
rose in some of these countries, but not in others. This question is explored
using a panel of data on savings and other key variables for 10 countries since
1960.

The paper shows that the countries with the highest saving rates in the
1980s were also the ones with the fastest real growth rates during 1960–84
and the ones that underwent a dramatic shift in their age distributions—from
over 40% under the age of 15 to barely 30%. Interestingly, even the Asian
countries with moderate saving rates that did not experience large demographic shifts exhibit strong correlations between real growth and savings.
For example, the two low-income countries in the sample experienced low
and variable growth rates during the years when real growth rates were low
and erratic. As growth rates stabilized at moderate positive levels, aggregate
savings rates in both countries began to rise.

The paper also looks at saving behavior disaggregated into households, corporations, and government where data are available. These data suggest that

most of the movement is concentrated in the household sector. In particular, the government does not seem to account for the increases in saving—at least not directly. Though provocative, these data suffer from serious measurement errors, especially in separating households from firms. Further analysis here requires additional data, preferably microlevel panels of firms and households.

Regressions analysis is used to separate out the determinants of savings over time and across countries. There are three key findings. First, the population share of children, the standard of living, and the real growth rate all enter significantly. Together, they explain a moderate portion of the variation in saving behavior. One area for future work will be to expand the sample so that additional socioeconomic factors can be entered as explanatory variables. Unfortunately, the sample cannot be extended much further in time. While additional countries can be added, the results may well be sensitive to the included countries.

Second, the results suggest structural differences in saving behavior between the low-income and the middle-income countries. In particular, household saving seems to be less sensitive to the age distribution and to changes in per capita income in the poorer countries. These findings are consistent with previous cross-country studies, which found structural differences between industrial and developing countries.

Third, the explanatory variables influence saving through two separate channels. On the one hand, living standards and the age distribution seem to have important structural effects on household behavior. On the other hand, changes in these variables tilt the mean age of consumption relative to the mean age of earnings in the economy. This second channel works interactively with the real growth rate. In contrast to some previous studies, the two channels are shown to work in opposite directions in this sample. Thus, omission of the interaction effects strongly biases the estimation results, suggesting, for example, that saving is not affected by the youth dependency ratio. However, the net effect for the middle-income countries is that a rise in dependency rates reduces saving—more so the higher the real growth rate. Similarly, the net effect of a rise in real per capita income is to raise aggregate savings—less so the higher the real growth rate.

Appendix
Savings Data Sources

BURMA: National income and gross savings data for 1960–81 were obtained from the *World Tables* (Baltimore: Johns Hopkins University Press for the World Bank), various issues. HONG KONG: National income and gross savings data for 1960–81 were obtained from the *World Tables,* various issues. INDONESIA: National income and gross savings data for 1960–85 were obtained from the *World Tables,* various issues. KOREA: National income and gross savings data for 1960–84 were obtained from Economic Planning Board (EPB), *Economic Statistics,* various issues. Urban and rural household savings data were obtained from EPB, *Annual Report on the Family Income and Expenditure Survey,* and Ministry of Agriculture & Fisheries, *Farm Household Economy Survey,* various issues. MALAYSIA: National income and gross savings data for 1960–85 were obtained from the International Monetary Fund, *International Financial Statistics (IFS)* and the *World Tables,* various issues. PHILIPPINES: National income data for 1959–86 were obtained from the *IFS,* gross and net savings data were obtained from the Philippine *Statistical Yearbook* (Manila: National Economic and Development Authority), various issues. SINGAPORE: National income data for 1960–85 were obtained from *IFS* and *World Tables,* gross savings data were obtained from *Yearbook of Statistics for Singapore* and *Economic and Social Statistics for Singapore,* various issues. TAIWAN: National income and savings data for 1960–86 were obtained from *Taiwan Statistical Data Book,* various issues. THAILAND: National income and savings data were obtained from *IFS* and *World Tables,* various issues. TURKEY: National income and savings data for 1960–85 were obtained from *IFS, World Tables,* and the Central Bank of Turkey.

Notes

1. The *World Development Report* (World Bank 1987) defines gross domestic savings as GDP less total consumption.
2. See Hammer (1985) for additional discussion of savings measures in cross-country studies. Hayashi (1986) provides a useful discussion of particular issues in measuring Japanese savings.
3. The countries are Argentina, Brazil, Costa Rica, El Salvador, Mexico, Panama, Peru, and Venezuela. These data come from *World Development Report* (World Bank 1987).
4. It is interesting to note that Williamson's (1978) study of Korean savings is entitled "Why Do Koreans Save 'So Little'?"
5. Japanese savings rates also peaked in the 1970s. It would be interesting to explore whether this saving pattern could be explained by temporarily high savings (especially corporate) during the rapid development phase, or the "big push" as suggested by Murphy, Shleifer and Vishny (1988).

References

Collins, Susan. 1988. Savings and Growth Experiences of Korea and Japan. *Journal of the Japanese and International Economies* 2:328–50.
Collins, Susan, and Won-Am Park. 1989. External Debt and Macroeconomic Performance in Korea. In *Developing Country Debt and Economic Performance,* vol. 3, ed. J. Sachs and S. Collins. Chicago: University of Chicago Press.

Deaton, Angus. 1989. Saving in Developing Countries: Theory and Review. *Proceedings of the World Bank Annual Conference on Development Economics, 1989.* Washington, D.C.:World Bank.

Dohner, Robert, and Ponciano Intal. 1989. Debt Crisis and Adjustment in the Philippines. In *Developing Country Debt and the World Economy*, ed. J. Sachs. Chicago: University of Chicago Press.

Fry, Maxwell, and Andrew Mason. 1982. The Variable Rate-of-Growth Effect in the Life-Cycle Saving Model. *Economic Inquiry* 20, no. 3 (July):426–44.

Gersovitz, Mark. 1988. Saving and Development. In *Handbook of Development Economics*, vol. 1, ed. H. Chenery and T. N. Srinivasan. Amsterdam: Elsevier.

Giovannini, Alberto. 1985. The Interest Rate Elasticity of Savings in Developing Countries: The Existing Evidence. *World Development* 11, no. 7.

Hammer, Jeffrey. 1985. Population Growth and Savings in Developing Countries. *World Bank Staff Working Paper* no. 687. Washington, D.C.

Hayashi, Fumio. 1986. Why Is Japan's Savings Rate so Apparently High? In *NBER Macroeconomics Annual 1986*, ed. S. Fischer. Cambridge, Mass.:MIT Press.

Leff, Nathaniel. 1980. Dependency Rates and Savings Rates: A New Look. In *Research in Population Economics*, ed. J. Simon and J. Da Vanza. Greenwich, Conn.: JAI Press.

Mason, Andrew. 1987. National Saving Rates and Population Growth: A New Model and New Evidence. In *Population Growth and Economic Development: Issues and Evidence*, ed. D. G. Johnson and R. Lee. Madison: University of Wisconsin Press.

———. 1988. Saving, Economic Growth and Demographic Change. *Population and Development Review* 14, no. 1 (March).

Mason, Andrew, et al. 1986. *Population Growth and Economic Development: Lessons From Selected Asian Countries.* United Nations Fund for Population Activities, Policy Development Study no. 10. New York: United Nations.

Murphy, Kevin, Andrei Shleifer and Robert Vishny. 1988. Industrialization and the Big Push. NBER Working Paper no. 2708.

Nam, Sang-woo. 1988. The Determinants of the Korean National Savings Ratio: A Sectoral Accounting Approach. World Bank, Washington, D.C. Mimeograph.

Ram, R. 1982. Dependency Rates and Aggregate Savings: A New Intertemporal Cross Section Study. *American Economic Review* 72 (June):537–44.

Summers, Robert, and Alan Heston. 1988. A New Set of International Comparisons of Real Product and Price Levels, Estimates for 130 Countries, 1950–1985. *The Review of Income and Wealth* 34:1–25.

Williamson, Jeffrey. 1978. Why Do Koreans Save 'So Little'? *Journal of Development Economics* 6:343–62.

Williamson, Jeffrey. 1988. Capital Deepening Along the Asian Pacific Rim. Discussion Paper no. 1363. Harvard Institute for Economic Research.

World Bank. 1987. *World Development Report.* New York: Oxford University Press for the World Bank.

Comment   Anne O. Krueger

A number of papers presented at the NBER conference on saving—including Sue Collins's interesting and important contribution—raise fundamental and

Anne O. Krueger is Arts and Sciences Professor of Economics at Duke University and a research associate of the National Bureau of Economic Research.

difficult questions about the determinants of economic growth. Historically, development economists have examined those determinants for developing countries, while others have raised the same questions in the context of the OECD countries. There is a great deal to learn by examining the entire range of country experiences, especially when it is recognized that some countries—including several in Sue Collins's group—have achieved more growth in per capita income in the past two decades than most now-industrialized countries did in the entire nineteenth century. This is especially so at a conference that focuses on savings and its determinants; some of the countries examined by Collins have experienced increases in their saving rates from less than 5 percent of GNP 30 years ago to 35 percent and more now.

Overall, I have little to quarrel with in Collins's paper. Moreover, the issues it raises are issues that have come up in several other papers in this volume, and I therefore wish to address some of these broader issues. The basic question that arises—with respect to Christopher Carroll and Lawrence Summers's paper, with regard to Robert Barro's, and to several others—is What are the determinants of growth? And how is growth related to savings? Growth as it has been experienced by the rapidly growing newly industrializing countries (NICs) of East Asia, and as it was experienced in the nineteenth century by the now-developed countries, transforms society. Almost by definition, all major economic variables move together. Poverty and low per capita incomes are such pervasive constraints on political, social, and economic behavior for poor countries that it is unthinkable that it could be otherwise. A major problem, therefore, is how to disentangle the simultaneous causation of growth from those exogenous stimuli that permit some countries to achieve rapid growth in per capita incomes while others grow, at best, slowly or even experience declining real per capita incomes and living standards. If, as Larry Summers suggested, saving is the activity that reflects the trade-off between the present and the future, it is clearly a central concern of those attempting to understand economic development and the growth process.

My unease is that it is not clear what savings we are focusing on and why we regard it as an interesting economic variable. To illustrate the basis of my concern, a useful starting point is to form the identity that the rate of growth of output is equal to the weighted average rate of factor accumulation plus the rate of growth of efficiency in factor use.

The increase in output, dY, is equal to the real rate of return on capital, r, times the increase in capital stock, dK, plus the return to everything else, w, times the change in everything else, dO. That is,

$$dY = rdK + wdO.$$

If we adhere to a conventional notion of savings and capital formation and ignore foreign capital inflows (which would not significantly alter the argument I want to make), then the rate of growth can be written as

$$dY/Y = rs + a \, dO/O,$$

where s is savings expressed as a fraction of output, and a is the share of all factors other than capital in output.

The point I wish to make is this: suppose, as Larry Summers's paper suggests and is often asserted by others, that the real return to capital does not vary much from 5 percent. Then, even with a high saving rate, say .3, the rate of growth of output that can be achieved will be only .3 $\times$ .05 = .015 or 1.5 percent. Considering the range of saving rates from .05 to .35 of income, with a real return to capital of .05, differences in saving behavior could explain at most 1 percentage point of differences in growth rates. Since we observe rates of growth of output of 10 and 12 percent in East Asia, and of 1 and 2 percent in sub-Saharan Africa, it seems clear that either we are misdefining savings and/or investment or the real return, or else savings and investment are relatively unimportant as determinants of growth.

Something is clearly wrong. What is it? I think there are several things. First, savings finances human capital as well as physical capital formation, especially at early stages of growth. Estimates from the human capital literature suggest real rates of return of 25 percent on primary education in developing countries, and certainly there is evidence that human capital formation is a vital component of the growth process. If savings were redefined to include expenditures (and forgone income) on human capital formation, the saving rates used in our growth equations would look quite different.

Second, measured savings fails to pick up a number of forms in which individuals save, especially in countries where the returns to saving in legal channels are low—a point to which I return in a moment. Measured savings in most developing countries fails to record capital flight (which is estimated cumulatively to have exceeded public external borrowing in a number of developing countries in the late 1970s), accumulation of gold (the stock of which in India is estimated to have been more than twice national income in the 1960s) and other precious metals and minerals, and savings destined for investment in the underground economy.

Third, the real rate of return to investors is a function of several variables, and there is a lot of suggestive evidence that it has fluctuated widely between countries and over time as a function of incentives afforded by economic policies. In Korea, for example, it is estimated that the real rate of return to investment in manufacturing exceeded 30 percent during the late 1960s and early 1970s; there is ample evidence that it remains very high. In the Korea of the 1950s, the evidence suggests that the real rate of return varied a great deal depending on the nature of the activity, but probably did not average more than 5 percent.

A final point, which is more relevant to estimating saving responses than it is to overall growth rates, is that, in many developing countries, financial markets are little developed and governments control the banking system and the allocation of credit. In these circumstances, real returns available to small savers through the financial system are negative and sometimes strongly so.

In Korea, for example, real returns to depositors in savings accounts were negative until 1964.

As these remarks imply, I am skeptical about using measured rates of saving as they are recorded in the national income accounts; I am even more skeptical about using 5 percent as a real rate of return on capital. While high growth rates clearly are a factor contributory to high saving rates in the rapidly growing countries, the real return to saving is also a factor, and it is questionable whether measurements of that return to date have adequately reflected returns to savings. Possibly even more important, factors (and especially governments' economic policies) governing the economic efficiency with which new resources are allocated, including the financial markets and the real returns they offer to savers, are clearly important in influencing the saving rate and its impact on the rate of economic growth.

Turning specifically to Sue Collins's paper in light of these considerations, I would only raise several issues. First, and most important, she does not investigate the role of the real rate of return to savers in affecting saving behavior. Second, she uses period averages as the saving rate for the countries involved. A major question there is why the evidence embodied in the very large changes in rates over time is not used. Third, I have some questions about the "sample" of countries used. Except for Turkey, it is entirely East and Southeast Asian—that part of the world (except Indonesia) has been subject to a relatively similar set of economic policies and incentives (as contrasted with sub-Saharan Africa and Latin America, for example): one wonders if the procedure is not akin to estimating determinants of height based on a sample of professional basketball players. Fourth, and less important, I have some misgivings about use of the dependency ratio as Collins uses it: in most rapidly growing developing countries, there is rapid migration from rural to urban areas and, with it, a drop in the number of children per family. As such, the dependency ratio is to a large extent a variable measuring lagged and cumulative migration, itself a function of the rate of economic growth.

Overall, the Collins paper, along with the other presented in this volume, provides a valuable contribution to the all-too-sparse literature on determinants of saving behavior in developing countries. It is to be hoped that her effort spurs further work, incorporating better estimates of real returns to savers, and alternative estimates of savings that more closely correspond to the concept relevant for economic growth.

Contributors

Alan J. Auerbach
Department of Economics
McNeil Building, Room 160
University of Pennsylvania
3718 Locust Walk
Philadelphia, PA 19104–6297

Philipe Bacchetta
ESADE
Avda. de Pedralbes 60–62
08034 Barcelona
Spain

Robert J. Barro
Department of Economics
Littauer Center 120
Harvard University
Cambridge, MA 02138

B. Douglas Bernheim
Department of Economics
210 Fisher Hall
Princeton University
Princeton, NJ 08544-1021

David F. Bradford
Woodrow Wilson School
Princeton University
Princeton, NJ 08544-1013

Christopher D. Carroll
Federal Reserve Board of Governors
R and S Division, EA Section
28th and C Streets, NW
Washington, DC 20007

Susan M. Collins
Department of Economics
Littauer M-7
Harvard University
Cambridge, MA 02138

James Davies
Department of Economics
Social Science Centre
University of Western Ontario
London, Ontario N6A 5C2
Canada

Angus S. Deaton
Woodrow Wilson School
221 Bentheim Hall
Princeton University
Princeton, NJ 08544-1013

Rudiger Dornbusch
Department of Economics
Room E52-357
Massachusetts Institute of Technology
Cambridge, MA 02139

Martin Feldstein
President and Chief Executive Officer
National Bureau of Economic Research
1050 Massachusetts Avenue
Cambridge, MA 02138–5398

Jeffrey A. Frankel
Department of Economics
Evans Hall
University of California
Berkeley, CA 94720

Robert E. Hall
Hoover Institution
Stanford University
Stanford, CA 94305-6010

Kevin Hassett
Graduate School of Business
Uris Hall
Columbia University
New York, NY 10027

Anne O. Krueger
Department of Economics
227 Social Science Building
Duke University
Durham, NC 27706

N. Gregory Mankiw
National Bureau of Economic Research
1050 Massachusetts Avenue
Cambridge, MA 02138-5398

Maurice Obstfeld
Department of Economics
Littauer Center M-7
Harvard University
Cambridge, MA 02138

James M. Poterba
Department of Economics
Room E52–350
Massachusetts Institute of Technology
Cambridge, MA 02139

Sherwin Rosen
Department of Economics
University of Chicago
1126 East 59th Street
Chicago, IL 60637

Michael Rothschild
Office of the Divisional Dean
Social Sciences
Mail Code Q-064
University of California at San Diego
La Jolla, CA 92093

John Karl Scholz
Department of Economics
Social Science Building
University of Wisconsin
1180 Observatory Drive
Madison, Wisconsin 53706

John B. Shoven
Department of Economics
Encina Hall
Stanford University
Stanford, CA 94305-6072

Joel Slemrod
Director, Office of Tax Policy Research
School of Business Administration
University of Michigan
Ann Arbor, MI 48109–1234

Joseph E. Stiglitz
Department of Economics
Encina Hall
Stanford University
Stanford, CA 93405-6072

Lawrence H. Summers
Department of Economics
Littaeur Center 229
Harvard University
Cambridge, MA 02138

James Tobin
Cowles Foundation for Research in
    Economics
Department of Economics
P.O. Box 2125, Yale Station
New Haven, CT 06520-2125

Steven F. Venti
Department of Economics
Rockefeller Center
Dartmouth College
Hanover, NH 03755

John Whalley
Department of Economics
Social Science Centre
University of Western Ontario
London, Ontario N6A 5C2
Canada

David A. Wise
National Bureau of Economic Research
1050 Massachusetts Avenue
Cambridge, MA 02138–5398

Author Index

Subject Index

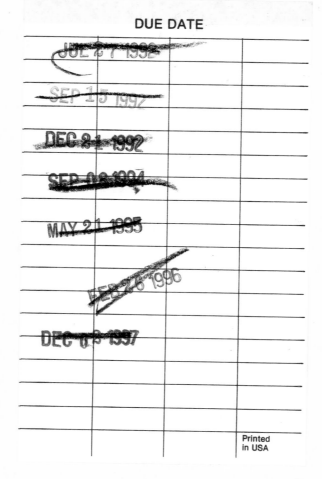

DUE DATE

JUL 27 1992			
SEP 15 1992			
DEC 21 1992			
SEP 08 1994			
MAY 21 1995			
FEB 26 1996			
DEC 03 1997			
			Printed in USA